THE HUMAN ENVIRONMENT

McGRAW-HILL SERIES IN POPULATION BIOLOGY

Consulting Editors
Paul R. Ehrlich/Stanford University
Richard W. Holm/Stanford University

THE HUMAN ENVIRONMENT

MICHAEL TRESHOW

Professor of Biology / University of Utah

McGRAW-HILL BOOK COMPANY

*New York / St. Louis / San Francisco / Auckland
Düsseldorf / Johannesburg / Kuala Lumpur / London
Mexico / Montreal / New Delhi / Panama / Paris
São Paulo / Singapore / Sydney / Tokyo / Toronto*

TO KAAREN, MIKE, AND PAUL

THE HUMAN ENVIRONMENT

1 2 3 4 5 6 7 8 9 0 D O D O 7 9 8 7 6

Library of Congress Cataloging in Publication Data

Treshow, Michael.
    The human environment.

    (McGraw-Hill series in population biology)
    Includes bibliographies.
    1. Human ecology. I. Title. [DNLM:
1. Ecology. 2. Environmental health. WA30
T797h]
GF41.T73   301.31   75-22270
ISBN 0-07-065136-1

This book was set in Times Roman by Black Dot, Inc.
The editors were William J. Willey and Douglas J. Marshall;
the cover was designed by Judith Michael;
the production supervisor was Judi Allen.
The drawings were done by J & R Services, Inc.
R. R. Donnelley & Sons Company was printer and binder.

Contents

PART TWO/TOWARD ENVIRONMENTAL HOMICIDE

Preface

Our destiny exercises its influence over us even where, as yet, we have not learned its nature: It is our future that lays down the law of our today.

Friedrich W. Nietzsche
Human, All Too Human

The human environment is more than our physical surroundings; it encompasses our social environment, including, most significantly, our social and cultural interaction. People create the human environment and are themselves its most important elements.

During the late 1940s and into the fifties, the belief persisted and grew that humankind had an unlimited future; that aided by our technological mastery, we would gain control over the earth and over our own destiny. Through a long period of steady economic growth and finally in the recently recognized era of environmental awakening, this view came to be questioned. Environmental problems from crowded cities and country-side, depletion of natural resources, and food shortages, to multifaceted pollution became increasingly recognized. Yet, little attention was given the real nature of the species *Homo sapiens* and its position in the total, finite world.

Many scientists who profess a belief in humankind's animal origins still ignore the possibility that our genetic nature might place serious constraints on our ability to survive in the new and changing environment we have generated around ourselves. Nevertheless, we are molded in a large measure by our environment—our behavior and culture are in part the product of our environment and genetics and determined by our response to it. The primitive gathering and hunting society, the early agricultural society, and the industrial-technological society all represented adaptations to the environment.

Throughout history, humankind's most significant achievements have been gained from our struggle to adjust to our environment and modify it for our security and well-being. The struggle for food has forced us to study and invent, often with little concern for the long-term consequences. The early hunter-gatherer was not a natural conservationist, and in quest of food and comfort, killed other species often until they were extinct. In providing shelter for humankind's increasing numbers, people "learned" to cut down forests for timber. They "learned" to burn prairies and clear forests to get game and, later, to provide land for their crops. They "learned" to poison fish and divert streams. For their comfort and material gain, they continue to deplete the earth's resources and to alter their environment.

Aspects of "progress" of humankind are shown in the material development of human history and the changes wrought by it in the human environment. Progress at the expense of the social, biotic, and physical environments cannot continue indefinitely, despite expectations that it will. The self-healing character of nature is not infinitely tolerant.

The problems of the next century are not so much those of the physical environment as those of understanding and controlling our needs. We must learn how we work and the interrelation of science and technology to society and culture. The complexity of society is fast becoming too great for us to understand, and its problems perhaps too great to resolve. Comprehension can be gained best by taking a holistic approach to the human environment and its infinite interrelationships and interdependencies.

In this text, we shall develop the story of the genetic and behavioral forces that have influenced humankind's interaction with the environment and led to our present position. We shall show how biological systems, of which we are but one part, are dependent and interrelated through the exchange of both genetic and behavioral information and the feedback that "operates" to maintain order and stability in the system. Through such understanding of our place in our environment, we should best be able to begin to perceive the problems of tomorrow. We must proceed into tomorrow with an understanding of yesterday and view ourselves as part of the complex ecological systems of nature. We must understand and accept our place in the universe as *Homo sapiens* so that we might fit comfortably and permanently into the human environment.

ACKNOWLEDGMENTS

Many people contributed much to this book. I particularly wish to gratefully acknowledge the special contributions of Helen Alvarez of Park City, Utah, in writing the first five chapters and offering many valuable ideas and suggestions on the full manuscript. I should also like to thank and express my appreciation to the many reviewers for their helpful suggestions on specific chapters, namely Richard Firenze, James Grosklags, Curtis Williams, Richard Holm, and Eric Charnov, and to Frank Anderson for his careful editing of the manuscript. Also many thanks to Maureen Vaughn for her patience in typing the numerous revisions of this volume.

Michael Treshow

Introduction

For me the world is weird because it is stupendous, awesome, mysterious, unfathomable; my interest has been to convince you that you must assume responsibility for being here, in this marvelous world, in this marvelous desert, in this marvelous time. I wanted to convince you that you must learn to make every act count, since you are going to be here for only a short while; in fact too short for witnessing all the marvels of it.

The Teachings of Don Juan
Carlos Castaneda

Over thousands of millenia the process of natural selection has operated on the species known as *Homo sapeins* to produce creatures admirably suited to the environment of the planet earth. The oxygen of the air is their life breath, and the chemical components of the plants and animals provide the essential nutrients for their growth and activity. The sun warms them in the day, and at night various strategies for conserving energy help them maintain their body temperature within the narrow range demanded by their physiology. The earth, sun, and moon program their activity. The plants and animals nourish them, and the colors, shapes, and variety of the earthly scene delight their senses. In short, humans are designed to act in the earth ecosystem and in that action to find pleasure.

Out of the diverse primate stock roaming Africa and the Indian subcontinent evolved a large-brained-animal of upright stance and sensitive and skilled hands, a gregarious animal with the talents of speech, learning, and abstraction which promoted a lively social life and a rich inner fantasy life. Over the generations, human animals came to be less dependent upon the inherent genetic programs which ensure survival-promoting behavior in most animals. Instead, their behavioral choices came to be governed more and more by past experience and future expectation. These human animals learned to modify their behavior in the face of environmental change and to remember successful strategies which could be used again and again.

Almost from the beginning, people explored, altered, and exploited their habitat. One creature joined another in co-operative effort, and the group came to achieve what the individual could not. One generation taught the next, and knowledge persisted through the ages, not only in the biological code but also in the oral and written communications of the people. Cultures developed and differentiated in response to the constraints of the habitat and the inventiveness of the inhabitants. Many humans began to live in a state far removed from simple dependence upon their immediate natural resources. Supported by a wide variety of artifacts and sheltered from the environment by many strategies, the people of the developed world forgot their humble origins, refusing even to recognize the common humanity of the native peoples disrupted by the colonial expansion of the European world.

Even then, the great success of the developed world was bought at a price, and the price was not bargained at the beginning, nor seemingly will it be questioned at the end. Many humans continue to live further and further from their physiological and behavioral tolerance, and the precarious balance of this artificial state is still maintained by ever-increasing demands upon the environment at the expense of the rest of the earth's human and animal populations.

Three people are supported in a spaceship shuttling between earth and the moon at an incredible expense in energy and resources. This same budget would support an entire tribe of hunter-gatherers in the African bush. One-fifth of the world's people squander 80 percent of the world's resources of energy and materials while millions live in hunger, barely able to earn or beg a living from an environment they neither understand nor control.

In the twentieth century, the mass communication systems bring visions of plenty to these poor and, conversely, nightmares of misery to the rich. The old primate signals, which convey loneliness, distress, and pain, are ignored in the close physical contact of the mob but are magnified through time and distance by the eye of the camera. Many onlookers refuse physically to help one individual murdered in a crowded public place, but give thousands of dollars in aid on the basis of one televised appeal picturing the famished of Africa or India. The hand in the pocket substitutes for the comforting caress, but no one measures the equivalency of the two modes of behavior. We belong to a species whose members evolved in a social milieu rich in repeated acts of physical and emotional sharing. Can we survive in a world where an individual holds oneself separate from others, allowing only brief encounters for the purpose of exchanging objects?

Suddenly, in the 1970s, our well-tailored physique and long-practiced behavior seem somehow inadequate, and the strategies of the ingenious brain only deceive as we find ourselves in a world awry. Longing for the simplicity of our origins and hardly understanding how we came so far from an imagined paradise, we depend on our technical expertise to right the wrongs.

In some corners of the earth, small groups of people still live well, neither demanding too much of their environment nor expecting too little. Yet, these examples are ignored as we refuse even to emulate some of the thriftier citizens of the Western world. The average energy consumption of the French is 35 percent that of Americans, yet the French can hardly be said to live impoverished lives. Still, we rush to exploit the remaining energy resources of the globe without thought of the future. Indeed, we express outrage and indignation when the citizens of the third world demand just reparations for their loss.

We recover, refine, and transport fossil fuels with the most sophisticated equipment and in the process spread oil and debris over the rich fishing grounds of the continental shelf and the lands of the earth. Our miracle plants and animals shame the biblical gift of loaves and fishes, and still thousands go to bed hungry each night. Our internal-combustion engines and power generators enable us to perform feats unimagined even in the herculean days of the Greek gods, but the air is polluted with the waste gases of these machines.

The clever mind is used for more than exploitation of the resources of the earth. With our lively imagination, we conjure visions and work beauty and terror in stone, wood, paper, and film. We explore every facet of our world from the physical and biological to the mystical. No aspect of the planet is safe from our attention. We turn our eye inward even onto ourselves and marvel at the unique capacity for self-analysis, and with that inward eye we construct the most insidious myth, the myth of special creation. We see ourselves as unique, special, apart from the natural world. Imagining for ourselves a supernatural beginning, we grant ourselves a supranatural existence. It is indeed ironic that the very special talent, the capacity to believe, which was crucial to our mastery of symbols and had been such an important element in the rise of humanity, should now threaten to become an important contributor to the destruction of the ecosystem.

Comforted by this capacity to believe, we refuse to accept the fact that the inventive, technological, and mobile human may be as subject to natural law as the fish in the ocean and the birds of the air. We equate technological mastery, cultural sophistication, and human proliferation over the earth with immunity from natural processes. This egocentricity, far from being harmless, prevents us from elucidating our relationship to nature. Instead of recognizing that our acts have consequences that can be demonstrated here and now, we construct elaborate codes of conduct, laws of behavior which postpone consequences and rewards of action to the unknowable, untestable future.

Although we grant that these codes of conduct often reenforce biologically sensible behavior, as with the incest taboo of many people, unless these codes can be questioned and analyzed, we have no way of determining their value to the preservation of the earth ecosystem and the human species. If we are to develop a sane environmental policy, we must continually question the results of our actions. Certainly we have altered, tampered with, and expanded our environment, but we have not escaped the operation of ecological consequence. We have, however, influenced the health of ecosystems in such a way as to impair the natural mechanisms of self-repair, which are basic to sustaining a viable ecosystem.

If we have seriously altered our environment and disrupted the natural systems in the past, then we must either change ourselves to suit the new environment or restore the environment to suit our ancient selves. Although little attention has been given to the former, it is not, within certain limits, beyond the realm of biological possibility. After all, we have genetically tailored nearly every other domestic animal and many plants to suit our own highly specialized environment and goals. Given the time and motivation, we could redesign ourselves. Inadvertently, we may already be doing so, both genetically and behaviorally. Indeed if we service our political and technological threats, time will inexorably change us to suit the environment by the same mechanism that brought us this far.

A far more attractive possibility is the rational management of our ecosystems to satisfy the biological, cultural, and social needs of all people. However, all our efforts at preservation of our physical environment will be self-defeating as long as our goals and motives are based on erroneous assumptions about ourselves and nature. It is as ecologically reckless to raise the aspirations of the underdeveloped countries to the American-European Madison Avenue life-style as it is to expect to maintain that style for less than one-fifth of the world's population in the midst of widespread misery for the remaining inhabitants. Nor can we solve our problems by that Pollyanna thinking which asserts that since our ancestors evolved on the savanna, our only hope is to return to nature to live from the land in some semiprimitive state.

We have arrived in the twentieth century with a population of over 3 billion attempting existence on a planet whose resources are rapidly being depleted. There is no going back to an underpopulated and underexploited world. Our only hope lies in a highly knowledgeable, holistic treatment of the future.

Armed with the foresight gained from knowledge and theory, we may come to understand the workings of the ecosystems of the earth and decide which components, if any, are expendable and at what price. Certainly, we will discover that we must protect, cherish, and defend certain threatened natural systems or jeopardize human survival, for upon their health, humanity depends. As an added bonus, the understanding of living processes will bring us nearer to a reconciliation with our own nature and our position in the web of life—for life processes are truly universal in all earth's creatures.

Part One

From Our
Beginnings

Chapter 1

The Unity of Life

He built gradually to a crying jag, during which he claimed to be deeply touched by the idea of an inhabited planet with an atmosphere that was eager to combine violently with almost everything the inhabitants held dear. He was speaking of earth and the element oxygen.

Kurt Vonnegut, Jr.
God Bless You, Mr. Rosewater

Longing for certainty, we are born into the precarious state so sadly perceived by Vonnegut's hero. The very processes that sustain life on earth are capable of destroying it. Oxygen, which is our life breath, sustains the violent conflagrations that destroy our possessions, our forests, our shelter, and often our loved ones. Oxygen also crumbles iron artifacts to rust and rots fruit. The elemental earth is an impartial habitat.

In a mountain meadow, a lone cowboy encourages the reaction of oxygen and plant material to produce a fire at which he warms himself. Nearby, his horse consumes the same materials, but without exhaling smoke and flames. In the next canyon, at the bottom of a ski run, a maintenance crew clears a mass of trees and brush into a low spot and covers it with dirt. In mid-January, the spot is smoldering and bare of snow.

Is there a fundamental difference in these reactions or are they essentially the same?

The fire and the compost pile are both releasing energy. We can feel the energy from the fire and see the work accomplished by the energy from the compost as the water molecules piled on top change from the solid state, snow, to the liquid state. In the physical environment, the plant material reacts with oxygen, and energy is dissipated to the atmosphere. In the horse, the energy that was present in the grass is conserved. The horse can carry the cowboy home or provide food for a hungry wolf. Living systems are able to store and transform energy.

ENERGY

The ultimate source of all the energy in our system is the sun. It is not difficult for us, even as laypeople, to define energy when we are discussing the sun. We can feel the heat from the sun and see the light. The sensory organs of our bodies perceive the changes in energy impinging upon them—we experience the energy. However, when energy in the form of light and heat is transformed into the chemical energy of covalent molecular bonds,[1] we are confounded in our attempt at definition. The concept has moved from the realm of the practical to the theoretical. We must depend upon experimental evidence and cognitive association for our definition. We can experience the chemical energy stored by plants once again when we burn wood, ride a horse, or eat a peanut butter and honey sandwich. The standard definition of energy as the capacity to do work seems somehow inadequate, but if we supplement that definition with personal experience, we can arrive at an intuitive concept that will aid enormously in our understanding of the living systems of the earth.

The energy captured from the sun and stored as chemical energy by plants permits all organisms to alter the environment from one hostile to life to one accommodating to life. The environment can be utilized, altered, or escaped by the organism because it is able to do mechanical work, to selectively transport and accumulate matter or electrical charges against concentration gradients, and to synthesize basic molecules to support growth, repair, and reproduction.

Mechanical Work

The general idea of mechanical work is obvious. Our bodies employ chemical energy from foodstuffs for muscle contraction. The ability of

---

[1]Covalent bonds are those between atoms created by the sharing of electrons.

muscle cells to contract is one of the most important facts of life to an animal. By the contraction of muscle fiber, we can support our bodies against the force of gravity, escape danger, and lift objects. A woman, man, or child can harvest the energy stored in plant products by gathering roots, seeds, and fruit. A miner can dig fossil fuels and use them to make machines work. We can build shelters that help maintain the body-heat balance suitable to life processes or shiver to increase our body heat when we stand in the cold. Most significantly for life, we may make love in order to perpetuate our own special brand of molecular order or purely for pleasure.

Because of our ability to perform mechanical work, we can express our fantasies and abstractions on canvas, in wood, stone, sound, or body movement. We can laugh, talk, sing, dance, and test ourselves in games of skill and chance. It is obvious that not only is movement by muscle contraction possible, but this movement may be highly ordered, precisely adjusted, and synchronized. This organized utilization of chemical energy for mechanical work is as much a property of the slowly flowing amoeba as it is of the hummingbird, as much a character of plants as of animals.

By virtue of mechanical work, a plant may escape an unfavorable environment as effectively as an animal might. Some plants escape air pollutants such as ozone by closing tiny openings, the stoma of the leaves. In a drying environment, leaves may also roll inward, thereby effectively conserving moisture and reducing the amount of surface exposed to the dry air.

Because the direct transfer of chemical into mechanical energy is ubiquitous in the living world, we tend to forget what a remarkable accomplishment it represents. If we reflect that the most ingenious and analytic species on the earth, humans, have not yet extensively utilized this direct transfer in their machines, we may be able to appreciate the marvel of it more fully. In nearly every practicable machine produced by humans, the chemical energy is first converted into heat energy before work can be accomplished. A coal-fired generator produces heat which boils water. The steam is used to turn a turbine which generates electricity. As the fossil fuel reserves of the earth are depleted, we have cause to regret every calorie lost in these inefficient conversion processes.

Osmotic Work

The second general category of cellular work is not quite so obvious. The organism, by virtue of its selective use of the earth's resources, must accumulate certain elements and rid itself of others. It must secrete waste products, sometimes creating in that secretion vastly differing chemical environments from one side of the cell to the other. At the same time, the cell accumulates raw materials, the molecular building blocks of cell tissue. Because of the natural tendency of molecules to move from an area of higher to an area of lower concentration until a uniform concentration of molecules is achieved, the concentration gradients necessary to life must be maintained at the expense of energy. Biologists have been aware of the active transport of molecules across living membranes, or osmotic work, for a very long time. Yet it is precisely our failure to consider this phenomenon that has produced some of our most pressing environmental problems. (See Appendix, "The Laws of Thermodynamics.") In setting allowable levels of contamination of soils around nuclear reactor sites, the AEC acted in complete ignorance of the ability of plants to concentrate such radioactive elements as strontium. Instead of a series of dilutions of the elements from soil to plant to cow to milk, we find a series of increasing concentrations. A similar phenomenon has been observed in the relationship between DDT, insects, and birds. In the year 2001, will cows graze around Hallam, Hanover, and Oak Ridge? Will the milk be fit to drink? Has the DDT moratorium come in time to save birds and fish? Is the concentration of DDT in human body fat harmless?

Our perception of and response to the environment are based upon the ability of nerve cells to differentially transport sodium and potassium across cell membranes against concentration gradients. Every action and reaction in our nervous system involves this active transport. We can easily comprehend that energy is expended in our response to environmental stimuli. It is less obvious to us that energy is involved in the perception and in the process of integrating that perception with past experience and future expectation to tailor an appropriate response. Energy is as much involved in the organization of a work of art as it is in its execution.

Chemical Work

Finally, solar energy as chemical energy is used by living organisms for the biosynthesis of very large organic molecules from smaller subunits. The glucose produced by the process of photosynthesis combines with oxygen in the process of respiration. The degradation of glucose in both plant and animal cells serves three purposes. The small organic fragments left by the degradation can be combined with other elements such as nitrogen and phosphorous for the production of protein molecules, the building blocks of living tissue. The energy released from glucose is conserved to be used in the union of the organic fragments and the minerals into proteins, and some of that energy is also available for the performance of osmotic and mechanical work.

In living systems, energy is conserved and transformed in two general processes. All living cells contain a number of compounds which are able to store energy by the addition of a phosphate molecule to their structure. This stored energy can be donated to another cell process by the loss of the phosphate molecule. One of the most common of these high-energy phosphate-bond compounds is adenosine triphosphate (ATP). When energy is needed for other cell processes, the ATP can be converted to adenosine disphosphate (ADP). Since only two phosphate molecules are involved in ADP, some of the energy of ATP has been surrendered to the purposes of the cell. This energy is available to do work. The ADP is also available for recharging by the donation of a new terminal phosphate bond. The ATP-ADP system of energy exchange is found in all living organisms from amoebas to human beings.

The second mode of energy transfer is by excited electrons. Certain compounds in the cell are able to transfer electrons down an energy scale. Again, some of the most common of these compounds are found in all living cells.

With rare exceptions, only the living cells containing chloroplasts are able to directly utilize the energy of the sun to excite electrons and thereby transform nuclear energy into chemical energy. By a complex many-stepped process, a photon of light excites an electron from the chlorophyll molecule into a higher-energy orbit. In this orbit, it can be picked up by an electron-accepting molecule such as cytochrome, an iron compound. The excited electron is passed by a cyclic path from one to another of a variety of electron-accepting and donating compounds. At each step, the accepting compound gains in energy while the energy level of the electron decreases. The electron eventually reaches its original energy level and returns to the chlorophyll molecule. At some point in the cycle, the energy donated by the excited electron is used to recharge ADP to ATP. The ATP energy is employed for the production of glucose from carbon dioxide and water. From glucose and the essential minerals obtained from the soil, all the compounds of the living chemical "factory" can be assembled. The analogy to a factory is deliberate. A living cell is not simply a sac of organic broth in which complex compounds float in random motion, but a highly organized assembly line. The components of the cell are arranged in precise juxtaposition upon molecular membranes. The functional units within a single cell are also highly organized. The chlorophyll energy transfer and glucose assembly systems are present in the green-colored bodies of plant cells, the chloroplasts. The ADP-ATP synthesis systems and the respiratory processes are organized in another small organelle found in both plant and animal cells, that is, the mitochondrion.

ORDER

One of the most important points about energy reactions within a living cell is that the energy-transforming systems are in no sense haphazard, dependent upon chance encounter or chance resource. They are sequential, precisely ordered events, not only in space but in time, and therein lies their fragility. They are processes which proceed only within well-defined temperature boundaries. Their susceptibility to poisoning stems from an organization in which the products of one reaction become the substrate of another.

Biological Systems

The organization of elements, energy, and events into sequential arrays is not limited to chemical reactions but is a general characteristic of biological systems. (We are not using the word *element* in its strict chemical application but in its more general meaning of "component, constituent, or member of.") Throughout the next five chapters, the word *order* will be used to denote the arrangement of elements and events in space and time, i.e., "sequence, disposition, arrangement, arranged or *regulated* condition" (Oxford Dictionary). We have italicized the word *regulated* to stress that it is an important characteristic of the systems we will be discussing. In thinking about ordered systems, the student should not visualize a one-dimensional, linear sequence of things, but rather a complex net of interrelated elements and events.

In the photosynthetic cycle we have discussed, the elements of the system are the molecules of chlorophyll, water, carbon dioxide, ATP, and a variety of other enzymes not mentioned in our effort to simplify the description. The energy is a photon of light. We define *events* as interactions between the other members of the series: e.g., the photon excites an electron in the chlorophyll molecule; the electron is transferred to the cytochrome molecule. It is axiomatic in biology that events are ordered on a priority basis. The electron from chlorophyll can only contribute energy to ADP after it has been excited by a photon of light. From this simple priority relationship, we might guess that biological processes are governed by conditions.

Priority, regulation, conditions: these words convey the idea that the arrangement is dynamic. Given certain conditions, we may expect certain arrangements; change the conditions, and what happens to the sequence of elements and events? Throughout the book we will return again and again to the concept of biological systems as regulated sequences of elements and events. This general definition applies equally well to such diverse phenomena as the organization of plants and animals on a segment of the land, the grouping of small molecules to form a macromolecule such as insulin, or the organization of nucleus, chloroplasts, ribosomes, and mitochondria in a cell. It applies as much to the healing process in wounded tissue as to the revegetation of the land following the retreat of the glaciers.

In every case we can ask the same questions. What are the elements of the sequence? How are they related to each other? If we disturb one, what will happen to the other? Why are the elements and events ordered as they are? How is the order maintained in spite of environmental perturbation? Can we predict the changes which will follow specified disturbances?

To answer these questions, we need to increase the precision of our knowledge. In science we do this by measuring. In any ordered sequence we are not so much concerned with the elements themselves as with certain measurable attributes of those elements. For example, we might measure the concentration of molecules in a cell, the number of animals in a population, the weight of plants growing on a plot of a certain size, the amount of heat produced by a population of weevils in a grain silo.

Any system may be analyzed at various levels, depending on the training and competence of the investigator and the purposes of the investigation. For example, a physicist studying photosynthesis would be concerned with the behavior of the electrons and their reactions to light. An ecologist studying photosynthetic efficiency in a forest will concentrate on the relationship between available energy and the mass of vegetative product. Each will measure different variables.

ENVIRONMENTAL PERTURBATION

Regulating Mechanisms

In this text, we are going to emphasize the problems common to all levels of analysis. For an environmental text, the central question is how biological systems respond to environmental perturbation. By definition, in any ordered system a change in the value of one variable will result in a change in the value of at least one other variable. Given this delicate interrelatedness of elements and events, how can we account for the evolution and existence of complex living systems in a changing environment? Certainly environmental disturbance is not unique to the twentieth century. The environment of the earth has always been characterized by change. Inasmuch as orderly biological systems continue to function in a varying environment, they must be protected from dislocation or have the potential to proceed along alternative pathways. In the systems we study, we will be discussing the sources of input which order the system and the variety of strategies for maintaining the steady state against environmental perturbation. These latter strategies can be classed under the general term *regulating mechanisms*. Anthropologist Roy Rappaport has defined a regulating mechanism as "one that maintains the value of one or more variables within a range or ranges that permit the continued existence of the system." A system which cannot be maintained by the operation of regulating mechanisms upon input data will change character. It may evolve into another ordered system or into a disordered collection of molecules. We begin to understand the difference between the horse, the fire, and the compost pile.

Fortunately for the human species and for the evolution of complex systems over long periods of time, biological systems are, within certain limits, self-regulating, self-adjusting, self-timing, and capable of self-repair. Unfortunately, systems of self-repair evolved through eons of exposure to the hazards of the natural environment.

One of the principal questions that concerns us in the twentieth century is whether or not organisms can evolve adaptations to new hazards that we are introducing to the environment. In pragmatic terms, the question is: How much experience does a living system need before an effective response to the disruption appears? We are well aware that rapid adjustment to dislocation is characteristic of certain groups. Flies resistant to DDT and bacteria resistant to antibiotics have evolved within very short spaces of time; however, such obvious and dramatic adaptations are not the only effective responses to disruption exhibited by organisms.

The effectiveness of DDT is based on its ability to disrupt the ADP-ATP cycle. The DDT-poisoned cell still produces energy from the respiration of glucose, but no mechanism exists for transferring that energy by the conversion of ADP to ATP. The cell, literally, has no access to the large amounts of energy released by respiration. Given the fact that the ATP system is a universal energy storage and transfer mechanism in all living cells, how have we accepted the risk to all life forms entailed in its use? We have risked a great deal for the benefit of destroying a few pests who have the ability to adapt quickly to the threat. Because DDT in small doses does not kill birds or small mammals, we long assumed that they were unaffected by the pesticide. However, careful analysis of animal tissue showed that DDT was concentrated in reproductive organs and developing embryos. The organism avoids poisoning by concentrating the poison in "expendable" tissue. Needless to say, embryos whose ADP-ATP systems have been poisoned by DDT do not survive. They have no energy resource to support the rapid growth and development necessary to bring a young animal to self-sufficiency. In human beings, the DDT is concentrated in fat reserves, where it is commonly thought to be harmless since little energy exchange goes on in that tissue.

ECOSYSTEMS

The old song "the head bone connected to the neck bone, the neck bone connected to the collar bone" expresses our intuitive recognition that the parts of an organism are intimately related to each other. Our relationship with parents, grandparents, aunts, uncles, and cousins teaches us that similar organisms are related through time. However, the combined lessons of clichés, personal experience, and learned treatises have not been able to convince us that organisms of diverse origin are related in time and space in a complex system of action and reaction. Even ecocatastrophes of startling proportions have not convinced us that diverse organisms in our environment operate as parts of well-integrated systems. Even when we define that system as an ecosystem and study its components, the pragmatic implication of the definition eludes us. We pay lip service to the definition of an *ecosystem* as a group of organisms living and interacting in association under certain environmental conditions, in other words, an ordered sequence of objects, energy, and events bounded by conditions, a system in which a change in one variable will produce a change in at least one other variable, but we seem surprised when we experience that relatedness.

In recent years, many of our inland waterways have become choked with vegetation. As the mass of vegetation growing in these waters increases, many organisms that formerly abounded in the lakes and streams disappear. The stress placed upon the oxygen resource by the growth and decay of masses of vegetation disrupts the entire system. Fish and microorganisms can no longer compete for the limited oxygen. The operative conditions are changed, and not surprisingly, the complex of organisms adapted to the system must change. The growth of vegetation is stimulated by large concentrations of phosphorus discharged into the system in runoff from fertilized fields, and as detergent residues in sewage effluent. In order to support our system of intensive monoculture, we apply heavy applications of fertilizer to the land to replace the nutrients consistently removed by the continued cultivation of a single species on the same field. The phosphate applied to the field transcends its original purpose as it flows into the lake and threatens our vital need for pure water. (The cultivated field is related to the lake by a phosphorus exchange.) The difference between intention and result is of far more import than the simple economic cost of squandered fertilizer. The dislocation produced in the lacustrine system threatens to destroy a resource vital to our survival—clean water. We attempt increased crop production and achieve foul water. We seek clean clothes and achieve massive stagnation in our ponds and lakes. Why? How did the result stray so far from the intent?

We continually fail to gauge the ramifications of our actions on natural systems because we are ignorant of their logic. We act in seemingly rational ways to achieve clearly defined goals and instead achieve chaos. In every area of human interaction with the earth's ecosystems, we exhibit our shortsightedness.

Predator-Prey Interactions

The success of biological control of pests was demonstrated before the beginning of the century by the control of the immigrant Australian pest of citrus, cottony-cushion scale, by a native Australian predator, the ladybug. This beetle was imported for the express purpose of saving the United States citrus industry. In spite of the beetle's admirable accomplishments in controlling the pest, farmers applied massive doses of the newly introduced DDT in the hope of completely wiping out the scale. Instead, they actually increased the number of scale insects by killing the predator, the ladybug, rather than the more resistant prey, the cottony-cushion scale. In an effort to describe the dynamic equilibrium that exists between predator and prey populations, the Italian mathematician Volterra developed a series of equations to predict the outcome of such interactions; however, we continue to ignore those possibilities in our desire to rid the earth of all its natural predators.

In the Western United States, the United States Division of Wildlife Resources supports predator-control programs expressedly designed to protect domestic sheep and livestock grazing on the public lands. The intent and the means seem logical and rational. We are trying to manage the primary energy resource, herbs, by protecting the harvesters, domestic grazing animals. Yet certain public lands subject to that management reach a state of disorder in which only a fraction of the potential grazing capacity can be achieved.

What has happened to our neatly conceived intent-method-result model? How many intervening links in the chain from predator to a healthy rangeland did we ignorantly alter? Who perceived the poison message other than the target species, the mountain lion and coyote?

The extent of such message perception can be seen in the Kaibab Plateau of Arizona. The control of native predators so altered the natural control of the native herbivore, the deer, that resulting wild fluctuations in the deer population nearly devastated the landscape. Even subsequent deer hunts failed to curb the population.

Organisms compete for the matter and energy resources of the environment. The ranchers and sheep raisers of the United States call for predator-control programs to protect their domestic animals (important energy resources for people) from being harvested as energy resources by wild animals. In certain areas where these programs are successful, the primary energy resource, the vegetation, is destroyed. In the natural system, people, coyotes, sheep, deer, and plants harvest energy. In the managed system, the efficiency of the herbs is greatly reduced because of overgrazing by deer. The cushion scale and the orchardist both compete for the products of the citrus tree. In the poorly managed system, the cushion scale increases its population and monopolizes the harvest. In the native Australian system, people, ladybugs, and cushion scale share the resource. In the lacustrine system, many organisms are able to harvest the energy resources of the ecosystem until phosphorus gives certain vegetative forms a competitive edge. The uncontrolled growth of those forms results in a virtual monopoly of the resources of the system.

Available Energy

It is a logical assumption that limiting competition will increase the available energy resource for the surviving organisms. However, is it also logical to believe that this state will correlate with maximum utilization of the energy resources? The examples given illustrate the importance of what seems to be a minor and subtle distinction. Is the maximum energy utilization in an ecosystem achieved by the interaction of many diverse organisms present in limited numbers or by the interaction of a few varieties of energy-converting forms present in large numbers? (See Figure 1-1.)

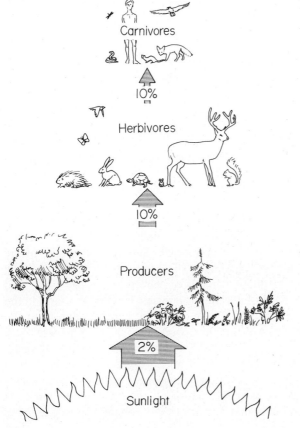

Figure 1-1 Energy flow and transformations in the food pyramid.

There is no easy answer to that question. It is a question that we will attempt to explore, in depth, in future chapters, as we judge the success of our attempt to manage our environment for maximum energy utilization.

The idea that the energy resources of the earth are finite would have been greeted with disbelief in the fifties and sixties. The sun rises each day without fail, flooding the planet with abundant cheap energy. For all practical purposes, the primary resource is infinite. Yet the strategies for harnessing this energy are definitely limited. In spite of all the protestations of the world's optimists, the capacity of the earth to produce green plant food is finite. In the closing months of 1974, we came to realize that even if problems of economics and distribution could be erased, there would not be enough food in the coming years to adequately feed all the people. Some must starve; many will starve because of circumstances.

One of the most obvious ways to increase the available energy reserves of the world is to operate on the primary process, the photosynthetic process. This research has received a good deal of attention and produced some fantastic results. The yield of all our major crops has been greatly increased by the introduction of high-yield, disease-resistant varieties which respond well to applications of large amounts of fertilizer. However, such an approach may only be successful under ideal conditions. All the miracle plants and fertilizers in the world cannot guarantee high crop yields from fields flooded late in the spring and covered by frost early in the fall. The farmers of the American Midwest had a vivid example of that fact in 1974.

A less obvious, largely ignored, but potentially more effective method for increasing the available energy reserves of the world is to manage entire ecosystems as units designed for maximum energy utilization, but how are we to achieve that management when we do not even understand the systems? (See Appendix, "Entropy.")

The problems of the twentieth century should have taught us that a simplistic definition of life as organized energy transformation has hardly been adequate in the solution of these problems. Neither does such a definition do justice to the variety, complexity, humor, and beauty of the solutions to the problem of existence. The earth is jammed with living organisms; they exist in almost unlimited variety, in every nook and cranny. We cannot, even in our wildest fantasies, imagine the earth in the absence of its living inhabitants. The magnificent canyon country of the Southwest is an alien environment, comprehensible to people only because of the biological surprises hidden in its barren vastness. A single redbud tree against a red canyon wall appears greener than an entire forest; a line of bright ferns along a seep spring on a sheer rock cliff delights our senses, promises water in a dry land, and confirms our faith that life is the common denominator of our environment. Because living things are common, we tend to take the processes that support them for granted. The claim of ecology action groups and humanists that life is fragile and that the living systems of the earth are in danger of mass destruction is no more than "crying wolf" to the citizen and politician confronted by the intransigence of the housefly, the rat, the dandelion, and the starving families of Africa and Asia.

In deserts, mountains, arctic wastes, and Yellowstone hot springs, we find living systems functioning and reproducing. Surrounded by a mass of living cells, we take ordered systems for granted. Except in reference to ourselves, we hardly consider that such order is unique to the physical world and highly unlikely from the postulates of physics and chemistry. The odds against such ordered existence are succinctly stated in the second law of thermodynamics: "In any isolated system entropy always tends to increase toward a maximum."

ENTROPY

Nevertheless, continued Callisto, he found in entropy or the measure of disorganization for a closed system an adequate metaphor to apply to certain phenomena in his own world.

Thomas Pynchon
Entropy

The word *entropy* as a section heading immediately signals the general education student: "Stop! Skip incomprehensible idea ahead." But stay with us as we try to explain a concept which has found its way from thermodynamics into literature (*Entropy,* a short story by Thomas Pynchon), into art (*Entropy and Art,* Rudolf Arnheim, 1971), and seemingly only slowly into the general biological literature, where it has the most potential for fruitful application.

We are not going to attempt to explain the concept in its most esoteric expressions or to consider the controversy which surrounds the refining, extension, and application of the concept to biological problems. The interested student can follow these arguments in the works of Gatlin, Morowitz, Mesarovic, and Pynchon listed in the bibliography. Our concern with the concept arises out of the fact that "the maximum entropy state is characterized by equiprobable, independent elementary events" (Gatlin, 1972). We note that this state is something quite different from the intimately related and ordered events and elements postulated for biological systems. If isolated systems tend to move toward maximum randomization according to the second law of thermodynamics, how can we explain the evolution and continued existence of systems in which events and elements are intimately related? We could counter with an explanation that biological systems are open rather than closed systems and therefore not subject to the second law of thermodynamics. Apart from the fact that such a simple explanation is wrong, we would miss an opportunity to learn a great deal about biological organizations if we dismissed the dilemma so easily. It is through exploring the wider application of a limited concept that we learn. The theory or its extension may later prove to be completely or partially in error, but that does not invalidate its usefulness in extending our understanding.

In spite of the fact that the theory and its extension and implications are in a state of almost constant revision, the general concept can be very useful in this text and to our understanding of environmental problems. If we are to achieve more efficient energy harvest on this planet, we must understand the efficient harvesters, the living systems, what we are doing to those systems, and the probable future state of any system given this action or that. The concept of entropy gives us a convenient shorthand expression to convey the progress of any living system along a continuum from ordered to disordered. It will help us understand the difference between a horse and a compost pile.

Consider a deck of cards. If we scatter the cards on the floor and then gather them up without any thought of arranging them, we will be dealing with a random sequence. Our chances of predicting the position of any card in the deck will be very low. Given a deck of 52 different cards, 13 each of four suits, the possible combinations or configurations of the sequence will be very high. It would be almost impossible to predict the order of any one of the possible sequences from a small random sampling of cards. Knowledge of the position of one card tells us very little about the position of the other 51. The only limit of freedom to the position of any card is physical; two cards cannot occupy the same space. The only statement we can make with absolute certainty is that any card drawn will not be found in any other position than the one it occupied.

Suppose that we decide to order the cards by some arbitrary set of rules. We will order them numerically from two to ten with the jack, queen, king, and ace following. To impose further order upon the system, we will arrange the suits in each set in the sequence, heart, diamond, club, and spade. Knowing the rules of ordering and the character of the items ordered, the position of any card in the deck can be predicted with absolute certainty. Even if we had no knowledge of the constraints upon the order but knew only the character of playing cards, we could deduce the rules by drawing a limited number of cards, noting the position of each card drawn, its character, and finally, its position relative to the preceding draw. With a larger sample, we might even deduce the character of the members of the system even if we had never seen a deck of cards. After such a random sample, we could predict, with a high degree of certainty, the positions of any of the remaining cards in the deck.

The two systems illustrate many of the important distinctions between systems with a high entropy and systems with a low entropy. In the ordered deck, the cards are not distributed randomly; the position of any card within the deck space can be predicted with accuracy. Once an arbitrary starting point has been chosen and the rules of arrangement fixed, the position of every member is fixed with respect to every other. Both the character of the elements ordered and the rules of order can be deduced by a small random sample from the space. In a low entropy system, the number of configurations the elements can assume is very low. Under the rules given for ordering the deck, only one configuration was possible. In a randomly ordered deck, the possible number of configurations is great because the items are independently distributed; the position of any card is not contingent upon the position of any other card. We can see readily then, any number of systems could be designed to lie along a continuum between the two examples. We could arrange the cards in numerical sequence by allowing the suits to vary or in suits allowing the order of the numbers and face cards to vary. In each of these two cases, the number of possible configurations the deck may assume increases but does not equal the possibilities for a completely mixed deck. The probability that we will accurately predict the position of any card decreases but again does not approach the error probability of the completely random system.

There is one other important but subtle difference in the two decks. The ordered system has the capacity to store and transmit meaning or knowledge. We may define *knowledge* in part as acquaintance with facts or principles as a result of investigation. We investigated the decks by drawing a number of cards. From a small random sample of the ordered deck, we could have deduced the fact of position of the other members of the space and the principles of the ordering. We could make sense of the system. In fact, one definition of sense, arising out of computer technology, is to "determine or locate the position or arrangement of." This definition of sense will be used again and again in our discussions. An ordered system is sensible. The disordered deck is nonsensical in terms of card position and relationship. We have arrived at a statement of another of the unique characteristics of living systems, the ability to store, convey, and process information. This ability is central to maintenance of organization in biological systems.

The relationships between organized systems, entropy, energy, and work have been well summarized for the general student by Harold J. Morowitz in his book *Entropy for Biologists:*

At all levels life is very much subject to the second law of thermodynamics. The sun as a high-temperature source and outer space as a low-temperature sink provide two effectively infinite isothermal reservoirs for the continuous performance of work. On the surface of the earth a portion of that work continually goes into building up ordered biological structures out of simple molecules such as CO_2, H_2O, N_2, NH_3, etc. Dissipative processes inherent in the random distribution of thermal energy act to constantly degrade biological structures and return the material to the small molecule pool. This tension between photosynthetic buildup and thermal degradation drives the global processes of the biosphere and leads to the great ecological cycles. The entire process is exentropic owing to the flow of energy from the sun to outer space, but the local processes may lead to great order such as a rotifer, a sonnet, or the smile on the face of Mona Lisa.

In this book we are not so much concerned with the processes that lead to order in a rotifer, a sonnet, or the smile of Mona Lisa as with the processes which have the potential to disrupt such order.

CONCLUSIONS

The ability to capture, store, utilize, and transfer energy is the basis of all life. Energy is used to perform mechanical work, transport and accumulate matter, get rid of wastes, and synthesize new molecules. The exchange of energy is a highly ordered process in both space and time. The processes are self-regulating, self-adjusting, and capable of self-repair through change and adaptation. Life systems are largely interdependent, and any disruption of one system is likely to affect the other systems. This is true at the molecular level of organization and holds for interactions at the organismal as well as ecological levels. The most efficient systems are those that are the best ordered—those that have the greatest ability to store, convey, and process information.

SELECTED READINGS

Gatlin, Lila L. *Information Theory and the Living System.* (New York: Columbia, 1972).
Lehninger, Albert L. *Bioenergetics. The Molecular Basis of Biological Energy Transformations.* (New York: W. A. Benjamin, 1965).
Mesarovic, M. D. (ed.). *Systems Theory and Biology.* (New York: Springer-Verlag, 1968).
Morowitz, Harold J. *Entropy for Biologists.* (New York: Academic, 1970).
Pynchon, Thomas. 1960. Entropy. *Kenyon Review,* Spring 1960, pp. 277–292.
Pynchon, Thomas. *Gravity's Rainbow.* (New York: Viking, 1973).

Chapter 2

The Exchange of Information

A tragic sigh, "Information, what's wrong with dope and women? Is it any wonder the world's gone insane with information come to be the only real medium of exchange?"

Thomas Pynchon
Gravity's Rainbow

A young man in China covers a wall along a busy thoroughfare with posters. The posters give a graphic description of the persecution of his sister by Communist party officials. In a Washington, D.C. square, a large number of demonstrators march and carry signs to protest the Vietnam war. In a box, in a small country town, a black cat has a litter of kittens, one gray and three black.

COMMUNICATION

These three disparate events have a common element. They are processes which involve communication. The young man in China and the war resisters take their message to the streets because they have no access to the official news channels. They disclose important truths by extraordinary channels. The cat, on the other hand, communicates the most extraordinary instructions without conscious effort. In a single fertilized egg cell, she and a tomcat have bequeathed to the next generation a master program for all the essential metabolic processes which will sustain life. It may seem farfetched to link these three events, but we do so to stress the common elements in every process of communication.

We do not need to be scientists or mathematicians to realize that living organisms are information-processing machines. We constantly receive messages from our environment, integrate those messages with stored knowledge in the brain, and respond according to conscious or unconscious goals. We communicate not only with our environment and with each other but with other organisms. I greet my dog in the morning and he goes into an ecstasy of motion, making several turns around the kitchen, presenting his neck to be rubbed, and wagging his tail. He obviously processes a message from me and communicates one in return. Two shoots emerge from a seed in the dark earth. One grows down to become a root and the other seeks the light to grow into a stem with photosynthetic leaves. Did the plant process a message from the environment?

A generation of students who grew up with the fine nature programs of American television needs little persuasion to believe that other organisms besides humans communicate effectively and precisely with each other. Anyone who has viewed the mating dance of cranes or the interaction between the bird called the *honey guide* and its eager human followers would grant that language is hardly a prerequisite for communication. We intuitively sense that communication is a universal process in living systems.

INFORMATION

As is usually the case with progress in science, however, our intuitive perception of a natural process leads to very little additional knowledge about that process. The intuitive ideas need to be given definition; assumptions need to be stated and tested before they can make a contribution to science. A few people begin to think about the processes in original ways. They state their ideas as tentative theories and give them mathematical expression. Suddenly, it seems there is an explosion of ideas, arguments, experimentation, and theorizing. The original theory is redefined, corrected, and broadly applied to diverse fields of human endeavor. This is exactly what has happened in the field of information theory.

Intuitive ideas about information were developing in many areas of study, but these were first given mathematical expression by Claude Shannon, who worked in the laboratories of the Bell Telephone Company. It was not immediately obvious to biologists that anything like the quantity defined by Shannon in his paper "The Mathematical Theory of Communication" could be important to living organisms. The problems he sought to encompass in his theory were more pertinent to engineers and electricians. These workers were trying to arrive at general answers to the questions of how much information could be transmitted along a certain channel and how that information should be coded for maximum efficiency and minimum error. They were trying to predict, using mathematical expressions, the probable state of a message as it changed from source to transmitter to receiver. At a more esoteric level, they were approaching a definition of the relationship between information, energy, and entropy.

Apart from the formidable mathematical barrier, another puzzling feature of the theory as it developed kept workers in other fields from appreciating its significance. This feature was the theorists' insistence that information theory had nothing to do with meaning. Henry Quastler, of the University of Illinois, stated the paradox thusly: "Information theory is a name remarkably apt to be misunderstood. The theory deals in a quantitative way with something called information, which, however, has nothing to do with meaning." Lila Gatlin, a theoretical physicist, realizing the difficulty that students might have with this paradox, tried to state a definition that anyone could grasp.

What is information? To be honest, information is an ultimately indefinable or intuitive first principle, like energy, whose precise definition always somehow seems to slip through our fingers like a shadow. We often define energy operationally as the capacity to do work, not the work itself. Similarly, we may define information operationally as the capacity to store and transmit meaning or knowledge, not the meaning or knowledge itself.

From this definition, we begin to understand the point mentioned at the end of Chapter 1. One important difference between ordered and disordered systems is the capacity of each to convey meaning or knowledge. We have already said that an ordered system is sensible. By *sensible* we mean that the arrangement of the elements of the sequence can be derived from a statistical sample of the system.

Is it not also obvious that a major difference between the horse and the compost pile is the capacity to store and transmit knowledge? Does this difference have any relationship to the differing capacity of each system to store and transform energy? It is readily apparent to all of us that a horse may transmit its knowledge of "being a horse" to the next generation through the reproduction and birth of a colt. However, the idea that a compost pile might communicate the knowledge of "being a compost pile" into the production of another compost pile is so ludicrous that we never even consider the impossibility of the proposition. Yet, sometimes thinking about ludicrous possibilities focuses our attention upon important relationships we might otherwise never consider. How does the capacity to process and transmit knowledge result in such vastly different future possibilities for the horse and the compost pile? Does the informational capacity of the horse have other important ramifications beyond the obvious import to reproduction and perception? Does a horse have more in common with an ordered deck of cards than with a compost pile? Can we learn something of value about communities and ecosystems from a consideration of the information capability of horses and other living systems?

The theoretical work of the communications engineer has caused us to turn our attention to several important parameters in the communications process that are liable to definition, generalization, understanding, and control. If we refer to our examples again, we will be able to see that informational processes of diverse meaning have many common elements. One of the primary problems for the horse, the cat, the young man in China, and the antiwar activists is not so much meaning but how to communicate that meaning most effectively. For the cat, is genetic coding of a skill a more effective method of transmitting survival-promoting information than experiential learning? Should a group of activists choose nonviolent intervention or terrorism as the most effective method of communication? Will self-immolation convey the same amount of information as a 50,000-person sit-in? In the sixties, we learned that a march by 50,000 people of all ages and social strata could convey the depth of the dissatisfaction with the war far more effectively than the published results of a public opinion poll showing that 50,000 opposed the war. The lessons of revolutionary politics are not lessons in meaning but lessons in the communication process. We might say lessons in "how-to." Could it be that the process of evolution constitutes lessons in "how-to" for living systems—how to communicate survival-promoting knowledge in the most efficient manner?

ERROR CONTROL

At the simplest level, every communication system is composed of at least three elements: a source or transmitter of the message, a channel, and a receiver. A message is usually thought of as a one-dimensional sequence of symbols, as seen on this page. However, mathematician

Norbert Wiener has considerably broadened the application of the information concept by defining a *message* as a "discrete or continuous sequence of measurable events distributed in time." We will use this definition again and again. In both living and nonliving systems, the sequence of symbols is ordered by a set of constraints. In the ordered deck of cards, the constraints are arbitrarily set by the character of the playing cards and our rules of ordering. One possibility for studying and understanding biological systems is to try and discover the set of constraints responsible for ordering those systems.

We may fail to see the relevance of this simple model of a communication system to biology because living systems are not so simple. A biological message may not be a one-dimensional sequence of symbols. A source or transmitter of the message is not always easily identifiable, and the channel is never as simple as a cable in a telephone communication system. In living systems, a channel is not simply a physical entity but a process involving interactions between the message and the receiver. At each interaction the message may be transformed. We have only to consider the example of visual perception to appreciate the complexity of the process. The message does not arrive at the receiver, the optical center of the brain, in the same form that it impinged upon the retina of the eye. Several transducers which change the energy from one form to another are imposed between the sighted object and the brain.

Especially in biological systems, the state of a transducer may affect its operations upon a message. Each of these interactions reduces the reliability of the transmission. One of the central problems in communications engineering remains how to increase the reliability of the transmission. One of the central problems in the evolution of living systems is also error reduction in message transmission. At the theoretical level, the problem studied by the engineer and the biologist is the same, and one theorem defines a solution in both cases. In his second theorem, Shannon formulated the idea that a message could be transmitted without error and without loss of message rate if the message had been properly encoded at the source, this in spite of the impossibility of eliminating *noise* in any system. [One definition of noise is as follows: "Any malfunction in the transmission mechanics which causes error in the message received." (Gatlin, 1972).] The interested student is referred to Gatlin for an exhaustive discussion of the application of Shannon's ideas to biological processes.

The telephone company and the living system face some of the same problems in the design of a communication system. Error control is one of the most perplexing of these problems. How much error is permissible in the system before its capacity to transmit knowledge is seriously impaired? We would suppose that the biological communication between generations exemplified by the cat and the kitten permits only low error. We suppose this because the survival of the kitten is so completely dependent upon the knowledge of how to convert the energy resources of the environment into cat flesh and bone. We suppose that a garbled message does not translate into cat survival.

Notice these are only suppositions. One of the principal stimulants to Claude Shannon's work was surely the desire of the Bell System to transmit as much information as possible at the lowest cost. In Chapter 1 we touched upon the idea that biological processes have a price that is paid in energy. Information processing also has an energy cost. Biological systems and the telephone company must both be concerned with the price of error-free transmission. Do the benefits gained from the reduction of error compensate for the cost? Cost/benefit ratios are as important to living systems as they are to the corporate executive.

Quite apart from the cost-of-error control is another subtle point. In the next three chapters of the book we shall explore the idea that error is necessary to and intimately related to the ability of living systems to adapt to environmental perturbation. The propensity for error in any communications process has been of great significance to the evolution of living systems in a changing environment.

HIGHER-ORDER SYSTEMS

From our example of visual perception, we can generalize that a communication network consists not only of hardware, in our example, the eye, the nervous system, and the brain, but also of relationships between those elements. This second point is fairly obvious, but the significance of it is not so easy to grasp. The information process in living systems can be described as a hierarchical ordering process. Symbols or message units are ordered or coded either according to some rule or by chance. However, the hardware and the processes are also ordered. According to Michael Polanyi, "each level of organization is subject to dual control: first, by the laws that apply to its elements in themselves and, second, by the laws that control the comprehensive entity formed by them." The definition of the rules of this ordering presents one of the most perplexing theoretical problems in modern scientific thought.

Once we have reduced a process to its basic elements, we can begin to sense its operation in hitherto unsuspected places. Can it be that our example from Chapter 1 (sewage effluent, lake, and vegetation) also represents a communication system processing a phosphate message? The sewage effluent is the source of the message, the lake and its living organisms constitute both a transducer of and receiver of the message, a message which has significant effect upon the ordering of the system.

Before the age of environmental awareness, so-called waste products were hardly considered at the end of the manufacturing process. We were finished with such materials and had no thought that they would continue to be processed by the environment. This attitude is one facet of the problem of environmental deterioration. "It's only hot water, dump it in the lake." In the halcyon days of industrial development of our country, there was little time or concern for questions of continuing process, and no time to consider what kind of messages we were generating into the information-processing systems of the environment and how those messages would influence the natural systems as they were integrated into them.

Our discussion has suddenly shifted emphasis from consideration of an organism as an information-processing being to consideration of an ecosystem as an information-processing system. Is this jump justified? Wiener believes that not only is it justified, but it is absolutely essential if we are to understand our environment. He has said that "it is manifest that the importance of information and communication as mechanisms of organization proceeds beyond the individual into the community." Wiener's statement stresses the relationship between information and order, which Shannon had defined by stating that entropy was the measure of the information capacity, and a relationship, which we have touched upon in our discussion of the ordered deck of cards. We stressed that the capacity of the ordered deck to convey information was related to the ordering of the elements of the deck. Does an ordered sequence of elements and events, defining an ecosystem, constitute an information-processing system? If so, what is the significance of the relationship between order and information in ecosystem dynamics?

Australians, Rabbits, and Myxomatosis

Let us examine another environmental problem to determine if the "capacity to store and transmit meaning or knowledge" has anything to do with the ordering of an ecosystem. The European colonists of Australia brought along many exotic species such as scotch pines and lombardy poplars to assuage their homesickness in a strange environment. They also brought rabbits to hunt and to supplement a diet of mutton and beef. The rabbits bred with their normal fecundity, producing a population explosion that threatened to decimate the already sparce vegetation of the semiarid country. Predation by humans and dogs, the Australian dingo, could not control the rabbits. Another source of biological control was sought and found—the myxomatosis virus that infects rabbits. In the first years after the introduction of the virus, the rabbit population declined and the vegetation began to recover from rabbit overgrazing. This happy condition prevailed for only a few years, however, after which the rabbit population increased again.

The Australian continent had long been separated from the principal landmasses of European experience. The energy exchange systems of that landmass differ from all others in the world in a significant feature. The ecosystems were organized around relationships between herbs and herbivores. For all practical purposes, large carnivores to harvest the herbivores were missing from that ecosystem organization. In other areas of the world, carnivores are a vital element in herbivore control. When rabbits were introduced to Australia, they were effectively freed from a significant population-control system, predation. A once-ordered habitat, supplying the energy and resource needs of herbs and kangaroos, deteriorated to a very low-productivity habitat. No mechanism or process existed in the Australian environment for the organization of such a fecund herbivore into the energy exchange system. The virus was introduced to the Australian system because scientists hoped that it would contribute to the organization of the rabbits into a stable relationship with the native herbivores and herbs. For a time, this hope was realized as the rabbit population was reduced to a level compatible with the survival of forage. However, after a time, the rabbit population again increased. Why?

Before we explore this question further, it may be well to examine some of the assumptions of our argument. The principal assumption is that communication or the transfer of information is vital to survival of living systems. Obviously, the cells of a kitten must possess some knowledge of how to conduct the metabolic processes that make energy transformations possible for the cat. It follows that the efficiency of the information-processing systems in living organisms is judged by their contribution to survival. But, in the Australian system, the survival of what? The rabbits, the virus, people, herbs, sheep? When we deal with the relationships between these organisms, we are dealing with a system at a higher level of organization and we have to revise our criterion. Now, we want to know the effect of that organization upon energy utilization of a segment of the landscape. Is the herbivore-herb system a more efficient energy-utilization system than the carnivore-herbivore-herb system? If we wish to understand the Australian system, or any ecosystem, we must understand it at successive levels of organization. To understand the relationship between the rabbits and the virus, we need to explore the information-processing systems as they operate at the cellular and molecular level in organisms.

PROTEINS

In any ecosystem under consideration, the ultimate source of the biological messages will be found in the molecular structures of the cell of a

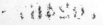

living organism. The work of many biologists, biochemists, and geneticists has permitted the definition of the information-processing systems that exist at the molecular level. In all organisms, there are two general classes of compounds whose primary function is informational. These two classes are proteins and nucleic acids.

Proteins function in a variety of ways in organisms, serving as structural components, as enzymes which catalyze the metabolic pathways, in sensory organs, in oxygen transport systems, as the contractive filaments in muscles, and in the immunological protection systems. A *Los Angeles Times* medical writer, describing research on cell-membrane proteins, gives a highly imaginative description of protein function. "These subs (proteins) also act as sensors that send messages to the cell's interior telling it what things are like topside. Among others, the cell uses this information to decide whether to divide or not. The subs even have tiny 'periscopes' that interact with 'war ships' cruising the area. The warships are antibodies screening all cells to make certain none is a diseased enemy."

In a developing seed, proteins serve to process messages from the environment in a manner which promotes orderly development. In the emerging tissue which is to become a root, hormones concentrated by gravity regulate cell division and growth in the surrounding tissue to produce downward growth of the root. In the emerging shoot, light influences the hormone concentration in a way which causes the plant to grow toward the light. These observations can be supported by very simple experiments with synthetic hormones and young seedlings. The response of the plant to its environment is governed by the differential reaction of shoot and root tissue to protein concentration. The concentration, structure, and hence, biological activity of the protein is in turn influenced by the environment. A plant can be said to process a message from the environment as surely as an animal can.

The structural and communicative functions of a protein molecule derive from the ordering of the amino acids which compose the molecule. A protein molecule may be thought of as a message composed of amino acids (symbols) ordered according to some constraint or set of rules. The symbol set used by the living cell consists of 20 different amino acids. The amino acid units are joined to form polypeptide chains which in turn join to form a complex protein molecule. The information content of the molecule depends not only on the sequence and repetition of amino acids but on the configuration of the macromolecule. This mode of communication is not incomprehensible to us as it is analogous to the mode we have in written communication. Words are formed from 26 different letters arranged in various combinations. These combinations are arranged to form sentences and the sentences to form paragraphs. At each successive level of operation, a different set of rules prescribes the ordering of the system. The ordering of amino acids into proteins and proteins into macromolecules and macromolecules into structures is an analogous system in three dimensions.

In the complex three-dimensional arrangement, the function of an individual amino acid is affected not only by its linear neighbors but by the juxtaposition to distant amino acids because of the twisting and folding of the chain. This three-dimensional structure is significant in the organization of supramolecular structures and organelles within the cell. The arrangement and exposure of the amino acids in one macromolecule may influence the type of molecules which will fit in structural array around it. A small change in the amino acid sequence of the protein molecule can thus produce a significant change in function and structure. If the changed protein is involved in many different enzymatic reactions of the organism, the result will be seen at many different stages of development.

The complex structure and position effects of the amino acids explain how many proteins—enzymes, for example—may possess a similar function in all organisms and yet exhibit a distinctive character in each species. The oxygen-transporting pigment, hemoglobin, is found performing the same function in a wide variety of animals and yet is distinctive in each. This characteristic of proteins can be explained by postulating the existence of certain invariant sequences and positions related to function and the variation at other sites related to species specificity. The possession of characteristic form permits the distinction of self from invader, so important to the integrity of the self.

When we consider the great number of different arrangements possible using 20 different amino acids and combine that versatility with three-dimensional variety, we can understand how protein variation can account for the great diversity exhibited by the living organisms of the earth. However, that simply begs the question of how to explain the diversity. One of the most obvious questions at this point is how the structure of the protein is determined.

CHROMOSOMES AND GENES

The observation that characteristics are passed from one generation to another in living organisms must be nearly as old as humanity. Ancient farmers, herders, pigeon fanciers, gardeners, and horse breeders selected and bred plants and animals for specific characters. In 1865, a monk, Gregor Mendel, working in a monastery garden, demonstrated that this inheritance could be mathematically expressed. He provided a scientific base for the selective breeding that has produced our "miracle" grains.

Mendel found that when a garden pea with round seeds was crossed to a variety that produced wrinkled seeds, all the offspring (F_1 generation) grew into plants with round seeds. However, when the offspring were crossed with each other, the next generation (F_2 generation) produced an assortment of plants, some with round seeds and some with wrinkled seeds. The types were present in the approximate ratio of one wrinkled-seed plant to three round-seeded plants. Mendel's work was largely ignored by the scientific community of the time.

In 1835, Hugo von Mohl observed small thread-shaped bodies in the nucleus of the cells. These bodies were later called *chromosomes* or "colored bodies" from their tendency to absorb dye dropped upon the tissue preparations. The number and shape of the chromosomes were observed to be constant in all the cells of an organism but to vary from species to species. During cell division, the chromosomes participate in an elegant series of maneuvers whereby they reproduce and redistribute themselves into the two halves of a dividing cell. In most organisms, chromosomes are present as pairs, that is in the diploid set. In ordinary cell division, the chromosomes reproduce and divide themselves so that each daughter cell has a full complement of chromosome pairs. In certain tissues of plants and animals, however, cell division produces not two cells with a full diploid set of chromosomes, but four cells called *gametes,* each with only half the number of chromosomes of the parent, that is, with a haploid set. These cells are then able to fuse with other haploid cells to restore the diploid number, that is, to produce paired sets of chromosomes once again. This process is diagramed in Figure 2-1. This cell division and subsequent union of haploid cells is the basis of sexual reproduction. The new diploid cell formed from the fusion of two haploid cells contains one set of chromosomes from each parent. This process is the basis of selective breeding. The contribution of one chromosome of a pair by each parent permits the recombination of desirable characters from two organisms into one offspring. In the transfer of chromosomes, cells transmit information to daughter cells. In the process of sexual reproduction, two parents may contribute to the information store of the new organisms.

By the time Mendel's work was rediscovered, the study of cell division and chromosome movements provided a physical explanation of his observations. It was postulated that the characters Mendel observed were determined by "genes" present upon the chromosomes. Thus, a strain of peas, which always produced round-seeded offspring, was thought to have two genes for round seeds, one on each of a pair of chromosomes. Conversely, the wrinkled-seeded varieties have two genes for wrinkled seeds. Somehow, when the two types were crossed, the gene for round seeds "dominated" the gene for wrinkled seeds and all the

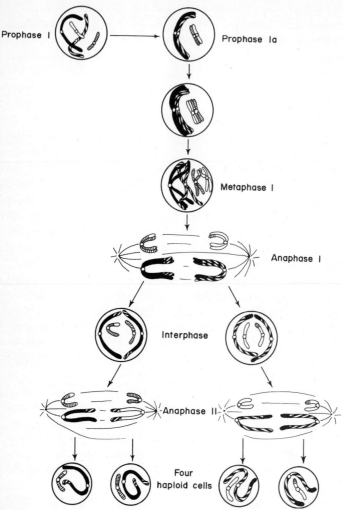

Prophase I

Prophase Ia

Metaphase I

Anaphase I

Interphase

Anaphase II

Four
haploid cells

Figure 2-1 Meiosis: The duplication of chromosomes and cells to form "daughter" cells.

offspring had round seeds. The gene for wrinkled seeds had not disappeared from the informational store of the plants. When that gene was sorted out by cell division in gamete production and that gamete combined with another having a gene for wrinkled seeds, a plant with wrinkled seeds appeared again. The two genes, *R* and *r,* which appear on homologous chromosomes and affect the same characteristic are called *alleles*. In the production of gametes the two alleles sort independently, one going to each gamete. (See Figure 2-2.)

Subsequent experimentation over many years illustrated that genes control the character of organisms by controlling enzyme synthesis. The original one-gene–one-enzyme hypothesis was eventually broadened to one-gene–one-protein.

DNA

Since a specific type of protein may be involved in many different processes and structures in the living organism, many characteristics can be affected by one gene. In spite of progress in chromosome mapping for location of genes controlling specific proteins and the success of selective breeding experiments, the specific nature of the hereditary material remained a mystery. In 1943, O. Avery and his coworkers demonstrated that deoxyribonucleic acid (DNA) was the genetically functional material.

The chemical structure of DNA was already known, but it gave no clues to how DNA might control the genetic transfer of information. The molecule was a combination of sugar and phosphate units and four bases: adenine (A), thymine (T), guanine (G), and cytosine (C). In all the DNA studied, the amount of adenine had been found to equal the amount of thymine, and the amount of cytosine to equal the amount of guanine. In any one plant or animal, the amount of DNA was identical in all tissues and exhibited a characteristic $A + T / G + C$ ratio. This ratio differed from

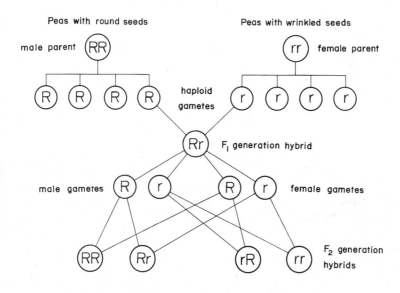

Figure 2-2 Diagrammatic illustration of Mendel's observations.

species to species as did the amount of DNA. It hardly seemed possible that this one molecule, common to all organisms and varying in seemingly insignificant ways, could code the infinite variety of the living world. Since the structure of the molecule was still unknown, no mechanism for the performance of its informational capability could be postulated. The hardware of the system was known, but the functioning system could not be understood until the relationship of the parts was revealed.

Watson-Crick Model

In 1953, James Watson and Francis Crick published a brilliant model for the DNA structure. Once elucidated, the Watson-Crick model proved almost too simple to be true, for it not only satisfied the evidence gathered from chemical analysis, x-ray crystallography, and physical chemistry, but it provided a relatively simple explanation for the biological activity of the molecule. The model readily satisfied the two important functions of information storage and transfer (see Figure 2-3).

Watson and Crick proposed that the molecule was formed from two thin polymeric chains twisted about each other in the form of a regular double helix. The two backbone chains were constructed from the regular sequence of a sugar and a phosphate group. The sugar and phosphate are joined in such a way that the two chains exhibit the property of direc-

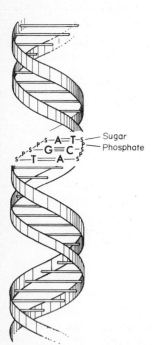

Sugar
Phosphate

Figure 2-3 Diagram of the Watson-Crick model of the DNA molecule. Two sugar and phosphate chains are intertwined in a helical coil and held together by hydrogen (H) bonds positioned between the complementary bases (adenine, thymine, guanine, or cytosine).

tion. Linking the two backbone chains as treads on a spiral staircase were the four bases. Adenine was always paired with thymine and cytosine with guanine. This linear arrangement of the bases along the chain constitutes a *message,* that is, a sequence of symbols ordered according to some constraints. Herein lies the capacity of the molecule to store and transmit knowledge.

The replication of DNA is postulated to occur by the simultaneous uncoiling and breaking of the hydrogen bonds which join the base pairs so that each strand, as it separates, is free to mate with complementary bases for the formation of a new daughter strand. Thus, two molecules are produced—each new helix comprises one parental and one daughter strand. Each strand of the DNA serves as a template for the production of its base complement. Obviously, the process is not as simple as depicted here. We have only given a bare outline of the process.

Protein Synthesis

The knowledge encoded in the DNA is brought to bear upon the activities of the cell through the mechanism of protein synthesis. Many independent investigations revealed that the information coded in the base sequence of the DNA, which is found in the nucleus of the cell, is conveyed to a ribosome, the site of protein synthesis in the cell cytoplasm, by another nucleic acid compound, messenger RNA (mRNA). The single-stranded mRNA is also composed of a ribose sugar phosphate backbone and four bases. The bases are the same as in DNA with the exception that the thymine of DNA is replaced by uracil in RNA. The mRNA is formed as a base complement to one strand of DNA. It follows from base complement coding that the two strands of the DNA molecule will code two strands of mRNA with different base sequences. The strands of mRNA code the sequence of amino acids in the formation of proteins. A schematic drawing of the process is given in Figure 2-4.

Codons

Since the relationship of DNA to protein synthesis had already been established, the problem remained to decipher how the sequence of bases on mRNA was read, if four different bases were to specify twenty different amino acids. If the bases were to be read as "two-letter words," or instructions, as is shown in Figure 2-5, only 4×4, or 16 different instructions would be possible. However, if the bases were read in triplets, as shown in Figure 2-6, then $4 \times 4 \times 4$, or 64, different combinations are possible. Within five years after the first discovery that UUU coded for the amino acid phenylalanine, the entire base code dictionary had been worked out. The numerous experiments, which produced these results, revealed that certain amino acids could be coded

G-G-T-A-T-C-G-T-T-G-A-A
· · · · · · · · · · ·
C-C-A-T-A-G-C-A-A-C-T-T
G-G-U-A-U-C-G-U-U-G-A-A

DNA molecule

mRNA strand

Figure 2-4 The coding of the mRNA from a single strand of the DNA molecule.

	A	**T**	**C**	**G**
A	AA	AT	AC	AG
T	TA	TT	TC	TG
C	CA	CT	CC	CG
G	GA	GT	GC	GG

Figure 2-5 Possible different word combinations, two-letter words.

GGU   AUC   GUU   GAA

Figure 2-6 Message using three-letter words on the mRNA strand illustrated in Figure 2-4.

Glycine   L-Isoleucine   L-Valine   L-Glutamic acid

Figure 2-7 Amino acid sequence.

by more than one codon. That is to be expected from the fact that 64 codons are available to code 20 amino acids. In Figures 2-4 through 2-7, we have given a much simplified representation of the coding process.

By a complex process involving several enzymes, ATP, and transfer RNA, the amino acids specified by the codons of the mRNA are gathered, assembled, and bonded in the precise sequence specified by the master program instruction from the DNA. A segment of DNA coding for one protein molecule is thought to represent a single gene. In general, it is postulated that dominant genes produce functional proteins, whereas the proteins coded by recessive genes are somehow nonfunctional. According to this hypothesis, the hybrid pea plants (*Rr*), observed by Mendel, would have a gene on one chromosome of the pair which produced functional protein and a recessive gene on the other chromosome producing a nonfunctional protein. However, sufficient metabolic product would be available to the plant to permit the orderly development of round seeds. In a homozygous recessive plant (*rr*) with the recessive gene appearing on both chromosomes of the pair, no functional protein for the development of round seeds is produced.

The long peptide chains produced by a ribosome, as it reads out the mRNA instructions, may have as many as 500 amino acids ordered in precise sequence. The code, illustrated in Figure 2-7, might be the beginning of the code for insulin. The insulin molecule is composed of 51 amino acids beginning with glycine. In general, the language of the DNA code is universally understood in all plant and animal systems. The protein-synthesizing systems of bacteria, mice, humans, and roses all translate the codons of mRNA into the same amino acids. However, recent experimental work has revealed that the code may be ambiguous under certain circumstances as triplets have been found which code two different amino acids. Some unknown controls must operate in the transcription process to permit the specification of the correct amino acid for the sequence being built. Gatlin has suggested that the ribosome functions as a "master craftsman," able to translate the sequence of triplets with the aid of contextual clues to determine the admissible information to the process.

Error

In spite of all the controls, we do know that errors in information transfer and processing occur. Mistakes are made in the transfer of DNA from cell to cell, in the formation of mRNA from the DNA strand, and in the transcription of the protein. For example, an informational error in human DNA has produced a gene which is nonfunctional for the production of the protein phenylalanine hydroxylase. This enzyme is necessary for the normal conversion of the amino acid phenylalanine to another amino acid, tyrosine. In the absence of the enzyme, the normal conversion is blocked and an alternate system producing a toxic product occurs. The amino acid phenylalanine and the toxic product accumulate in the cerebral fluid. The presence of these compounds in the cerebral fluid alters the environment of the developing cells of the brain. In the absence of any regulating mechanism to restore the cerebral environment to the normal state, the brain is unable to develop and function normally. Individuals affected by this genetic change exhibit severe mental retardation and motor impairment. An error in communication at the molecular level influences orderly development at many successive levels of organization. An internal chemical message originating in the DNA and communicated through many transformations influences the ability of the organism to operate in the ecosystem. Since the by-products of abnormal phenylalanine metabolism appear in the urine as well as the cerebral fluid, a simple test for the condition, phenylketonuria (PKU), is available. If the affected infant is placed on a diet low in phenylalanine for the first 6 years of life, it may develop normally, since the brain cells are apparently not receptive to a *PKU message* after that age. Medical science provides the regulating system which maintains the environment of the brain in the steady state necessary to normal development.

The discovery of the relationship between DNA and protein synthesis has raised the hope that genetic defects might be treated by "repair" of DNA segments. However, the prospect is far from reality. The DNA of human chromosomes are incredibly long molecules, the smallest containing over a thousand million nucleotide units. Two experimenters have calculated that if the chemical identity of the bases could be revealed at the rate of one base per second, it would take over 100 years to map the entire base sequence of the DNA of a mammal.

However, DNA represents an ordered system. We have already discussed the fact that ordered systems exhibit the characteristics of predictability. Obviously, the problem of predicting base order in DNA is not as simple as predicting the arrangement of the cards in the ordered deck, but the theoretical considerations are the same. A great deal is being learned about the structure and informational capacity of DNA as it is analyzed by means of the theoretical concepts developed in the field of information theory.

In the treatment of genetic disorders, the potential remains for the introduction of segments of functional DNA into cells with "defective genes." This phenomenon is already an operative process in nature, as viruses have been discovered to transfer resistance to antibiotics from one bacterial cell to another. A virus is a DNA or RNA molecule shielded by a protein coat. The virus attaches itself to a host cell, dissolves the cell wall, and inserts its genetic program into the host cell. Within the host, the viral chromosome somehow inactivates the host cell's own instructional program and utilizes the protein-synthesizing machinery of the host to reproduce viral DNA and protein coat. Occasionally in this process, segments of host DNA are incorporated into the virus chromosome and can in this manner be communicated to another cell. In the operation of viruses, we see the fundamental nature of the DNA informational system. Carrying only a set of instructions, the virus can communicate its nature into new virus particles by appropriating the functional metabolic systems of other living organisms. A functioning cell usually dies once it has aided the production of a number of virus particles. The viral life cycle is diagramed in Figure 2-8.

The DNA code, transmitted from parent to offspring by the chromosomes, in effect transmits the vital protein blueprint from generation to generation. In order to produce a duplicate set of plans for the offspring, the parental DNA must duplicate itself. The observed variation in the world of plants and animals is evidence that the copying process is not error-free. Base pair deletions, replacements, and insertions of extra base pairs are all possible during DNA replication. These events, which change

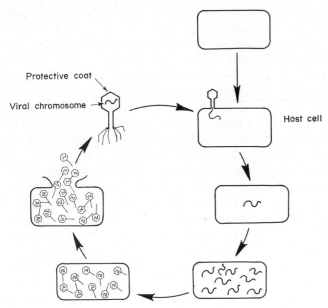

Figure 2-8 The life cycle of a virus. The virus first attaches to a host cell, then penetrates to where the viral genetic material substitutes for that of the cell, thus perpetuating more viral material. *(Based on Watson, J. D., Molecular biology of the gene.)*

the fundamental structure of the DNA, are commonly called *mutations.* Balanced against this possibility for error are numerous systems which promote stability and unvarying duplication. In addition to the systems briefly mentioned for screening the mRNA sequence and selecting the proper translation of the condon, the DNA molecule itself possesses significant powers of self-repair. Such systems constitute effective safe- guards against the action of mutagens, which have been a common feature of the environment of evolving organisms. One well-studied repair system is the thymine dimer system. The absorption of ultraviolet light by adjacent thymine bases in the DNA chain results in their fusion, and thus prevents the normal operation of that segment of the DNA. An elaborate system of enzymes exists which functions to dissolve that dimer. Without the evolution of repair systems, a reliable information transfer system could not function and the DNA molecule would never have achieved its importance as a genetic message in an environment fraught with hazards.

Yet, while recognizing the importance of error-free transmission, we must recognize that error has been almost as important to survival and evolution of living systems as the capacity for error control. Without the possibility for error, the Australian rabbits would never have become resistant to the myxomatosis virus. By an accident of replication, new information conferring resistance to the virus is incorporated into the DNA of rabbit embryos. Those rabbits produce subsequent generations exhibiting the resistance. The virus, in effect, acts to eliminate the nonresistant varieties of rabbit from the population.

We begin to grasp the magnitude of the difference between a horse and a compost pile. The horse possesses in DNA a master program for the construction and operation of functional systems to organize matter and energy. Furthermore, a horse can replicate itself by replication of the master program to "project" "horse systems" in a space-time continuum. The capacity of the living system to transmit knowledge resides not only in the original specification of the protein structure but in the subsequent organization of the proteins into orderly processes and tissues. Because of the propensity of the system for error, it may produce "trial" variants which can be tested for effectiveness in the varied environments of the earth.

Error in the transfer of information and the recombination of mutant forms by several processes, including sexual reproduction, have resulted in a tremendous variety of forms of life that are able to exploit the energy resources of the earth. Primary among the many causes of variation in organisms are changes in the DNA structure. Changes in the DNA molecule may be localized, as with gene mutation, or they may involve large portions of DNA, as when the structure or number of chromosomes is altered. In the duplication of chromosomes that occurs before cell division, the chromosomes often break and rejoin. Thus, two chromosomes may exchange genetic material with each other. Within certain limits determined by the chemical nature of the DNA, the errors which produce variation can be considered random. The most important point for the student to grasp is that the mutation or change in the genetic material does not originate or arise from any knowledge relative to need or desirability. Neither the organism nor the DNA molecule possesses a priori knowledge of the probability of success. Out of the inconceivable variety of possible forms and systems, only the most efficient energy transformers survive. Life progresses by the most inefficient of processes, trial and error.

CONCLUSION

The character of an organism can be regarded to be a compromise between the effects of many different genes worked out over the course of evolution. The prevalence of a gene in the population is maintained in relation to the balance between its advantageous and deleterious effects. If the characters it regulates are favorable to a population, interacting most efficiently with the environment from conception to maturity, the gene will appear most frequently.

Evolution is opportunistic. In no sense does natural selection produce species perfectly structured along any one adaptive line. Selection produces compromises. What evolves depends on what came before. New types, from proteins to populations, must be molded within the constraints of old adaptations. Evolution is "directed" by the constraints of the past and not the vision of the future, and *Homo sapiens* provides the best example of this fact.

Homeostatic mechanisms are vital to maintaining the integrity of species. These mechanisms, operating at all levels of organization, balance flexibility or variability in the system against stability. Exchange of information is critical at every step of the way. The potential for variation is essential for the population to "keep up" with changes in environment. It is also valuable in utilizing unoccupied, or inefficiently occupied, niches in the environment. Stability is essential in maintaining the efficiency of mechanisms that have been successful over the course of time.

In spite of the effectiveness of the environment in producing improvement in many functions and structures, this trend is not inevitably destined to proceed to perfection. The implications and warnings of this for humans are obvious in that it leaves little reason to consider humans to be the "ultimate" organism, or that everything we do is for the "better." We may be only another stage in the continuing diversification of DNA and life.

SELECTED READINGS

Abramson, Norman. *Information Theory and Coding.* (New York: McGraw-Hill, 1963).

Gatlin, Lila L. *Information Theory and the Living System.* (New York: Columbia, 1972).

Koller, Peo C. *Chromosomes and Genes: The Biological Basis of Heredity.* (New York: Norton, 1972).

Oparin, A. I. *Life; Its Nature, Origin and Development.* Trans. by Ann Syrge. (New York: Academic, 1964).

Polanyi, Michael. *The Tacit Dimension.* (Garden City, N.Y.: Anchor Books, Doubleday, 1967).

Quastler, Henry (ed.). *Essays on the Use of Information Theory in Biology.* (Urbana: University of Illinois Press, 1953).

Watson, James D. *Molecular Biology of the Gene.* (New York: W. A. Benjamin, 1970).

———. *The Double Helix.* (New York: Atheneum, 1968).

Wiener, Norbert. *Cybernetics or Control and Communication in the Animal and the Machine.* (Cambridge, Mass.: MIT, 1962).

Chapter 3

Stability and Variation

It is part, part of an old and clandestine drama for which the human body serves only as a set of very allusive, often cryptic programme-notes—it's as if the body we can measure is a scrap of this programme found outside in the street, near a magnificent stone theatre we cannot enter.

Thomas Pynchon
Gravity's Rainbow

A young black mother watches in anguish as a doctor examines her baby, who screams in pain. His muscles and joints ache, his head pounds, and his heart races to rush oxygen to the cells of his body. He is suffering a sickle cell crisis. Over and over, she puts down the persistent "why?" "Why should one so young endure so much pain?" She can hardly imagine that the answer to her "why" is to be found in a small, seemingly insignificant change in DNA in a population of distant ancestors living in a malaria-infested area of the African bush. The pain of her baby is intimately related to the survival of her ancestors. She can only hope that awakened consciousness of her race in American has forced attention and research into the long-neglected disease in time to save her child from further pain and eventual death in an acute crisis.

VARIATION

Sexual Reproduction

In Chapter 2, we attributed variation in the genetic information to a change in the DNA structure. However, there is a much more significant source of change in the genetic message communicated from one generation to the next. The enormous depth and range of the diversity, which permits a wide and varied utilization of the earth's resources, developed out of the sexual system of reproduction. As a method of sampling and pooling genes, sexual reproduction represents a nearly perfect experimental design, combining random sampling, which ensures an abundant source of variation, with a high degree of specification or limitation of choice, which ensures genetic stability and continuity.

In the process of sexual reproduction, the total message stored in the parent is randomly assorted into halves. As in a secret code that must be matched to another portion to constitute a message, one gamete must fuse with another to produce an operational message unit. Chance plays an important role in both the random assortment of chromosomes and the fusion of gametes. Another possibility for variation arises in that information may be exchanged between two chromosomes.

Random Assortment

We can begin to appreciate the potential for variation in sexual reproduction if we follow only six genes distributed upon three pair of chromosomes. Suppose the parental genotype is heterozygous for all three characters. By *heterozygous* we mean that the alleles on the homologous chromosomes are different. We can represent the parental genotype as *AaBbCc*. By halving its message, the parent can produce the following different gametes: *ABC, ABc, Abc, AbC, aBC, aBc, abC, abc.* Each chromosome segregates independently of the others. Within certain limits, the gametes also combine at random. A sperm bearing the *abc* chromosomes has an equal chance of mating with any of the eight egg types listed. Now try to imagine the possible variation in the species *Homo sapiens* with 23 pairs of chromosomes, each with a very large number of genes.

Crossing-over A second source of variation in sexual reproduction is the process of crossing-over. In the reduction division that precedes gamete formation the homologous chromosomes (each consisting of two chromatids) pair, the chromatids break and recombine to produce chromosomes that carry information from two different sources. Again let us construct a sample genotype for an insect. This time we will diagram only one pair of homologous chromosomes but will follow two genes, one for eye color and one for wing type. When two genes occur together on the same chromosome, we call those genes *linked*. The genes occur in two allelic forms. The gene for red eyes is linked to the gene for long wings We will make white eyes recessive to red eyes and vestigial wings recessive to long wings. Three different genotypes (but only two different phenotypes) are possible in the flies: *RRLL* and *RrLl* (red eyes, long wings) and *rrll* (white eyes and vestigial). If we follow the diagram in Figure 3-1, we can see that crossing-over can produce the possibility for two new genotypes detectable as two new phenotypes. Crossing-over recombines the linked genes so that we have the possibility for a white-eyed, long-winged fly or a red-eyed, vestigial-winged fly.

The possibility for variation from crossing-over is limited by the structure of the chromosomes and the distance between genes. Certain linked genes are rarely separated by crossing-over. They seem to be "protected" from crossing-over. In the way gene combinations with survival value remain linked.

NATURAL SELECTION

Simple admission to the DNA or chromosome structure is no guarantee that a variation will become a member of the society of information for the propagation of living systems. The effect of the variation will be tested at successive levels of complexity and over a long period of time. The new information must prove, over and over again, its fitness for inclusion in the ordered systems that characterize the living world. Fitness need not be resolved with simple yes/no decisions, however; instead, fitness is a matter of compromise, for the test is focused on the total environmental system, of which the change is but one small part.

DNA can change, but the changed DNA must retain its molecular identity; it must code functional mRNA. The codons of the mRNA must be translated into the production of essential, meaningful proteins. The proteins must permit and abet the development of a coherent organization. The organism bearing the change must operate within a highly specified segment of the environment. If the organism is able to reproduce, the change contributes to the informational store of the population.

The survival and replication of new genotypes will depend upon the information capability of the change relative to order. Can the new information be integrated into previously existing ordered systems without unduly stressing the regulatory mechanisms which permit the continued existence of the system? In any well-regulated system, a change may be simply countered by minor adjustments in the other variables. In

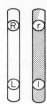

1.   Homologous pair of chromosomes

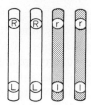

2.   Four strand stage of meiosis

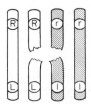

3.   Breakage of 2 chromatids

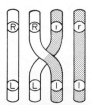

4. Crosswise reunion of broken chromatids

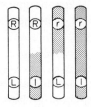

5.   Crossover products

Figure 3-1 The process of crossing over, during which segments of different chromosomes exchange positions, thereby altering the genetic nature of the cell.

many cases, new genetic information can result in a suitable adjustment to changing information from the environment. Thus a change in genetic information may permit a population to exploit a new niche in the environment. A change may confer an advantage in energy-processing potential for one population compared to another, or it may confer a disadvantage. The change is judged against one simple criterion: Can the changed system continue to supply its energy demands from the resources of the environment?

Successive Trials

Notice that we have not specified the level of the system. It may be molecular or metabolic, an organ, organisms, or population. By definition any variation in an ordered system must produce a change in at least one other variable. In a hierarchical, ordered system, the influence of a variation will be communicated from its source in one level to many other levels. At each level the variation will be tested against the criterion of continued operation of the system. The judgment of success or failure will vary at each level of organization. This is a significant point which we tend to forget in any discussion of natural selection.

We can begin to understand continual reappraisal of the variation by referring to the phenylketonuria (PKU) example. Apparently the coding error which produces PKU does not disrupt the DNA-RNA system at the molecular level. The fetus bearing the changed information develops normally and in all appearances is normal at birth. It is only with the ingestion of milk that the anomaly appears. The affected infant can not metabolize the phenylalanine in milk. At the metabolic level, an alternate system for phenylalanine metabolism replaces the normal pathway. At the level of interaction between the environment and the developing brain, the anomaly becomes obvious. Behavior of the organism is influenced in such a way as to preclude its unaided survival in the ecosystem. The variation arises at the molecular level, but the judgment for or against survival is made (in this case) at the ecosystem level.

Once we begin to think about this concept of successive trials, it is not difficult to grasp. A variation may be sensible (contribute to order) in the cellular system yet create havoc within the tissue organization, as is the case with certain types of cancerous tumors. The modified information may be sensible to the extent of producing a functioning organism, but may produce an organism whose functioning is nonsensical in an ecological context.

Sickle Cell Mutation

The sickle cell mutation of human hemoglobin is sensible at the level of molecular organization, for in terms of the beta chain architecture, the substitution of valine for glutamic acid at the sixth position does not disrupt the organization of that chain. In essence, the beta chain does not distinguish between the two amino acids. However, anomalies begin to appear in the organization of the alpha and beta chains into the hemoglobin molecule. Under conditions of oxygen stress, the cells containing the S hemoglobin type will assume a sickled shape. These sickled cells accumulate in the walls of the smallest vessels and prevent the normal flow of oxygenated blood to the cells of the body. A seemingly insignificant change in amino acid order in the beta chain is magnified into a significant change in the hemoglobin molecule. The change influences every oxygen-dependent system of the body. In the African bush, where the sickle gene is common, individuals homozygous for sickle cell die before reproductive age.

In the African environment and many others around the world, the influence of the new bit of information embodied in the S hemoglobin extends beyond the individual to the ecosystem. The mutation of hemoglobin, which produces sickling, also produces a red blood cell which is a less acceptable host to the malaria-causing organism, *Plasmodium falciparum*. In tropical climates, children heterozygous for sickle cell have a degree of resistance to *P. falciparum* infestation. Carriers of the trait are more likely to survive to reproductive age than noncarriers. They are more fit in a malarial environment than individuals with regular hemoglobin. Falciparum malaria is common in all areas of India, Africa, and Europe where a high percentage of the population exhibits the sickle cell trait. However, the ecological relationships between the mutant gene and malaria are not quite as simple as we have illustrated. In certain groups of African herdspeople living in falciparum environments, the sickle cell trait is very uncommon. It has been suggested by some investigators that the cattle which are closely associated with these pastoral peoples provide an alternate resource for mosquitoes. If this is a valid interpretation, then life-style becomes as important as genetic strategies of resistance to falciparum malaria. Will political pressures upon the African herders to abandon their herds translate into an increased incidence of malaria and consequent selection in favor of the sickle cell gene? From even a simplified exposition of the parameters of the sickle cell mutation, we become aware that the sense or nonsense of the information embodied in DNA is interpreted in an ecological context. Do we consider this context when we intentionally or inadvertently reorganize the animal and human populations of the earth?

VARIABILITY VERSUS RELIABILITY

In the opening paragraphs of this chapter, we emphasized the proposition that change has been tremendously important to the evolution and survival of organisms. Let us now stop and consider that the opposite strategy, that is, the ability to resist change, is also vital to the success of living systems. From purely theoretical considerations, both variety and reliability are essential to the information process. A DNA molecule, composed of a long invariant string of adenine bases, would convey no message, but neither would a highly variable strand, which could not be read as meaningful triplets. Any regulating mechanisms that balance the tension between variability and reliability are of such importance to the survival of living systems that they are themselves subject to strong selection pressure.

Control of Variation

A multitude of strategies for maintaining the integrity of successful forms balances the large variation which results from immigration of genes from one gene pool to another, from mutation, from crossing-over, and from the random assortment of chromosomes and the chance fusion of gametes. We have already alluded to some of the limitations to variation in DNA and to the role of natural selection in controlling variation. In the last 10 years, scientists have begun to define an incredible number of regulating mechanisms that operate at all levels of organization to maintain the steady state, that is, to counteract change forced by perturbations in the *genetic message* or *in the environment.* At the level of molecular organization, a number of systems limit crossing-over in chromosomes to preserve gene combinations of high adaptive value. The thiamine dimer system, mentioned in Chapter 2, is another strategy for counteracting change.

Superimposed upon systems to maintain genetic integrity are systems which support the strong tendency of organisms to maintain phenotypic uniformity. In spite of the tremendously varied genetic programs they represent, all individuals of a species conform to each other in many characters and processes. This conformity has a number of parameters, including not only appearance, but life-style, occupation, habitat, and range. The sum total of this integrated development permits us to say with certainty that this organism is a monkey and that an ape. Not only a monkey, but a rhesus monkey, *Macaca mulata.* This conformity is not achieved or imposed by fiat of the taxonomist with a desire to classify organisms. Rather, it reflects the subtle integration of instructions from the genetic program and the environment. The functioning individual, which develops from this integration, is called the *phenotype.* We might think of the genetic blueprint as defining the range of possibilities within which structures and processes can function. Where a system comes to lie within that range will depend upon the information provided by the environment. For example, the aquatic buttercup produces two types of leaves: finely dissected water leaves and simple, entire air leaves.

The specific shape of each leaf produced depends upon the environmental context in which the leaf develops.

Precisely because of the importance of maintaining phenotypic stability, many strategies have evolved to ensure orderly development toward the typical form. One of the most common in all organisms is genetic dominance. The Australian genetist J. M. Rendel has characterized the dominant gene as "a gene which, in the course of evolution, has come to acquire considerable flexibility. This enables it to react to a number of disturbing circumstances in such a way that the phenotype is preserved. One of these disturbing circumstances is the failure of its partner gene." In some complex way, enzyme production by a gene is influenced by its allele. Even if we cannot understand the specific mechanism of this regulation, we can understand the general characteristics of such mechanisms.

CYBERNETIC SYSTEMS

Negative Feedback

The word *cybernetic* comes from the Greek word meaning "steersman" or "helmsman," a good descriptive term for the regulatory mechanisms which permit systems to adjust to perturbation. Regulatory systems function by relating input to output. The input may be energy, as is most commonly the case in machines, with the output represented by work. In the classic example, that is, the thermostat of an iron, the input is electricity and the output heat. A good biological example of a similar mechanism is the light-regulating system of the eye. The input, light, is regulated by the size of the pupil, which is, itself, responsive to the output, a "light message" from the retina to the muscles of the iris. In both of these examples, the relationship between the input and the output is inverse. We term this a *negative feedback monitoring system.* As the iron becomes hotter and hotter, the input is reduced to some level in order to bring the output within the range determined by the setting of the iron.

Positive Feedback

Another mode of control, less commonly seen but very important in certain situations, is termed *positive feedback.* As the name implies, the input and the output are directly related. Positive feedback can be illustrated by the rewiring of an iron. In the positive-feedback iron, as the heat increases the input is increased, effectively making the iron hotter and hotter. Below a certain threshold value, the opposite would occur, as the heat decreases the input would be decreased. It is at once obvious that this type of operation has the potential for what is termed *runaway*— runaway to zero in the case of decreasing output, and runaway to maximum in the case of increasing output. In either case, the result is disaster, if the goal is to finish the weekly ironing.

On the other hand, if the goal can be achieved best by the expenditure of maximum effort over a short period of time, a system of positive feedback is an ideal control system. The adrenaline system, which regulates and organizes the flight or fight responses of mammals, is an example of positive-feedback monitoring.

The regulation of numbers in animal populations also illustrates positive feedback. The more organisms produced, the more individuals will be reproducing in the next generation. In sexually reproducing animals, the potential runaway to zero may be realized when the population falls below a certain threshold level. This is why certain species are threatened with extinction even though a few individuals can still be found in the wild. The potential runaway to maximum or to zero in animal populations is further regulated by a number of negative-feedback mechanisms which prevent drastic fluctuations in the population.

Homeostatic Systems

The methods developed in the science of cybernetics have great potential for the analysis and understanding of the cost/benefit ratios of homeostatic systems. The ecologist Richard Levins has attempted to define mathematically the relationship between homeostasis and optimum adaptation in a varying environment. His general conclusions are that homeostatic mechanisms increase fitness in an unstable environment, in spite of their cost in energy expended. In a stable environment, the cost/fitness ratio changes. The value of a homeostatic system depends upon the environment. The widespread ecological replacement of reptiles by mammals is often ascribed to the increased fitness of the warm-blooded animals during a period of environmental instability. After a cold night, the snakes and lizards of the desert must lie in the sun to raise their body temperature to a level conducive to metabolic processes. Cold-blooded animals are capable only of very sluggish responses until their body temperature reaches a certain level. A warm-blooded animal like the kangaroo rat, however, wakes ready for the day. He can run, feed, and explore immediately because his metabolic systems have been going all night, under the control of a homeostatic system, to maintain his body temperature within a narrow range. Does the advantage he obtains from this readiness for the day offset the metabolic cost of maintaining a constant body temperature?

Pollution, Moths, and Birds

One more example, perhaps, can clarify the role of cybernetic systems in controlling variation to permit continued existence of organic systems.

Two forms of the moth *Biston betualaria* are known in England. The percentage of the two forms in the population varies throughout the country, the dark form predominating in industrial areas and the light form in unpolluted habitats (Figure 3-2). The differential mortality of the two forms, while having some physiologic parameters, can be directly related to differential predation. In natural habitats, the dark forms are quickly eliminated by birds whereas the cryptically colored white forms pass unnoticed on natural birch bark. The opposite holds in industrial areas, where the tree trunks are covered by soot. The birds effectively control the proportion of dark genes within the gene pool of the moth population. Differential predation constitutes a form of regulation translated into differential survival and, hence, differential reproduction of one form or the other of the moth.

The gene for black color in *Biston* contributes to moth survival in the industrial environment. A change in genetic information translates into an effective homeostatic response to perturbation. The gene pool with a reservoir of variability has a better chance of responding to changes in the environment with successful adaptations. As pollution control programs in England have become more effective, the proportion of white moths in the population is increasing. Again the system responds to change by survival. The effectiveness of the response is determined by the predator-prey relationship between birds and moths.

This example clearly illustrates a fundamental premise of this text. The judgment of the value of any genetic or environmental information is a function of the operational system. We continually fail to consider this fact as we introduce human value judgments into ecosystems.

FIRE AS A REGULATING MECHANISM

For example, we have long been taught that fire represents an unmitigated disaster in the ecosystems of the United States. Yet in the ecosystems of the Southeastern United States, fire is a vital element to maintaining the open water areas of the swamps of Georgia and the Everglades of Florida. Periodic burning of these areas maintains the balance between grassland and forest and promotes the slight variation in elevation essential to the hydrologic balance of those areas. Given all the assumptions that we often make about fire and water, this is a totally unexpected relationship. (See Figure 3-3.)

As early as A.D. 1200, the Indians of the Southwest had utilized fire to maintain the unbroken expanse of waving grass that supported the great herds of buffalo upon which the Indians depended for food, clothing, and shelter. The undulating green sea that stirred the imagination of the pioneers and is still evoked as the epitome of the pristine landscape

Figure 3-2 The dark and light forms of the peppered moth photographed against a natural, lichen-encrusted trunk of an oak in an unpolluted countryside (upper); and dark, soot-covered oak trunk near Birmingham, England (lower). *(Courtesy of H.B.D. Kettlewell, University of Oxford.)*

Figure 3-3 Sawgrass wetlands of the Florida Everglades showing the vegetation character and hummocks. *(Courtesy of U.S. Forest Service, Ocala, Fla.)*

existed because the Indians periodically set it ablaze. They understood the relationship between grazing animals, grass, shrubs, trees, and fire.

In 1932, Herbert L. Stoddard of the United States Biological Survey concluded that quail and many associated wild species could not maintain adequate population levels in habitats from which fire was excluded. He early recommended the controlled use of fire as a tool for successful wildlife management in certain areas of the Southwest. However, it was not until very recently that the National Park Service came to recognize fire as an integral component of the information grid of the native ecosystems under their protection. The ecosystems of the United States organize fire into orderly development because they have been continually subject to natural lightning fires over their long evolutionary history. That history ensures the success of the pyrotechnics of Indians, sheepherders, and the early loggers of the Southeast and belies the wisdom of Smoky the Bear. Natural fires, in certain areas of the national parks, are now left to burn themselves out, controlled only by natural barriers to their progress.

PREDICTIVE INFORMATION

In the changing environment which might result from climatic change, fire, or pollution, several futures of a population may be predicted. The individual members may adapt to the change phenotypically or homeostatically, or the population may adapt genetically. What strategies are employed and in what combinations and with what degree of success depend upon many variables. A few of these are the genetic character of the population, the breeding system, the generation time of the organism relative to the change, and the character of the changes in the environment. Are the changes sudden, short-lived, steady, slow, or fluctuating? (Can the organism predict the change in advance?) One important factor is the ability of individual organisms to respond in an appropriate way before the change. That is, to prepare for the change before it comes. Richard Levins has attributed this ability to the predictive quality of certain events in the environment, to the presence of signals which precede the change. The prophetic character of these signals lies, however, not in the clairvoyance of the organism but in the statistical correlation, experienced by the population over a period of time, between the signal and the subsequent change. In essence, natural selection favors those organisms which respond *as if* they possessed the ability to recognize the correlation.

Levins has hypothesized that "there is no necessary relation between the physical form of the signal and the response evoked." This point is a reflection of the fact that the vital element in the capacity to transmit meaning resides in the reliability of the correlation between the signal and the change. In the earth's temperate zone, a certain number of days of freezing or near-freezing weather is inevitably followed by spring. Many plants of these regions respond to this "cold day message" by preparing for warmer weather. The seeds of many species will not germinate in the absence of cold, for to do so in the natural world would be to germinate before conditions favorable to growth existed. Day length is another important predictive signal in the life of temperate-region plants and animals. Many animals mate and migrate at appropriate times because they are genetically programmed to correlate day length and the environmental conditions of the coming season. In the forests of the Western United States, the lodgepole pine has recognized the correlation between fire and open-plant communities by producing cones which do not release their seeds until they are exposed to heat. The seeds thus released germinate in the open environment favorable to the growth of the species.

The ability of organisms to respond to predictive information leads to the possibility of biological control of certain organisms by "confounding their information," i.e., introducing the appropriate sequence of signals at an inappropriate time. This technique is especially appropriate to the control of insects in which dormancy is related to predictive information. Seed germination and flowering in many plants are already manipulated by controlling the information input in germination chambers and greenhouses.

One of the seemingly insurmountable problems in environmental change generated by people arises from the fact that natural systems possess no inherent mechanisms for defining "sensible" responses to change. No homeostatic systems exist for integrating the new information into the old order. For example, native and cultivated species of plants have had no evolutionary experience with the high levels of such substances as SO_2, PAN, and ozone that we are introducing into the atmosphere in air pollutants. Since populations of organisms with the ability to respond homeostatically to the change do not exist, large segments of the landscape may be left barren or with a greatly impoverished flora and fauna. This is very commonly the condition of the landscape around the copper smelters of the Western United States. The barren land is exposed to the full erosive force of the physical environment (Figure 3-4).

One important aspect of this general problem is that groups of organisms do exist that have the ability to evolve interpretive systems relative to new information. The key element in the organization of a genetic response is the generation time of the organism relative to the duration of the change. Organisms capable of producing many generations in a short period of time might fortuitously generate DNA combina-

Figure 3-4 The response of an ecosystem to air pollution, illustrating positive feedback whereby sulfur dioxide killed the sensitive species, reducing the shade, thereby altering the environment and rendering it less suitable for even sulfur dioxide–tolerant species.

tions that code resistance to the pollutant. Bacteria, insects, and annual plants all fit this criterion. The problem with this response, in terms of restoring the landscape around the smelters, is the fact that annual plants, which possess the ability to respond to the change genetically, seem to offer but slight potential for restoring the environment. In a severely eroding landscape, they may be completely ineffective.

ECOLOGICAL NICHE

The Population

Throughout this chapter, we have hinted at two important points. The first is that over the millions of years of evolution of living systems, until very recent times, there has been one unvarying criterion of success: reproduction. Darwin stated it simply, "what pays off is success in leaving progeny." Secondly, although natural selection operates through the death or survival and reproduction of the individual, it is the population that evolves. Harvard University biologist Ernst Mayr has characterized the individual as "only a temporary vessel, holding a small portion of the gene pool for a short period of time." If the individual reproduces, the genes "it held" remain part of the informational store of the population. If the individual dies without reproducing, that particular copy of genetic information is lost to the population. Increasingly in modern biology the population has become the unit of study and observation. Mayr restricts the term *population* to the "local population, that is, the community of potentially interbreeding individuals at a given locality." We can grasp the significance of this definition if we compare Mayr's definition to Wiener's definition of the *community*, "properly speaking the community extends only so far as there extends an effectual transmission of information." We readily see that the population is defined by the transmission and exchange of genetic information; that is, of DNA. This exchange or the prevention of it is very significant to the utilization of the earth's resources by living organisms. When the effectual exchange of genetic information is prevented, we have the potential for the creation of two populations which may, over a period of time, become separate species. This development depends exclusively on the failure of communication between the two groups. This failure may have many different causes, the important fact being that barriers to crossbreeding protect the genetic integrity of each group, effectively preserving the variability between the groups and, also, limiting the variability within each population. The most significant point about the separation of the two populations is that they begin to utilize different segments of the environment. Competition between the two modes of DNA for energy resources and space is drastically reduced. At first, this difference may be simply spatial. That is, the two populations fill the same ecological niche in different areas of the landscape. Over a period of time, the genetic variation that develops between the two groups will expand the parameters of their differential exploitation of the environment. In short, they will evolve to fill different niches.

As we try to define the niche concept, we begin to understand the ways in which the resources of the planet are divided among the various living systems occupying the earth. We begin to recognize, appreciate, and value the subtle balance between competition and cooperation, between dependence and predation, and between utilization and renewal.

A *niche* is an abstraction, a definition of an environmental space in which an organism operates most efficiently. We can further characterize that space by defining the variables which interact in informational ways with the organism. We may generalize about the niche of a species or define the specific way in which varieties of the species fulfill the generalized model. The niche of a species may be broad or strictly specified. For example, the niche of the species *Homo sapiens* is broad including many diverse environments and a wide variety of resources. In contrast, the niche of *Myxotricha parodoxa* is very limited, being defined by the variables in the digestive tract of Australian termites. The problem of defining the niche of a species is complicated by the fact that the realized niche may represent only a segment of the potential niche of the species.

The Serengeti Plain

The niche dimensions of many species exist in dynamic relationship with each other in the earth's ecosystems. Richard Bell has provided a very interesting analysis of niche interaction on the grazing ecosystems of the Serengeti Plain of Africa. Not only do the buffalo, zebra, wildebeest, topi, and Thomson's gazelle utilize different portions of the vegetation, but they utilize them most effectively in a successional regime.

During part of the season, the animals graze in mixed herds on hills where short grass is common. The short-grass plains represent the optimum environment for all groups because the animals can satisfy their protein requirements without excessive grazing effort. As this resource is depleted, the largest animals, who require the greatest bulk of food, move into the depressions where the vegetation is a heterogeneous mix of tall grasses, short grasses, and herbs. In this plant community the greatest concentration of protein is at ground level. The zebra and buffalo graze the stems and tops of the tallest grasses. As they graze these areas they trample and soften the vegetation. The wildebeests follow the zebra and buffalo into the lower areas. After the dense grass stands are opened by the larger animals, the wildebeests can efficiently graze the middle level of the vegetation. This level consists of a greater proportion of leaves to stem and represents the least departure from the wildebeests' optimum resource. As the vegetation is successively trampled, the fruits of the grasses are knocked off and concentrated on the ground. The Thomson's gazelles, the last animals to move into the trampled areas, graze the leaves, herbs, and fruits at ground level. These grazing patterns are intimately related to digestive tolerances for protein/cellulose ratios, to body size, and to effective grazing time. The student is urged to read Bell's complete analysis, for it includes a detailed discussion of the energy needs of each herbivore and how those needs are satisfied through the interaction of the environment, the vegetation, and the behavior of each group of animals.

Bell notes that a disturbance of the animal populations at the upper grazing levels would seriously reduce the grazing efficiency of the wildebeest and gazelle. He also makes the point that pastoral people have long been a component of this ecosystem and, as such, exist in dynamic equilibrium with it. The pastoralists who graze domestic animals and regularly burn areas of the plain help to maintain the short-grass community most favorable to the native species.

Succession

Through studies such as Bell's, we are beginning to understand how species are organized into informational grids. The extinction or removal of one species produces a dislocation in the entire system. In the course of the long-term evolution of one species into another, or the gradual disappearance of a species over a long period of time, the other components have a chance to organize adaptations to the changing information. However, with the rapid changes we often impose, only organisms that produce new generations in a matter of minutes or weeks may organize appropriate responses. Through our ignorance and disregard for the interdependence of organisms, we may cause the extinction of entire ecosystems.

It was obvious, once such perceptive individuals as the early ecologists, Kerner, Cowles, and Clements, had shown it, that many species by virtue of their occupation of the landscape alter the environment away from their own optimum niche toward the optimum niche of another species. A striking example of this phenomenon can be seen in the Rocky Mountains, where the aspen forests are commonly nurseries for the spruce and fir trees that will eventually replace aspen on undisturbed sites (Figure 3-5). The aspen cover alters the light reaching the understory, in essence changing the value of one of the variables of the environmental space. A change in the ratio of aspen to spruce-fir reproduction is the response to the new variable. In this system, aspen

Figure 3-5 The changing ratio of firs to aspen as the shade provided by the aspen makes the environment more suitable to the fir.

acts as a kind of thermostat, a cybernetic mechanism regulating the vegetative output of the landscape by regulating the energy input. The regulatory character of aspen provides for the rapid recovery of the spruce-fir forest after a disturbance from fire or a small-scale timbering operation. Any disturbance of the forest canopy alters the light reaching the understory. Light-tolerant species, such as aspen and lodgepole pine, grow rapidly in the opening, gradually restoring the forest canopy and again altering the light input. This alteration creates an environment more favorable to young spruce and fir trees, which are very shade-tolerant.

REGULATION IN ECOSYSTEMS

From the early studies of succession in ecosystems, we should have learned that the ability of any ecosystem to recover from a disturbance depends upon the extent of the damage to the self-regulatory mechanisms of the system. However, we do not learn. We continue to assault the essential elements of self-regulatory systems in the environment. This is the very reason why predator control programs have such a disruptive effect upon ecosystems. Predators are vital links in the system of negative feedback that balances the two basic trophic levels of the food chain, the herbs and the herbivores. This is not to imply that predation is the only mode of population control. We have simplified these systems in order to illustrate the principles. Our logical inclination is to assume that the most effective regulator of the herbivores would be the supply and condition of the herbage. The only trouble with this mode of control is the time lag inherent in it. By the time that the vegetation is sufficiently decimated to affect the population of herbivores dependent upon it, the vegetation itself may be beyond saving. The ecosystem approaches the potential runaway to complete disorder. In anthropomorphic terms, it is in the best interest of the predator to maintain the health of his primary resource, the pasturage of prey.

The study and manipulation of the regulatory mechanisms of ecosystems can help us understand the dynamic relationships that exist between organisms. This technique has been cleverly and effectively utilized by a number of animal ecologists. R. T. Paine removed predatory starfish from a stretch of intertidal shore in order to study competition between organisms. The removal of the starfish initiated successive deletions from the ecosystem. The barnacles, grazing chitons, and limpets were eventually crowded out by the mussels. These and similar experiments have led to the surprising generalization that predation reduces competition, and, thereby, promotes diversity of organisms in an area. Predation is an effective strategy for maintaining the niche diversity of the habitat, which enables a multitude of DNA forms to share the resources of the landscape.

Fire is another element which may promote niche diversity in an area. If niche diversity and productivity are as intimately related as some ecologists believe, these results are of more than theoretical interest. The experimental results obtained by Paine and others should influence our determination of how we may best harvest the finite energy resources of the earth. Can the energy of the sun be most effectively harnessed on an area of the landscape exhibiting maximum species diversity or maximum development for a few species? Modern agriculture has opted for the latter, but reasons for the choice may be specious at best. A choice based on expediency and tradition without reference to biological principles may, in the end, be a very poor choice. The relationship between maximum utilization of the landscape and species specialization and diversity needs to be carefully studied.

In all the expedient choices that we make, we may be aiding the operation of a fundamental ecological principle—succession. Are we altering our habitat away from our niche optimum? Are we generating information which disorders ecosystems? Does *Homo sapiens* have a future in a disordered world? Considering our long apprenticeship in the carefully orchestrated symphony of theme and variation, can we ever hope to function in a disordered environment? How much will the attempt stress the homeostatic systems of our bodies, our social groups, and our native ecosystems? Homeostatic systems operate only at a cost in energy and resources. Have we calculated the price? Can we afford it? Do we want to pay the price? These are important questions which we will consider in the second part of the text.

CONCLUSIONS

Information is a vital force in determining the order, or efficiency, of a system. Nonsensical, as well as sensical, information must be processed and interpreted at every level of organization. Any organism that fails to "interpret" its environment will not survive. Some of this interpretation is at a cellular, or genetic, level of organization. The stability of natural systems is closely regulated by various mechanisms of both positive and negative feedback. The most critical of these include food resources, disease, and the interactions of predators and prey.

Millions of years of evolution have provided many organisms the capacity to genetically "predict" future environmental changes. But we have come to rely more on logic and learned behavior. This can be dangerous since we often respond to environmental perturbations as though we understood the future consequences or appropriateness of the actions. We behave as though we could predict all the consequences, while in reality the facts for interpretation are lacking or have been grossly misinterpreted. Often, through intuitive reasoning, we unwittingly postpone the ultimate consequences, ignoring the systems of negative or positive feedback that might have regulated any effects upon the environment.

Our behavior will determine our success in interpreting information correctly to increase stability and homeostasis in the system. But to understand why we respond as we do, one must first understand the nature of humans and the forces underlying our behavior.

SELECTED READINGS

Bell, Richard. 1971. A grazing ecosystem of the Serengeti. Scientific American, vol. 225, no. 11, pp. 86–93.

Levins, Richard. *Evolution in Changing Environments.* (Princeton, N.J.: Princeton, 1968).

Lewontin, Richard C. (ed.). *Population Biology and Evolution.* (Syracuse, N.Y.: Syracuse, 1967).

MacArthur, R. H., and J. Connel. *The Biology of Populations.* (New York: Wiley, 1966).

Mayr, Ernst. *Populations, Species and Evolution,* an abridgment of *Animal Species and Evolution.* (Cambridge, Mass.: Belknap Press of Harvard, 1970).

Monod, Jacques. *Chance and Necessity.* (New York: Knopf, 1971).

Pianka, Eric R. 1966. Latitudinal gradients in species diversity, a review of concepts. American Naturalist, vol. 100, pp. 33–46.

Proceedings Tall Timbers Fire Ecology Conference, annually from 1962. (For the basic research on influence of fire in the ecosystems of the earth.)

Stanley-Jones, D., and K. Stanley-Jones. *The Cybernetics of Natural Systems.* (New York: Pergamon, 1960).

Thomas, Lewis. *The Lives of a Cell.* (New York: Viking, 1974).

Wiener, Norbert. *Cybernetics or Control and Communication in the Animal and the Machine.* (Cambridge, Mass.: MIT, 1962.)

Chapter 4

The Behavior Strategy

Then she opens her nightgown, baring her large breasts, and puts her arms gently around the sick woman, whispering inaudible words of comfort, cradling her, kissing her mouth and cheeks, holding her tight.

Ingmar Berman
Cries and Whispers

In the late 1890s a tired sailor on a whaling ship, many months out of a New England port with no success, stares dully at the horizon. At first his tired eyes hardly register the difference between the waves and the shiny round backs of the whales rolling through the sea. But in an instant, all the men on board have seen the whales and within minutes the small boats are in the water and the best and oldest harpoonist of the crew has fixed his target. His boat pursues one of the smallest bodies in the water, a young calf, now trailing behind its mother as she speeds away from the boats. The old whaler knows if he succeeds in harpooning the calf, the mother and some of her companions will turn in the water and come to the aid of the injured calf. They will move under the struggling body and attempt to push it up in the water. In their care-giving desperation, they will be an easy target for the whalers.

Half a world and more than a half a century away, Jane Goodall sits quietly at the edge of a clearing observing a chance encounter between two groups of chimpanzees. As the animals sight each other, the dominant male of one group, hair standing on end, begins a loud hooting. At this signal all males, females, and young of the group scatter out of the way. All but one infant, that is, who, heedless of the changes in its environment, moves toward the displaying male. The infant is immediately seized, a convenient display object, and dragged screaming along the ground. In an unprecedented action, the mother of the infant hurls herself at the dominant male. The infant is picked up by another male who seems not to know whether to comfort him or display with him.

In a completely different social setting, turmoil rends another group. The normal low buzz of conversation in a second-grade classroom changes to hysteria as one child stands, pounding upon another, yelling, and crying. It's Jim again, wiggling, poking, and punching until one child, tired of bearing the torment from his hyperactive neighbor, turns around and punches Jim in the nose. The teacher grabs Jim and forcefully removes him from the blows of his classmate. Struggling against competing impulses to cuff and comfort him, the teacher solves the immediate problem by removing him from the scene of the turmoil into the hall where he can be calmed.

SURVIVAL

There are millions of ways in which an organism can die, but there is only a very narrow range of ways in which it can survive and leave offspring.

Niko Tinbergen

Whales, adults, chimps, and children: all organisms react to perturbations in the environment. We call this active response *behavior* and judge it morally or socially good, as the reader judges the behavior in the examples, according to our ethical, cultural, or scientific bias. Yet such judgments hardly help us to understand the phenomena we observe. In earlier chapters, we stressed that the logic of any biological process can only be understood in an environmental context. When we study the behavior of an animal, we want to know how that behavior relates to the survival of the organism. If the organism lives in a group, then the question must be extended to include the survival of the population. We have tried to convey the idea that the earth is an impartial habitat and natural selection an impartial arbitrator. Yet, life is so common, so abundant on earth, and death so hidden, made invisible, that natural selection and death exist for us only in the geologic past. We forget that the long historical process is an accumulation of moments. The genetic and nongenetic information generated by each of us in this moment of time will influence the future. If you doubt that natural selection is still a force in human evolution, you have only to think of how many genetic combinations have been lost to the human species through the folly of the keepers. How many fatal accidents might have been avoided by slight changes in behavior? Individuals and populations survive only if their choices are energy-wise. Behavior is as intimately related to those choices as are anatomy or physiology. We are back to the fundamental question of how the finite energy resources of a segment of the landscape can best be exploited by living organisms.

We seem to take for granted that animals and humans "know" the ways in which to satisfy the basic requirements of life. Behavior which has obvious survival value—habits of food-gathering, shelter-seeking, mating, and the rearing of young—is rarely questioned by any but a few interested researchers. Yet upon close examination, we find that we really have very little knowledge about even the most essential behavior.

How does a cat "know" that it is suited to catch and eat rodents while a deer "knows" that it should browse leaves? Why do herbivores flee and carnivores fight, and is there a measurable physiological difference between this flight and fight tendency? Why does a meadow mouse build its nest in a meadow and a woodland mouse in a woodland? When offered a choice, how do laboratory-reared mice choose the habitat appropriate to their species?

Why does a pintail duck mate with another pintail, and how do the male and female pintails find and recognize each other in a habitat shared with mallards, coots, grebes, sculps, and countless other swimming and wading birds? Why are hybrids between pintails and mallards rare in nature when they are possible and viable in domestic habitats? How do we "know" that we are destined to mate with a human and not some closely related primate such as, for example, a chimpanzee? And what is the source of the revulsion the very reading of the idea engenders in us? Is this revulsion innate, cultural, learned, superficial, an indefinable illusory mood, or a measurable physiologic change of state?

Tests such as these are met daily by every organism, including humans. Any animal failing many such tests fails to survive, and failing to survive guarantees that its genes will not be transmitted to future generations. Any population composed of a high percentage of such failure is doomed to extinction.

We might suspect that knowledge so essential to survival would be communicated via the DNA system from generation to generation, and such is precisely the case for many patterns of behavior. However, we have also emphasized that evolution is pragmatic. If a system of nongenetic transfer of survival-promoting behavior works, then individuals survive and procreate. In humans and animals a multitude of nongenetic strategies serve to communicate and reenforce survival-wise behavior. Unfortunately, we too often stress the importance of our learned behavior and deny ourselves the right to inherited behavior patterns in the erroneous philosophical illusion that the possession and use of genetic information somehow diminish the worth and accomplishment of the human species.

The evidence for the continued operation of innately coded patterns of response in human behavior is being gathered by many investigators in the fields of behavior, psychology, and genetics. Anyone who doubts the existence of these responses need only view the films of Ingmar Bergman, especially *Cries and Whispers*. Bergman is a master of the orchestration of innate and cultural elements in human response. In his films these two elements of human behavior are subtly interwoven in some episodes and boldly counterpointed in others. More than many scientists, Bergman has grasped the tension in human behavior produced by heredity and learning and beautifully and horribly conveyed that tension through the medium of film.

As an axiom to the denial of inherited behavior in humans we refuse to animals the nongenetic transfer of behavior or at least qualify learning in animals to distinguish it from learning in humans. In this chapter, we want to develop the idea that in all the various cultures of *Homo sapiens* and in the characteristic behavior of all group-living animals, heredity and learning are as intimately and irreversibly intertwined as the lovers in Rodin's bronze.

BEHAVIOR AND ENVIRONMENT

Our first concern in an environmental text is with the influence of the behavior of an organism or a group of organisms upon resource use. Many ecologists have noted that behavior can increase the niche possibilities of an area beyond that provided by the physical resources of the environment. For example, consider two species of birds, both with sharp curved beaks and talons, keen eyes, and large strong wings. Both are well designed to harvest the small animals which are an energy resource capable of sustaining large predators through hours or days of fruitless hunting. Competition between the two similar species for the same energy resource can be reduced and the niche diversity of the habitat increased by a slight divergence in behavior. If one species hunts during the daylight hours and the other at night, or one hunts near or in the water and the other on land, the two groups cease to compete. Behavior is an important parameter in the realization of ecological niche.

Owls, ospreys, and hawks occupy different ecological niches by virtue of both morphological and behavior differences. Evolution might be thought of as a process in which genetic and environmental information serves to integrate the morphology, physiology, and behavior of a species within the constraints of the environment. We can appreciate how intimately related are behavior and form in an organism if we simply try to imagine a house finch attempting to catch and eat a mouse.

Within a population of similar organisms, behavioral strategies are important to the reduction of competition and to the adjustment of population numbers to the resources of the landscape. In birds which exhibit territorial behavior, only individuals who can claim a section of the landscape and discourage others from intruding upon it can attract a mate and breed. This behavior has the ecological effect of ensuring a mated pair adequate resources for rearing the young. Individuals who do not secure territory do not breed and are often more susceptible to predation.

Rank-Order

In a wide variety of species from insects through mammals, individuals are ordered in a priority system by some type of ranking behavior. The priority may relate to access to food, use of space, mating, and decision making. In many gregarious animals, the dominant organism exercises a leadership function and regulates group interaction. In some animals, rank-order behavior produces a rigidly structured group in which social status relates to every aspect of life whereas in others dominance relationships influence only certain aspects of life or operate only during certain periods of the life cycle. In either case, rank-order systems serve to reduce competition for resources between organisms with similar demands. During hard times, limited resources are not equally shared. Lower-ranking animals may be so consistently prevented from feeding, resting, social interaction, and mating that they die. The ecological sense of this strategy can readily be appreciated, for it ensures the continuation of the group even at the expense of individual survival.

Lifeboat Ethics

The ecological force of these strategies has begun to influence contemporary thought. The best definition of what has come to be called *lifeboat ethics* comes from the biologist Garrett Hardin. He has warned that since earth will not support the hordes of people demanding subsistence from it, the developed countries should be prepared to act as "lifeboats." The food and space resources of these areas should be carefully husbanded and not distributed over the world where they serve only to maintain thousands at a minimal subsistence level. Using the metaphor of the lifeboat, he notes that the boat is only effective if those inside prevent those in the water from climbing aboard; the only effect of trying to save everyone is to swamp the boat.

Obviously adjustment of population density to environment is not simply a problem for animal populations. We are well aware that the problem is critical for *Homo sapiens.* Disagreement over this problem centers only on estimates of the carrying capacity of the earth. What has not been obvious until very recently is that behavioral strategies have long been effective in the adjustment of human populations to resources. Many of these strategies probably have their origin in the prehistory of the race. Recently, several gifted anthropologists who have a keen understanding of ecological principles have detailed the ways in which complex cultural behavior patterns stabilize populations and resources.

Ecological Niche Diversity in *Homo Sapiens*

In his analysis of the ethnic groups of the Swat and Indus River Valleys of Pakistan, Frederick Barth related subsistence activities to ecological niche. He concluded that behavioral differences serve to reduce competition between the three neighboring groups and result in a full utilization of a varied landscape. The Pahtans occupy the valley floors where soils and climatic conditions permit the raising of two crops each season. The Kohistanis raise a single crop and herd animals in the upper valleys and on the mountain slopes. The uppermost valleys and slopes are left to the nomadic Guhars who supplement herding activities with seasonal labor in the fields of the Pahtans. Exchanges of energy and goods between the three groups integrate them in such a way that a dislocation in one population will affect the others. The differences in subsistence habits between the three groups are further reenforced by differences in political and social organization.

Taboo and Ritual as Regulating Mechanisms

A good deal of seemingly irrational behavior in humans can be understood when the activity is analyzed in an environmental context. For example, the taboo against pork, which is shared by two otherwise antithetical religious groups, Jews and Moslems, can be understood if we relate the taboo to the historical habitat of the people. The anthropologist William Harris has explained why pigs are a burden in a semiarid environment:

> Pigs don't provide milk, they are a pain to herd over long distances, they can't live on grass alone as cows and sheep do—in fact, they eat the same

food as human beings, which makes them competitors and they don't live comfortably in climates over 84 degrees as sheep and goats do. Because pigs can't sweat, in hot temperatures they must cover themselves with something wet to cool down.

Since the environment does not provide a suitable niche for pigs, a good deal of energy must be expended to maintain the pigs. It is obviously ecologically senseless for nomadic desert-living populations to attempt to raise pigs. The same energy output will produce a higher return when expended upon sheep, goats, or cows since the ecological requirements of these animals and the niche spaces in the environment more nearly coincide. Yet the taste of pork is such a strong reenforcement for herding pigs that an equally strong proscription is needed to ensure against futile attempts to keep them. In this case, religious taboo becomes an effective energy conservation measure.

Note that the raising of pigs is not impossible in that environment. We are clever enough to manipulate the environment to suit our whims. However, this regulation is costly. We might ask ourselves how many possible but expensive and environmentally contrary policies practiced in the United States reduce our efficiency. Is the extensive use of private automobiles, for example, one such environmentally insane habit we might well discard as too extravagant? Once a habit is deeply ingrained in the fabric of our behavior, we come to regard it as an inalienable right and its regulation as an abrogation of freedom. How many inalienable rights does an individual member of the species *Homo sapiens* really have? Do we individually have the right to destroy the habitat and thereby endanger the survival of future generations of *Homo sapiens?* Is there a subtle difference between religious taboo and legislation as regulating mechanisms which makes one acceptable to the species and the other abhorrent? Can this difference be exploited to ensure the well-being of the ecosystems of the earth?

Religious ritual has been effectively used by many human populations to protect the environment. In these groups, ritual operates as a homeostatic system adjusting human, animal, and plant populations to the environment. In his book *Pigs for the Ancestors,* Roy Rappaport details the operation of one such behavioral system of the Tsembaga in New Guinea. The Tsembaga he studied tend gardens and keep pigs. The gardens provide a variety of greens and starchy tubers for a diet which is adequate in calories but probably just marginal in proteins. The pigs clean garbage and feces from around the dwellings, cultivate fallow garden plots, and figure importantly in ritual as they are never eaten except in a ritual context. In an elaborate behavioral pattern which may cycle through as many as 10 years, the pigs serve to regulate human population grouping, fighting between enemy groups, and energy and material exchanges between friendly groups. The rituals associated with pig killing and eating often coincide with times of stress. It is significant to the success of the Tsembaga life-style that protein is made available to them at precisely the times when the body is drawing down its protein reserves. During these rituals, small numbers of animals are killed and eaten. When a cycle of fighting with neighboring groups ends in victory, a few pigs are killed and eaten. In the ensuing years, fighting is prohibited and the pig population is allowed to increase until sufficient animals are available for a feast worthy of the ancestors to whom the victory in the battle is credited. However, this point is always reached before the pig population exceeds the carrying capacity of the land. As the pig population increases, pigs disturb gardens, create friction between neighbors, and demand excessive care. The nucleated settlement expands outward until pigs begin to seriously compete with humans for the produce of the gardens. At a certain point the people no longer tolerate the "pig pressure" and a prolonged ritual termed the *Kaiko* begins. During this period, large numbers of pigs are regularly killed and eaten, the dispersed population contracts in the ritual celebrations that follow, and relatives and allies from distant areas are invited to feasts where dancing, trading, and courting take place. Through the operation of ritual, the group ensures itself a large number of allies through generous gifts of pork. The high-protein food is distributed through the group, and the environment is protected from overpopulation by pigs. The ritual functions not only in the exchange of energy but also in the exchange of information, both genetic and nongenetic. At the rituals, intergroup marriage may be arranged, and the visiting warriors communicate through dancing skill their probable value as allies in the next battle. It is important that outsiders are bonded to the host groups by ties of kinship and obligation, since at the end of the *Kaiko* fighting may begin again. The ritual behavior pattern can be seen to have important ecological consequences.

No one would argue that the Tsembaga ritual is an example of genetically encoded behavior. However, neither is it exclusively dependent upon learning and cultural reenforcement. The ritual cycle illustrates the complex interaction of biological and cultural information because the foundation of the entire system is firmly rooted in genetic information. The dietary needs of the people, the physiologic requirements of the pigs, their competition with people for food, and their rooting behavior—all are regulated by genetic information. Further, were we to observe a film of the courtship behavior of the people, we could easily interpret the meaning of the actions. We would understand the facial and body expressions because they would be little different from those at a Midwestern box social. Are these elements learned or inherited?

GENETIC CODING

There is no longer any doubt that DNA can code complex patterns of action. The genetic inheritance of motor action patterns in certain animals has been thoroughly studied, and impressive evidence exists that certain specific patterns of action are similarly inherited in many species. One example will be given as an illustration of the fact. (We do not intend to imply from this example that all behavior in all animals is inherited or that all the behavior of any one species of animal is completely controlled by either heredity or environment.)

Hygienic Behavior in Bees

The geneticist W. C. Rothenbulier studied the resistance of two different inbred colonies of bees to American foulbrood disease. He found that the two colonies differed in the removal of dead larvae from the brood cells. Breeding experiments showed that the nest-cleaning behavior of bees depends on at least two genes, both recessive in hygienic bees. An individual recessive for the first gene but dominant for the second would uncap the cells of dead larvae but not remove the larvae, while individuals dominant for the first and recessive for the second would not uncap cells but would remove dead larvae from cells uncapped by the investigator. Only individuals recessive for both genes would uncap the cells and remove the dead larvae within a sufficiently short period of time to affect the spread of the disease-causing organism.

Environmentally Resistant Behavior

After many years of studying the behavior of diverse animals, the Nobel prize winner, Niko Tinbergen, believes that patterns of behavior can be ranked on a scale from more to less resistant to environmental modification. At one extreme end of the scale we find inherited patterns which are completely resistant to environmental input. One of the most invariable behavioral units seen in the animal kingdom is the cocoon-spinning behavior of the *Cupiennius* spider. Once the spinning begins, the program is strictly followed through the egg-laying process regardless of any environmental perturbation generated by an interfering experimenter. The spider is unable to repair any damage to the cocoon, instead proceeding as if the job were well done. Eggs will be deposited in a cocoon from which an experimenter has removed the bottom.

It hardly seems possible that stringently programmed, environmentally resistant action patterns are still part of the behavioral repertory of *Homo sapiens*. An absolute answer to this possibility can hardly be given inasmuch as very little experimental work has been undertaken in the genetic study of human behavior. Cross-cultural comparisons which might reveal environmentally resistant behavior are being made by German ethologists, but this work is little known in the United States. H. Hass and I. Eibl-Eibesfeldt have compiled a film library of human facial and body expression in diverse cultural groups. By cross-cultural comparisons, they hope to identify the common elements in the social behavior of all *Homo sapiens*. These comparisons will undoubtedly show that people with diverse cultural experience share many common action patterns. Whether or not these common patterns are inherited or reinforced by experience will still be untested. Whichever the case may be, we know the effect is a shared pattern of response comprehensible to all organisms of the species. How else are we to explain the ease of communication between the stone-age Tasaday people discovered in the Philippine jungle and their twentieth-century visitors? Why should we take for granted that two humans of such drastically different experience should be able to communicate goodwill by facial expression and body language? Does the successful peaceful contact between the two indicate that certain patterns of action, especially those involved in social communication, are very old in the scheme of human evolution and very resistant to environmental interference? On the other hand, perhaps the experiential social environment of *Homo sapiens* is so similar throughout the world that common patterns of response are to be expected. Still, why should that social experience have so many common elements?

Genetic Coding and Human Behavior

Even though we have no direct evidence that complex sequences of action in humans are genetically coded, we do have circumstantial evidence that the DNA of the chromosomes influences human behavior. In the human species an extra Y chromosome turns up in 1 out of every 1000 males, but the frequency of the XYY genotype is significantly higher in the prison population of the United States. This correlation in itself does not "prove" that behavior defined by our society as criminal is mediated by genetic constitution. It does, however, indicate that a cause-and-effect relationship *might* exist between aberrant behavior and genetic abnormalities.

There is an accumulating body of evidence that the internal chemical balance of the body is intimately related to distinctive behavior patterns in humans. Many of the behavioral symptoms exhibited by schizophrenics can be modified by manipulating the internal chemical environment of the body. In recent years, doctors have shown that symptoms exhibited by some hyperactive children can be relieved by placing the child on a diet which restricts artificial coloring and flavoring agents common in processed food. Obviously the behavior of these children is related to body chemical reactions to certain compounds, but the chemistry of the reactions and the relationship to the genotype of the individual has not been thoroughly investigated.

Many of the objections to the idea that *Homo sapiens* might exhibit inherited patterns of behavior arise from poor understanding of biological processes. The most vocal critics of this idea demand to see complete action patterns in human behavior similar to those exhibited by the *Cupiennius* spider. Instead, they find only confusing and complex variation in human activity.

Inasmuch as elements of behavior are genetically coded and inherited, they are subject to the same generalizations applied to morphological and physiologic characters. The expression of the behavior may depend upon the environment much as the phenotypic expression of a morphological character depends upon the interaction of the environment and genotype. This point is often overlooked by those who fail to understand that species-typical patterns of action need not be invariable in all members of a species. Just as we have come to expect variation in many inherited physical characters, we should expect variation in genetically coded behavior.

Because of the error potential in the DNA informational process, we should expect genetically coded behavior to evolve in much the same way that morphological and physiologic characters evolve. Action patterns may lose their original purpose and new functions be superimposed on old patterns. Evolution is pragmatic, new characters are organized out of existing possibilities, and the resulting pattern is of necessity a compromise imposed by the constraints of the DNA-RNA system, the physiology and anatomy of the organism, the history of the population, and the exigencies of the environment.

We can readily appreciate this fact if we consider how our own system of temperature regulation has been adapted to serve our emotional response systems. It is no accident that we refer to love as an affair of the heart, and flushed cheeks and goose bumps are as common in life as in literature.

As with morphological and physiologic characters, natural selection does not result in patterns of superefficient behavior. The criterion of survival is acceptibility, not perfection. Innate recognition of the infant by the mother would seem to be a logical necessity of the pattern of extended infant care. Yet this recognition has simply developed through the evolution of other systems, without following the logic of inherent necessity. In most of these systems environmental stimuli and genetic information are intricately interwoven to ensure that the mother and the infant will be bonded to each other. Natural selection reflects the outcome of a gamble; if a system works most of the time, it does not matter to population survival that it fails some of the time.

In goats, the recognition and subsequent acceptance of the young develops out of a specific pattern of behavior by the mother. Soon after birth the mother licks and sniffs the young. Deprived of this opportunity, the mother will not accept the young and refuses to exercise normal patterns of maternal care toward it.

In many species, the social attachment of the child to the mother contains an element of chance. In such diverse animals as goats and geese, the *following response* of the child to the mother is quite unspecific. The newborn animal simply follows the first large moving object in its environment and continues to in spite of the fact that the relationship may be nonsensical. In the wild, the error probability of this system is low. It is only in domesticated animals that these old strategies become risky, but even there the survival risk is low because the farmer exercises an *in loco parentis* relationship toward the animals.

Several investigators have remarked that the "modern method" of child care in the United States almost certainly has implications relative to the early and important relationship between the mother and the infant, but no serious studies have been undertaken to explore this possibility. Seemingly, the only persons concerned about this critical period in the life of the human young were the young Americans who developed the counterculture of the 1960s.

A MODEL: DOG DRINKING WATER

When genetic programming does not provide a fully developed built-in solution to environmental perturbation, the challenge of survival is met by individually tailored reactions responsive to environmental input. Viewed in the harsh reality of existence, the old argument as to whether behavior is primarily innate or learned becomes unimportant. Recent works linking memory of learned pattern to changes in DNA, the basic molecule of the genetic memory, have forced the consideration that instinctual and learned behavior may share more common elements than previously suspected.

The question central to any behavioral act is how the information from many sources is perceived, integrated, stored, retrieved, and acted upon. How is the communication integrated between sensory and motor control areas? How is the internal state of the animal related to the sensory process and the motor activity? Is mnemonic information stored in the brain encoded and transcribed by systems similar to the DNA-RNA systems which transmit genetic information? How is the "goodness of fit" between the intention, the action, and the result tested? Does the result, by some feedback process, alter the model or process used in future situations?

When we begin to think about these question, we realize the

incredible complexity of even such a simple behavior pattern as drinking water. For every animal dependent on an external source of water this simple act involves communication of need, recognition of the relationship of environmental water to internal need, identification of water, motor competence to move the water from the external to the internal environment, and finally, communication of sufficiency.

Much of our knowledge of this process comes from studies with dogs. In the dog, the information of water need is communicated from sensory organs in the hypothalamus which monitor the water level in the blood. When the water level falls below some preset standard, the dog searches for a stimulus which will release the motor action pattern by which water may be obtained. Ethologists call this behavior *appetitive behavior*. The order of stimuli and response patterns in this model illustrates a generalization that applies to many forms of behavior. The need for water does not directly release the motor pattern of drinking. Simple hunger does not, in a dog, release salivation and the mechanical motions of eating. A second stimulus more directly related to the satisfaction of the need must be sought. The first stimulus releases the behavior, active searching, for the second stimulus.

Around the turn of the century, the Russian behaviorist Pavlov demonstrated through an elegant series of experiments that dogs could be conditioned to a wide variety of stimuli for the release of specific patterns of behavior.

The recognition of the second stimulus depends upon the animal's sensory equipment. The dog's neural circuitry obviously is not loaded with a complicated definition of water. Instead, the dog responds to one characteristic of water. Cattle easily identify water by olfactory stimuli, whereas people depend almost entirely upon visual or auditory stimuli.

Once the motor pattern of drinking has been initiated, the problem shifts to that of goal accomplishment. The simple technique of inserting a rubber balloon into a dog's stomach and blowing it up demonstrated that receptors in the stomach report filling. In the drinking dog, internal sensory perception of "full" is integrated with other types of comparative information to initiate the stop-action sequence.

Experimental work with other animals has shown that the stop-action sequence is often not related to the accomplishment of the obvious goal. Rather, the performance of the motor pattern in itself constitutes the source of goal-accomplishment information. When two groups of human infants are fed the same quantity of food, one through nipples with very large openings requiring little sucking to exhaust the milk supply and the second group through normal nipples allowing a long period of sucking, the first group will show various signs of hunger. These signs include restlessness, crying, and in vacuo sucking. The stop-sucking program is seemingly not initiated by a comparison of food sufficiency but by a comparison to an innate program reading "satisfactory number of sucking movements." This relationship between sucking and hunger symptoms has been observed in a number of mammals.

One of the most creative controversies of modern science centers on the answer to one final question that we might ask about our drinking dog: Does the satisfaction achieved by the drinking behavior pattern influence the future operation of that behavior? B. F. Skinner is the spokesman for the school of thought which maintains that "behavior is shaped and maintained by its consequences." The other school of thought believes that the shaping is accomplished by natural selection and that much of behavior is maintained by genetic programming.

The emotional attacks of each school on the other emphasize their differences, which center mainly on the degree of genetic versus learned programming. The arguments from both sides obscure the fact that all those involved would agree with Skinner's statement that "all reinforcers eventually derive their power from evolutionary selection."

A GENERALIZED MODEL

If we further generalize our model, we will come to appreciate the enormous difficulty in trying to sort behavior into nature-nurture cubbyholes. In the following section we have borrowed freely from the ideas and data published in *Systems Theory and Biology,* edited by M. D. Mesarovic. The purpose of our model is strictly instructional; that is, to focus on the common elements of diverse behavior.

READ SUBPROGRAM

The first step in the program diagrammed in Figure 4-1 is the organization of the input. Input information has three sources: mnemonic information stored in the brain and acquired by experience, sensory information from both the external and internal environment of the organism, and genetic information acquired in the DNA code inherited from previous generations.

Reduction of Input

There is a wealth of experimental evidence which permits us to make several generalizations about this step of the behavioral process. Recognizing that cost/benefit ratios are important to organic systems, we might suspect that successful behavior patterns are best characterized by economy of information processing. We have already mentioned that dogs, cows, and people react to a very simple definition of water. Some of the earliest evidence on reduction of information came from the work

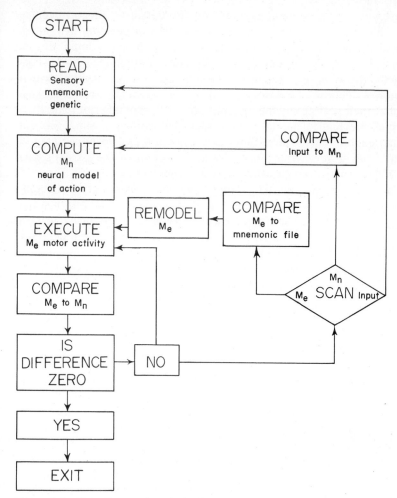

Figure 4-1 Flow diagram for a behavior program model.

of the animal ecologist D. Lack. As early as 1943, he demonstrated that the aggressive behavior of male robins could be released simply by a bundle of red feathers attached to a "wire leg." This model represented the greatest reduction of effective stimuli and proved a more effective releaser than a stuffed robin without red breast feathers.

The generalization that animals, including people, often process only very limited aspects of environmental stimuli, instead of integrating the abundant and diverse aspects of sensory stimuli available to them, has since been corroborated by many scientists.

Imaginative experiments have shown that schooling behavior in fish is a response to prominent markers on the dorsal fin of conspecifics, rather than to the gestalt of the fish, and that in courting fish, single strategically located body stripes constitute effective stimuli. In sea urchins, defensive and fleeing behavior can be stimulated by a single chemical, the odor of predatory starfish. For every survival, critical behavior reduction of sensory input seems to be the rule. Turkeys recognize their goslings by their peeping and will respond preferentially to a peeping mechanical model over a silent but moving gosling. Even in humans, experiments with infants have shown that a response may be elicited from a very young baby by a simulation of the parent's face consisting of but a triangle with two spots representing eyes.

The reduction of stimuli to simple elements is characteristic not only of innate behavior patterns but often pertains even in situations in which learning plays an important role. Nearly everyone has had the experience of being "stimulus bound." I have looked vainly over my own desk for, say, a gray stapler, thereby missing completely a blue stapler in plain view. My behavior program simply kept reiterating the gray model. The phenomenon of stimulus fixation may also be an important parameter in such common occurrences as persons freezing to death in snowbound automobiles when they are surrounded with flammable materials and gasoline. In this situation, there seems to be no simple sensory input leading to a fire-building behavior program.

In general, animals first attend to specific and limited sensory information, ignoring the total configuration of objects presented to them. The psychologist D. O. Hebb has noted that in test situations rats often focus on room cues rather than food-dish cues. When the food dish is changed, the first program tried by the rat in finding the dish is a response to the room cue which worked in the previous trial. The stimulus is not the food dish but some other cue. Hebb theorized that the "animal mainly perceives and responds to the least-variable objects in his environment, which are the ones at the greatest distance." (This habit does not develop out of cognitive recognition by the rat that door frames are immovable, but out of the environmental history of the species in which distant objects were consistently less variable than near objects.) Hebb's conclusions are very similar to those of the ethologist Konrad Lorenz that innate releasing stimuli are characterized by very simple character relationships. He noted they are characterized by "a maximum general improbability of form" which ensures that the releasing stimuli will not be accidentally met often in the environment. Simplicity, lack of ambiguity, and stability are characteristic of effective stimuli in both conditioned and innate responses. The power of the stimulus in both cases derives from the correlation of stimuli and success in the execution of the behavioral program. The correlation may be computed by an individual organism through experience or by a population of organisms adapting genetically.

Influence of Internal Chemical Balance

The information permissible to the READ subprogram is determined by the constellation of external and internal information available to the organisms. Even from our admittedly limited understanding of the principles of information theory, we can postulate that certain groups of symbols received and ordered concurrently constitute a readable message unit. It is obvious to even the most casual bird watcher that red feathers do not signal aggressive behavior in robins during the midsummer and autumn flocking seasons. "Red feathers" is not permissible to the male robin's READ program until it can be organized into a sequence with an internal message. We can theorize that the coincidence of the red-feathers stimulus and a specific hormonal stimulus produces an ordered sequence which communicates information via the READ program. Similarily, the first experience of a large moving object in the young goat's environment determines the subsequent admissible input to the following-behavior program.

Psychologists and neurophysicists have long recognized that the internal mood, or state of mind, of the animal influences which external stimuli will be recognized in the nerve cell. This idea is expressed in the concept of set, attitude, or attention by the psychologists and dominating motivation of the neurophysicists. Attention or dominating motivation of the organism is related to past behavior or metabolic and hormonal reactions. The physiologic origin of "feelings" such as thirst and hunger, which operate in the realm of subsistence, is readily accepted as important to the behavior program, but moods such as loneliness, apprehension, or joy also undoubtedly have physiologic parameters which can become a source of sensory input to the READ program.

The fact that an organism's hormonal balance influences sensory perception can hardly be argued. Hormones influence sensitivity to external stimuli and serve to direct, focus, and control the stimuli-seeking and attention-giving activities of animals and humans. It has been demonstrated that sexually mature human females are sensitive to the odor of musk, which males and immature females cannot detect. However, males injected with female sex hormones are sensitive to the odor. Further, there is experimental evidence that in the female this sensitivity increases at ovulation. Does this heightened sensitivity during the period when mating behavior is most effective for reproduction indicate that odor plays a more important role in human behavior than previously suspected? The investigation of this possibility is a new and rapidly developing research field.

Internal sensory input which influences attention to external stimuli is also subject to modification from external stimuli. The estrogen balance of female rats, for example, can be influenced by mating behavior in their cage mates or even by the presence of males in the cage. Jane Goodall observed one example of this phenomenon in the wild chimpanzees of the Gombe stream when an older female developed the pink swellings of the estrous cycle entirely "out of phase" and seemingly in response to competition from several young females displaying at that time.

The message unit admitted to the READ program serves to decipher a neural model of action which in turn calls up a motor EXECUTE program. In order to simplify, we have diagramed the motor EXECUTE step without including the numerous cybernetic loops assuredly involved in it. For example, in the drinking-dog model, organs such as legs, muzzle, and tongue must have constantly changing positional information relative to the water. This information is processed via subprograms complete in the periphery of the central nervous system and involving the brain only in an after-the-fact way.

The problem with any model is that the process modeled is never as simple as illustrated. We should have multiple arrows between the READ, COMPUTE, and EXECUTE subprograms of the diagram to illustrate that motor activity constitutes a form of input to the READ program permitting constant readjustment to the entire sequence.

Serial Stimuli

In its natural habitat during the mating season, a male toad responds to all moving objects by clasping them. Through a long period of evolution, such nonspecific response must have achieved a high probability of success. In the toad's native habitat, the number of possible "claspable" objects is limited. If the toad chances to clasp another male, its defensive call causes the release of the grip and the toad is ready for a reiteration of the program. When a female is clasped, her response constitutes the stimulus for the next subprogram. The reaction of the male and female to each other sequentially generates the subprograms by which mating is finally achieved. The same system of serial releasing stimuli is beautifully illustrated in the intricately choreographed mating dance of many birds.

Compute Neural Model

The COMPUTE-neural-model step embodies the concepts of goal or intention. However, in this discussion the words *goal* or *intention* are not used in the commonly understood sense of cognitive recognition. Even in patterns of behavior in which learning is an important element, the result and the expressed intent may be quite different. Rappaport stressed, in his study of the Tsembaga, that the intent of the people and the actual ecological achievement were not cognitively related.

He did not work out the ritual relationships between pigs and environment by asking the Tsembage what they were doing but by observing the behavior and its results in relationship to the environment.

The cognitive intent of the Tsembaga is the appeasement of ancestors and the discharge of debts to allies. This behavior is reinforced by the pleasurable experiences associated with the ritual as well as by the practical advantages that ensue from it. For survival, the significant point is not the intent but the ecological effect. This is not to imply that what the people think they are doing is unimportant. In fact, this cognitive input is vital to the behavior program.

In order to solve the environmental problems of the twentieth century, we need to analyze the ecological effects of our actions; but perhaps in order to change ecologically reckless behavior, we should operate on the intent input to the neural model. If a people cannot or will not abandon "reckless intent," then it may be possible to couple that intent to a more "sane" EXECUTE program.

The encoding of neural model of the action is a complex research problem posing many unanswered questions; however, something is known about the process for certain animal behavior programs. The neural model may be genetically encoded and entirely environmentally resistant, as is the case with the *Cupiennius* spider, genetically encoded to be responsive to environmental influence, or experientially acquired but responsive to genetic influence.

Imprinting

One generalized process by which neural models are acquired is termed *imprinting.* Young goats and young geese are imprinted to the parental model through environmental experience. Imprinting may provide a neural model for an immediately useful pattern of action as in the following behavior of the young kid or it may provide a model that will not be used until a long period of time after it is acquired.

The neural model for the species-typical song in many birds is experientially acquired, but the period of life in which the experience will influence the model is genetically determined. If a white-crowned sparrow is isolation-reared, it subsequently sings distinctive individualized songs. However, if the birds are isolated only after feathering, they sing the typical dialect songs of their group. The song heard from the parents between hatching and feathering is stored to become the internal auditory template to which the young bird compares its own efforts. This example should not be taken as a general rule for the coding of bird songs. In some nest parasites, the pattern of the foster parents is used as a template whereas in others the typical species pattern, which is never experienced in early life, is somehow encoded as the neural model. The phenomenon of the storage of complex behavior templates to be used at some later stage of maturity is common to many species. The psychologist Frank Beach found that young mice treated with hormones could exhibit the full range of adult mating behavior. A neural model is available to the mouse-mating program long before the coincidence of hormonal readiness and environmental stimuli in the READ program.

EXECUTE Model

The EXECUTE model defines the specific action by which the neural model may be accomplished. Again, we have simplified by omitting the innumerable subprograms involved at this step. We have already noted the number of cybernetic loops between organs and spinal cord running in the drinking-dog model. In a complex behavior pattern, a number of subprograms may be involved, and these subprograms may or may not be specific to one "master program." Konrad Lorenz has formulated the concept of tool activities to indicate that a particular activity may be useful in many behavior programs. For example, running, grasping, and digging are generalized activities which can be utilized in many different contexts and in response to a variety of stimulus patterns. Further, even more highly specified patterns of action may appear in the service of more than one function. In dogs, greeting behavior contains elements of submissive, greeting, and food-begging patterns. The care-giving behavior exhibited by dolphins and whales is demonstrated in response to the distress of both adults and young and has even been reported in response to drowning humans. The adaptation of patterns of action to many diverse situations further illustrates the principle of economy of organization.

Compare-Remodel

As the action progresses, a comparison of M_e to M_n occurs in order to specify the END command. From experimental evidence and observation, we know that the input to this subprogram may vary from simple comparison of number of motor movements as in the sucking program of kittens, calves, and babies to the integration of the wide range of external and internal sensory data called up by an artist deciding that a painting is finished. In the sucking baby and the *Cupiennius* spider, the comparison of M_e to M_n is entirely internalized. No external input is admissible to the program to permit remodeling of the neural template. The spider operates through three stages of our model while the artist creatively commands the entire range of options implied by the expanded model.

Creativity

In defining these options, we should be careful to again qualify their range. In any species, we find certain facets of behavioral repertoire extremely resistant to remodeling and others highly plastic. We can theorize that invariable behavior patterns are not linked to the COMPARE-REMODEL subprograms. Further, in behavior patterns which represent the full implications of the model, the sophistication with which animals scan the data and remodel the neural model of behavior may vary tremendously between species and between individuals within a species. One parameter of the creative process in humans must surely be the sensitivity and precision of judgment for the END command.

Intelligence

The difference between the spider and the artist represents a subtle change of enormous evolutionary significance. With the inclusion of the COMPARE-REMODEL subprograms, behavior is no longer simply an expression of a stringently choreographed life cycle. Rather, behavior becomes an effective immediate response to environmental perturbation. In a stable environment, the spider cocoon-spinning program is sufficient to survival, but its inability to adjust the program severely limits its ability to respond to environmental perturbation. For *Cupiennius,* the only effective response to repeated environmental disturbance of that behavior is the genetic adaptation of the population. Once each separate response to change is no longer dependent upon genetic reorganization, the time interval between perturbation and response is shortened from generations to seconds. Individual adaptation to change replaces genetic adaptation of the population and the possibility for variation in response is enormously increased since the result is no longer dependent upon the permutation of 20-odd amino acids in sets of 3 but is limited only by the ingenuity of the organism working within the constraints of its architecture.

The multitude of options implied in our expanded model can be reduced to one word—*intelligence.* The animal behaviorist Keller Breland has defined intelligence as "the breakdown of the instinctive fixity increasing the potential for recombination, both within the musculature and the environment." The fact that this potential for recombination is organized out of preexisting models and possibilities explains why we find it impossible to separate the influence of heredity and learning in behavior. An intelligent animal can learn to organize genetically coded subprograms into a variety of new master programs. Similarly, specific elements of an innately coded program may be amenable to change through experience.

Innovation

The age-old criterion for success, reproduction, is joined by another criterion, innovation. Any population that adapts to environmental perturbation through the inventiveness of some of its members is bound to have an edge in the struggle for survival. When that edge is transmitted to the next generation, whether by imitation or teaching, with or without symbols, that character is as surely subject to natural selection as is any character genetically transmitted.

Before we congratulate ourselves on our facility with this new survival tool, we had perhaps consider one more point. Slobodkin, in defining a model for evolutionary success, has concluded that successful organisms will "respond to environmental perturbations in such a way that they not only minimize the departure from the steady state conditions caused by the perturbation but also maximize their ability to withstand further perturbations."

Inasmuch as we are concerned not only with our own survival through the next 50 years but also with the survival of our children and grandchildren, may it not be well to ask ourselves if our behavioral responses are maximizing the ability of the human race to withstand further environmental perturbation?

CONCLUSION

Although the nature of our most fundamental behavior may reside in our genetic template, evolution has favored a trend toward an increased capacity for learning and flexible behavior. There is often a subtle interaction between this learned behavior and what is innate, and the two cannot be clearly separated.

Much has been written concerning our innate behavior. Such traits as aggressiveness and territoriality are presumed by some to be part of our genetic code and professed to explain much of contemporary behavior. But if we accept that we are basically violent, then there can be little optimism in predicting our destiny. On the other hand, if we recognize that we are largely a product of experience and learning, then the prospects of a peaceful benevolent future become encouraging. The ability to learn and transmit information, coupled with an increased capacity to respond to any environmental pressures, has provided *Homo sapiens* with a tremendous selective advantage over every other animal. This advantage has enabled us to become earth's most malleable creature, occupying every global niche, and forming multitudes of diverse societies, or cultures, each in response to the local environment.

SELECTED READINGS

Beach, F. A. 1947. Evolutionary changes in the physiological control of mating behavior in mammals. Psychology Review, vol. 54, pp. 297–315.
Eibl-Eibesfeldt, I. *Ethology, the Biology of Behavior.* (New York: Holt, 1970).
Goodall, Jane. 1968. The behavior of free-living chimpanzees in the Gombe Stream area. *Animal Behavior Monographs.* 1 part (3) 161–311.
Hall, Ed T. *The Silent Language.* (New York: Fawcett, 1959).
Hebb, D. O. *The Organization of Behavior.* (New York: Wiley, 1949).
Lehrman, D. S., and J. S. Rosenblatt. The study of behavioral development. *The*

Ontogeny of Vertebrate Behavior. Howard Moltz (ed.). (New York: Academic, 1971).

Lorenz, Konrad. *Studies in Animal and Human Behavior.* Vol. 11. (Cambridge, Mass.: Harvard, 1971).

Marler, Peter, and Paul Mundinger. Vocal learning in birds. *The Ontogeny of Vertebrate Behavior.* Howard Moltz (ed.). (New York: Academic, 1971).

Skinner, B. F. *Beyond Freedom and Dignity.* (New York: Knopf, 1971).

Slobodkin, Lawrence B. *Growth and Regulation of Animal Populations.* (New York: Holt, 1961).

Stanley-Jones, D. *Kybernetics of Mind and Brain.* (Springfield, Ill.: Charles C Thomas, 1970).

Tiger, Lionel, and Robin Fox. *The Imperial Animal.* (New York: Holt, 1971).

Waterman, T. H. Systems theory and biology - view of a biologist. *Systems Theory and Biology.* M. D. Mesarovic (ed.). (New York: Springer-Verlag, 1968).

Chapter 5

The Emergence of Culture

Enough. Now they had no children. Let him *wrack his head for how they would live. She would not exchange her solitude for anything.* Never again to be forced to move to the rhythms of others.

Tillie Olsen
Tell Me a Riddle

It is 1938. Across the country, Americans are just beginning to recover from the economic plight of the Great Depression, but in rural areas, in the dust bowl that is the American Midwest and in the coal mining areas of Appalachia and the Rocky Mountain West, the times are hard. In a Western mining camp, an injured miner with a broken toe hobbles around his garden. He picks the potatoes and cabbage which will provide the only meal his family will have that night. The same meal they had last night and the night before and all the nights for the past month. When the potatoes and cabbage are cooked, his three children eat first. Only when they have finished will he sit with his wife to finish the meager meal.

In India, in 1974, an American television camera scans a mealtime scene. A woman cooks a handful of rice with a few drops of oil in a pan many times too big. When the rice is ready, she measures out small portions to six children and her husband. She herself eats only the tiny amount left in the pan after all have been served.

In a mountain village in Africa, an old woman huddles over a piece of food found beside a forest trail. She furtively tries to stuff the entire bit in her mouth but she is too late. A group of youngsters, ravished by hunger, pounce on her and steal the food from her mouth. When we read Colin Turnbull's account of her rapacious people, the Iks, we are shocked. Shocked because we are accustomed to sharing. The selfish, aggressive behavior of the Iks, who abandon their children and steal food from their old people, is repugnant to us, foreign to our experience, and alien, we believe, to human nature. We identify only with the single family who managed to migrate to a distant part of the forest where they lived in the "human" fashion, sharing space and food.

LIVING IN GROUPS

For all our recorded history we have lived in groups. We share space and resources and find contact with other humans pleasurable. Even the Iks who fight over food seek social interaction. For all group-living animals, isolation is as serious a threat to the health of the individual as is starvation. Social animals are programmed genetically and experientially to seek social contact. Young, old, male, and female find pleasure in physical and emotional interaction. Deprived of that opportunity, social animals show signs of stress and withdrawal. The tendency to live in groups is supported by strong biological imperatives.

Throughout the first four chapters, we developed the idea that the energy resources of the earth are limited and that organisms compete for those limited resources. The competition may be tempered by physiologic and behavioral differences which separate species into different ecological niches. Still, within any population, the individuals with similar requirements must compete with each other. Given this intense and unremitting competition, how can we explain the commonly observed tendency of many species of animals to live in groups? Considering the possibilities for environmental devastation and conspecific conflict inherent in the social state, how and why did societies evolve?

Advantages of Group Living

The numerous ecological advantages of grouping together are reviewed by Peter Klopfer in *An Introduction to Animal Behavior.* Groups may vary from simple aggregations of individuals to highly integrated, complex societies. In highly ordered groups, the individuals recognize each other and respond to each other through well-defined relationships.

The need for grouping, at least during the mating season, is obvious for sexually reproducing animals with internal fertilization, but mating cannot be considered the primary stimulus for grouping. In many species, the most stable groups are formed in the periods between mating, and the mating season is more often characterized by conflict, competition, segregation, and territorial behavior.

A group of animals may be more successful than a single animal in the search for food, the perception of and escape from danger, and in the response to environmental perturbation. The advantages in food gathering are especially marked when the food is found in large quantities but irregularly distributed. Animals feeding in groups are able to spend more time feeding and less watching when the watching duties are shared by many. Further, a group of animals presents a greater challenge to a predator than does a single individual, and young animals are afforded greater protection within the group. Small animals may even chase away a large predator by acting together. The mobbing of predators by birds is a common behavior pattern.

Intragroup Conflict

The advantages of living in groups must be significant to outweigh the disadvantages, for group living stresses not only the resources of the environment but the homeostatic systems of the individuals. In a social setting, the probability of interpersonal contacts increases with the number of individuals. Each individual becomes a potential perturbation in the environment of others. Intragroup conflict must be minimized if the social group is to remain stable. If individuals learn to predict with reasonable accuracy the probable behavior of others, conflict can be avoided. Stuart A. Altmann, in a study of monkeys, concluded that the "relative success or failure of any individual depended very greatly on his ability to make the appropriate response to different individuals under a variety of circumstances." In highly organized groups of individuals who maintain close contact throughout the year, familiarity with each other promotes social harmony. Strangers disrupt the social scene because they introduce an element of uncertainty into the order. In a well-integrated group, the size may be constrained by the limit to the number of individuals that any one animal may know well. In many primates the effective group size is further limited by the visual range of facial expressions and hand and eye signals. The community is defined by the limits to the transfer of information.

Is the size of human groups similarily constrained? Some

architects and educators have theorized that the optimum size of
an elementary school is determined by the number of pupils that the
principal may recognize and know by name. The infantry patrol leader,
the host, and the young gang leader all know that there is a limit to the
effective size of a patrol, a dinner party, or a gang, but little attention
seems to be given this fact in the planning of humane cities and shopping
centers in modern America. The difficulties inherent in attempts to
interact with large numbers of strangers are evident in every phase of
modern life. The inherent difficulty in these interactions may explain why
encounters with strangers are often defined by cultural ritual and taboo.

Social Stability

In the preceding chapter we have briefly mentioned some of the strategies
which permit economy of response and reduce friction in social interaction. One of the most common mechanisms regulating social interaction is
order or rank. These systems vary from the inflexible, highly stereotyped
pecking order system seen in chicken flocks to the fluid, imaginative, and
flexible dominance systems exhibited by the chimpanzee and other
primates. Dominance relationships and the attendant behavior reduce
ambiguous information, increase predictability, and provide for economy
of response. The result is a more stable social climate.

Territorial behavior also serves to limit social contact. In birds,
territoriality not only ensures an adequate resource supply, but the
exclusion of other conspecifics from the area reduces the necessity for
social interaction. All the energies of the mated pair can be concentrated
on the rearing of the young. In wide-ranging pack animals, such as dogs,
territoriality limits the possibility of contact with strangers. In all animals,
patterns of greeting, grooming, submissive, and aggressive behavior serve
to promote social stability. (Dominance relationships are maintained by
the threat of aggression, and in this sense aggression contributes to order.)

As Rappaport showed in his description of the Kaiko ritual, in human
societies behavior which promotes social stability becomes ritualized. In
the Alaskan eskimo, serious disputes were settled in ridicule song rituals.
The two adversaries sang outrageous insults at each other to the great
delight of the other members of the community. In societies such as the
modern Zuni, where aggressive interaction is regularly suppressed and
older ritual forms of regulation have been abandoned, neurosis, anxiety,
and social bickering are common.

The careful attention to the behavior of others, which is a feature of
social life, is important not only to stability but in the adaptation to
change. The great titmice of England are gregarious birds who became a
nuisance because of their habit of tearing the tops from milk bottles left

on doorsteps. Such an innovation, had it occurred in solitary-living birds, would have no population significance. Animals who live alone do not watch each other, but social animals who watch each other closely imitate and learn from one another. Other titmice, imitating the first innovator, learned that milk bottles were a reliable source of high-protein food. The habit quickly spread through England. In a social group, the innovations of individual members may contribute to the survival of the group.

PARENT-INFANT BOND

The classic explanation for the evolution of social life in the primates was that sexual attraction served to keep organisms in groups. Recent studies of free-living primates, however, have shown that in species with a marked breeding season, social contact does not diminish in the period between breeding seasons. Throughout the year males, juveniles, and females move together in homogeneous or heterogeneous groups. In these groups, many patterns of behavior serve to reinforce the social bond Further, as mentioned earlier, the breeding season is often the most disruptive period in the social cycle.

Extended Infancy

In fact, it is the helplessness of the infant rather than the sexual prowess of the adult that provides the foundation for the social order. In all social animals, from insects through fish and mammals including humans, the care, protection, and rearing of the young provide the foundation for the social bond. In any species in which the young undergo a long period of helplessness and delayed maturation, infant care is one of the chief determinants of behavior. It is no accident that politicians cuddle and kiss babies, because such behavior communicates a potent biological message.

Systems of extended care of the young could hardly have evolved in the absence of the evolution of systems which ensured the protection of the young from predacious parents or conspecifics. The care-dependency relationship of the parents to the young is guaranteed by genetically coded patterns of behavior and reinforced by experience. The biological necessity and force of the protection-dependency relationship explain why infantile gestures are used by adults as appeasement signs in response to conspecific aggression. The behavior patterns which ensure the care and training of the young and those which regulate social interaction are intimately related. Many of the responses which the infant first uses relating to the mother are employed in more complex patterns in all subsequent social interaction. These behavioral responses permit individuals to live harmoniously in close contact and ensure the care and training of the young who are themselves capable of learning. The young learn from the parents and from their littermates and peers in a sheltered environment free from some of the constraints of food getting, choice of shelter, knowledge of danger, etc.

The parent-infant relationship extends beyond simple sustenance. E. Count has described the relationship as one of ecology: "The mother is the environment of the offspring, originally mechanical and physiological with psychological dimensions supravening in measure as the mechanical and physiological retire." During the period when the infant's essential needs are provided by the parents and the immature body is undergoing a long period of growth and development, the young animal gains the competence to ensure his own survival. Stability is extremely important in the infant's environment because the young animal's adaptive range is narrow and undifferentiated. It does not possess well-developed regulatory systems for countering change in the environment.

In the early stages of development, the mother is the center of the infant's world, and the environment near the healthy mother is one in which the infant feels most secure to explore and test his abilities. Anyone watching an infant visiting with his mother in a strange home can observe this fact. It is as if the baby were attached to the mother by an invisible, elastic unbilical cord. The baby ventures a little distance into the strange environment and periodically returns to the mother. An offered toy or cookie is taken to the mother for her examination before it is played with or eaten. The behavior is exactly that of any young social animal who periodically returns to the center of security, the mother. The same pattern can be observed in young puppies first venturing forth from the den or litter box.

Stability and Healthy Personality

The full import of this early period of development can hardly be overstressed in a time when increasing numbers of human children are battered, abandoned, and emotionally disturbed. Child psychologists have long recognized that the self-confidence and trust in fellow humans developed in the infant become the basis for the healthy adult personality. David Hubbard, a psychoanalyst who studied airline highjackers, has developed a novel theory of the relationship between infant security and emotional disturbance. Humans and many other animals orient to the environment through the movement of tiny crystals located in the vestibular apparatus of the inner ear. If these crystals are defective at birth, the infant develops poor muscle tone, has difficulty standing, learns to walk at a late age, and otherwise relates poorly to his environment. Such an infant grows up in an unsteady world in which his own responses are uncertain. Hubbard believes that such a physical defect could produce severe personality disorders in children and adults.

Deprivation Rearing

We already have ample evidence that disturbances in the environment of infant primates produce abnormal adult responses. These relationships have been intensively studied by zoologist H. F. Harlow, who tested the effects of early rearing conditions on later behavior. Rhesus monkeys were reared in various degrees of isolation. Some were provided with surrogate mothers such as terry-cloth–covered forms with eyes and nipples that dispensed milk (Figure 5-1). Other surrogates consisted only of a wire-mesh frame with nipples. Other infants were not provided with surrogates at all but simply isolation-raised. Food and shelter were provided for all the animals. Monkeys raised without real mothers exhibited extremely abnormal behavior. They spent most of their time in self-clutching, rocking, vacant staring, and self-mutilation. They exhibited many of the same symptoms characteristic of autistic and schizophrenic

Figure 5-1   Surrogate terry-cloth mother and rhesus monkey. *(Courtesy of Dr. Harry F. Harlow, University of Wisconsin Primate Laboratory.)*

children. In the monkeys deprivation-rearing devastates all social re-actions. They exhibit abnormal and unsuitable responses in every aspect of social behavior from peer interaction to mating and maternal behavior.

In the deprivation-rearing experiments, the relevant situation in the mother-child interaction has been destroyed. The experiments introduce an important parameter whose total effect cannot be assessed—the inertness of the surrogate. A natural mother is never inert. Lehrman and Rosenblatt, in an excellent discussion of the dynamic development of the mother-child relationship, have stressed that the active reaction of the mother to the infant is an important element of the relationship. As the physiologic and psychological state of the mother changes as a consequence of her contact with the infant, so does the infant's state change as a consequence of its contact with her. As might be expected from the behavior model developed in Chapter 4, the hormonal state of the mother is a relevant component of the infant-mother environment. Considering this relationship, it is surprising that we have not explored the behavioral consequences of ending the lactation period of the human mother so abruptly by the artificial feeding of cow's milk to human infants.

The Bonding Process

We do not mean to imply, from this discussion, that the bond between mother and infant is innately coded. As with other behavior patterns, genetic elements and experientially reinforced patterns are interwoven as the bond develops. The bond is the result of an evolving relationship between two dynamic organisms, each changing in subtle and important ways. The fact that young parents often feel intense animosity toward their babies is sometimes cited as evidence against innate behavioral responses toward the human infant. However, this very animosity tells us that the bonding process is complex and important to the survival of the infant. David Hamburg in a study of emotions and human evolution has stated the problem well.

> But the human mother is practically hairless, and in any event the motor equipment of the human infant does not permit effective clinging. Yet, how is this adaptive problem resolved? Simple, the mother must hold the baby; sometimes for long periods, under very difficult circumstances. In that event the mother must want to hold the baby. . . .

A human baby is an exasperating burden, demanding and helpless; it limits the mobility and restricts the freedom of the parents. If the parents were not bonded to the infant by strong behavioral ties, it is quite likely that all babies would be abandoned. The fact that some are does not "prove" that interaction between the mother and infant is not reinforcing.

Instead of denying the existence of such bonds, we should be exploring the reasons for the failure of the bonding process in certain cases.

Fortunately for human evolution, the *Homo sapiens* infant is provided with innate responses that he cleverly learns to use to maximum effect. We have already noted the response of very young infants to a simulation of the mother's face. Anyone who has been a parent has felt the pleasure and excitement at this first sign of recognition, and it is obvious to all parents that the human baby early learns to manipulate the parents through the use of even a limited behavioral repertory. The child begins very early to accumulate a store of information from the environment which can be integrated with genetic information to elicit desirable behavior from the parents.

The mother also exhibits certain seemingly innate patterns of behavior in her interaction with the baby. If we observe an inexperienced human mother with her first-born infant, we find that when she talks to the baby she does a quite surprising thing; she puts her face very close to the baby's face, a distance she uses in no other social interaction except one, sexual behavior. Why should the mother act as if she knows what investigators such as B. J. Cratty discovered only after careful observation and experiment: "The newborn infant can generally accommodate (visually) at a distance of about $7^{1}/_{2}$ inches and this accommodation seems to be initially locked in at this distance." Is this approximately the "eye contact" distance between the mother and the infant at the breast? No doubt the mother's behavior in regard to communication with the baby is reinforced by the response of the infant, but her first use of this distance may reveal innate coding of the pattern. (See Figure 5-2.)

The bond between mother and infant develops through the days and months of close contact imposed by the inability of the infant to operate effectively in the world. Naturally if parents ignore the infant, they will not experience the feeling of being bonded to it. Neither, however, will the infant survive unless it finds a competent, stable, and loving surrogate. Needless to say, if infants do not survive, populations do not develop and evolve.

Orphan Survival

Jane Goodall observed that the survival of chimpanzee orphans in the wild was dependent upon their ability to find substitute mothers, usually mature female siblings, who provided a sense of security comparable to that provided by an experienced mother. This sense of security and the way it affects all subsequent behavior are even more important than the provision of food or protection from danger. The sense of security achieved by the infant is intimately related to the maturity and sense of security exhibited by the surrogate.

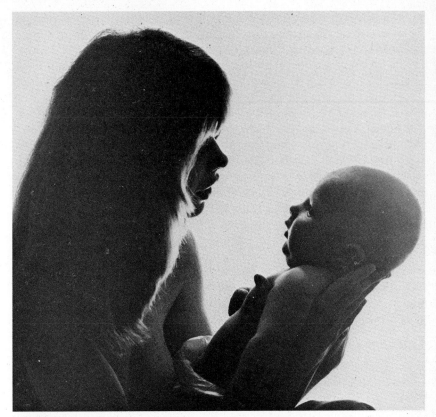

Figure 5-2 Mother with baby held at the natural distance of about 7¹/₂ inches.

Throughout the world of social animals, the resulting bond established between mother and infant is often very long-lasting. Margaret Altman has observed that the mother-infant bond in herd animals such as deer produces a kind of tribe led by the oldest female "grandmother." In chimpanzees, the most common social grouping is a female and her various aged young, the uterine kin. Goodall has speculated that the close and long-lasting male friendships she observed in free-living chimpanzees were based on uterine kinship.

THE EMERGENCE OF *HOMO SAPIENS*

Sharing

The gradually increasing maturation period of the primate infant which culminated in the long infancy of the *Homo sapiens* produced a drastically different set of selection pressures upon the bearer of the ovum and the bearer of the sperm. The survival of a helpless, demanding, and tiresome creature in a state of prolonged infancy probably depended upon the evolution of a caring, compassionate, patient, inventive, and attentive mother. In contrast to her primate relatives and her unburdened male companions, she had to share her food, shelter, and personal space for long periods of time. In order to accomplish this feat it was necessary for nature to modify her responses from the general primate pattern. What was needed was a change from the typical habit of "to each his own" in food gathering to a state more similar to the habit of the carnivorous pack dogs of food sharing. The part that the male played in this search for and sharing of food was almost certainly determined by the environment. In environments where food was scarce and the sources widely scattered, male help would have been essential to the survival of the mother and child. However, in areas of abundant food resources a mother could have easily fed herself and several children by simple gathering activities. Given the primary importance, to the survival of the species, of the mother-infant interaction, it is surprising how little consideration is given in the literature of skeletal-motor and behavioral adaptations to the ways in which the demands of infant care have shaped human evolution.

General Primate Characteristics

It is generally thought that the genus *Homo* arose from a common ancestral stock which also gave birth to the other modern primates, the gibbons, orangutans, gorillas, and the chimpanzee. The evidence of this close relationship is to be found in the fossil record and in the careful physiologic and anatomic comparisons of the living primates. Among the many works which discuss the similarities and differences between the other primates and *Homo sapiens,* the student is referred to the works of Adolph Schultz and John Napier in anatomy and Morris Goodman and Vincent Sarich in serum proteins.

Even today we share many of our talents with our primate relatives and owe much of our uniqueness to the evolution of the ancestral gene pool. The stereoscopic color vision, the increasing importance of visual and auditory stimuli as opposed to the common mammalian reliance on olfactory stimuli, the flattening of the face, the grasping hand, the lively social life, and the diverse range of behavioral responses, all are attributes selected in the long internship in the forest and savanna environment. Even the vaunted large brain, the tendency toward enlargement of the cranial capacity compared to body size, is a general primate trend. The extraordinary complexity and differentiation of the human brain is a phylogenetically recent development.

Uniquely Human

A number of characteristics have been important in the evolution of humans from primate stock. Among these are the bipedal habit, the complex brain, the sensitive and skilled hand, the extended immaturity of the young, the survival of postmenopausal females, the loss of estrus in the female, the general loss of body hair in both sexes, and the acquisition of language.

Loss of Estrus

The loss of estrus may well have been one of the most important differences acting to separate *Homo sapiens* from other primates. The loss, in the female of the species, of a distinct estrus cycle accompanied by visual changes in the body tissue and overt sexual behavior gave rise to a myriad of behavioral modifications. The loss of estrus demanded radical adjustments in the typical primate pattern of mating. This change undoubtedly influenced social organization and child rearing. The evolution of a female with the ability to achieve repeated pleasurable orgasms and the capacity to bear children at any time of the year must have been accompanied by important adjustments in other parts of the system if the population were to remain in balance with its food and land resources. One can imagine the reproductive chaos if the constant fertility of the male had been combined with a comparative female receptiveness. Instead, a rather neat balance was achieved in the emerging species. A receptive, insatiable female periodically releasing a few gametes (in the ovulatory phase of her monthly cycle) was balanced by a continually fertile male who was rapidly satiated by an easily achieved orgasm.

The sexual excitement and disruptive social behavior characteristic of other primate groups during the estrus of females were profoundly modified. The loss of seasonal mating readiness accompanied by overt physical and behavioral signs may have facilitated a more stable social climate. In free-living primate groups, the mating season is a time of social tension in which the mother-infant bond is disrupted and the infants are exposed to danger in the ensuing social conflict. The year-round availability of receptive females could have tempered the disruption of the mother-uterine kin "family" that has been observed in the free-living chimpanzee when the mother again achieves estrus. The loss of estrus may also be part of a complex of factors which resulted in the establishment of the human animal of stable male-female bonds.

Bipedalism

There is a universal agreement in the literature of human origins that *bipedalism* (walking erect) is the singularly most important character in the evolution of *Homo sapiens*. Bipedalism freed the forelimbs for all manner of tasks whose performance and perfection led to cultural development and altered selection pressure on the hand and brain. The forelimbs could be used to carry food, objects, or infants and to wield tools or weapons. Apart from the theories that bipedalism arose out of the general primate locomotor pattern in response to a changing, more arid environment, there is no satisfactory explanation for the adoption of what must have initially been a very inefficient mode of locomotion. A mode that evolved by the radical realignment of the primate skeleton must have conferred significant advantages to outweigh the disadvantages of stress upon the spine and the awkward balance of the head and internal organs which still plague humans.

"Man the Hunter"

Almost every investigator of this problem has admitted that in the beginning bipedalism would have been very inefficient compared to the well-developed locomotor patterns from which it diverged, but all have gone on to assume that the advantages that they propose would have been sufficiently compensatory. These assumptions are succinctly stated by Kenneth Oakley. "There are good reasons for supposing that the earliest erect hominoids were tool users, for bipedalism is initially disadvantageous unless there is some compensating factor, and in the case of the hominoids this can surely only have been the ability to wield weapons while moving." None of the proponents of this position have explained how an efficient quadruped evolving into an initially inefficient biped could have wielded weapons with sufficient skill and accuracy to survive and reproduce.

It seems obvious to us that the elements of an initial, experimental, inefficient bipedalism were consolidated in a far less hazardous and demanding ecological niche than that occupied by the early hunters.

It is unfortunate that the evolution of *Homo sapiens* in the hunting niche has been expounded by the most eloquent contributors to the literature of human origins. Many of the theories developed out of the emphasis on hunting as a singularly important human activity need reexamining, but the competence and authority of the proponents of the hypotheses discourage informed dissent. Evolution in the hunting niche has been used to explain such diverse human developments as bipedalism, anterior dental reduction, superior manual dexterity, war, language, home base, and most ingeniously, the reproductive anatomy of women, frontal sex, and male-female pair bonding. The student can review the theories in the works of Desmond Morris and Sherwood Washburn.

Hunting is a spectacular activity, involving a constant threat to survival that leaves a lasting impression on a person's memory and providing many stories which become part of the cultural heritage of a people. Since the artifacts of the hunt are as persistent as the mental images, they serve to distort the archeological records. The implements, tools, weapons, and bones of the hunt are much better preserved than the digging sticks, gathering baskets, seeds, fruits, vegetables, grubs, and eggs that have almost certainly been important to humans throughout their history, but are only poorly represented in the archeological record.

In a thorough analysis of a group of hunter-gathers living in the Kalahari desert, Richard Lee found that small human groups are living well in what might be considered marginal habitats. Even in this semiarid region the women are able, in two or three days work, to gather enough plant food for a week. Vegetable foods constitute 60 to 80 percent of the diet, with the remainder being made up of animal food secured by male hunting parties. In the same expenditure of time and effort, the women provide two to three times the food by weight as do the men. Lee concluded that the tribe could live exclusively on vegetable food, but animal food is highly prized for the variety it affords in the diet and the opportunities for adventure provided by the hunting. In every hunting-gathering tribe studied except the eskimo, only a small fraction of the diet is satisfied by meat, and hunting occupies but a fraction of the time of males.

Even in the eskimo, whose environment dictates the meat and fish diet, hunting is not necessarily an impressive communal activity demanding the elaborate preparation and loud communication which supposedly exerted strong selection pressure on the earliest attempts at vocalization. The eskimo seal hunter squats, with infinite patience and in quiet solitude, above a hole in the ice, his eyes trained to the nearly imperceptible movement of the bit of down he has placed above the hole to detect the breathing of the seal beneath. In any environment the hunt is characterized by stealth. Only when animals are driven into nets or over cliffs does the hunt provide an opportunity for vocalization.

Just how pervasive an influence on modern thought has been exercised by the idea of "man the hunter" was illustrated at a 1966 symposium on hunting-gathering peoples. "The symposium agreed to consider as hunters all cases presented, at least in the first instance. It was also generally agreed to use the term 'hunters' as a convenient short hand, despite the fact that the majority of peoples considered subsisted primarily on sources *other than meat*—mainly wild plants and fish." (Lee and DeVore, 1968). We can see that bureaucrats have no monopoly on newspeak. Obviously the hunt is one of the most beautiful inventions of scientific people for with it they have ingeniously explained every character that distinguishes humans from their primate ancestors. Each unique acquisition from language to big breasts, from home den to huge territory has been attributed to evolution in the hunting niche. Certainly that niche helped to shape human evolution, but the precise ways need to be reconsidered. The impact of gathering as a survival strategy has received almost no attention in the literature of human origins.

Periodic Environments

One of the most widely accepted human traits that we may profitably reexamine is our supposedly huge territory. S. Washburn and V. Avis have again related this to the hunting habit:

> The acquisition of hunting habits must have been accompanied by a great enlargement of territory, since the source of food was now more erratic and mobile . . . whether early man scavenged from the kills of the big carnivores, followed herds looking for a chance to kill, drove game or followed a wounded animal, his range of operations must have been greatly increased over that of the arboreal apes.

However, the fact is that we did not historically, nor do we at present, occupy a large territory. It is a fallacy to equate human proliferation over the globe to the ability to occupy a large territory; the territory of individuals and bands is small. Out-migrations have obviously occurred repeatedly, but extensive utilization of land by single individuals or small groups within a few generations is purely an artifact of the imagination.

Even most of the free-ranging animals upon which humans would have preyed occupy small, limited ranges, as do the wild carnivores. Hunting success for carnivores, *Homo sapiens* included, is predicated upon detailed knowledge of the area being hunted. It is likely that hunting success for both humans and animals is inversely proportional to the distance from the familiar range.

The origin of nomadism in humans is probably not so much related to a carnivorous habit as much as to the occupation of areas whose ecological imperatives were quite different from the subtropical savannah of our origin. An ecological theory advanced by M. J. Dunbar of McGill University in Quebec can give us some idea of those imperatives. Dunbar proposes that a species exploits the productivity of its environment in such a way as to avoid the large oscillations that are harmful to the survival of the species and even the entire ecosystem. Such oscillations are "absent in tropical and subtropical environments which foster much more complex ecosystems in which there is a great multiplicity of energy paths along which overloading can be released." These environments are characterized by year-round productivity, whereas the temperate and semidesert environments exhibit seasonal or fluctuating surges of productivity. Breeding seasonality, migration, and population controls help to synchronize resource availability and utilization in periodic environments.

The tacit assumption in most accounts of human origins is that competitive pressure, associated with shrinking forests during a period of climatic change, was responsible for the radiation of the ancestral hominids onto the open country. These accounts fail to consider the tension that would have been created between the opposing forces of competition and the natural conservatism of the primates. Studies of free-living primates have demonstrated the reluctance of groups to move outside of the habitual range. Washburn and Hamburg (1965) relate this conservatism to the adaptive value of learning and to the need for familiarity in order to fully exploit the habitat.

No modern primate species approaches the propensity of humans to exploit new areas, and we would expect that the ancestral stock would have been even more conservative than modern primates. We suspect, further, that the exploitative character of *Homo sapiens* is much overrated being, in fact, an artifact of the modern period of history. The very long period of tool development and the continuation of certain types of tools over thousands of years support the idea that *H. sapiens* are inherently conservative.

The exploitation of new habitats by a population must be related to behavior and population genetics as well as to competitive pressure. Every population has the potential for accumulating genetic variability, and this variability is often greatest in peripheral populations. We imagine that a segment of the ancestral population became, by small increments of change, less well adapted to the old habitat. Under normal conditions of habitat stability and gene flow, the potential variation would be checked; but given proximity to a new niche, the variant segments of the population would have a chance for survival, separation from the parental gene pool, and eventual consolidation of their differences.

I. M. Tattersall of Yale University has produced some evidence that the early stages of human evolution proceeded in environments which fit Dunbar's description of minimum oscillation. From a study of the Nagri flora and fauna of the Tertiary Siwalik deposits of India, in which one of the earliest probable hominids, *Ramapithecus,* is found, he concluded that the Nagri environment was characterized by tropical forests interspersed with broad rivers and tree savanna. In just such an environment the earliest human ancestors could have gradually changed from an arboreal species to a ground-living form. They could have evolved into a niche proposed by Clifford Jolly of New York University. From an extensive comparison of the dentition and anatomy of the jaws of fossil forms, Jolly concludes that our ancestors were seed eaters.

The ability to exploit grass seeds as a staple is not seen in other mammals of comparable size, though it is seen in birds and rodents, presumably because the agile hand and hand-eye co-ordination of a higher primate is a necessary pre-adaptation to picking up such small objects fast enough to support a large animal. With these pre-adaptations and the adaptive characters of jaws, teeth, and limbs the basal hominids would have faced little competition in the exploitation of a concentrated high energy food. They would thus have attained a stable, adaptive plateau upon which they could have persisted for millions of years, peacefully accumulating the physiological adaptations of a terrestrial, open-country species.

Jolly's model not only provides a more reasonable explanation than the "hunting man" hypotheses for the anterior dental reduction and evolution of the hominid jaw, but it also provides an explanation for the survival of an initially maladapted species in the open country. More importantly, his model postulates the occupation of a competition-free niche in which the elements of an initial, experimental, inefficient bipedalism could have been consolidated.

Speculations on the Origin of *Homo Sapiens*

We cannot resist the temptation to speculate that prehominids may have been forced into the savanna niche by the demands of infant care. An essentially hairless mother and infant responding to the problems of infant transport could have initiated many of the hominid behavior patterns that came to be so important to the hunting society. The home den, food sharing, male help in infant care, and the division of labor could have originated from the restricted mobility of mothers who had to carry babies. It seems to us that the trend to nakedness, the loss of estrus, the habitual occupation of the ground, and the adoption of bipedalism may have evolved together as part of a complex pattern of physiologic, behavioral, and ecological differentiation from the basic primate stock. However, until further investigations clarify the problem, this model is purely speculative.

Dispersal

As the climate became more dry, a trend indicated by fossil floras and faunas, a somewhat preadapted biped could have become more nomadic. Hunting-gathering peoples move not so much with the migration of big game herds as with the development of the plant resources that are the main component of their diet. With the acquisition of domestic herd animals much later in human evolution, nomadic peoples moved with the developing plant resources upon which their herd animals depend. All nomadic peoples move along well-defined paths dictated by the seasonality of the vegetation and familiarity with the terrain and the resources.

There is a second type of human dispersal across the landscape which is quite different from nomadism. That is the periodic and often violent dispersal of individuals from population centers. In an area of increasing population and stable resources, the resources will be depleted unless some alternatives to overcrowding are found. In many animal groups, young males of reproductive age find themselves pushed to the fringes of the social group. The net result of this isolation is to prevent them from effectively breeding and contributing to the population.

The "walk-about" rites of the Australian aboriginal tribes were an effective dispersal mechanism with the added advantage that they exerted strong selection pressure for the survival of the most fit individuals. The tendency to walk about almost certainly has both biological and cultural determinants (Figure 5-3).

In any out-migration, the survival of the migrants depends on their ability to function in unfamiliar terrain. John Greene at the University of Colorado was one of the first anthropologists to suggest that the cruel and

Figure 5-3 A party of Aboriginals camped in desert country near the MacDonnell Ranges in Australia's Northern Territory. *(Photo courtesy of the Australian Information Service.)*

seemingly senseless puberty rites of the Australian aborigines were ecologically meaningful. He reasoned that the pain of the rites left an indelible memory, in the mind of the boy, not only of the rite but of the extremely important information conveyed to the young in that rite; information upon which his life would depend.

Probably one of the single most important causes of mortality in animals, whether from predators, starvation, or other natural causes, is unfamiliarity with the terrain. Familiarity and predictability are vital to maximum utilization of the environment. This is as true for humans as for any other animal. In a strange environment there is little chance for the neural systems of the animal to construct visual projections of feeding, watering, and sheltering locations which promote day-to-day survival. Countless experiments have shown that such unfamiliarity spells disaster. Mice released in productive ecosystems identical to, but outside, their home territory simply do not survive. In human groups the communication of the individual memory for such sites, from individual to individual and generation to generation, is an additional factor dictating habitual use of familiar terrain.

Learning and Teaching

The consequences of the extended period of infant dependency are felt in every aspect of human life. We can hardly imagine the shape of human culture given any other system of individual growth and development to maturity. The parents not only provide for the physical well-being of the infant and inscribe the original affectational system which influences all subsequent behavior, but they also transmit information vital to the survival of the young once it leaves their care. The importance of mnemonic information to the survival of *Homo sapiens* has had significant consequence in the evolution of the species and the development of culture.

Postmenopausal Survival

In humans the importance of the mother-infant bond to the organization of the social group confers special significance to the mother as a carrier and transmitter of survival-promoting information. We can appreciate the biological force of this function if we reflect that it is the only reasonable explanation for the survival of postmenopausal females. The *Homo sapiens* female is the only female primate who spends a significant portion of her mature life cycle in a nonreproductive state. There is absolutely no biological sense to this survival if reproduction were the only criterion of evolutionary success. But the survival of knowledgeable members of a social group is very understandable when information creatively organized in the mind of one individual can be transmitted by imitation or by teaching to influence the survival of others. The survival of the human female long after her child-bearing years are over is testimony to her importance as the transmitter, first by passive example, and later somewhere in the protohuman stock by active teaching of information which permits a more effective response to changes in the environment.

Capacity to Believe

Any animal who learns much of his survival-promoting behavior from another must have the capacity to believe what he observes or is shown. There must be some guarantee, innately coded or experientially reinforced, that one will do as one is told. A young animal learns to heed the warning calls of his social group, to eat foods which his mother eats, to sleep in the sheltered place she chooses, and to accept her judgment in a thousand vital decisions. Each time that acceptance produces success, the tendency to follow advice is reinforced. As the infant develops and the relationship between mother and child changes in subtle and important ways, the force of her authority wanes.

However, the predisposition to authority is not completely thrown off by the attainment of sexual maturity and freedom from parental care. The capacity to believe, so vital to the learning young animal, predisposes the adult to authoritarian doctrine, dogma, and propaganda. If the predisposition to dogma represents the dark side of the capacity to believe, we can also find this same capacity at the foundation of a more stunning human achievement, the development of language. For a symbol to be effective, those to whom it serves as communication must accept it in place of the thing that it symbolizes. The communication of a nectar source from one bee to another involves symbolism in the form of dancing. However, this symbolic giving of direction is reinforced by the odor of nectar on the returning worker, so the information is never conveyed "secondhand." Only the directions of a worker actually returning from the fields with the physical evidence will be followed by other bees. Obviously language communication in humans involves a far greater commitment to belief, but that commitment develops out of the same prosaic contingencies as learning what to eat and where to find it, where to sleep, and who your enemies are and how to avoid them.

Teaching Behavior

The predisposition to learn by imitation leads to the possiblity of learning from teaching. It might at first seem that teaching behavior is nothing more than the correlate of learning, but we believe that a distinction can be made between learning by imitation and learning from teaching. In the behavior model developed in Chapter 4 we described learning as an internalized individual process. The individual integrates sensory, genetic, and mnemonic information, acts, compares the results of his action to some neural model of intention, and readjusts his action pattern to achieve the desired effect. If the achievement of the goal results in the remodeling of the neural model to influence the future behavior, we say the organism learns. The organism learns when it remodels its behavior after observation, practice, and experience.

In all the behavior recorded by Goodall for chimpanzees, learning occurred by imitation, practice, and positive and negative reinforcement. She reported few instances where the mother actively aided the learning. The one exception may be made in the instance, common to the animal world, where the parents or mother encourages or pushes the infant to try a new form of behavior. The parent in effect determines the time at which the infant is ready for certain patterns. Birds determine when the young shall begin flying practice. In the chimpanzee, the mother determines the time the infant will change from the ventral to the dorsal riding position and somewhat passively aids in the first clumsy standing and climbing movements of the infant.

In no aspect of behavior is this lack of teaching more evident than in termite-fishing behavior of the chimpanzee. The infant apparently learns all the aspects of this behavior, from the choice of an adequate tool to the specific way to manipulate it, by imitation, practice, and positive reinforcement. Imitative behavior is characterized by the passive participation of the model being imitated; the imitated parent or individual does not actively intervene in the learning process or in any way aid that process.

George Schaller has reported some evidence of teaching behavior in the gorilla, and Gene Sackett reported one remarkable example observed in the primate laboratory: A macque monkey trained to correlate a colored ball with an electric shock warned another monkey against the choice of that ball by physically pushing the other away from the choice. This behavior represents a remarkable feat of extrapolation depending on the transfer of the result of the internalized behavioral model to another individual—the essence of the teaching behavior.

Teaching implies the ability to abstract many elements of the behavioral program, to transfer the neural and execute models to the behavior of another individual, and to convey the ways in which the action may be more effectively remodeled. Teaching becomes more remarkable and significant to the human evolutionary progress when the ability to symbolize the stimulus and the result, and thereby to convey an abstraction of the behavioral model to another individual, is added.

Altruism

Konrad Lorenz said in a speech to University of Colorado medical school students that "the other incentive for wanting to know is wanting to help." We believe that the *sapiens* characteristic of wanting to help is a facet of altruism, the unselfish concern for the welfare of others. Although not exclusively a human character, altruism has certainly been important in human evolution. The trait can be observed in many animal groups. Jackdaws attack predators carrying other jackdaws; dolphins tend sick dolphins for days; and birds issue warning calls when predators are spotted.

The evolution of such altruistic behavior has eluded genetic analysis. The classical mathematical models show that selection pressure operating on a gene that conferred an advantage to the group at the expense of the individual would prevent that gene from being established in the group in sufficient numbers to establish the trait. However, it has been argued that if altruism benefited the bearer's nearest relatives, those most likely to bear the altruistic genotype, conferring an advantage on them over that enjoyed by families lacking the genotype, such a character could become established in the breeding population in spite of the risk it entailed for the individual bearer. The problem hinges on the element of risk involved in the behavior. It is noteworthy in this respect that the warning calls of many birds are produced in an accoustical pattern that is diffuse and without directional or source quality so that a predator is unable to use the call to locate the signaling bird.

In its early development in *Homo sapiens* altruism could have developed in the context of the teaching behavior pattern, a pattern of enormous benefit to the group but without risk to the individual. The value of teaching behavior would have been as great in a gathering society, where a good deal of botanical information is exchanged between individuals and generations, as it would have been in a hunting society where cooperation is vital to success. The development of language makes more sense in the context of the teaching behavior than it does in any other pattern of human action.

With the development of language, new ideas creatively organized in the mind of one individual could be communicated to another. Information vital to survival could be exchanged between organisms, successful responses to perturbation could be shared. The mnemonic information of the individual was enriched by the accumulated knowledge of the group. Information persisted through time not only in the DNA code but in the heritage of the people.

CONCLUSIONS

Like other species, *Homo sapiens* evolved genetically and fit neatly into the environment for countless millennia. But throughout the course of this period, unlike other species, we developed the unique ability, or strategy, to modify our behavior in response to the environment. We evolved the capacity to learn from experience and, most significantly, pass this information along to other members of our group and to their progeny through teaching. This new system was as responsive to selective forces as the old genetic one on which it was founded, and with which it continues to interact.

For the mechanism to succeed though, we had to believe what we were taught. This capacity facilitated our success and the development of culture; at the same time, it made us subject to authority, giving our society stability. The species succeeded in proportion to the sensibility of the information transmitted. The conveyance of erroneous information would be expected to be detrimental to the species success and survival.

The potential for cultural alteration is not limitless. Yet we have the capacity to relearn and unlearn illogical information provided that the social, or perhaps economic, motivation exists. The human capacity to believe gives us a tremendous flexibility and advantage in responding to environmental perturbation. But, again, the information input must be sensible. As the world becomes increasingly more crowded, more constraints may be called for to maintain a stable and viable culture. The biological limits to our cultural modification may be as vital to our continued success as the solutions to any resource, energy, or food limitations.

SELECTED READINGS

Altmann, S. A. Social behavior of anthropoid primates: Analysis of recent concepts, *Roots of Behavior.* Eugene Bliss (ed.). (New York: Harper, 1962).

Count, E. W. *Being and Becoming Human: Essays on the Biogram.* (Princeton, N.J.: Van Nostrand, 1973).

Dunbar, M. J. The evolution of stability in marine environments; natural selection at the level of the ecosystem, *Group Selection.* George C. Williams (ed.). (Chicago: Aldine-Atherton, 1971).

Goodman, Morris. 1963. Serological analysis of the phyletic relationships of recent hominoids. *Human Biology,* vol. 35, pp. 377–436.

Hamburg, David A. Emotions in the perspective of human evolution, *Perspectives on Human Evolution.* S. L. Washburn and Phyllis C. Jay (eds.). (New York: Holt, 1968).

Hamilton, W. D. The evolution of altruistic behavior, *Behavioral Ecology.* Peter H. Klopfer (ed.). (Belmont, Calif.: Dickenson, 1970).

Illingsworth, R. A. The development of the infant and young child, *Normal and Abnormal.* (Baltimore: Williams and Wilkins, 1971).

Jolly, Clifford J. 1970. The seed-eaters; a new model of hominid differentiation based on a baboon analogy. *Man,* vol. 5, pp. 5–26.

Klopfer, P. H. *An Introduction to Animal Behavior.* (Englewood Cliffs, N.J.: Prentice-Hall, 1974).

Lancaster, J. Primate communication systems and the emergence of human language, *Primate Studies in Adaptation and Variability*. Phyllis Jay (ed.). (New York: Holt, 1968).

Lehrman, D. S., and J. S. Rosenblatt. *The study of behavioral development in the ontogeny of vertebrate behavior*. Howard Moltz (ed.). (New York: Academic, 1971).

Milgram, S. 1963. Behavioral study of obedience, *Journal of Abnormal Social Psychology*, vol. 67, pp. 372–378.

Morris, Desmond. *The Naked Ape*. (New York: McGraw-Hill, 1969).

Napier, J. R. 1970. *The Roots of Mankind*. (Washington, D. C.: Smithsonian Institution Press, 1970).

Oakley, Kenneth P. The earliest tool makers, *Evolution and Hominisation*. Guttfried Kurth (ed.). (Stuttgart: Gustav Fisher Verlag, 1968).

Olson, Everett, C. 1959. The evolution of mammalian characters. *Evolution*, vol. 13, p. 344.

Schultz, Adolph H. The recent hominoid primates, *Perspectives on Human Evolution*. S. L. Washburn and Phyllis C. Jay (eds.). (New York: Holt, 1968).

Tattersall, Ian. 1969. Ecology of North Indian *Ramapithecus*. *Nature*, vol. 221, pp. 451–452.

Turnbull, Colin. *The Mountain People*. (New York: Simon and Schuster, 1972).

Waddington, C. H. *The Ethical Animal*. (New York: Antheneum, 1961).

Washburn, S. L., and David A. Hamburg. The implications of primate research, *Primate Behavior*. Irven DeVore (ed.). (New York: Holt, 1965).

Washburn, S. L., and Virginia Avis. Evolution of human behavior, *Behavior and Evolution*. (New Haven: Yale, 1958).

Chapter 6

Agriculture and
Population Growth

The basic question is not how many people can share the earth, but whether they can devise means of sharing it at all.

Otto Friedrich, 1971

Already in that bright dawn of civilization when our remotest ancestors first claimed dominion over the earth, they had begun to strain the ecological balance of which we are so intimate a part. Even before the ancient Egyptians first tilled the fertile flood plains of the Nile or the farmers of Sumer sowed seeds of barley along the Euphrates, early humans were supporting increasing numbers with roots and tubers planted in the tropical soils of Southeast Asia and harvesting grain in the hills of Mesopotamia and China. Every morning men and women set out to gather any of a hundred or more kinds of plants that served as food. Each evening, or sooner, they would drift back to pool their collected resources.

MEETING BASIC ENERGY NEEDS

The older, more stable plant communities of tropical lands provided a relatively constant food source adequate for the needs of the populations that had evolved with them and whose cultures and mores were consistent with limiting numbers to those compatible with the food resource, i.e., to the carrying capacity of the land. Life flourished with the ability of men, women, and children to get food, to gather or kill enough edible material to provide the energy and nutrition needed to satiate the pangs of hunger and sustain life. Food-getting was the primary activity, but how much energy and time were consumed in attaining it? A good idea was provided by the studies of anthropologist Richard Lee of the University of Toronto who calculated the subsistence energy budget for the modern hunting-gathering society of the Kung bushmen.[1] This would approximate that of similar primitive cultures of the past and present.

The Kung of the Dobe area of Botswana live in a marginal area surrounded by a nearly waterless desert, but they are entirely self-sufficient in terms of subsistence. During an average season, each productive individual supported himself or herself in 2 to 3 days of gathering per week, leaving the remaining days for such other activities as resting or visiting, and particularly in games and gambling. Certainly, tribes in more productive areas would spend even less time and effort gathering food. The only drawback to this mode of life, if it could be considered one, lies in the ecological limits to the numbers that can be supported. About 600 square miles were required to support 248 Bushmen. Not all the land was used, though, and the effective population density was found to be 25 per 100 square miles or 4 square miles per person.

Primitive people had always been food-gatherers and hunters, moving with the shifting food resources and avoiding areas of scarcity. Humans began as an intimate part of the ecosystem but rarely remained so. For the most part, their numbers were limited by the natural carrying capacity of the land and could only increase as new food sources were discovered or cultivated.

Human beings, like every other organism, occupy a position, or niche, in the ecosystem and survive only to the extent that we maintain the landscape within the dimensions of the niche. We expanded beyond our original niche only in proportion to our capacity to exploit other habitats and displace the organisms that once occupied them. As human populations increased, more and more habitats and niches were altered.

[1]The correct spelling is !Kung. The exclamation point was introduced to denote the pronunciation. We omit it for simplicity.

Still. the human population might have remained in balance, or *homeostatic*, with the system if agriculture had not been discovered, which allowed our numbers to increase tremendously.

The universal ability to hunt and gather food provided a base for culture and agriculture. Probably by the end of the last Ice Age, humans learned how to cook, collected stones for grinding seeds into flour, and could make pots to store grain. Hunter-gatherers in Southwest Asia lived by collecting seeds of wild wheat, barley, and other grains. They harvested large-seeded legumes and collected the energy-rich dates, almonds, grapes, apples, and pears native to the region. They may have been aware that seeds dropped along the trail, or scattered about the threshing area, germinated; but it was still a major step to intentionally cultivate them. It demanded the abstract ability to conceptualize the future.

PRIMITIVE AGRICULTURE

The enormity of this step, its impact on humans and the total environment, must be appreciated. It has proved to be the single most important intervention we have ever made in our environment. It was one thing to pick fruits from mature plants or dig up their roots; it was a profound jump in imagination to realize that if certain seeds were placed in the ground, they would germinate some months later and grow up to produce more fruit. Perhaps some early gatherers in an already fairly permanent fishing village by a river or sea noticed the green sprouts arising from stored grain that they had failed to keep dry and drew the correct conclusions. However it came about, the relation of seeds to the mature plant may have been discovered again and again, perhaps over a period of tens of thousands of years, by people throughout the world.

On the other hand, many anthropologists believe that agriculture was discovered only once. If so, the partly wooded foothills of the Zagros and Taurus Mountains of Iran and Turkey are then considered the most logical birthplace. The discovery of long-buried seeds of cultivated wheat and barley has revealed that primitive farmers were raising crops there as early as 7000 B.C. Here were all the plants and animals thought to be so essential to a transition from food gathering to farming—wild barley and wheat, the wild sheep and goat, and even cattle and horses.

In either case, agriculture most likely evolved gradually, over thousands of years, from a natural response to an environment that provided a convenient source of food. Even today, where native wild wheats grow on the few undisturbed rocky slopes of the Taurus Mountains, during the three-week ripening season, a family can gather more grain than it could eat in a year.

It seemed only natural for people to prefer settling in areas where edible plants were most abundant and grains could be easily gathered and stored. The need to wander over the countryside, collecting large numbers of various other edible plants, was reduced.

As more land was altered and planted with these few species, more and more of the native plants that might once have provided some of man's diet were eliminated. The farmer became more dependent on what could be grown. This dependency on a few plant species may have been encouraged by another much earlier development. When bones are excavated from the deepest, oldest deposits of cave sites in the Zagros Mountains, one finds that the meat eaten 20,000 years ago came mostly from such large, hoofed animals as wild sheep, cattle, and goats. The debris from slightly younger deposits shows a gradual substitution of lesser creatures—fish, crabs, and water birds. It would seem that the large mammals became scarce, perhaps in response to hunting pressure. This shortage may have created a greater need to rely on plant foods.

According to the most widely accepted views, the environment of the Nile and lower Mesopotamia Rivers was perhaps even more amenable to the development of permanent agriculture once the concepts of farming had been discovered. Here, in the broad river valleys of the Nile, Euphrates, and Tigris Rivers, agriculture flourished. The land was inundated each spring with a fine silt and organic debris from the mountains, providing a planting bed rich in nitrogen and other nutrients essential to the rapid growth of the high-yielding annual species that came to dominate the agriculture of that area.

The environment of the American tropics was different, as was *H. sapiens'* response. Natural lightning fires had always burned local areas of the jungle, and people couldn't help observing the lush crop of annual plants that quickly filled the new clearings. Over the course of time, they learned to set the fires intentionally and plant the clearings in edible species. Such "swidden agriculture" of cutting and burning is still practiced by primitive tribes in South America and the Pacific islands (Figure 6-1). Trunks and branches are stacked and burned, and the ashes used for fertilizer. Digging sticks are used to plant the seeds or cuttings. The Haununoo of the Philippines plant as many as 50 different kinds of plants in their plots, and the crops are harvested as they ripen throughout the year, but any one small area is only planted for a few years, thus maintaining the richness of the soil. The plants used were determined by the ecological conditions of the region. In

Figure 6-1 Swidden agriculture consisting of burning natural forest areas to provide clearings in which to plant crops. Newly cut area in Simbai Valley, New Guinea. *(Courtesy of Dr. Roy Rappaport, University of Michigan.)*

Thailand, rice and other native plants were cultivated perhaps 15,000 years ago.

The New World lacked the river systems and flood plains, where fertility was naturally restored each year and permitted intensive and sustained cropping, but other methods and crops were used. In Latin America, bottle gourds and avocados were first grown about 7000 B.C. and beans, a thousand years later. Peppers, pumpkins, and corn have been grown for 5000 years in Mexico. The mountain terrain of Mexico and Central America provided a rich diversity of habitats and growing conditions that supported an enormous variety of edible wild plants. Elias Yanovsky of the United States Department of Agriculture listed 1112 different species of plants that furnished food for Indians of North America. Gradually the most desirable of these, including corn and potatoes, were selected for cultivation, and people developed an increasing dependency on a few of the most reliable species.

By 7000 B.C., another "improvement" in obtaining food was emerging: the domestication of animals. It may have begun when village children discovered a newborn lamb or goat and brought it home as a pet.

Even today, these animals have a warm appeal, and they readily accept humans because of their easy capacity for imprinting. Over the centuries, the neolithic farmer came to accept these animals and provide for their needs. In return, the animals provided meat and milk and could utilize lands that were too rocky or too steep for crops.

Cost to the Land

At first the nomadic hunters and gatherers probably disturbed the ground little, scattering only a few wild grains about semipermanent settlements. Cultivated food contributed little to their diet. As more people aggregated in these areas of abundance, and populations grew, however, the adequacy of these natural foods must gradually have diminished. The need for food could be met only by cultivating plants more intensively, and they came to depend more and more on these planted crops, just as is done today in clearing new land. Herds of gazelle, wild pigs, and other game were available, but their numbers were limited, and cropping provided a more reliable food source.

In every temperate region of earth, people took advantage of the most abundant food plants and developed ways of encouraging their growth. They might have been expected to overreact to the benevolence of the land as they did when clearing large areas of land for farming. The nutrients that plants need to grow are to a very great extent stored in the plants themselves. When these plants are removed from the land, whether by burning or by being used continually for food, the nutrients are lost. The land becomes increasingly less fertile, and production gradually decreases. This is most pronounced in forests where trees store so much of the nutrients. Burning this cover releases some of the nutrients, particularly the phosphates and potash, into the ash, where it is available to the rapidly emerging annual plants. Nevertheless, after two or three years, the rains have leached away the nutrients, and the land becomes unproductive. New forests must then be cleared and the cycle repeated.

Such may have been the case with the early Mayan civilization, where exposure of the tropical soils could have led to the ultimate ruin of both the land and the civilization. In more permanently stable societies, however, people evolved cultural practices, taboos, rituals, and sacrifices that kept numbers in balance with the capacity of the land to support them. In such instances, the intervention over the landscape was limited, and they fit harmoniously into the ecosystem information web; here, the cultural and behavioral evolution was slow enough for people to adjust and interact continuously in the ecosystem.

Such a continued balance, though, apparently was the exception. For most cultures, agriculture had far more implications than anyone could perceive. The most obvious impact was on the land itself. Through the course of evolution, plant communities had developed that were best suited to each particular area. The plants complemented each other to occupy the land in a manner most consistent with the stability of the total ecosystem. When these plants were removed to make way for the few main crop plants, this stability was destroyed. The balanced relationship between plant and the insect and animal species that lived in this system was also shattered. Most significantly, the balance between the plants and the land was lost together with the interactions of one plant with another.

Quite conspicuously, the natural habitat was altered to best suit human needs. Game was driven off or killed, forests were slashed and burned, and grasslands plowed up or overgrazed. When allowed to graze too intensively, or in too large numbers, goats, sheep, or any other livestock eat away the cover of plants that protect the land from erosion. The impact of this excessive feeding can still be seen after some 5000 years.

Human disregard or misunderstanding of a balanced relation with the ecosystem, that is, the long-term carrying capacity of the land, is well illustrated by the abuse of Mesopotamia and North Africa. Here, human culture failed to maintain the balance with nature as it expanded far beyond its niche. The land became sacrificed for immediate gain.

In the city of Kish, first capital of Mesopotamia after the "great flood," the record of ignorance was left in a thick deposit of brown alluvium. Already 5 millennia before Christ, the pastoral hills had been overgrazed, removing the protective cover, and enabling the rains to wash away the surface soils into the rivers and irrigation ditches. The hill people raised more and more goats and sheep, and the farmlands below were inundated with silt from the wasted lands above. Lands that in biblical times were said to have supported over 20 million people now support less than 5 million at a bare subsistence level. Irrigation ditches once servicing 21,000 square miles gradually filled with silt as the surface soils of the once fertile crescent washed away.

Syria was once famed for its oats, wheat fields, and well-nourished herds, and a quarter of a million people lived in its ancient center, Jerash, which is now only a village of a few thousand seminomads. The springs have dried out and the soils washed to bedrock because of human failure to understand the changing environment.

The slopes of the Zagros Mountains originally were covered with rich grains and scattered trees and brush. It is easy to imagine early people cutting away this woody, protective cover with stone axes to make room for more food plants. Since the earliest days of farming, the land has been modified for expedience. Inevitably, as the decline in the soil's fertility began, its capacity to provide crops was reduced, and the number of people it could support diminished. The obvious response was to till new land, putting more land in a single crop, and leaving less uncultivated land from which nature's once diverse bounty could be gathered.

About 3000 years ago, a Semitic tribe spread out from central Mesopotamia and occupied what is now Lebanon. The narrow coastal plain could not support a growing population long, and these ancient Phoenicians soon spread from the coast and began to cultivate the forested inland hills. They farmed these forests as they had their own flat alluvial valleys, since it was the only way they knew. Forests that protected the soil were cleared and the slopes cultivated. But the environment was not the same and the land responded differently. Soil quickly eroded under seasonal winter rains. The tribe responded by building retaining walls across the slopes; slopes up to grades of 76 percent were terraced, but the battle was a losing one (Figure 6-2).

The ancient cedars of Lebanon once covering 2000 square miles were cleared for farming and to provide timber for King Solomon, who supplied 80,000 lumberjacks to work in the forest and 70,000 to skid the logs to the sea.

The same story was repeated in China, where ancient farmers failed

Figure 6-2 The wasted lands of Mesopotamia with the sparse grasses. *(Courtesy of U.S. Soil Conservation Service.)*

to understand their environment. The Chinese of 4000 B.C. came to depend on millet as their main food resource. When the early farmers cleared away some of the native plants that competed with the grain to make room for millet, they removed the cover that had protected the soil from erosion. As more and more land was cleared and cultivated, the deep, fine-textured loess (unstratified) soils began to wash into the rivers that drained the area. Now, the silt-laden channel of the Yellow River runs 40 feet above the plains over the 400-mile course to its delta, held in place by dikes built over the period of farming in the area. Gullies 600 feet deep have been eaten out of the once forested uplands. Remnants of temple forests provide a clue as to the original nature of much of this land.

The record is the same almost wherever people grazed animals or tilled soil. The original ignorance was understandable, but the continued, deliberate disregard of knowledge gained over 5000 years is disastrous. In Asia, Europe, and America, environmental disregard was the same—we seem by our nature to place immediate needs above the long-term environmental balance. Farmers utilized the resources intensively and seemingly efficiently in an attempt to bring order to their environment and make life easier. In the short run, they were successful. The new practices were endorsed and transmitted through culture, since they contributed to the survival and comfort of those who practiced them. Farming brought the potential for stability through permanent settlement and gave the opportunity for a growing population that nomadism could not support.

Social Consequences

Despite the pronounced impact of agriculture on the land, its greatest influence was on the people. Agriculture apparently solved the problem of providing a ready supply of food throughout the year, but it also generated many more problems. Partly through the attempts to resolve these new problems, agriculture opened the way to all the complex societies and civilizations that followed. Before the rise of farming, people were relatively inconspicuous inhabitants of the earth. They lived on the casual bounty of nature and modified the land but slightly to increase their food supply. All people on earth were originally hunters and gatherers, and with rare exception lived in small bands that wandered about in search of food. With the constant local food source provided by agriculture, they no longer had to wander since a small area of land could support many more families. Four square miles could support 100 early farmers.

Primitive people lived in intimate contact with the natural world, sharing their habitat with the wild animals and crossing each other's paths daily. They lived in small groups or bands that were part of a still larger group, the tribe. Over the course of evolution, people became socially, if not genetically, attuned to associating with a limited number of people. They were social animals, but only to the extent that they could know and directly communicate with their associates.

The ability to raise their own food encouraged permanent settlements where more people could associate with each other than ever before. Individuals were now compelled to relate to more people than they may have been genetically capable of comfortably associating with. Psychologically, people became removed from the natural world and substituted an environment of their own creation.

The social impact of agriculture in creating this substitution is rarely considered, yet agriculture permitted the aggregation of far larger numbers of people than could ever have been accommodated before. Hunting-gathering societies typically associate in bands of about 25, the number with whom any one individual can maintain communication at a given time. Anthropologists consider this a natural number for primate associations that prevails even in the gorilla, baboon, and chimpanzee bands. Primitive tribes typically consist of about 500 members, the number that any one human can know by name. Such a tribe is formed from the affiliation of the smaller bands.

Agriculture made possible the close associations of far more than this number. The association of large numbers of people was not a function of agriculture alone; the permanent farming villages remain small even today. But agriculture made possible a much larger population, the city, and with it a vast increase in trade and commerce. The human social structure was completely altered. Indirectly, agriculture precipitated social changes and new cultures and must have been one of the strongest forces in shaping the present human environment.

Today, our numbers make it difficult to interrelate with others the way we did as a hunter-gatherer, and we seek to compensate for this lost heritage. Through various mechanisms, recreation, and social groups, we still seem to seek out relatively small groups with which we can be comfortable. We work alone, or as part of a much larger group, but rarely do we have continued interactions with the number of persons that our inheritance may have directed. This departure, in turn, may lead to psychological and political uncertainty.

The possible long-range social consequences were not foreseen by the early farmers and were not weighed against the immediate advantages. They became increasingly dependent on one basic crop and on the environment. The weather, for instance, was critical to the development of the crop. Drought or fire could mean failure. Plant diseases and insects, which became more prevalent with the larger acreages of fewer plant species, became a serious threat to survival. Their crop was also subject to flooding, a hazard unknown so long as we depended on a diversity of plants in an undisturbed system.

Nevertheless, the surplus of food usually available to the early farmers provided a resource they could trade for tools and luxuries, stimulating trade and commerce. The sedentary agricultural life often encouraged skills, crafts, and various forms of art. Permanency gave rise to possessions that nomads could not carry—another major step in the evolution of culture. Most important of all, agriculture gave rise to permanent dwelling places that arose to meet the environmental conditions of the day.

POPULATION SURGES

Tool Making

Demographer Edward S. Deevey, at the University of Florida, suggests that human population growth has shown three great surges (Figure 6-3): The first occurred perhaps a million years ago with the advent of tool making, but as a recent product of evolution, human numbers remained relatively few and in easy balance with the capacity of the land to support them until rather recent times—perhaps 30,000 years ago. By then the increase of human numbers throughout a long history as tool-using

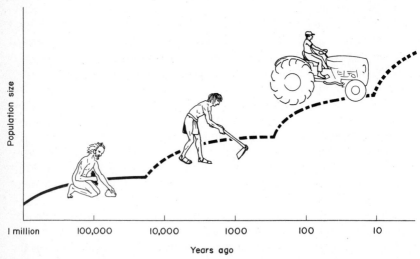

Figure 6-3 Logarithmic population-growth curves illustrating periods of accelerated growth during the first cultural, or tool-making, era over 100,000 years ago. Neolithic agricultural "revolution" following the last ice age; the scientific-industrial surge of the past 200 years. A fourth, most recent, surge has been added resulting largely from the control of the death rate during modern times. *(Based on Deevey, The Human Population.)*

hunters and gatherers had enabled us to broaden our territory into Europe, Asia, and through the Americas.

Neolithic Agricultural Surge

Population growth was temporarily slowed, or perhaps the population was crowded into already occupied lands by periods of glaciation. By the time the last ice age receded, the population had increased to such a density in some areas that people relied more on foods they raised themselves. Over a period of a thousand years or more, agriculture became the major source of subsistence in many parts of the world. The great reliability of the food resource, beginning about 10,000 B.C., led to more permanence of settlements and the next great surge in population growth.

Throughout the ensuing millennia, religious curbs, warfare, disease, famine, and other cultural and social forces restrained population growth, but all proved only to be delaying mechanisms. The continued interaction of these forces may explain why a few societies in the Southwestern United States deserts, Africa, Australia, New Guinea, and parts of Southeast Asia have not suffered the maladjustment of overpopulation and abuse of the environment. As Deevey states, "The environment, of course, sets upper limits, but these are, in fact, almost never reached. Instead, the limitation falls at a much lower level through such bottlenecks as social interaction, territoriality, and antagonisms."

Cultural checks were significant for centuries but now serve to keep but a few populations in balance with their environment. Abandoning the aged, sick, and wounded, and infanticide involving as many as half the births, once common in many cultures, are now rarely tolerated. Among Polynesians, any weakly or malformed child was disposed of as a matter of course; even the retention of healthy children was questioned. Taboos against sexual intercourse during the 1- to 3-year lactation period spaced out births in many cultures. The institution of marriage, and the accompanying mores, also limited births, especially when postponed until a suitor could afford a spouse. Even in recent times, marriage in England was not socially sanctioned until the couple could get their own cottage. The cultural practices of the Aborigines of Australia have limited their density to numbers that can be supported by the meager resources. Circumcision, subincision, and widely prevalent superficial mutilation inflicted during initiation ceremonies often caused fatal infections.

Homo sapiens' presumed aggressive behavior and predisposition to fight have been postulated also to have helped maintain a balance with the environment. Anthropologist Anthony Vayda suggests that warfare has a survival value largely through adjustment of male-female ratios in the population and prevention of population increases leading to over-exploitation of the habitat. Primitive wars came about because "a diminishing per capita food supply and increasing intragroup competition for resources generate intense domestic frustration and other intragroup tensions." Vayda postulates that when tensions reach a certain level, release may be sought through warfare.

Religious and political tensions helped restrict populations throughout the Middle Ages. In Europe, the Hundred Years' War of the fifteenth century and the Thirty Years' War of the seventeenth century, to name but two, caused hundreds of thousands of direct fatalities, many to the reproducing segment of the population, slowing population growth for over a century.

Pestilence and disease, often associated with wars, further restrict population growth, especially in an urban situation. Populations adapted to a seminomadic subsistence are small and distributed over a wide area; the small population size would limit the types of infectious disease mostly to those caused by parasites such as lice, internal protozoa, pinworms, and yaws, or to those transmitted by insects, such as sleeping sickness. Isolated populations and their parasites tend to adapt to accommodate each other. Wars, urbanization, or other disturbances tend to disrupt this "genetic-immunologic" balance. Urban living created environments more amenable to cholera, typhus, smallpox, a multitude of viral diseases, and malaria. Malaria served as a vital environmental message limiting populations, especially where they had expanded into tropical habitats in which certain mosquitoes abounded, until DDT removed this check. The Black Death provided another curb. The disease, erupting principally in association with urbanization, killed at least a fourth of Europe's population in the fourteenth century.

When war and pestilence no longer kept population down, famine often ensued. Over the ages, local famines numbered in the hundreds of thousands. They have had a tremendous impact, especially on subsequent populations. One major famine in India killed an estimated 3 million people in 1769–1770. During the same period, populations in Europe and China also reached critical numbers for the food resource, and millions perished.

Scientific-Industrial Surge

All these mechanisms became inadequate about the eighteenth century, giving rise to a third major world population surge. New agricultural methods, crop introductions, and technology provided more food; diseases no longer contributed significantly to mortality; and a period of relative peace ensued.

Reduced Death Rate

Populations grew steadily into the twentieth century, and growth again accelerated in what might be considered a fourth surge resulting largely from control of the death rate, particularly since World War II, with no diminution of births. Control of malaria, yellow fever, cholera, and smallpox has been especially significant in accelerating population growth, which is disrupting any vestige of equilibrium or stability that may have once existed in the human environment.

GROWTH AND LIMITS TO BIOLOGICAL POPULATIONS

The growth rate of any biological population is determined by fertility and mortality—the birthrate and death rate—as well as by its initial numbers. Many animal populations are characterized by a sigmoid, or S-shaped, growth curve in which a population, after a brief, gradual increase, soon increases at an accelerating rate, so long as conditions are favorable, until various factors begin to reduce the rate of growth (Figure 6-4). Food, space, habitat, predation, disease, and competition may all be limiting. All of these interplay to determine the carrying capacity, the numbers that can be supported in any given environment; together with social factors such as territorial behavior, social rivalry, and social hierarchy, they determine the ultimate numbers at which the growth curve will stabilize.

Presently, the human population continues along the log, or exponential phase, of growth, and the ultimate time when the slope may stabilize remains unknown. In fact, there is considerable doubt if the S-curve will be pursued, or if, at some point along the line of exponential growth, the population growth rate will suddenly drop to a near-zero point or even reach it. Such a curve is exhibited by some vertebrates such as arctic rodents. Growth builds up until stopped suddenly by some drastic limiting factor, and then ceases. Several reputable scientists feel that the human population is pursuing such a curve. They believe that the earth's carrying capacity has already been critically overextended and the

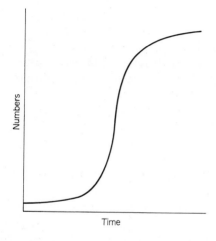

Figure 6-4 Characteristic population-growth curve showing the sigmoid or "S" shape of a gradual build-up, rapid growth, and final stabilization.

population growth rate will crash catastrophically, at least in some parts of the world.

Natural Increase and Doubling Times

The rate of natural increase is determined by subtracting the rate of deaths from the rate of births. Theoretically, if the world birthrate was 34 births per 1000 people, and the death rate 14, the population growth rate would be 20 per 1000, or 2 percent. Mathematically, a 2 percent growth rate doubles the population in 35 years—not simply because we add two people per year to a population of 100, but because those added are also reproducing.

Such doubling, assuming a constant life-style or degree of affluence, is significant since it requires doubling every resource—housing, roads, food, and energy requirements. In those countries such as Mexico and Ecuador with an annual population increase of over 3 percent, the population doubles every 23 years. In the United States, Europe, and Russia, the increase in 1972 was just over 1 percent, with a doubling time of 70 years. In Sweden and the United Kingdom, the percent increase is below 0.8 percent, with a doubling time of close to 100 years.

If continued, the average world growth rate of 2 percent would certainly strain the world's ecosystem for food, water, and mineral resources. Natural ecosystems would be replaced by those most productive to people, and the quality of life would diminish drastically.

When human numbers were few, the rate of increase was not too significant since even a rapid growth rate would not involve substantial numbers, and resources were plentiful. However, with increasing numbers, birth and death rates assumed greater significance.

Death Rates

So long as the number of births are balanced by deaths, a population would remain in partial equilibrium and grow fairly slowly, but as soon as death rates are controlled, growth accelerates. Similarly, controlling infant mortality has a tremendous impact on population growth. Even a slight increase of the birthrate over the death rate would soon vastly increase the number of individuals in a population. Conversely, a higher mortality rate would lead to extinction.

Age Structure

But there is more to population size than the growth rate. Age structure, sex ratio, and population density are also important. Most significant is the percent of the population of childbearing age, as shown by the age structure of a population (Figure 6-5). Where most of the people are young, as in Latin America and South Asia, the potential for reproduction is greatest.

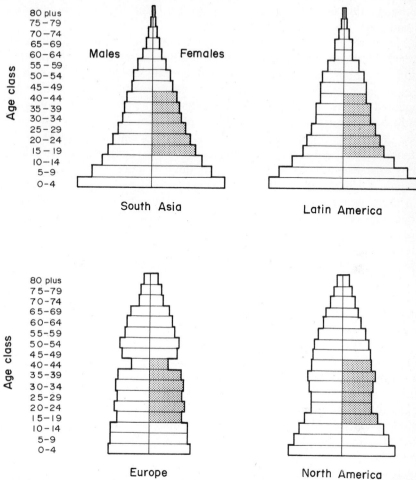

Figure 6-5 Age structure of populations in representative regions. The most stable population exists in Europe where only 26 percent of the population is below the reproductive age. The least stable population exists in Latin America, where 41 percent of the population will reach a reproducing age in the next 15 years. Shaded area denotes the reproductive sector of the population. *(Adapted from Davis, W. H. (ed.), Readings in Human Population Ecology.)*

Picture the population of a newly developing country where the death rate has been curbed and medicine has begun to reduce infant mortality. Since World War II, when public health measures were widely introduced over much of the world and DDT began controlling malaria, such conditions have prevalied. During this period the age class of young inflated greatly while the older classes remained fairly stable. The postwar babies have now reached a reproductive age, further enhancing the potential for inflating the population base of the population profile, although this potential is not being realized due to attitudes favoring smaller families.

Picture next a population in which the younger individuals have migrated, leaving only the older, nonreproductive segment of the population, or a population in which the members of reproductive age choose not to have children. In these cases, the population profile would be pinched at the base, indicating the smaller numbers of reproducing individuals, and a potentially declining population.

Age ratios are an important element of population structure, since they indicate future trends and portend potential dangers. Age structure may disclose a population in which only a small percentage of the population is under 15. In such a case, as best exemplified in the age structure of Europe, the growth rate will slow down as these people reach their reproductive years. The population, however, may continue to increase for many decades before actually stabilizing. The declining population growth rate would reflect a condition in which an effective birth control program or natural checks have reduced the young segment of the population.

Age structure also may represent a more uniform distribution of persons in each age group. The growth rate may have stabilized, but the population will continue to increase until the number of persons reaching a reproductive age no longer exceeds those leaving it. A stable population, in which both high birth and death rates prevailed, was most characteristic of primitive societies and persisted until recent times. The pyramid for the United States is fairly equilateral but with a pronounced bulge for the age group born in the prosperous twenties and a pinching in during the Depression and World War II days. In the nonindustrial countries in South Asia, Latin America, and Africa, where the increasing control of infant mortality has greatly inflated the proportion in younger age groups, over 40 percent of the population may be under 15 years of age. As this segment of the population reaches the reproducing age of from about fifteen to forty-five years of age, the population density will become especially critical.

The age pyramid for India provides a good example of the consequences of unrelenting population growth. Each year the number of young people reaching a reproducing age far exceeds the number of older people who move out of their reproductive years or who die. This trend will persist through subsequent generations until their progeny gradually diminish in numbers proportionate to those leaving the reproductive age. If fertility were reduced to the replacement level of 2 percent by 1985, the population, which was 570 million in 1971, would still exceed a billion before it stabilized around the middle of the twenty-first century. If the 1970 growth rate persisted, the population would reach 1.5 billion by the year 2000. On a world basis, the population would grow to some 6.3 billion even if all reproduction rates were brought down to replacement levels by 1980.

Most children are born to women between twenty and twenty-nine years of age. Consequently, delaying marriage, or more realistically, delaying childbearing, until even age twenty-five could slow down population growth since it would reduce the number of childbearing years. Reducing the number of births to older women would similarly help. For instance, birth rates for Taiwanese females over twenty-nine dropped sharply between 1950 and 1964, with a resultant decline in population growth. The attitude of many young United States women toward smaller families is producing a similar sharp decline in population growth rate in the United States.

CULTURAL INFLUENCES ON POPULATION PROJECTIONS

Many cultural factors also affect population growth and projections; for instance, the "sexual revolution" or "new morality"—a freer attitude toward premarital and extramarital sex—tends to delay or reduce marriage and birthrates so long as birth-control methods are used. Women's liberation, with more freedom of choice and better job opportunities, is similarly delaying childbearing. Some years ago, population growth in China was considered critical. Now, China may become the first developing country to succeed in controlling growth. Chairman Mao "asked" women to postpone marriage until age twenty-three, and supported the request with strong economic incentives. Premarital sex in China is virtually nonexistent due, in part, to public opinion and peer pressure. In China, the "pill" and intrauterine devices are free and popular. By 1972, the annual rate of natural increase had dropped to 1.24 in Peking and 0.69 in Shanghai.

Everyone seems interested in the populations projected for the future; but the world is changing so fast that today's trends are unlikely to reflect tomorrow's. Projections consistently have been wrong in the slower moving past, and they are unlikely to improve in the future. Our attitudes are too variable, and our behavior rarely consistent for long. Projections are low when given in periods of low birthrates and high when given during periods of high birthrates. In the United States, the projection for the year 2000 fell by 60 million people in the 5 years from 1960 to 1965. Predicting populations is more than a mathematical numbers game; it is a prediction of future attitudes extending perhaps to legislation.

Population growth along with attitudes depend in part on the economy. In the prosperous 1920s, who would have predicted the depression of the 1930s that so drastically reduced the numbers producing children? Growth in France has been slow ever since the Revolution;

peasants there have not wanted to subdivide their lands, and opportunities for their sons and daughters in cities were limited. The birthrate of about 16 per 1000 people reflects this sentiment. The same attitude and response have reached North America. No longer are children needed to work the farm. State welfare is replacing children as "old-age insurance," and the social desirability of large families is lessening, in spite of the resistence of some socially conservative elements of society.

Nathan Keyfitz of the University of California projected population growth in the United States based on varying degrees of fertility, that is, the actual number of children produced. At 3.4 children, the population in A.D. 2000 would be 356 million, whereas at 2.5 children, the population would be 280 million. This range is wide enough to be reasonably reliable, yet births might well exceed 3.4 or, more conceivably, stop at less than 2.

The birthrate of Europe, where birth control is more widespread than in the United States, is stabilizing more rapidly. Large families have been too expensive for decades and rarely a measure of status. The same is true for most of the industrialized countries.

The real threat comes from the nonindustrialized (or developing) countries where two-thirds of the world population lives. The relative contribution of these countries to global population is most critical (Figure 6-6). In Africa and Latin America, where the population is

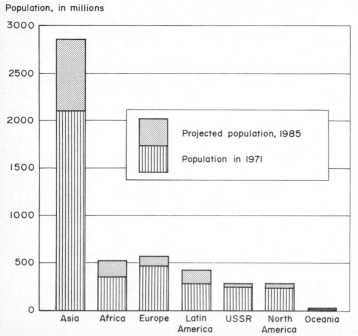

Population, in millions

Figure 6-6   Projected world population growth by area, from 1971 to 1985.

projected to nearly double between 1965 and 1985, the cost of birth control may be prohibitive and children are often a measure of status. Also, lack of education often makes contraception impractical. Religious discouragement of birth control may have been advantageous to an agrarian society a century or more earlier, but is now impairing the quality of life of millions in South America.

While birthrates in the industrialized countries appear to be slowing, those in the nonindustrial countries are not. The accelerating population rise in the nonindustrial countries results from the sharp drop in mortality, especially infant mortality. Although children once died from all kinds of communicable diseases, they now live, thanks to modern public health practices. And there is much room for further "improvement." The death rate in many countries is only 9 to 10 per 1000 (Table 6-1). The death rate in Africa is twice this, leaving a potential for vastly accelerating population growth there. There are a great many young children in proportion to the total population so the potential future growth is even more serious if the existing fertility rate persists another generation. Most critically, the overpopulated countries equate growth with prosperity and are not interested in limiting the size of families. Birth control programs are viewed as a myth of the rich to subjugate and exploit the poor.

Even a 1 percent increase is too much to tolerate for long and would yield a world population of 60 billion in 300 years. To maintain a steady population in the United States, the birthrate would have to drop from 17.6 per 1000 per year to equal the death rate of 9.6 per year while all immigration stopped. The net reproduction rate, that is, the difference between birth and death rates, would have to be less than 0.5 percent. The number of children per family would have to be held to 1.2—lower than for any human population in recorded history.

It is important to stress the time lag in making projections. For instance, at a replacement rate of 2.0, about the number needed to maintain constant population, the population would take at least 70 years to stabilize. This is exemplified in the United States where, by 1972, the population growth rate had slowed to zero with two births per couple. Although the population continues to grow, it should level off at about 320 million by 2040, *if the trend continues.*

CONCLUSIONS

Agriculture gave humans surplus food, settlement, and the beginnings of civilization, but at the same time it provided the basis for an increasing and perhaps unnatural population density and the drudgery of unremitting, year-round agricultural toil. Agriculture, although fostering comfort and security, created the peasant and condemned the majority to a sedentary and servile existence. Subsequently, technology freed many

Table 6-1 World Population Trends and Data.

Country	Annual births per 1000 population	Annual deaths per 1000 population	Annual rate of population growth (%)	Number of years to double population	Population estimates 1971 (millions)	Population projection to 1985 (millions)
North Africa	47	16	3.1	23	89	140
Western Africa	49	23	2.6	27	104	155
Eastern Africa	47	21	2.6	27	100	149
Middle Africa	46	23	2.2	32	37	52
South Africa	41	17	2.4	29	23	34
Southwest Asia	44	15	2.9	24	79	121
Middle South Asia	44	16	2.7	26	783	1137
Southeast Asia	43	15	2.8	25	295	434
East Asia	30	13	1.8	39	946	1182
North America	18	9	1.2	58	229	280
Latin America	38	9	2.9	24	291	435
Middle America	43	9	3.4	21	70	112
Caribbean	34	10	2.2	32	26	36
Tropical South America	39	9	3.0	24	155	236
Temperate South America	26	9	1.8	39	40	51
Northern Europe	16	11	0.6	117	81	90
Western Europe	16	11	0.6	117	150	163
Eastern Europe	17	10	0.8	88	105	116
Southern Europe	19	9	0.9	78	130	146
U.S.S.R.	17	8	1.0	70	245	287
Oceania	25	10	2.0	35	20	27
World	34	14	2.0	35	3706	4933

Source: Based on Population Reference Bureau Data Sheet, August 1971.

from agricultural toil only to relegate them to industrial toil; often more tedious, monotonous, and less satisfactory in terms of a million years of nomadic heritage.

Anthropologists Lionel Tiger and Robin Fox regard agriculture as "a great leap backward," returning the majority to a restrictive food-getting state of our primitive past, but all the while confining us to smaller and smaller space and taking us farther from our inherent place in the natural ecosystem.

Agriculture made possible a tremendous surge in human numbers, but it also created dependency on it for support. Lands put into single crops no longer accommodated a varied diversity of plants. Ultimately, agriculture alone became inadequate; ever-increasing human numbers could be supported only as technological methods were developed and applied to agriculture. Irreversibly, technology also became an inseparable part of the human environment.

If a global population explosion and expected subsequent crash are to be averted, some means of stabilizing the population must be achieved. Progress has been dramatic in a few countries, such as East Germany, which has a growth rate of 0.1 percent, and a doubling rate of 700 years. The population of tiny Malta is actually diminishing, with a negative growth rate of -0.8 percent. But these are exceptions brought about by massive emigration resulting from economic and political imperatives. A few countries are making substantial progress, such as West Germany and Finland, with growth rates of 0.4 percent. Japan, largely through a coordinated government program, has reduced its growth rate to 1.1 percent, but its population will still double in 60 years. Population increases in the underdeveloped countries are most rapid, and control will ultimately occur through development or catastrophe.

Certainly there is room for many more bodies on the planet Earth, but the question of how many is academic; it is hoped that it will never be resolved, because the population will stabilize at some much lower number. This number will be determined by the information input of the environment and especially by human behavioral and cultural response. The more we have, the more difficult and complex is the social and economic system required to maintain order. The real question is not the theoretical number the earth can support, but the number it can support comfortably. How much does the quality of life suffer with each increment increase in population? Even now the quality of life has diminished for many. Tremendous improvements in agricultural and industrial technology have made it possible to support literally billions more than a hunting and gathering society could. Perhaps new scientific or sociological developments will further extend the capacity to support our numbers. But what are the costs to the human environment?

SELECTED READINGS

Cohen, Yehudi, A. *Man in Adaptation. The Biosocial Background.* (Chicago: Aldine, 1968).

Daugherty, H. E. The ecology of human population growth and control, *In The Nation's Environment.* (Johnson City: East Tennessee State University, 1971).

Deevey, E. S. 1960. The human population. *Scientific American,* vol. 203, no. 9, pp. 195–204.

Denevan, W. M. 1970. Aboriginal drained field cultivation in the Americas. *Science,* vol. 169, pp. 647–654.

Flannery, Kent V. 1965. The ecology of early food production in Mesopotamia. *Science,* vol. 147, pp. 1247–1256.

Harris, David R. 1967. New light on plant domestication and the origins of agriculture. A review. *Geographical Review,* vol. 57, pp. 90–107.

Isaac, E. *Geography of Domestication.* (Englewood Cliffs, N.J.: Prentice-Hall, 1970).

Keyfitz, Nathan. United States and World Populations. *In Resources and Man.* National Research Council. (San Francisco: W. H. Freeman, 1969).

Lee, Richard B. 1966. !Kung bushman subsistence: An input-output analysis. Ecological essays: *Proceedings of the Conference of Cultural Ecology.* National Museum of Canada.

Lowdermilk, W. C. 1950. Conquest of the land through 7000 years. United States Department of Agriculture and Soil Conservation Services, SCS MP-32.

Murdock, G. P. *Africa: Its People and Their Culture History.* (New York: McGraw-Hill, 1959).

Sauer, Carl O. *Agricultural Origins and Dispersals.* (Cambridge, Mass.: MIT Press, 1952).

Solheim, W. G. 1972. An earlier agricultural revolution. *Scientific American,* vol. 226, no. 4, pp. 34–41.

Stott, D. H. Cultural and natural checks on population growth. In Smith, R. L. *The Ecology of Man.* (New York: Harper, 1972).

Ucko, P. J., and G. W. Dimbleby (eds.). *The Domestication and Exploitation of Plants and Animals.* (Chicago: Aldine, 1969).

Vayda, A. P. 1961. Expansion of warfare among Swidden agriculturists. *American Anthropologist,* vol. 63, pp. 346–358.

Part Two

Toward Environmental Homicide

Chapter 7

Industry and Agriculture

Our true Diety is mechanism. It has subdued external nature for us, and we think it will do all other things.

Carlyle
Signs of the Times, 1829

In Paris, Dickens's Madame Defarge was knitting the destiny of French aristocrats; in London, Parliament was expressing concern over discontent in the Colonies; and in the Colonies, Ben Franklin was tirelessly striving for the unification and freedom of his country in the diplomatic spheres of Europe. The decade of the 1770s, Dickens's setting for *A Tale of Two Cities,* also set the stage for the emergence of a new age—that of the Industrial Revolution.

For several decades, the machines and factories of industry had been drawing people from pastoral farms of rural Europe in ever-increasing numbers, and events were transpiring that were destined to lead the United States and the countries of Europe into an era of industrial power and dependency—an era of leisure and freedom toward which the entire world had unwittingly been striving since human origins. It was an era destined to confirm our belief in our uniqueness from other animals but also one that ultimately made us aware of our position in the total environment.

It was an era whose seed spawned the environmental chaos which we were not to recognize for two centuries—when modern people viewed the bounded limits of the planet from space and saw first hand that there was no escape from the increasing wastes and numbers. Actually, a plethora of environmental ills accompanied industry from the start, and a few visionaries decried environmental destruction centuries ago. But the problems were largely ignored because of more overwhelming social problems.

The acrid, soot-laden air of industrial England, the continual deafening clatter of the steam engine, and the outrageously dangerous and crowded working conditions were appalling even in their own time. Such problems emerged insidiously though, and became the accepted price for what then seemed a better life. The problems evolved because scientific theories were too rapidly applied to technological progress with no regard as to the possible environmental consequences and no understanding of the position of technology in the total system.

THE RISE OF TECHNOLOGY

The era of progress or enlightenment, as Arnold Toynbee first described it, had an earlier inception, going back to the upheaval in traditional religious thought and political philosophy of the seventeenth century. Basic tenets of religion and state were questioned, particularly the belief that Deity did not intervene at will in human affairs; also questioned was the "divine right" by which monarchs had claimed to rule. Monarchs became less revered, and their absolute dominion over human destiny was questioned. Increasingly they were regarded as merely heads of government; if a ruler failed to respect individual rights, the subjects believed they were justified in overthrowing the government.

These concepts had been espoused in earlier times, but such heresy had been put down effectively. Not until the eighteenth century were people ready and in a position to listen and read. Most significantly, only then did sufficient numbers possess the freedom and affluence to speak out. The questioning of divine rule, coupled with the spread of liberal, democratic ideas, and free thought were becoming rampant and were major contributors to the industrial revolution.

People were struggling to dispel a trait of their animal origins that traced back to prosimian ancestors. In any population there is always a dominant animal, the one to which others defer. Such animals dominate the social structure of the ape communities, and their counterparts dominate the political structure and systems of humans. In common, the societies share the same concerns of survival, perpetuating the group, defending it, and keeping social order.

It seems to be our animal heritage, with our capacity to believe, that demands we be subservient to a dominant being or entity while striving for a higher rank within the system. Human political systems from monarchies to democracies and communism are based on a hierarchy and struggle for status.

Social systems seem to be so strongly programmed into our inheritance, and society so fixed on a rigorously rank-ordered basis, that the system or feudal principle itself is rarely challenged, only those who run it. It was challenged by Spartacus in Roman times, the revolutionaries of the eighteenth century, and it is challenged by the New Left of contemporary America. Even in a democracy, which gives an equal chance for everyone to become unequal, the central core is threatened—not so much the system as the leadership.

The relatively stable constitutional monarchy of nineteenth-century England afforded the opportunity for one to speak out against the injustice of government as represented by prime ministers, while still accepting subservience to the dominant Queen Victoria. This flexibility within stability may have been the most significant of many factors that launched the Industrial Revolution.

Initially, only Great Britain possessed the uniquely fortuitous combination of circumstances—unity of purpose, resources, and responsiveness of leaders—to bring about the birth of a new epoch. Enterprise had freed the nation from the guild system still prevailing on the continent. Guilds had dictated designs and prices, inhibited innovation, restricted the movement of workers, and curbed their initiative. Also, English society lacked the social pressures that dissuaded French and German nobles and their sons and daughters from entering business.

The political unification of Great Britain further served to its advantage. No tolls existed between its regions, and by remaining largely aloof from foreign wars, the country's energies and monies were not wasted in maintaining armies, but rather, directed toward capitalization and growth.

Perhaps most important, England's highly developed finance system, led by the mighty Bank of England, enabled an accumulation of great funds of capital. The extensive system of banks offered credit, often on a long-term basis. New business could readily be established, or old ones expanded, on borrowed money.

The tremendous changes transpiring in England were observed

covetously by the nations on the continent. The industrial growth was viewed as progressive and desirable and was vigorously emulated. Progress was change, and change was always for the better. This dogma, which was to become a virtual doctrine, has persisted essentially unchallenged for centuries. Few in nineteenth-century England expressed the negative concern that commerce was to become a religion and the factory a shrine.

Except for England, most of early nineteenth-century Europe was just emerging from centuries of feudal rivalries. Germany consisted of a loose confederation of small, jealous states. Italy was constituted of a number of hostile principalities divided since the fall of Rome; the Scandinavian countries were isolated and divided. France was in revolution and all but bankrupt from it. Eastern Europe and the Slavic states remained part of the Turkish Empire until the Greeks were able to cast them out in 1829. The United States was but a newly emerging nation whose resources remained untapped and its strengths undeveloped.

In England, however, discoveries and events were transpiring that were making possible the increasing substitution of machines for human labor. Changes in religious attitudes, liberalization of politics, and advances in technology and science gradually also combined in other nations of Europe to broaden the scope of the startling new age and establish an increasing dependence on technology. Industrialization flourished. The closing decades of the eighteenth century saw a tenfold increase in the number of patents granted for inventions in England. Inventions like James Hargreaves's spinning jenny in 1769 made a particularly notable contribution by rapidly accelerating production in the textile mills. A person could now spin thread simultaneously on dozens of spools, not just one. Soon the jenny was run by steam.

The Steam Engine

When James Watt received a patent on a vastly improved, highly functional steam engine, also in 1769, no one could have foreseen the astounding social changes that were to follow. Few foresaw the social consequences this one engine would have as continously improved models came to be used not only in the textile mills but also in coal mines, forges, breweries, and finally to transport people and materials over land and sea. By the early 1800s, such traditional trades as sewing, flour milling, brewing, and shoemaking all were becoming mechanized. These developments required more iron and more coal to produce the iron, as well as to provide the energy to drive the machines.

Steel

Henry Bessemer's invention to convert pig iron to steel, in which impurities were burned out of molten iron by forcing a draft of air through it, was also critical to the Industrial Revolution, although it did not come until 1857. Prior to then, since the early eighteenth century, iron had been smelted cheaply by roasting it over coke. A hundred years earlier, charcoal obtained from wood had been used, but England's once majestic oak forests that had provided that wood were now exhausted. In our haste for economic gain we had failed to recognize the limits of one more resource. Fortunately for the iron industry, an abundant supply of coal was available that provided a suitable substitute for wood once its volatile impurities were driven off by heating it to form coke. Early industry was largely founded on this wedding of iron and coal; the nations possessing them soon became the leaders of industry.

With steel, the construction of railroads, bridges, heavy machines, and even skyscrapers, formerly limited by the inadequate structural properties of iron, was possible. Steam-driven trains could now run over durable steel rails, and lightweight steel plates could provide ships more strength, buoyancy, and cargo space than ever before. World steel production soared from 500,000 tons in 1870 to 28 million tons in 1900.

Chemicals and Petroleum

The chemical industry grew proportionately, unwittingly imposing its impact on the environment. Illuminating gas from coal was introduced in 1802 and came to be widely used in urban lighting before being gradually replaced by electricity less than a century later.

Ultimately the petroleum industry lent its impact. Though the naptha component was known as a lighting fuel even in Babylonian times, its value as a lubricant and fuel was not truly recognized until the mid-1800s. When the internal combustion engine became practical in the 1900s, petroleum products became indispensable and added their wastes to the environment.

Copper

Copper was also to find new uses. Before the nineteenth century, this element was prized in coins and jewelry, used in tools and utensils, or heated with zinc or tin to make brass or bronze. Nearly pure copper ores had been used since early Egyptian times when Neolithic cultures found copper provided a remarkably malleable material that could be easily fashioned into jewelry or tools or weapons that proved vastly superior to wood. For several millennia its supply was restricted to what could be extracted from fairly high-grade ores, but within a decade after cheap steel was introduced, James Elkington, an American metallurgist, developed a process for refining copper from lower-grade ores. This discovery was especially timely in coinciding with the emergence of the electrical industry. Electric dynamos were in commercial use in the 1840s to generate arc light and to electroplate base metals with gold, silver, and copper, but uses were limited in that electricity had to be generated on the spot where it was used. Widespread, everyday use of electricity waited for Thomas Edison to develop a new kind of generator that produced a steady current at half the fuel cost of any previous generator. Once the power lines were built, the current could be transmitted through copper wires wherever desired. Electricity was made practical and soon became indispensable. It was dependent on copper, which was refined with the emergence of a vast new industry producing and consuming another resource. The new uses of materials in ever-greater quantities added to the complexity of our ecosystem and the concomitant chance of bringing about its failure.

THE LABOR SUPPLY

The birth of the industrial age coincided fortuitously with a plentiful supply of labor. Many factors contributed to a labor surplus. There was a declining death rate coupled with an increased life expectancy. Also, there were fewer wars controlling population. Already in the eighteenth century a population explosion was underway. The checks which had held down the population through the Middle Ages had been lifted. For the past century, Europe had been free from the ravages of plague and typhoid, which between 1708 and 1711 had killed one-sixth of the population of Köningsberg in East Prussia and left 60,000 farms deserted. The "Black Death" claimed nearly 20 million European lives in the fourteenth century and 10 million in the seventeenth century. The devastating wars of the seventeenth century, which claimed millions of lives, had also quieted. According to the United Nations estimate, the population of Europe more than doubled between 1800 and 1900, despite common practices of infanticide and abortion. The number of Europeans was rapidly exceeding the capacity of cultivated land to produce enough food. Britain had to import large quantities of grain, but fortuitously, this was made possible by the new grainfields of the United States and larger ships; the European lowlands fared little better. The Eastern European principalities were more fortunate. These less-populous lands still had available good, fertile agricultural lands once the dense beech forests were cleared away. Once again a majestic resource was destroyed to make room for expanding civilization.

Much of the labor force for the new factories came from the farms. Until about 1730, farming practices in England had changed little from those of the Middle Ages. During this period, the great landholders became increasingly aware that farming could be made more profitable if new practices were introduced—practices that included new methods of cultivation, improved care and breeding of farm animals, more effective farm implements, and testing of new crops. Experiments with all sorts of crops, machines, fertilizers, and new breeds of animals were widely pursued. Added acreages of once communal land were enclosed to make the experiments more feasible; many tenant farmers were thus dispossessed and driven to seek work in the cities.

With the more efficient farming methods, and greater numbers of people competing for fewer jobs on the farm, life on medieval farms grew increasingly harsh, especially in Great Britain where the age-old custom of serfdom was first to be abolished and to disappear. Peasants were released from bondage to the land. They were in a sense dispossessed with no place to go and no landholder responsible for their welfare. They had sacrificed security for freedom.

Freed to leave the farm, and often forced to since they were unable to make a living on it, peasants sought work in the city. This migration to the city was ultimately to become responsible for the initial congestion of urbanization. Competition for jobs was acute among the poor, and labor was cheap. This was rationalized by the archaic capitalistic view that labor was a commodity subject to the fluctuations of supply and demand, and its exploitation would lead to the greatest good for the greatest number. In truth, it led to great profits for a few and great misery for countless others.

Misery was not confined to the city, but prevailed wherever the number of people exceeded their resources, or resource exploitation was short-sighted, or ill-conceived. The population explosion was devastating in the city, but disastrous in the country. Although the poorest laborer in England lived on oat gruel, bread, and potatoes, the farmer lived almost exclusively on potatoes. Such conditions were well illustrated in Ireland where the population had grown from 1¹/₂ million in 1800 to over 8 million in 1845. The population explosion had been made possible by advances in agricultural technology. Potatoes had been introduced during the Napoleonic wars, replacing oats as the basic staple on which the burgeoning population depended. Cereal yields were too low to keep pace with the need, and potatoes roughly quadrupled the number of calories that could be produced on an acre of land. Potatoes at first provided the needed calories, but in the long run allowed the population to increase disastrously, and most significantly made the peasant dependent on a monoculture agriculture. The desirability of monoculture was temporarily reinforced by the adequate food it provided, but when a single deleterious force, the potato blight disease, was imposed and destroyed the crop, the consequences were ruinous. The potatoes were all the farmer had to eat. Millions starved and millions more emigrated to America. No wonder farmers were eager to migrate to the city—and migrate they did. By 1851 there were more people living in the cities of Great Britain than in the country; by 1901, three times as many lived there.

The cities were not built to accommodate such masses, and housing failed to keep pace with the migration. Living conditions were abominable. Families crowded together in attics, cellars, or the corner of a room shared by many others. Open trenches running down the middle of dirt or cobblestone streets served as sewers. Water was a luxury and often brown with fecal particles. Parks were nonexistent in the working-class areas and scarce elsewhere. Epidemics of cholera and typhus periodically ravaged the cities. Tuberculosis and diptheria were common, and continued to be until medical technology caught up with crowding and brought these and other diseases under control, ultimately allowing the population to swell unabated.

Factory owners hired and fired according to their needs and whims, and paid a bargain price for labor with no regard for the welfare of the employees. Man, woman, and child worked endlessly to sustain their paltry existences. Small children typically worked from 6 A.M. to dark. With life on the farm still more grim, competition for employment was fierce, and the employer had complete control. These social conditions, brought about by technology, were to have far-reaching consequences demonstrating the interaction of people with their environment and social philosophy.

A tremendous rift arose between the laborers and capitalist owners, and laborers could do little or nothing to improve their lot. The feudal society of the Middle Ages, consisting of aristocracy and peasantry, was rapidly giving way to a new social order—an order of capitalist and laborer. Such were the conditions in England, which inspired Karl Marx to cry out for the need of equality in the theoretically classless society of communism.

There were few individuals as enlightened as Adam Smith. In his "Wealth of Nations" he asserted that if each man were free to improve his own economic position, and conversely, if economic systems were free to utilize the best skills of each man, then everyone from laborer to manufacturer would benefit. He recognized that wages were a continuing source of irritation between workers and industrialists, but he advocated high wages as an incentive to production and a benefit to society.

Gradually there emerged an agency of reform, the trade union. Although entirely forbidden by law before 1824, and many of its activities deemed illegal for decades to come, unions operated surreptitiously in England, growing in size and power, until the inequality between capitalist and labor diminished.

Whether coerced through the pressures of labor unions, compelled by governmental decree, as in Bismarck's Germany, or inspired by political philosophy, as in the United States and Great Britain, working and social conditions gradually improved, together with wages for the laborer. The worker had more money to spend and thus became a major consumer. The wealth of nations became more widely dispersed.

ENVIRONMENTAL EFFECTS

Benefits for the individual were obvious, but what of the total human welfare. The higher wages generated increased purchasing power even in the nineteenth century. More consumers were able to make demands upon the environment and to reap the bounty of its resources. Affluent people shared and consumed resources in ever-greater quantities, and depleted them with accelerating haste. Resources were consumed in proportion to the ability to procure them from the capital-deficient nations and people.

Great Britain, France, and Germany led in providing the needed capital to develop or exploit the resources of the colonies. The immediate gains realized by the colonies encouraged their development, and few nonindustrial countries were in a position to object.

Goods could only be economically produced proportionate to their sale. Increase of production, or "progress," was possible only with expanded markets. For instance, the steam engine gave rise to the locomotive and railroads, which required tremendous volumes of steel for rails, thus greatly expanding the markets for this product. Improved quality of steel made possible its wide use in building and shipping. Widespread, practical use of electricity demanded more copper and improved technology to extract it from increasingly lower-quality ores. More power demands required more generation and use of coal, oil, and gas. Raw materials were being drawn from as far away as China, India, and Japan, as well as the ports of Africa and the Americas.

Outlets for the manufactured products were first met by this tremendous growth of new uses. Outlets subsequently were created by the added consumers of a burgeoning population, their improved purchasing power, and their accelerated quest for an improved material quality of life. Had quality of life been equated with asthetic values, the continuous growth that placed such a burden on natural resources might never have arisen. The need for a market also made growth and prosperity largely dependent on an ever-increasing population.

To maintain a level of industrial activity sufficient to employ the increasing population, industry had to expand, new markets had to be found, and resources consumed in ever-increasing quantities. It must not be implied that the objectives of expansion were to provide employment or markets per se. The stimulus was simply economic, and more basically the quest for a more comfortable life. This and the profit motive have always been behind the quest for new markets and the development of resources. These factors and more blended to achieve a flourishing economy. Everyone appeared to be better off, but in seeking improvements, there was scarcely any room to consider the consequences of technology.

AGRICULTURAL GROWTH

Throughout the eighteenth and nineteenth centuries, increasing industrial growth and population pressures brought new demands for more food and production. Europe's numbers rose from 120 million in 1750 to over 180 million by 1800. Within the next century, 200 million more had been added. Improved medical knowledge almost eliminated many formerly devastating diseases. Smallpox, typhus, typhoid, and diptheria no longer sustained their death toll.

By 1800, much of Europe was in a precarious position but did not know it. The population had simply outgrown the food supply. Many European countries were no longer self-sufficient for food. An earlier food crisis had appeared imminent, but had been delayed when such new high-producing crops as potatoes and sugar beets were introduced and improved farming practices utilized. The crisis was delayed further by mass migrations largely to America and Australia. The discovery and development of America were perhaps more timely than anyone envisioned in averting disaster in Europe.

With the discovery of America, new land became available for the taking. And taken it was! Here lay the richest unspoiled reservoir of resources on earth. Endless forests, virgin meadows, and vast reserves of mineral ores provided the potential for enormous wealth and prosperity. But for how long? The immediate success of the new nation depended on the ability of the pioneers to exploit the land as quickly, efficiently, and completely as possible.

England was anxious to colonize the new land to heighten its own prestige and establish its claim before other European countries could strengthen their position. Europe sought new lands to replenish already diminishing supplies of resources and to accommodate its expanding population. More realistically, the ambitious and dominant Europeans sought to increase their wealth and position. Before the American Revolution the King of England played his role by dispensing land in America. Land was also dispensed by trading companies established to become governing bodies for land settlement. The Virginia Company, chartered by the Crown, was composed of London entrepreneurs who received large land grants from the King. This was subsequently divided and sold. The sale price was reasonable, and farmers and laborers alike, seeking escape from feudal monarchies, clamored for a fresh start, again sacrificing their modicum of security for greater freedom. But their freedom was bought at the expense and freedom of the existing culture. The native American Indian was displaced or killed to make room for the invading settlers.

Population growth was rapid. Already by 1640 there were 28,000 settlers in America. This swelled to 85,000 by 1660 and to over 2 million

100 years later. Despite the initial small farm holdings, large estates evolved in a remarkably short time. Labor was scarce and competition for it fierce. The great land holders spent huge sums recruiting tenant farmers from Europe and paying their passage. Settlers of every trade filled every ship to escape the degradation and despair of England.

Governments fostered emigration and colonization for other reasons. Overpopulation in England was evident from the increase in vagrancy and unemployment, and these threatened the country's stability. If the undesirable poor were shipped to the Colonies, they could produce the raw materials needed at home. They would also be customers for England's surplus of manufactured goods. The industrial revolution was beginning to have a profound influence in creating the attitude that population increases were desirable, and growth was good. New markets meant more profits.

Credit became available through newly evolving banking methods that favored large, prosperous landowners who could readily purchase new land as their soil became exhausted. Credit, together with slavery, also helped maintain the large labor supply and supported the plantation owners' luxurious standard of living.

Subsidies provided by the mercantile capitalists paid off handsomely in providing products that formerly had to be bought from foreign nations. Timber from New England and tobacco from Virginia quickly assured the financial success of the Colonies.

Timber was felled and lush forests and fertile valleys put to the plow. Abundance of land provided ample food for the colonists and an abundance for markets abroad. Specialized crops were grown for export throughout the South with no regard for the future of the boundless lands.

Tobacco introduced to Europe by Sir Walter Raleigh in 1612 rapidly took the peoples' fancy and created a demand undaunted even by laws King James passed to prohibit its use. Thousands of acres of dense Virginia woodland were cleared to plant the neat, verdant rows of tobacco. The fertile soils and seemingly endless availability of land permitted the most improvident cultural practices. Year after year the same crops were grown on the same land until it ran out. Growers then moved onto fresh land and soon laid it to waste. Such methods were widespread in the north and south alike. They had been practiced since the earliest times, but always there had been fresh lands.

Perhaps a few farmers understood the consequences of what we now recognize as land abuse, but even had they enjoyed perfect knowledge of soil management, social and economic limitations would have prevented them from following the management practices they knew they must. Abundance of resources and strong individualism would encourage only methods yielding the greatest immediate profit.

Farming practices that had been used successfully in England proved ruinous in America. Farmers in Europe had little trouble with soil erosion. Rains came more as mists than downpours, and crops consisted mostly of grasses and grains. The gentle, sod-covered slopes of Europe presented problems more of rotation, seed selection, and cultivation methods. The settlers were unfamiliar with the interaction between the new crop and the environment.

From the earliest days of agriculture, we have managed our land more for immediate expedience than long-term returns; but the consequences of adverse agricultural practices were vastly intensified with mechanization.

Farming techniques were improved continuously; yields increased still more with the introduction of new, more productive crops in the fifteenth and sixteenth centuries, but they were not yet needed. Black death, with war to spread it, so set the population back that when the disastrous plague of the Middle Ages waned, much of Europe with its abandoned farms had to be colonized anew. By 1700, though, Europe's resurgent population growth exerted an unyielding pressure on the land.

By 1850 the stage had been set. Although wooden plows penetrated the earth no more than a few inches and were barely adequate to scratch out the weeds and prepare a shallow seedbed, the new iron plows were capable of gouging deep into the soil. Power was available, crops with greater productivity were being grown, and cultural practices such as manuring and rotation were better understood. Cultivation of such forage crops as alfalfa made possible greater milk and livestock production, in turn providing sustenance for a still greater population. Scientific societies for agriculture and farmer education were being formed. Improvements in the printing press contributed substantially in spreading the newfound knowledge of better agricultural methods. Production soared. The numbers of people soared even faster, providing an ever-greater incentive for increasing yields and bringing new land into cultivation. Europe could no longer provide for its own, but the technology of transportation and agriculture made it possible to exploit new lands thousands of miles away.

Pressure on governments exerted by the hungry populaces toward the middle of the nineteenth century, especially in England, slowly forced a loosening of tariffs, opening the door for importing grains from abroad. Demands for food arose at a time when vast new lands were opening in America following the Civil War. The lands alone would not have been enough, but steam power had been made portable about the same time, and steam engines were soon adapted to the farm. Deep, rich grassland soils of the plains were plowed, tilled, and planted with the help of machines. John Deere's steel plow patented in 1837 especially made possible the conquest of the prairie soils. At harvest, newly developed mowing and threshing machines and efficient combines took over. Although horses continued to outnumber tractors for many years, improved designs in plows made it possible to plow an acre a day with a team and driver. A widening network of railroads and great new steel-hulled steamships made it possible to ship the crops abroad in vast quantities.

Horses and mules continued as the major working force tilling the great plains into the 1920s, when an incident occurred that illustrated the interplay of events that can produce drastic change. A devastating epidemic of equine encephalitis struck, killing tens of thousands of horses. Rather than risk losing fresh horses to this plague, farmers switched to the mechanical tractors that John Deere, Henry Ford, and others had brought out at a price they could afford.

Arid lands of the Western Great Plains were unsuited to cereal grains, but provided a superb range for extensive herds of cattle, once the native herds of foraging buffalo were destroyed. The railroad provided the essential means for transporting cattle to the marketplace. Railheads increased in number, and the numbers of range cattle and sheep increased rapidly. Herds were moved from one range to another, beyond the plains and over the Great Basin and Southwest, eating away the protective cover of grasses as they went. By 1900 there were no more places to go. The land could support but a fraction of its former potential. All that remained was the picked-over, the by-passed, or the land that was too dry, too steep, or so infertile that it could not be expected to yield a crop. The remaining arid grasslands were transformed to parched deserts in but 3 decades.

The last of the world's great available agricultural resources disappeared with the wasting of the West. No new agricultural lands remained that could be suitably developed using existing methods. For all practical purposes, land had run out by the turn of the century. What now? The world's population continued to accelerate at a prodigious rate, seeped in ignorance and motivated by an innate egocentric drive for growth and status.

CONCLUSIONS

The gradual emergence of free thought late in the Middle Ages initiated an era of discovery that gave birth to an age of technology and industry. The steam engine, especially, was influential in changing society from farming to one of industry. Applied to agriculture, technology brought new efficiencies, greatly increasing production, and made possible, or even necessary, the vast migration of populations to the city. With machines to replace much of human effort, growth and material wealth in Western civilization improved rapidly during the nineteenth century—but not without costs to once-productive lands and the natural ecosystems. The rise of technology may have answered many of our needs, but it may also have created more problems than it resolved.

SELECTED READINGS

Burchell, S. C. *Great Ages of Man. Age of Progress.* (New York: Time, 1966).

Cottam, W. P. *Our Renewable Wild Lands—A Challenge.* (Salt Lake City: University of Utah Press, 1961).

Fussell, G. E. *Farming Techniques from Prehistoric to Modern Times.* (London: Pergamon, 1965).

Gay, Peter. *Great Ages of Man. Age of Enlightenment.* (New York: Time, Inc., 1966).

Lowdermilk, W. C. 1950. Conquest of the land through 7000 years. United States Department of Agriculture and Soil Conservation Services, SCS MP-32.

Tiger, Lionel, and Robin Fox. *The Imperial Animal.* (New York: Holt, 1971).

Toynbee, Arnold. 1884. Lectures on the Industrial Revolution in England. (Boston: Beacon Press, 1884, reprinted 1956).

Weisberger, Bernard A. *The Life History of the United States. The Age of Steel and Steam.* (New York: Time, Inc., 1964).

Chapter 8

Carrying Capacity of the Land

The history of man is the record of a hungry creature in search of food.

H. Van Loon

MALTHUS'S DISMAL THEOREM

There were too many people in 1798. There were too many because already large numbers were miserable and hungry in the "civilized" world. Although ignorant of the population explosion echoing over Europe, Thomas Robert Malthus recognized and espoused the threat of overpopulation. Among his observations were the postulates that (1) "food is necessary to the existence of man," and (2) "the passion between the sexes is necessary and will remain nearly at its present state."

Malthus postulated further that (3) "the power of population to grow is infinitely greater than the power of the earth to produce subsistence for man." He ,proposed that population increased in a geometric ratio but subsistence increased only in an arithmetic ratio (Figure 8-1). Since food was necessary to life, the two unequal powers must be kept equal.

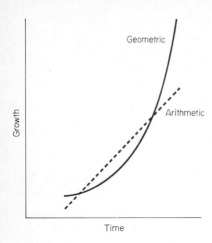

Figure 8-1 Theoretical geometric growth of populations compared with the presumed arithmetic growth of agricultural production.

Production must be increased at more than an arithmetic ratio or population must be restrained at less than a geometric ratio. Gradually, as the gap between production and population widens, more people must share less food; ultimately a large segment of the population will go hungry.

This gave rise to what is often called the dismal theorem, which was proposed by Malthus in 1803 in an enlarged edition of his book "An Essay on the Principle of Populations as It Affects the Future Improvement of Mankind." His basic propositions were:

1 Population is necessarily limited by the means of subsistence.

2 Population invariably increases where the means of subsistence increases, unless prevented by some very powerful and obvious checks.

3 These checks, and the checks which repress the power of population and keep its effects on a level with the means of subsistence, are all resoluble into moral restraints, vice, and misery (including disease and starvation).

While food certainly places the ultimate limit on the population of animals, including humans, the "dismal theorem" allowed for technological and other improvements in agriculture that would presumably increase production so that more people might be sufficiently fed for some indefinite period in the future.

Kenneth Boulding of the University of Colorado carried the postulates one step further in his "utterly dismal theorem" proposed in 1958: "If the only check on the growth of population is starvation and misery, then any technological improvement will have the ultimate effect of increasing the sum of human misery, as it permits a larger population to live in precisely the same state of misery and starvation as before the change."

This theorem must be kept in mind throughout the following discussions. Barring some drastic future improvements and innovations in providing more food, a limit must ultimately be reached when there is not enough food for all. Possibly this limit has already been reached. In this case, all postulates on the numbers of additional people which can be fed are hypothetical; and furthermore, other factors may limit our numbers before the food supply is exhausted.

The extent to which production can be improved only determines how large a population can ultimately be supported. The number is finite. Improvements in agricultural technology only determine the period of time we have in which to impose adequate restraints on population. At the same time more consideration must be given to what constitutes an optimum population, if such could ever be attained. Improving production must be viewed only as a means of buying time to stabilize populations at an equitable number. The day of reckoning can never be averted, only delayed. Meanwhile, the delay hastens environmental degradation. Increased production is bought at the price of disrupting environmental systems evolved over the millennia.

FOOD NEEDS

Just how much food does it take to support a person? Naturally, this is dependent upon size and physical activity, but it also depends on how we define *food*. The most immediately apparent food requirement is calories consumed. Each day we must consume sufficient food to provide us with the potential energy we will need for breathing, respiring, assimilating, and simply moving around. The energy comes largely from carbohydrates, mostly in the form of sugar or starch. The calorie is the unit of energy used in describing one's energy requirement. Sleeping contently during the day might consume as little as 1500 calories. Working or playing actively though, one would require more than twice this. On the average, 2000 to 2500 calories are considered essential to sustain a person each day.

Actually, calories are not too hard to obtain. They are often abundant in inexpensive foods and obtainable in the poorest countries. The hungry masses of India each receive close to 2000 calories per day. So do those in the Philippines and Africa. Despite this, in 1960, nearly 2 billion persons lived in countries where the calorie intake was less than the recommended minimum.

Calories are not enough; proteins are also essential. Proteins are made up of various combinations of some 22 amino acids required for life. All can be synthesized by plants, but we are unable to manufacture some of them, the *essential amino acids,* and must eat foods that contain them. (See Appendix, "Essential Amino Acids.") Some plants contain a fair amount of these, but nowhere near the quantity found in animal products. Most of our protein supply comes from plants, especially cereals, which provide some 70 percent, but their content of essential amino acids is inadequate for a healthy diet. A richer supply is found in soybeans, peanuts, peas, and beans, but these are rather low-yielding, and we still rely largely on such animal products as milk, meat, fish, and eggs for the essential amino acids.

Such foods are virtually unknown to children in the forests of Africa or to the Indians of South America. They are scarce in India, Pakistan, Indonesia, and most of the rest of the world. The children show this protein deficiency in the swollen bellies of their emaciated bodies, their spindly, swollen limbs, and pigmented or serpentlike skin. Kwashiorkor, meaning in West African "the disease the infant gets when another baby is born," or the "red baby" disease, affects some 2 to 10 percent of the children in developing countries. Nearly half the population shows milder degrees of malnutrition. Hunger may be satisfied by the cheap calories in starch, flour, or sugar, but normal development is impossible without the essential amino acids found in protein of the right kind.

The availability of protein, not carbohydrate, provides the best gauge of nutrition. It also shows the tragic nutritional disparity between the have and have-not nations of the world. The daily diet in Western Europe and the United States contains close to 100 grams of protein. A diet in the Congo basin or Far East may well have less than 50. Nutritionists say we require 57 grams of protein containing the appropriate amino acids each day.

For those with the price of a meal, neither calories nor protein need present much of a problem. Some economists have argued that food shortages are not a dilemma of too little food but of too little money to purchase it. There is certainly some truth in the view that poverty is the underlying cause of malnutrition. One can purchase a meal or groceries in even the poorest country if one has the price. Unfortunately, many don't have the price. They are unemployed or subsisting on marginal farm land. Perhaps the food shortages are largely economic and social problems—problems resolvable more to greater income than greater production. Yet if everyone could afford to eat their fill, how far might the world's food resource go?

If more food were produced, creating a surplus, the price should theoretically decrease so that more people could afford to be adequately nourished. Over half the world's population cannot. Any discussions on the amount of food which can be produced should bear in mind that someone must pay for it—not only in money, but in land, labor, fertilizer, fuel, and machines; and in energy consumed in production. Consequently, a discussion of the amount of arable land necessary to support a given population becomes rather hypothetical, particularly if we assume that infertile, exhausted lands can produce up to the capacity of some of the world's most fertile acreage.

With this in mind, let's look at the amount of food that can be produced on the existing land, and then look at the land available and other ways in which potential world food resources could be expanded.

IMPROVING PRODUCTIVITY

Agricultural production has many limitations, not the least of which is the potential productivity of the existing arable land. What is the potential for increasing production on presently cultivated lands? Production has constantly increased in the past, but there is no justification to believe it can continue to do so indefinitely. There have been genetic improvements, improved pest control methods, better water use, and improved cultural practices. But all have their limits, despite the optimism afforded by the "green revolution."

The Green Revolution

The green revolution is no revolution. It does not provide a solution to the world food problem but only a means of buying time. The term simply denotes an especially astounding increase in yields on a given acreage through agricultural technology. It is the sum total of all agricultural advances, but particularly the breeding of especially productive crops, most notably rice and wheat. Farmers have been impartially selecting improved varieties of crops for thousands of years, but recently the advances have been truly remarkable.

The miracle rice varieties IR8 and C4-63 represent the most dramatic advances in productivity. They are the result of a multipronged research effort by the International Rice Research Institute and the University of the Philippines College of Agriculture. Both varieties have the capacity to produce 4000 to 8000 pounds of rice per acre compared with the national average of 1200 pounds per acre. Yields of wheat in Mexico rose from 495 to 680 pounds per acre. The yield increase was brought about by breeding and selecting primarily for a more favorable response to nitrogen fertilizer. The plants are short and thick, and able to support the heavy grain crop. They have their drawbacks though in their high nitrogen and water requirements, and increased disease susceptibility. But better yields and resistance characteristics are continuing to be bred into still newer varieties. The IR-26 variety, for instance, released in 1973, is a least moderately resistant to every Asian disease of rice.

A main advantage of the new grains is that they mature rapidly and are relatively insensitive to day length so that two or three crops per year can be grown. The acreage of high-yielding varieties increased from 200 in the 1964–1965 crop year to about 39 million acres of wheat by 1973. About 35 percent of Asia's wheatland is covered, and 20 percent of the rice acreage—about all that can be, largely due to limitations of nitrogen and water.

Plant breeding for productive characters is clearly the basic means of increasing yields. The energy expended in incorporating the new genetic information to the plant is minimal compared to the gain in desirable traits achieved. It should cost little to utilize the solar energy more thoroughly and efficiently.

Physiological Improvements

There are physiological limits to the possible productivity of a crop in different soils and climatic environments. There is a limit to how efficiently a plant can absorb light energy and store it in the chemical warehouse of carbohydrates. To put it another way, there is a limit to the photosynthetic efficiency. Plants rarely can utilize more than 1 percent of the radiant energy they absorb; there would seem to be considerable room for improvement.

Conceivably, photosynthetic efficiency might be improved through reducing respiration by altering the morphology of the plant so as to maximize the interception of light by the canopy, or by enhancing the rate of carbon dioxide utilization. One means of improving the efficiency is through plant breeding to design plants that have a larger amount of photosynthetic surface, that is, leaves and stems exposed to light. Often the seed- or fruit-bearing structures are uppermost on the plant and shade the leaf area. If plants could be designed so the leaves had maximum exposure to light, they would be able to manufacture more carbohydrates. To take advantage of this though, plants would also have to be bred that transported a high percentage of this food to the edible parts, whether it be fruit, leaves, or roots. A good example of this is the production of dwarf grain varieties with upright upper leaves and spreading lower ones that intercept the greatest amount of light. Soybeans are already "built" this way, bearing fruits along a central stem and surrounded by leaves. Use of the growth-regulating chemical, TIBA, causes such normally rounded plants as soybean to assume a pyramidal shape; the greater exposure to sunlight results in a consequent increase in seed weight.

Together with developing plants that have a greater surface area exposed to light, more efficient plants might be developed that obtain maximum photosynthetic productivity per unit area. Many efforts to significantly influence photosynthesis for the purpose of increasing yields have failed. But this is no cause for overt pessimism. Certainly, there must be some chemical or other mechanism that would systematically stimulate the rate of carbon dioxide uptake and utilization.

Multiple Cropping

Another way in which greater yields could be harvested from a given acre of land would be to raise more than a single crop during the year. This has been done for years in areas having a long growing season. A related approach would be to breed a greater tolerance to low temperatures so that a crop could be planted earlier or harvested later in the year. Geneticists have worked toward this end for many years with no major breakthrough.

Plant Adaptations

Plant breeders have had the greatest success in improving yields of developing plants that are able to utilize greater quantities of nitrogen, possibly because this is where the emphasis has been placed. This has provided the major breakthrough in the so-called green revolution. These potentially highly productive plants can attain their potential only when provided large amounts of nitrogen fertilizer. Without it, such rice varieties as TR-8 are no more productive than the old ones. New varieties may also be developed to extend their range northward or into more arid regions once suitable only for grasses.

The improved grain varieties are also able to utilize water more effectively but are so dependent on it they cannot be grown successfully without irrigation. Hence, there is a limit to the acreage on which they can be grown. Water, or lack of it, already imposes a serious limitation on the amount of potentially arable land on which crops can be raised. The deserts of the world can sustain only sparse populations of the most highly specialized and adapted species. Much of the world's land resources, while not true deserts, still receive insufficient precipitation to grow food crops. True, some native forage crops, desert grasses, and chaparrel may grow, but not traditional food plants.

Few plants able to endure such harsh, dry environments are suitable for food. Traditional crop plants constitute but a small fraction of the plant world. Conceivably, palatable species or varieties of prevalent wild species might be developed, or existing flora rendered edible, but growth would be slow and limited. Dry lands might best be utilized by raising naturally occurring plants or adapted grazing or browsing animals and harvesting these. The vast cattle ranches of the American Southwestern deserts, and sheep ranches in the barren expanses of southwest Australia, afford examples of this. But there has been limited research to seek animals that might be better adapted and more productive than the traditional livestock under these conditions. Possibly breeds could be developed that are better adapted, or entirely new; perhaps native animals could be raised. Kangaroos, for instance, thrive in regions too harsh for even sheep or goats.

Taking another approach, much of the food consumed by livestock could go to people. Livestock feed could consist of the many plant residues that cannot be digested by humans, such as sugar cane bagasse, citrus pulp, straw, leaves, corncobs, and stems of various grain crops.

WATER LIMITATIONS

George Borgstrom, Professor of Food Science at Michigan State University, calculated the water needs of agriculture to be truly astounding—up to 500 pounds to produce a single pound of wheat, 800 pounds for a pound of potatoes, 5000 pounds for a pound of vegetables, 10,000 pounds for a pound of milk, and up to 50,000 pounds of water to produce a single pound of meat.

On a worldwide basis, water is abundant. Unfortunately, fresh water is often most abundant in areas unsuited to agriculture. Some of the world's greatest rivers flow in practically uninhabitable areas—the Amazon of Brazil, the Ob, Yenisey, and Lena of Siberia, and the MacKenzie of the Canadian Arctic.

Much of the usable water is drawn from vast underground resources left from the Ice Age. Until recently, we were limited to the shallow groundwater, but with the advanced technology of modern pumping, huge new sources have been made available. These include those of the high plains from Texas to Nebraska, the San Joaquin Valley in California, and the deserts around Lake Chad in North Africa. Ever deeper strata are tapped as the groundwater levels fall; pumping ceases only when the level drops to where the cost of pumping becomes prohibitive. Pumping in Saudi Arabia and parts of Israel is no longer economically sound—the energy required is too great. Pumping is nearly prohibitive over large irrigated areas of Texas and Arizona. The world water reserves continue to diminish as they are used faster than they can be recharged. Further losses arise from the contamination of the remaining reserves by wastes.

Supplying water for arid lands from distant mountain sources has often been discussed. Water is already being transported to the deserts of California from over 800 miles distant. Around mountains, over ridges, and across plains, water is pumped, but only at the expense of large quantities of electric power. Plans have long been discussed to divert water from the Columbia River to the south, but costs are tremendous and protests remain strong. Even more grandiose are the plans of the North Atlantic Water and Power Alliance (NAWAPA) to divert huge amounts of water from northern Canada and Alaska to the western deserts and Mexico. Again costs in energy and dollars are the greatest deterrent, although the prospective environmental disruption provides a second limitation.

Similar plans have been proposed to divert water from Siberia to more temperate regions. Such possibilities will become increasingly feasible with the increasing demand for food; but the possible far-reaching consequences of reversing entire river systems must be considered. According to Dr. Tinco E. A. Van Hylckama of Texas Tech University, reversing the rivers now flowing into the Arctic seas could "alter oceanic currents, change climates drastically, affect the flora and fauna of oceans, and even the food chain." Centuries would be required to restore environmental equilibrium or homeostasis.

Water for irrigating might also be taken from the sea. Towing icebergs from Greenland or the Antarctic sounds preposterous but would actually be cheaper than the most efficient desalinization plants. Nevertheless, desalinization remains more feasible although it is far too costly, both in energy and dollars, to use the water for agriculture. If the land were needed and food sufficiently in demand, however, desalinization could provide additional productive acreage despite any costs in terms of power required.

Even if the technical problems of cheap desalinization were conquered, there would remain the problem of disposing of the huge mountains of salt that would rise around the desalinization plants. Borgstrom points out that 35 tons of salt would be produced as a by-product to get 1 ton of water. Very likely, all the salt could not be contained, and much would be blown into the atmosphere, adding to the particulate air pollution.

FARMING PRACTICES AND LAND USE

Farming practices have by far the greatest impact in limiting production or facilitating maximum yields. Traditional methods of farming drastically limit production not only in the nonindustrial regions of the world, but in many industrial lands. Only one crop is harvested every year over large parts of Africa and Latin America even on irrigated land. Farming over much of Europe still depends on heavy utilization of hand labor with little mechanization. Many agrarian countries simply lack the capital resources to purchase the tools and tractors of modern technology. Production then can only keep up with expanding populations by increasing the acreage farmed. Most often new farming land comes from pasture and forest land, with the permanent loss of these resources. The marginal quality of such lands for farming is shown by the 21 percent rise in cultivated land in developing areas between 1959 and 1966 that provided only a 10 percent increase in yields.

If yields are to be improved, traditional farming methods must be modernized. This can only be done if farmers are convinced it will be profitable and they can afford the improvements. Where farmers are reluctant to adopt new techniques, government price supports are sometimes necessary to provide the incentive to motivate them to try new varieties and methods. This has been the successful approach introducing the new cereal varieties which have been widely planted in much of Asia.

A major disruptive side effect of the new varieties is that the costs of production are greater so that only the larger farmers can make best use of them. The higher production sometimes drives down the price of the crop so that small farmers cannot make enough profit from their meager crop to earn a living.

Intelligent use of pesticides has further increased production by reducing the toll taken by the fungi, bacteria, insects, weeds, and other pests. The use of pesticides remains in its infancy even in many of the industrial countries of the world; their use is virtually absent in less-developed areas. Yet it is in many of these tropical countries that losses to insects are most staggering. Pests continue competing with people for sustenance, often limiting production as much as 50 percent. Introduction of more effective control methods could easily increase world food production 10 to 20 percent.

Cropping intensity could be improved along with yields. More than half of the arable land in much of North Africa and the Near East lies fallow each year. Leguminous fodder crops could survive over much of the area, providing food for the undernourished livestock and improving the soil quality. Still better yields could be obtained if better adapted varieties were used together with the proper pesticides and fertilizers, improved irrigation, and intensive crop rotations.

Lack of one mineral nutrient or another, mostly nitrogen, has limited production since we scratched our first seed hole. Nitrogen metabolism has been understood scarcely more than a century, and nitrogen deficiencies have yet to be adequately corrected over much of the world's agricultural land. A tenfold increase in world fertilizer utilization is envisioned between 1962 and 1985, mostly in the irrigated areas of Asia, the Near East, and northwest Africa. Yields would rise concomitantly. But where would the fertilizer come from? The cost of producing fertilizer far exceeds the economic capacity of developing nations to produce or use it. This was ironical for some years when there was a surplus of fertilizers in developed countries that the poor nations could not afford—but the surplus was short-lived.

WORLD PRODUCTION POTENTIAL

Land Use

Modern agricultural technology enables the Dutch to feed 385 people well on a single square kilometer of farmland, although much food is imported or drawn from the world's oceans and subsidized with proteins from the soybean fields of North America. Yet in Africa and North America, a square kilometer supports only 11 people. Between these extremes, Asia supports 68 persons per square kilometer, Western Europe 147, and Japan and Southeast Asia 200 to 270. The numbers of persons that might hypothetically be sustained on a given acreage is misleading though, since much of the land in many countries is not arable. It would be more valid to indicate the amount of available cultivable land available per person (Table 8-1). This indicates better the increased numbers of persons the country might feed. (See Appendix, "The Productive Capacity of a Nation.")

Most of the world's lands are simply not suited for cultivation. Land often is far too rough or steep, or the soils too poor. More often because of climate, it is suited only to grazing or forestry and is sensitive and responsive to the destructive forces of erosion.

In 1798, when land in America was plentiful, Thomas Jefferson reportedly wrote, "we can buy an acre of new land cheaper than we can manure an old one." Now, there is no new land immediately suitable to cultivation. Productivity can be increased mostly from more intensive use of lands, or changing their use where possible. With sufficient ingenuity, more acreage might be claimed from deserts and swamps, but the best grazing lands have already been taken.

Table 8-1   Available Cultivable Area Per Person; in Acres

Australia and New Zealand	2.9
U.S.A.	2.68
U.S.S.R.	2.59
Africa	1.3
South America	1.0
India	0.82
China	0.50
Germany	0.48
United Kingdom	0.42
Japan	0.17

Source: Adapted from International Botanical Congress Symposium on World Food Supply, Seattle, Wash., 1969.

Forest lands are often best left in forest. For instance, the lush teak jungles of Java and giant firs of the Pacific Northwest are most highly valued for their timber. Such rugged, mountainous lands are unsuited for cultivation. Traditional crop plants can be grown on less than one-fourth of the world's 32 billion acres. Another fourth of the lands is best suited for grazing, largely because of limited water or a climate unsuited for crops. The remaining half includes wastelands, tundra, desert, and mountains. Of the 8 billion acres that might be considered potentially arable, less than half is now cultivated. About half the range land is also in use. These 3.5 billion acres provide the chief source of food for the present 3.7 billion people on earth—roughly an acre of cultivated land and an acre of rangeland per person. Some of these are not too productive. The best land is gone. The available land is unevenly distributed over the world, with over 80 percent cultivated in Europe and Asia and as little as 2 percent in Australia. Production on a large percentage is limited by the harshness of desert or tropical environments. A third of the potentially arable land lies in the humid tropics (Figure 8-2).

Tropical Lands

The tropical rain forests of the Amazon, an empire larger than all Europe, Southeast Asia, Australia, and Africa, only superficially appear to provide lands that are neither too profitable for other purposes, nor too rugged to farm.

The quality of the soil in such tropic rain forests is too poor to make

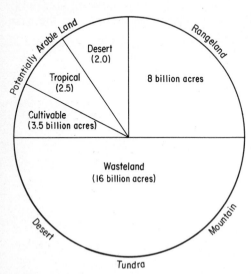

Figure 8-2 Distribution of the world's land mass according to its potential for raising crops.

cultivation at all probable, at least with traditional modern agricultural technology. There are fertile soils in the tropics, such as the rice bowl of the Mekong delta, and the deep black soils of Bali and Java; but in the former, nutrients are renewed annually by flooding, while in Java, the soils have been deposited from rich volcanic ash. The productive tropical lands here and in Madagascar and the Rift Valley of Africa support about 80 million people on 25 million arable acres, but even here the saturation point has been reached. Overpopulation is critical, and foods must be imported.

Heavy rains continually leach out the minerals from tropical soils, and all the nutrients not bound in the existing plants are soon lost to the sea in the endless flow of waters. The prevailing dampness and high temperature combine to favor rich populations of bacteria, insects, and other organisms that quickly break down any humus and allow oxygen to permeate soils not covered by the natural luxurious vegetation, soon oxidizing its iron and aluminum to form an impervious crust as much as 70 feet thick. Vast areas have even been converted to ores concentrated enough to mine for aluminum or iron. Once tilled, the red lateritic soils, high in iron and aluminum often harden nearly to the texture of brick and are rendered useless for farming.

The tropics were the first lands settled by *H. sapiens* and have long suffered the pressures of overpopulation. Africa, first settled millennia ago, has suffered the greatest land abuse. Famine along the Ganges in ancient India long ago forced emigration to the infertile areas of the south, where even the difficult lateritic soils must be tilled. The Mayan civilization of Yucatan may well have declined from abuse of lateritic soils in that region. The early Indian civilizations were no more aware or conscious of land utilization than the invading Europeans of the sixteenth century.

Improper management of these soils has left a permanent record of disaster. Drought and the pressure of overpopulation, which forced too-intensive cultivation, destroyed the Mayan civilization, and the baked lands remain untilled. In Cambodia, ancient temples such as Angkor Wat built of sandstone laterite still persist. Physical artifacts of the Khmer civilization which ruled the area from the ninth to sixteenth centuries remain. The laterite clays endured for centuries in magnificent edifices, but were disastrous to an expanding agriculture.

The Indians native to the Amazon till such tropic lands successfully, but on a small scale. Only small areas are cleared, with most of a given area left under natural cover. Trees from the clearings are burned and the ashes left to provide the nutrients. Crops are sown by hand after the first rains. Crops are never grown in one place for more than 3 to 5 years; land is then allowed to return to native vegetation and left undisturbed for 15 to 20 years. Using such simple methods over a wider area, or improving on them, might increase productivity substantially without destroying the land, but only so long as the natural balance between the land, mineral cycling, and the plants is not disrupted.

Economic and Social Limitations

Theoretically, world agricultural production could be vastly increased, but the economic, social, and educational obstacles are formidable. A major difference in agriculture in industrial and nonindustrial countries is economical. Specifically, the difference relates to the amount of capital invested in farming and farming technology. The availability of capital for investing in agriculture has been a major stimulus to success. Farms in the developing areas have been too small to obtain investment capital. Farming is mostly subsistence with little left for marketing. Rent, interest, and taxes devour profits from any meager surplus. Most important, interest rates in these countries are often exhorbitant. One estimate puts the average annual interest rate in these countries at 36 percent, but sometimes it reaches as much as 400 percent, which permanently precludes adequate investment.

The profit-taking landlords are less likely to invest in farm improvements and more apt to use their money in trading or more lending, or to acquire more land. The small farmer has nothing to invest. In Africa, cattle have prestige value and are acquired at the expense of the land. In Asia, profits are likely to be hoarded in gold or jewelry, not better seed or farm equipment. To compound the problems, many agrarian cultures place a higher premium on leisure than on profit so the farmer is unlikely to work harder than absolutely necessary. The transition to market production and mechanization to increase profits and yields is slow.

Overcoming the economic obstacles to improving productivity will require major action by the government and farmer alike. Action will come only with motivation and investment. Only government can provide the needed agricultural extension services, capital, and impetus to transform traditional agriculture—if this is the best course to steer.

In Latin America much of the land of some countries remains bound and uncultivated in large estates descended from the colonial era. In other countries land is poorly utilized because of laws or export regulations restricting production. Transportation is another factor, and is often entirely inadequate to move crops from potentially productive land to market. Often the rural farmer has neither the incentive nor the capacity to improve production. If land reform were affected and linked with modernization of agricultural techniques to raise productivity, income would be redistributed, increasing the purchasing power for the rural population. Land reform legislation has been passed in some countries, but few acts have been implemented for the simple reason that those who passed the laws would be divesting themselves of their land and power. One must also bear in mind that each Latin American country has its own unique problems. Countries with the greatest acreage of cultivable land such as Argentina do not necessarily have the population density motivating high productivity. Countries such as Colombia or Venezuela with dense populations lack the land resource. Dissention or lack of cooperation among Latin American countries, and even within countries, precludes sharing or trade agreements that might make lands or resources most available where needed.

A further dilemma is the lack of people trained in modern agriculture. Agricultural methods can be improved only through education—through technical personnel in the rural areas of the developing countries who are able to demonstrate the most effective farming methods.

Production in the communist countries is limited by the lack of incentive for farmers in the large cooperatives to obtain maximum yields. Their initiative is directed more toward their small, privately owned plots where the profits are their own. Yields on this intensively cultivated ground are high and account for a substantial percent of the agricultural production.

CONCLUSIONS

The best land resources are now occupied, and all resources are known to some degree. The National Academy of Sciences Committee on Resources and Man recognizes four extreme types of regions in regard to food and land:

1 The highly developed countries with adequate land technology to increase food production severalfold (United States and Soviet Union).

2 Developed countries unable to provide sufficient food but drawing on imports at an increasing rate (England and Japan).

3 Poorly developed countries with extensive land resources (Argentina and Philippines).

4 Countries with lands fully exploited and still unable to support themselves within their boundaries (Indonesia and Haiti).

The food situation is obviously critical in these last two groups although Group 3 countries have the potential to support themselves. Plant selection and pest control might even buy the fourth group some time. Nevertheless, how much can world food production be increased and equitably distributed before population overwhelms production and the situation becomes hopeless?

Contrary to Malthus's tenet, perhaps production may continue to increase geometrically, not arithmetically for some time longer. During the 1960s, world agricultural production increased at a rate of 2.7 percent annually, while population growth increased at 2 percent each year.

Conservative estimates by the National Academy of Science Committee on Resources and Man place the maximum theoretical potential production at about 16 times the present—or capable of sustaining nearly 60 billion people. This presumes optimal utilization of all the available land, agricultural technology, and achieving every social and economic reform needed for maximum production. Half the number might be more realistic. Less conservative estimates range far higher. Eliminating all meat-eating animals on land and sea that compete with people for the energy stored in plants, and utilizing plankton directly could provide food for still greater populations. Most significantly though, what might be the economic, environmental, and social consequences of attempting to feed so many? Ultimately, the only solution to meeting the world's food needs is to limit the global human population.

SELECTED READINGS

Aldrich, Daniel O. (ed.). 1970. Research for the world food crises. Publication no. 92. *American Association for the Advancement of Science.*

Boerma, Addeke H. 1970. A world agricultural plan. *Scientific American,* vol. 223, August, pp. 54–69.

Borgstrom, Georg. *The Hungry Planet.* (London: Collier-MacMillan, 1967).

Brown, L. R. *Seeds of Change: The Green Revolution and Development in the 1970's.* (New York: Praeger, 1970).

Brown, L. R., and G. Finsterbush. Man, food and environment. In W. W. Murdoch. *Environment.* (Stanford, Conn.: Sinauer, 1971).

Committee on Resources and Man. 1970. *Resources and Man.* (San Francisco: W. H. Freeman, 1970).

Grigg, David. *The Harsh Lands.* (London: Macmillan, 1970).

Hardin, C. E. *Overcoming World Hunger.* (Englewood Cliffs, N.J.: Prentice-Hall, 1969).

International Botanical Congress. All Congress Symposium: World Food Supply. Seattle, Wash. 1969.

McNeil, Mary. Lateritic Soils. In *Man and the Ecosphere.* (San Francisco: W. H. Freeman, 1970).

Van Hylckama, T. E. A. 1971. Water resources. In W. W. Murdoch. *Environment.* (Stanford, Conn.: Sinauer, 1971).

Chapter 9

Seafood, Synthetics, and Other Protein Sources

Yes, Professor, the sea supplies all my wants. Sometimes I cast my nets in tow, and I draw them in ready to break. Sometimes I hunt in the midst of this element, which appears to be inaccessible to man, and quarry the game which dwells in my submarine forests.

Captain Nemo, in Jules Verne,
Twenty Thousand Leagues Under the Sea

The writers of science and fiction alike have long portrayed the sea as a cornucopia of delicious sustenance—a utopia of boundless resources capable of supporting populations without end. Science has dipped well into the ocean resource, yet found such dreams unlikely to be realized.

Biological production in the world's oceans is nearly as varied as on land, ranging from the richly productive waters of the narrow bands of coastal shelves to the vast expanses of the open sea. As on land, the green plants—diatoms, dinoflagellates, and other algae—using the energy from the sun are the primary producers.

PRODUCERS AND CONSUMERS OF THE SEA

Primary Producers

By measuring rates of photosynthesis at varied depths at stations scattered over the oceans, estimates of net plant production by the microscopic algae have been made. One widely accepted figure is that of Koblenz-Mishke who estimates that 130 billion metric tons of plant material are produced in the world's seas each year (Figure 9-1). This is a tremendous resource, but it is distributed over such a huge area and at such great depths that harvesting would present a major obstacle. And what if this hurdle were vaulted? Plankton flavors are anything but enticing. The salt content is high, the silica skeletons of many present

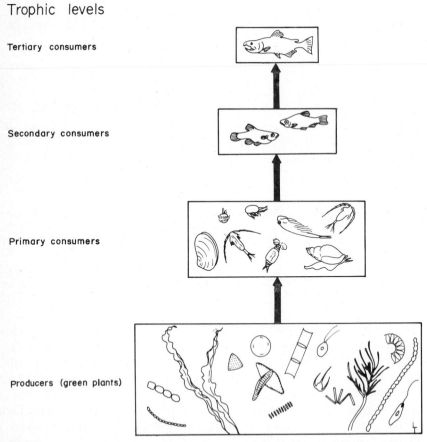

Figure 9-1 Simplified aquatic food pyramid, illustrating the direct route for conversion of plant material into animal tissue.

further problems, and the taste and smell are nauseous at best. More critically, if plankton were removed in any quantity, the seas would be depleted of the food base on which all other life in the sea depends.

What of the larger algae or seaweeds? The use of algae as food is by no means a new idea. Ancient farmers from the Orient to Ireland have utilized the nutritious thallus of the kelps, but nowhere are algae used so abundantly for food as in Japan, where 20 different species are eaten. The red algae *Prophyra* is cultivated over 155,000 acres of shallow seas using techniques over 200 years old. Yields could likely be increased substantially by utilizing modern techniques.

Primary Consumers

More food might be obtained from the oysters, clams, and mussels, the primary consumers that filter plankton, or the surface-grazing abalones and anchovies. The greatest promise in raising animals for food in the sea appears to lie in raising more shellfish and fish in coastal waters, a process that is not new. Aristotle discusses the cultivation of oysters in Greece, and Pliny describes oyster farming in Roman times; methods have changed little in 2 millennia, only the quantities have increased. Australian mariculture provides some 60 million oysters per year in its brackish estuaries. Potential yields of 4000 pounds of fish per acre in Mangrove swamps of southeast Asia hold still greater prospects. In the Bay of Fantanto in Italy, 108,000 pounds of mussels per acre per year are raised. Collectively, shellfish and other primary consumers compose a fifth of the animals being harvested from water—about 13 billion metric tons of organic matter per year.

Secondary Consumers

The secondary consumers, feeding largely on rotifers and other herbivorous animal plankton, form the next trophic level of the aquatic food chain. These sardine and herring, flounder, and shrimp provide a potential 2 billion metric tons of food per year but are vital to the larger species which form a major resource for people.

Tertiary Consumers

An estimated 300 million tons of halibut, tuna, salmon, and large cod composing the tertiary trophic level, that is, the tertiary consumers that feed on herring and other smaller fish, might also be harvested. But what segment of this can actually be reaped? Roughly half of this mass is scattered in densities too sparse to harvest or at depths impractical to reach. This would still leave 150 million tons that might be harvested each year. Continued improvements in sound-detecting gear, satellite detection, and other methods to track down the wandering schools of fish might whittle down this potential still further. The number and size of fishing vessels have increased greatly in recent decades, as have improvements in technology to detect the schools. The catch has risen proportionately. The energy in fuel expended is tremendous, however, and the costs rise disproportionately to the yields as the fish resource is depleted.

INCREASING YIELDS

Theoretically, fish yields could be increased if the amount of plankton could be increased. In seas where upwelling occurs, bringing up minerals from the bottom, including the often growth-limiting (by its absence) phosphorus, which serves to fertilize the green plankton, fish are most abundant. Artificially induced upwelling has been suggested, but it is considered impractical for the near future, and energy costs would be tremendous.

Fertilizing closed or nearly closed bodies of water seems far more reasonable, yet there are still problems. Waters are often too cold and the growing season too short for a response. In smaller lakes, oxygen becomes depleted below the thin photosynthetic layer and cold-water fish cannot survive; in shallow waters weed growth becomes excessive.

Controlled fish culture in ponds appears most promising. This is roughly comparable to grazing stock on fertilized pastures or fattening them in a feed lot. Yields are little better than on land but have the advantage that such nonarable land as swamps might be utilized.

The total fish taken from the sea in 1970 approached 65 million tons, roughly half the theoretical potential, suggesting that twice as much protein could be taken from the sea. This is misleading though, and in reality the quality of the catch has declined for several decades, as the numbers of more desirable species have been depleted. Over-fishing of Plaice in the North Sea became evident as early as 1890. Catches of salmon, Atlantoscandian herring, cod, menhaden, and tuna have diminished to where harvesting more than a sustained yield is unlikely. Nevertheless yields of 100 million tons a year have been predicted, even with no radically new technology.

Yields from the sea could be further increased by harvesting at lower trophic levels, but this would be at the expense of the larger fish species that we now eat and on which the secondary consumers depend.

POTENTIAL PROTEIN SOURCES

Algae

The next logical step is to cultivate the tiny unicellular algae forming the base of the aquatic food chain as we do crops on the land. Without tampering with the 130 billion tons of plankton on which life in the sea depends, we could farm algae in ponds, estuaries, or conceivably, the open sea.

Attention has been given in the research laboratories to cultivating *Chlorella* and *Scenedesmus*. These single-celled green algae abound in the fresh waters of the world over a wide temperature range. They duplicate themselves once every 12 hours and are tolerant of changes in environment and attack by other organisms. Equally important, the rapidly growing cells are rich in protein and vitamins. About 50 percent of the dry weight is protein containing all amino acids essential to people. They are equally rich in minerals. These algae can be cultivated in various ways, and yields have been obtained corresponding to 20 tons per acre of pond each year. This can be compared with the next most productive crop, grass, yielding but 600 pounds of protein.

There is an obvious drawback. The flavor and seaweed taste of dry algal powders are not always favorable. Algae might be palatable in small quantities, but not in quantities required to provide adequate nutrition. A major problem with this single-cell protein (SCP) is the high content of nucleic acids. When these are digested, they produce urea and uric acid, which can cause gout. Methods are being developed to remove this or breed strains with a lower nucleic acid content, but all this adds to the cost. Convincing people that SCP is food presents another problem. Still, SCP provides a valuable potential protein source, and the sea may well make its most valuable contribution in providing the needed supplies.

Fish Protein

Fish protein concentrate (FPC) is frequently promoted as the answer to the world's protein needs, and for good reason. When the fish oils are removed, the dried, powdered solids contain 80 percent protein. FPC meal can be incorporated with flour and other food staples to supplement diets otherwise deficient in the essential amino acids.

Nevertheless, the product is still expensive in that those who need it most can least afford it. Even if the taste could be completely disguised, there is no assurance that the undernourished would modify their eating habits and purchase it. Also, much of the FPC comes from the approximately 10 million tons of anchovies harvested each year off the shores of Peru. Although FPC could be made from trash fish not usually eaten, most still comes from the small species that provide the main food source for tuna, salmon, and other desirable species. The harvest of these fish is declining in part because of the depletion of their food supply.

Yeast and Bacteria

Yeasts and bacteria have the potential of providing additional sources of single-cell protein. In 1952, Felix Just, a German biologist, succeeded in growing yeasts on crude oil. Less than 20 years later, in Grange Mouth,

Scotland, British Petroleum began producing animal-grade protein by fermentation. Bacteria and yeasts are able to utilize a diverse range of organic materials for food, including petroleum. Certain selected species can transform the hydrocarbons to the protein, carbohydrates, and fats we require. The hydrocarbon used is gas oil, a fraction between kerosene and lubricating oil. The yeasts feed principally on wax in the oil, but more ubiquitous strains might be selected to better utilize the entire substrate.

Yeasts and other fungi contain up to 60 percent crude protein and can be made edible and delectable regardless of the substrate on which they grow. There are about 2000 edible kinds of fungi, although only 20 or so are commonly used as food. More might well be utilized. Yeasts could be grown on such wastes as the sulfite solutions of pump mills, or sugar cane wastes, or even the sewage of large cities. Despite the distasteful character, such short-chain cycling represents the ultimate in efficient energy utilization.

Cereals and Fortification

Lack of protein is the most critical type of malnutrition, and providing the essential protein supplement is the greatest challenge to food scientists. Protein deficiency may not kill directly, but leaves its victims vulnerable to other diseases. Since protein is in the shortest supply of all nutrients, only a small segment of the world's population can afford the luxury of animal protein; for the most part, we depend on the less-expensive grain crops for most of our protein. One approach to supplement protein in cereals is to breed varieties high in the essential amino acids. This has met with some success in corn, especially for feeding animals. Dale Harpstead of Michigan State University reported that pigs fed 130 days on corn high in the essential amino acid lysine had gained 73.2 pounds, whereas the weight gain on normal corn was only 6.6 pounds. Thus the efficiency of production was substantially increased by altering the genetic message or information content with no increase in the amount of energy expended. Studies with malnourished children in Colombia were conducted with similar results. Children fed supplements of the high-lysine corn rapidly recovered their vital functions; even children hospitalized from malnutrition soon recovered.

Food scientists are enriching the protein content of wheat and rice in the milling process, but this adds far more to the cost of the product than breeding in a high lysine-content medium. Fortifying these grains with lysine and other essential amino acids is becoming increasingly important, but remains expensive.

Protein and other nutrients from varied sources are being used and studied. They include soybean, cottonseed, peanut, sunflower seed, sesame, fish protein concentrate, and single-celled microorganisms such as algae, fungi, yeast, and bacteria. Soybean is cheapest and most widely used. Mostly, it goes to animal foods, but its use in dehydrated products for human consumption is increasing rapidly. As the demand for soybeans increases, the cost goes up, making it less plentiful for the poor.

Other Plants

Cottonseeds might become an important source of protein in areas such as India, which normally produce cotton but do not utilize the seed. First, the toxic pigment gossypol in the seed must be removed or rendered physiologically ineffective, which increases the cost, or gossypol-free varieties must be bred. Still, cottonseed protein concentrates are fed to poultry and swine, and small quantities have been used in bakery products for 30 years.

Green plants such as alfalfa are unlikely to provide much protein because of their bulk and the difficulty in transporting them. Furthermore, the green paste extracted is unattractive in both appearance and taste.

Roasted, crushed, or boiled, the peanut is eaten and enjoyed almost everywhere. As peanut butter, it makes an indispensable American sandwich. Elsewhere it is processed for oil and protein concentrate. Peanut protein does not provide the essential amino acids of soybean or cottonseed, but it can be fortified. The greatest difficulty with peanuts in most tropical regions is the threat of aflatoxin, a chemical formed from mold products developing in the peanuts after digging. This problem must be solved before peanuts will make much more of a contribution to the global protein supply.

CONCLUSIONS

Aside from the economic and social limitations, the problem of feeding the world's increasing hordes is providing each individual with sufficient high-quality protein and something over 2000 calories of food energy each day. According to the National Academy of Sciences, the sea provides about a fourth of the protein requirement for the present population. This might be improved to keep pace with the increasing population until the end of the century. The remaining protein comes mostly from grains, which could be fortified to meet the needs of the growing population, and animal protein, which is already too costly for many people.

The sea could also provide about 20 percent of the food energy requirements of the 7 billion people anticipated by the end of the century. The land could easily provide the remainder.

Despite the pessimistic tenets of Malthus, agricultural production has increased at a rate even greater than population. Within a century of the

Industrial Revolution, scientific theory was applied to agriculture, leading to the emergence of an era of accelerated agricultural productivity. Scientific farming programs have been especially successful in breeding more productive crops. Varieties were developed that not only outyielded earlier ones severalfold, and were resistant to disease and insect pests, but lent themselves better to mechanical harvest. Still, greater production was sought. Diseases, insects, and competition with weeds continued to limit yields substantially. In some years a disease might destroy half or more of a grower's crop. Even with the use of modern pesticides, plant pests continue to reduce production 20 percent. Without pesticides, yields would be cut in half and food costs would soar unpredictably. More realistically, farmers seeking greater profits were not going to sit by idly and contribute their crop to sustain competing plant pests. The mechanism for controlling the pests existed in chemicals developed to eliminate them, but the way these chemicals interacted as a new component of the environment was largely unknown, and a further technological threat to the human environment was introduced.

SELECTED READINGS

Borgstrom, Georg. *The Hungry Planet.* (London: Collier-MacMillan, 1967).

Clark, Colin. 1958. World population. *Nature,* vol. 181, pp. 1235–1236.

Food: Proteins for humans. *Chemical Engineering News,* November 24, 1969, pp. 68–81.

Fortified foods: The next revolution. *Chemical Engineering News,* August 10, 1970, pp. 36–44.

Grigg, David. *The Harsh Lands.* (London: Macmillan, 1970).

Harpstead, Dale D. 1971. High-lysine corn. *Scientific American,* vol. 225, pp. 34-47.

Holt, S. J. The food resources of the ocean. In *Man and the Ecosphere.* (San Francisco: W. H. Freeman, 1970).

Koblenz-Mishke, O. I. 1965. The magnitude of the primary production of the Pacific Ocean (in Russian). *Okeanologiya,* vol. 5, no. 2, pp. 325–337.

Pinchot, Gifford B. 1970. Marine farming. *Scientific American,* vol. 223, no. 6, pp. 14–21.

Tamiya, Hiroshi. 1959. Role of algae as food. *Proceedings of Symposium on Algology.* UNESCO South Asia Science Corp. Office.

The New Priorities. Food: Preventing hunger and malnutrition. *Chemical Engineering News,* March 8, 1971, pp. 19–22.

World Food Supply. 1969. International Botanical Congress Symposium, Seattle, Wash.

Chapter 10

Agricultural Pest Control

Man may not be a climax and the culmination of evolution but a planetary disease.

Loren Eisely

Pliny called it "the greatest pest of crops"; the Romans had a god for it—Robigus; wherever grains have provided the principal staple, stem rust has influenced production and the quality of life. Over the course of history, it has been among the most destructive of all plant diseases, completely capable of destroying a wheat crop covering hundreds of acres, and causing the people who depend on it to go hungry. Such is said to have been the case in ancient Rome, whose decline is in part attributed to a succession of severe epidemics of the disease. The only control was prayer: "Stern Robigus, spare the herbage of the cereals." And a yellow dog was sacrificed to Robigus.

PLANT PESTS AS PART OF THE ENVIRONMENT

Plant pests have always been accepted as part of agriculture. Fungi, insects, and other pests have competed with us for food energy since we first disrupted the natural ecosystems and grew but a few plant species where many had grown before. Blasting and mildew have caused dramatic crop losses since earliest times, as described in the Bible, but the only control was prayer and righteous living. "If there be famine in the land, if there be pestilence, blasting, mildew, locust, or if there be caterpillar; if the enemy (insects) besiege them in the land of their cities . . . then hear thou in heaven." The ancient Hebrews considered diseases to be God's punishment for human wrongdoings.

Since ancient times, farmers have wisely selected the most vigorous and disease-free plants for their seed source. In any population, a few plants possess some degree of tolerance to most diseases. Selection of these for future crops helps reduce losses, but the organisms which cause disease also change and adapt, and by sheer chance a few evolve that adjust to the new environmental message and become capable of attacking once-resistant strains.

Throughout history, pests have taken their toll, particularly when a single plant species has been relied on for survival. Such competition became increasingly serious as the human population grew. In 1845 and 1846, weather conditions were particularly favorable for the potato blight fungus in Northern Europe and especially in Ireland, where the potato was virtually the only crop grown. Prayers went unanswered. The fungus turned the crop, both harvested and unharvested, into slimy ooze, and over 1 million people died in Ireland alone as a direct result of the famine; 1½ million more emigrated. Another fungus, *Helminthesporium,* destroyed a third of the corn crop in the United States in 1970. Currently in Latin America, insects often reap a fourth of the crop.

Rice is vital to the sustenance of over half the world's population. Each year blasts and blights limit production, and each year thousands starve because of meager yields. An insect or disease outbreak lasting 2 or 3 years could be disastrous to millions.

Insects and fungi are natural components of the environment. They only become pests when we impose our influence on their natural habitat, altering it in such a way that conditions favor their abnormal development. The Colorado potato beetle, for instance, normally feeds on wild members of the potato family. When we began farming its habitat, the potato beetle was able to increase its numbers and range, causing extensive damage.

Simply plowing the land reduces biological diversity, which can lead to outbreaks of pests. Before the virgin steppes of Kazakhstan in the U.S.S.R. were plowed up for planting, the land contained twice as many species of insects as nearby wheat fields, although the density of pest species was only half that of the cultivated land, but after only 2 years of farming, most of the dominant insect species found in the newly planted fields were important pests. The natural balance of insect populations had been destroyed, to be replaced by overwhelming numbers of pest species.

THE NEED FOR PEST CONTROL

When medical science and pest control technology lifted the barriers of disease that once restrained human population growth, and world populations swelled, more food was needed; agriculture became more intensive, and the habitats and composition of more and more insects and fungi were altered, with many of their species becoming pests. The need for controlling them became critical to feeding the increasing population. Treating the crops with chemicals toxic to the pest provided one effective and popular means of control.

Pesticides

Use of pesticides is but a crude attempt to correct an ecologically unbalanced or disrupted ecosystem. The early approach to restoring balance was to kill—kill the target species and anything else happening to get in the way. The broad-spectrum chemicals that were used killed a wide range of different kinds of insects, not just the harmful ones. The poisons were nonselective, and their impact extended well beyond the intended target.

Chemicals basically affect insects in two ways. Some cover or coat the leaf or fruit so that when the chewing insect feeds, it consumes a lethal dose of the poison. Insects such as aphids and leafhoppers, however, suck the cell sap from within the plant and escape such stomach poisons. Killing them requires a chemical that kills on contact or is poisonous when inhaled, or a systemic poison which is taken up by the plant and accumulates within the cells so the insect is killed when it feeds. Contact poisons can be short-lived, breaking down to a harmless form within hours or days and still be effective. Stomach poisons, on the other hand, should remain toxic as long as possible; in other words, their biocidal activity should be persistent for weeks or months. And thereby arises a major problem.

The principal group of stomach poisons used is almost too good with respect to persistence. These are the chlorinated hydrocarbons, of which DDT is the best-known member. These chemicals last for years, being transferred throughout the ecosystem, passing along the food chain, accumulating as they go. Such inorganic pesticides as arsenic and copper also last many years.

Several groups of unrelated chemicals are effective as contact poisons, but the principal group is the organic phosphates derived from the nerve gases developed in World War II which have a very high dermal and respiratory toxicity. The group includes parathion, TEPP, guthion, malathion, and many more. Their toxicity and stability vary tremendously; most are extremely toxic since they destroy the enzyme cholinesterase that is a necessary part of the process of message transmission at the nerve ends. Many of the organic phosphates have a systemic action whereby they are absorbed into the plant and persist for 1 to 2 months, but compared with the chlorinated hydrocarbons, they are relatively nonpersistent, lasting in the environment only a few days or weeks. They are not passed through the food chain to any degree.

These chemicals do the job that was intended—kill insects, but it must always be kept in mind that controlling pests is not primarily a chemical problem; it is a biological problem requiring a biological approach. The population of a harmful species must be reduced without affecting desirable species. Many insects are beneficial to the environment and must be spared. Such is the case with bees, which are essential to pollination of cultivated crops and native plants alike, and such is the case with the predaceous and parasitic insects that normally hold down populations of destructive insects. All are part of the natural ecosystem.

Natural, Biological Controls

Plant-feeding insects are under constant attack by parasites and predators. Parasites, commonly tiny wasps less than $1/16$ inch in length, attack and develop in the bodies of caterpillars, scale insects, mealybugs, and eggs of aphids and even mites. Their reproductive rate is prodigious, and they can readily hold a population of pest insects in check if environmental conditions are favorable for their development. Unfortunately, conditions are often unfavorable, and it is difficult to raise parasites in sufficient numbers to be effective. Also, parasites are generally most effective only when densities of the pest species are intolerably high already having caused serious crop injury. Although a parasite might be successfully introduced on one generation of host insects, food availability and weather might not permit bridging the gap to the next generation.

Ladybugs, lacewings, dragonflies, and other predators are scattered widely throughout the insect world. They are ravenous in their consumption of pest species, and one would think such predators would provide an effective means of biological control (Figure 10-1), but it is not that simple. Ladybugs, for instance, have their own natural enemies. Their numbers are further reduced by chemicals used in control programs. Many more predators require alternate hosts and will succumb in their absence. Weather conditions are also critical to survival of the predacious and parasitic insects. Low winter temperatures may eliminate a population, necessitating annual release, a practice which is prohibitively expensive. The host species of insect pest often has a far wider range than

Figure 10-1 Predacious lacewing larvae attacking an aphid pest. *(Courtesy of Max E. Badgley, University of California at Riverside.)*

a given predator so that at best predators can provide an effective control only in limited areas. Still, where the environment is favorable, ladybugs can aid control.

Viruses, bacteria, and fungi cause disease in insects and plants just as they do in humans. Occasionally these can be used in a sort of biological warfare against pests. The milky disease of the Japanese beetle, caused by a bacteria, has been highly effective in controlling this pest.

Natural enemies such as birds, small animals, reptiles, and fish also help hold down insect populations. Over 100 species of birds feed on scale insects, wood-boring larvae, grasshoppers, and other pests. In an undisturbed ecosystem, they generally prevent destructive outbreaks of a pest, but not always. Recent outbreaks of forest pests in New England and the Rocky Mountains have spread unchecked and continue to confound the experts. The fuzzy brown caterpillars of the gypsy moths have stripped foliage throughout forests of the Northeast. The populations of natural enemies were wiped out by DDT and have not caught up with outbreaks of the pest. The balance of insect populations is easily upset and difficult to restore.

Biological control, whether from parasite, predator, or pathogen, has the tremendous value that, if successful, it becomes self-sustaining and integrated into the normal environment of the control area. Unfortunately, nonchemical control methods are not likely to provide widescale control for many years. For the present, crop-destroying insects are most effectively controlled when natural, biological controls are coupled with the use of the right chemicals. Thorough scientific knowledge of the chemicals and host-parasite interaction is essential to the application of such an integrated approach. Too often this is lacking, and chemicals continue to be used indiscriminately.

PESTICIDES IN THE ECOSYSTEM

Each year over 100 million acres of cropland receive one or more applications of chemical pesticides in the United States alone. Five million acres of Montana forests have been sprayed with DDT. Where does it all go? Some gets on the crops sprayed, some drifts onto surrounding vegetation, more settles onto the soil, and a little gets on the target pest; but in the long run, all the persistent chemical enters the ecosystem. The more persistent the chemical, the longer it stays, the further it is transferred in the food chain, the more dispersed it becomes in the biotic web, the greater the cumulative concentrations, and the greater the potential hazard to the biota.

At least one study has attempted to account for all the DDT used in a given location. When the amount of DDT present in soil, plants, and runoff from one orchard was measured over a period of 20 years, only 50 percent could be accounted for. The remaining half was suspected to have entered the atmosphere during application. The chemical may then be dispersed over great distances. DDT and related chemicals have been found in atmospheric dust over the Barbados Islands, from the Shetland Islands to high in the Sierra Mountains of California.

In our sometimes overzealous efforts to thwart the persevering intrusion of plant pests, we may have imposed a further limitation on production. Insecticides, fungicides, and of course herbicides, can all impair plant growth. All are metabolic poisons rarely restricted to their intended target. In almost every instance, the benefits far exceed the hazards; yet there are local instances where certain chemicals have accumulated in the soil to where they have actually caused a decline in production.

Accumulation

The dangers of toxic chemicals to the environment have been enumerated again and again. They are characteristic of all pesticides. The hazards depend on several factors: initial toxicity of the chemical to humans and other biota is obviously of prime importance, but the persistence is more significant in the long run. A short-lived chemical, regardless of how toxic it is, soon breaks down to harmless components. A stable chemical, on the other hand, persists. It not only may become a fairly permanent part of the environment, passing from the tissues of one living thing to another as they are consumed, but can become increasingly concentrated as it is passed through a food sequence. As the chemical becomes concentrated, it may prove lethal to organisms anywhere along the food chain, or the effects may be more insidious.

One of the most striking and well-documented examples of the insidious and delayed effects occurred in the 1950s in Clear Lake, a large, shallow lake in northern California. Excellent fishing there is marred by the Clear Lake gnat, whose dense numbers present a terrific nuisance. Naturally, everyone was delighted when scientists discovered that treating the water with less than 0.02 ppm of DDD (a close relative of DDT) was enough to kill the larvae that bred in the muck at the bottom of the lake. But more DDD was needed the second year, still more the third. In 3 years the control was no longer effective. More significantly, a decline in the numbers of grebes became apparent. Over 100 were known to have died in a single year. Analysis of the fatty tissues of these fish-eating birds revealed a concentration of 1600 parts per million DDD—80,000 times more than that applied to the lake. Analysis of other biota along the food pathway or food chain revealed that the algae had accumulated an average of 5 ppm; carp 40 ppm; bluegill 125–254 ppm; largemouth bass 1550–1700 ppm, and white catfish up to 2375 ppm. The plankton showed a 265-fold increase, small fishes a 500-fold increase, and predaceous fishes and birds an 85,000-fold increase in DDD (Figure 10-2). A thorough study of a salt marsh community bordering Long Island Sound provides another striking illustration of residual contamination. While DDT residues in the water were only about 0.00005 ppm (.05 ppb), the chemical was accumulated in the algae and in the herbivorous fish. Birds near the top of the food chain that fed on these fish had concentrated the chemical a million times. The literature is replete with examples of pesticide accumulation

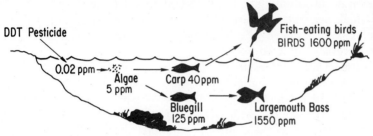

Figure 10-2   Buildup of chemicals along a representative food chain.

both in aquatic and terrestrial systems, but the principles remain the same.

Such accumulation would be irrelevant except for the toxicity of the chemicals in the higher concentrations. Birds are among the more seriously affected forms of life. Chlorinated hydrocarbons are most damaging to reproduction of birds because of their effect on the eggshells. High levels of the hormone estrogen are associated with and necessary for the formation of calcium reserves in birds. The chlorinated hydrocarbons activate enzymes that transform estrogen into a more water-soluble compound that is readily eliminated. Thus the estrogen needed for calcium storage is lacking and the reserves are too low for the formation of strong eggshells. The weight of the bird is sufficient to collapse the shell, and the offspring never develop.

A decline in the thickness of the eggshells of the Peregrine falcon has been linked with time and confirmed experimentally. There was little population change until 1947, when the eggshell thickness began to diminish markedly. The same effects have been demonstrated on eggs of western grebes and brown pelicans.

Biologists were alarmed at the widespread use of DDT even by 1948, but 2 decades of data revealing the harmful effects were necessary to slow its use. Fortunately, few pesticides are so persistent as DDD or DDT, and few examples of accumulation or delayed expression exist implicating other than chlorinated hydrocarbons.

Insecticides are particularly harmful to natural systems when they get into the water. The aquatic insects, the mayflies, caddis flies, and stoneflies, are especially sensitive to many pesticides. These are the same insects on which the native trout, steelhead, and other gamefish depend for their food. Destruction of the insect larvae causes the secondary effect of starving desirable fish species.

A still more insidious side effect might be to the marine algae. Environmental biologist Charles Wurster of the State University of New York has reported that DDT reduced photosynthesis in both experimental cultures and natural communities of marine phytoplankton. If such suppression occurred in a large scale, it could reduce the earth's oxygen supply, which originates in part from these algae. Secondly, if the algae populations were reduced, life in the sea that depends on these plants could be adversely affected.

Nevertheless, pesticides are often not as bad as they are made out. A number of malefic myths concerning DDT have become part of the pesticide lore. The myth that it causes cancer is especially misleading. In actuality, long-term studies with DDT workers show they have a lower incidence of cancer than the control population.

Chemical Alteration

Chemicals may occasionally be unexpectedly hazardous if their break-down products are more toxic than the original chemical. Chemicals are degraded to various products and are taken into the leaves and roots of plants growing in contaminated areas. What might be the effects of such degradation compounds? Most compounds are detoxified and excreted; there are those that pass through unchanged and unmetabolized; but most critically, there are those that accumulate faster than they can be excreted or are chemically altered. The organism may affect the compound by altering its chemical nature or metabolizing it. In studying the effects of a chemical, it is desirable to understand the total effect and to account for the total dose—how it is distributed, excreted, altered, and metabolized. Both the efficiency and safety of a pesticide depend on the interrelation-ship of a compound with the organisms it might contact. Chemical reactions may take place within the organism, making the pesticide either more stable or perhaps more toxic than the initial chemical. Recent work suggests that parathion on foliage is converted to paraxon, which is not only more stable but 10 times as toxic as parathion.

Chemical Resistance

The effectiveness of a chemical depends not only on the general toxicity of the chemical but the inherent resistance of the target species. Pesti-cides, or more specifically, herbicides, designed to kill weeds, often are designed to block a specific metabolic pathway, for instance a step in photosynthesis. The chemical kills by interfering with this pathway; as humans, animals, and insects lack this pathway, the chemical is unlikely to harm them. Consequently, herbicides are rarely toxic to biota other than plants, even at high concentrations. However, there are exceptions; the phenoxyacetic acids (2,4-D, 2,4, 5-T, and relatives) act as natural plant hormones. In excess they encourage excessive water uptake and disrupt normal cytoplasmic activity, causing anomalous growth and death, and there are indications that the same chemicals cause human birth defects.

The same principle applies to other pests. The more closely related a pest is to humans phylogenetically, the more likely it is that a chemical effective in its control will also be toxic to humans. Chemicals used for predator control are particularly dangerous. Sodium fluoacetate, strych-nine, and cyanide, the most widely used chemicals, are deadly to coyote and people alike. Poisonous baits strewn over western rangeland are taken not only by coyotes but by all carrion-feeding animals and birds including the hawks, vultures, and the rapidly disappearing golden and bald eagles.

Predator-control programs are directed toward eliminating animals and birds of prey that feed on young cattle or sheep. In reality, the effort is misguided, since the predators rarely feed on healthy livestock. Rather, they prefer rodents and rabbits—the same animals that compete with livestock for forage. Thus, by not understanding the environmental message, the ranchers are doing themselves a disservice in destroying the very animals that would hold down the rodent populations that are really detrimental and competitive.

Another hazard risked in allowing rodent populations to build up through predator control is that the disease germs they carry could build up to a degree that an epidemic of some disease such as plague might occur. In the same way, control of leopards in Africa, largely through the demand for leopard skins, has made baboons a serious crop pest, again illustrating the interaction in the ecosystem.

In almost any population of insects, a few individuals have some degree of resistance to almost any chemical. These genetically tolerant individuals will continue to reproduce, and this selective action, with the prodigious reproductive capacity of most insect species, will enable their progeny to soon replace the sensitive members of the population.

Resistance is nothing new. In 1908, San José scale insects in apple orchards were observed to develop some resistance to lime sulfur. By 1928, codling moths were developing a tolerance to arsenic. Within 2 years of its introduction in 1944, populations of houseflies were found resistant to DDT. More than 120 species of insects and arachnids are known to have developed resistance to various insecticides; more than 30 species of insects are resistant to DDT.

This doesn't mean that chemists must develop more poisonous chemicals; rather, they must find chemicals with a different and more specific mode of action, that is, affecting some other metabolic process. Such chemicals actually may be safer to people.

CONCLUSIONS

When the newer organic pesticides were first developed, they gave great promise of solving all our pest problems in restoring a balance or order to monoculture. These same chemicals and more are now being applied in the developing countries in response to the pest problems arising on the vast new acreages planted in single crops, but their use is being questioned.

Dr. Norman E. Borlaug, renowned for his research in producing the "miracle" high-yield strains of wheat, asserts that the probable hazards of pesticides are a matter only for the concern of a society like the United States, where food is plentiful. He warns that if agricultural chemicals such as DDT are banned, the world will be doomed not by chemical poisoning but by starvation, but some balance might result because such human diseases as malaria would again reduce human numbers, diminishing the amount of food needed. Pesticides have given us more food but also allowed more people to live.

It is hoped that the lessons learned in the past will be remembered. As biologist Robert Rudd of the University of California has stated, "The mainstream is in integrated control (utilizing both biological and chemical technology) and as the new techniques of field ecology and systems analysis become developed its position will become more and more assured."

Chemicals used for pest control are not necessarily highly toxic; their hazards are often more insidious than direct. Every pesticide imposes a new factor into the environment, a factor to which the biota, over millions of years of communal evolution, have had no opportunity to adjust. Ultimately the ecosystem will evolve in response to the imposition of pesticides, but there is no need for the consequences to be drastic or intolerable if pesticides are used correctly and the hazards recognized and avoided.

In the long run, the varied hazards to the environment, including subtle secondary effects of pesticides on nontarget species as behavior modification, must be critically and intelligently evaluated before using them. Similarly, the possible hazards of discontinuing use of existing chemicals must be considered.

Pesticides have helped people increase food production and reduce starvation. Further, they have been instrumental in controlling certain diseases and reducing mortality. Thus, they have helped increase the world population, ultimately imposing a still greater burden on the world's energy and food resources. For example, control of the tsetse fly in Africa opened millions of acres to agriculture, but in so doing enabled people to invade and disrupt vast acreages of natural ecosystems. Pesticides have aided us in our quest for growth and dominance, but as we have attempted to impose order by applying pesticides to eliminate one pest, we have occasionally disrupted the total system, creating unwanted side effects or disorder in the environment.

SELECTED READINGS

Borlaug, N. E. 1972. Mankind and civilization at another crossroad. In balance with nature—a biological myth. *Bioscience,* vol. 22, pp. 41–44.

DeBach, Paul (ed.). *Biological Control of Insect Pests and Weeds.* (New York: Reinhold, 1964).

Farvar, M. T. et al. 1971. The pollution of Asia. *Environment,* vol. 13, no. 8, pp. 10–17.

Frost, J. 1969. Earth, air, water. *Environment,* vol. 11, pp. 14–28, 31–33.

Miller, M. W., and A. A. Berg (eds.). *Chemical Fallout—Current Research on Persistent Pesticides.* (Springfield, Ill.: Charles C Thomas, 1969).

Nash, R. G., and C. A. Woolson. 1967. Persistence of chlorinated hydrocarbon insecticides in soils. *Science,* vol. 157, pp. 924–927.

Peakall, David B. 1970. Pesticides and the reproduction of birds. *Scientific American,* vol. 224, no. 4, pp. 72–83.

Risebrough, R. W., R. G. Huggett, J. J. Griffin, and E. D. Goldberg. 1968. Pesticides: Transatlantic movements in the Northeast trader. *Science,* vol. 159, pp. 1233–1236.

Rudd, R. L. *Pesticides in the Living Landscape.* (Madison: University of Wisconsin Press, 1964).

Rudd, R. L. Pesticides, in W. W. Murdoch, *Environment: Resources, Pollution and Society.* (Stanford, Conn.: Sinauer, 1971).

Woodwell, G. M., C. F. Wurster, and P. A. Isaacson. 1967. DDT residues in an East Coast estuary: A case of biological concentration of a persistent insecticide. *Science,* vol. 156, pp. 821–824.

Chapter 11

The Energy Era

Toward what ultimate point is society tending by its industrial progress? When the progress ceases, in what condition are we to expect that it will leave mankind?

John Stuart Mill, 1857

In the age of Byzantium when people rarely ventured beyond the walled cities, and knights traveled the pristine forests and fields of Western Europe, farmers learned to use the power of wind to turn the lofty sails of windmills. They supplemented and substituted for the mechanical energy of human and animal muscle, once the sole source of power for running the mills and lifting water for irrigation, greatly advancing technology.

Water power, exploiting natural differences in elevation, has been used for irrigation from the earliest times and was used to grind the grain to flour in Imperial Rome. By the seventeenth century, waterwheels were being used to compress and pump air into the bellows of the forge and drive the pounding mills used in the manufacture of cloth. More and more, toward the middle of the eighteenth century, waterwheels were being used in industry to replace human and animal power.

Throughout all but a tiny portion of human history, the energy available to lighten our burden has been limited to what we could harness from the falling waters, the wind, animals, and our own muscle. Farmers with their simple tools, the hoe, mattock, sickle, and scythe, remained the backbone of the economy. Except for the wind and water, energy came from the metabolism of food, and its production required most of our efforts (Figure 11-1).

ENERGY "NEEDS"

Early Man

Before the advent of fire, primitive people produced and consumed little more than the 2000 to 3000 calories a day they needed to stay alive. The introduction and use of fire for heating and cooking may have raised the energy consumption of the hunter-gatherer to about 4000 calories. The use of domestic animals in the primitive agricultural societies raised the rate to perhaps 12000 calories according to geologist Earl Cook of Texas A & M, and this comprised virtually all the energy consumed. The energy

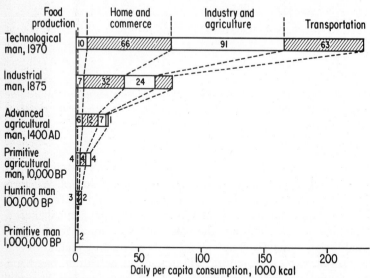

Figure 11-1 Daily per capita energy consumption showing the increases as man discovered new ways to lessen his own burdens. Primitive man had only the energy from the food he ate. Hunting man burned wood for heat and cooking. Primitive agricultural man domesticated animals and utilized their power. Advanced agricultural man also employed the power of wind and water. Industrial man had the steam engine. Technological man added electricity. (*Adapted from Earl Cook. The flow of energy in an industrial society, Sci. Amer. 224(3): 135–144. 1971.*)

budget remained relatively simple as people consumed little more fuel than needed for their survival or to nourish the soldiers, tradesmen, and aristocracy. Peasants tilled the soil and lived on it in servitude. They toiled from dawn to dusk caring for the livestock and raising sufficient food for themselves and the landlord. Of every 10 families, 9 lived on the farm, turning the soil with a wooden plow drawn by oxen or family members, sowing the seed by hand, hoeing out weeds through the long summer, and harvesting the crop with scythe or hand. The meager produce was carried to market on a person's back, or by animal or cart.

Industrial Man

Within a century after James Watt refined his steam engine, making it a practical force in driving industries yet unimagined, the daily per capita energy consumption was to reach 70000 calories in England, Germany, and the United States.

The early eighteenth-century engines were developed primarily in response to what might well be considered an environmental problem— flooding of deep coal mines by ground water. Removing this water was far beyond the capacity of animal or man-driven pumps, although water mills sufficed where this power source was available. By making power available some distance from water, another environmental problem, that of water pollution by coal dust, was eliminated, but more environmental problems were to be posed than resolved. The interacting forces of the environment were poorly understood.

The limitations of water and wind were gradually lifted as steam engines of increasing efficiency supplemented the power of these primitive sources. Engines burning coal for their energy were soon turning wheels that milled grain and replacing the people and horses that had turned the grinding wheels that crushed zinc and copper ores. Engines soon turned the treadmills used to compress bulky cotton to manageable bales; they were applied in such diverse activities as spinning cotton, threshing grain, driving the bellows of the blast furnaces, and making iron. All these applications and more gave employment to thousands in industry and more in cutting the logs or mining the coal to run the engines.

When James Watt patented his steam engine, transportation was almost exclusively by foot. Horses were enjoyed only by the wealthy, and carriages were rare. When George Washington traveled from Philadelphia to Cambridge to take command of the American army in 1775, it took him 12 days. People begrudged the time wasted in travel as much as we do today, but there was no choice. Centralized industry meant goods had to be transported in greater quantity and over greater distances than ever before, creating a need for hastening travel and communication. In the United States the rapidly expanding population was migrating west. The

West produced food and raw materials needed in the East, and in the East, finished products were sought by western markets. Wagon transport was prohibitively slow and expensive. Americans turned to the inland waterways and an expanding network of canals.

Water travel in the eighteenth century was scarcely advanced over that of the ancient Phoenicians. Travel was essentially all downstream; upstream progress was arduous and rare. Typically, boats were made near the headwaters and sold at their destination for the wood they contained.

A fertile imagination was needed to envision the awkward, snorting steam engines churning the water from an iron hull, or mounted on wheels. Yet, there were those possessed of such vision.

The strenuous toil of the boatmen ended in the late eighteenth century, when the hulls of wooden barges were successfully fitted with steam engines that utilized the energy stored in wood and coal (Figure 11-2). By 1820, steam was pushing great vessels against the currents from the Hudson to the Missouri. Coal, but mosty timber, was consumed to power these ships, and the dense black plumes of smoke gave ample notice that the riverboat was coming. Thriving ports all along the Mississippi were jammed with steam-driven river traffic by 1830 when rail transport was just emerging.

People tried for years to harness an engine to wheels. By 1829, primitive locomotives that could run at 30 miles per hour were developed,

Figure 11-2 The Clermont. The first vessel to demonstrate the practicability of using the steam engine for river transportation. *(Courtesy of the New York Public Library.)*

Figure 11-3 The Crystal Palace. The Great Exhibition of 1851 in which was displayed all the great discoveries inaugerating the Age of Power.

and an era was opened during which trains rapidly replaced the dusty, tiring stagecoach. Within 2 decades, 6000 miles of track had been laid in England and 3000 miles served the major cities of the United States from New England to Georgia. The coal-consuming engines of the iron horse and riverboat were to replace hay and sweat as a fuel for industry and transport. Rapidly expanding transportation created a market for steel and a vast demand for iron ore. Smelters and foundries emerged in the industrial East and throughout Europe wherever ore deposits were discovered.

THE RISE OF INDUSTRY

An era of industry and power had clearly emerged by the midnineteenth century when the iron gates of the Great Exhibition opened in Victorian England (Figure 11-3). A half century earlier most of Europe had lived in a rural world of farms, dirt roads, and barge canals. Wealth came from the soil. Textiles and tools were wrought by craftsmen. Power came from wind, water, or animals. Now on display at the Crystal Palace was a world of iron, coal, and steam, machinery and engines and of railroads and steamships. Ingenious new devices were making life easier: the water closet, bathtub, and the gas range for cooking. There were hydraulic presses and power looms, a 31-ton locomotive capable of traveling at an astonishing 60 miles per hour, and a printing press that turned out 5000 copies of the Illustrated London News in an hour.

The magnificent edifice constructed of 300,000 panes of glass set in newly wrought iron girders glistened in the morning light, but dimmed with the evening. Its splendid exhibits fell into darkness as the gates closed at 6 P.M. The industrial world still lacked effective artificial light.

That same year, Samuel M. Kier of Pittsburgh set up a one-barrel still to produce a pale-yellow "carbon oil" to light the lamps and lanterns of a young country. Eight years later in 1859, Edwin L. Drake drilled a hole 69.5 feet into the ground in the backwoods village of Titusville, Pennsylvania and brought in the first commercial oil well.

The oil had been there for ages, formed in the prehistoric marine ooze, but there had been little use for it. Indians used it as a medicine, and the white man later sold it as Seneco Oil to cure rheumatism, but mostly it was a nuisance, and much of the oil found its way to pollute the streams and canals.

In 1851 whale oil was the most common illuminant known. Valued in both candles and lamps, whale oil was gathered by 700 whaling ships that ranged the Seven Seas to gather it. During the peak years of whaling, from 1835 to 1872, oil from 292,714 whales was burned. The whaling era dwindled only as petroleum products were refined to provide a superior fuel for lighting streets, homes, and factories, but not permanently. A resurgence in whaling, using highly efficient factory ships, again threaten the survival of these giant marine mammals; in the 1973 season alone, 44,000 whales were killed mostly for their oil and meat—85 percent by whalers of the U.S.S.R. and Japan. Still more critically, more whales have had to be killed in recent years because the larger species, yielding the greater quantities of whale oil, have been all but killed off. The biggest, most productive, blue and fin whales were near extinction by 1970, the smaller sei and sperm whale species are threatened, and the whaling industry itself is heading toward self-destruction, since only the Soviet Union and Japan still operate at a profit. The short-term approach is most vividly reflected by the Soviet Union's harvesting of krill, the antarctic shrimp that is the primary food source for most whales.

The few steam engines and machines of the midnineteenth century were constantly breaking down for lack of proper lubricants, whale oil being the best. Petroleum better filled the need, though, and soon found an added role as a fuel for cooking and heating, but another 5 decades passed before its greatest economic use was recognized. The internal combustion engine, for which petroleum products were to excel, was largely unknown; the coaches, carts, and carriages still depended on horses for locomotion.

The uses of wind and water power, and even the mechanical power of the steam engine were limited partly by human imagination but more by their nature. The energy produced was available only where it was produced. It could not be transported or transmitted. Factories were congested around whatever power sources were available. The location of industrial centers still was determined to a large measure by the availability of wind and water for power, as well as proximity to rivers or the sea for ready transport.

THE EMERGENCE OF ELECTRICITY

The smoldering dragon of electric power slumbered in the womb of darkness for eons until aroused by the scientific genius of Michael Faraday and fully awakened by the alert mind of Thomas Edison. Electricity waited for their imagination to catalyze proven theories into a practical, functional force. As with all great discoveries, however, electric power was built on a foundation of knowledge laid over the course of history by equally keen minds.

Electricity, known in the form of magnetism since the days before Confucius, remained an idle laboratory curiosity until the Italian physician Alessandra Volta announced his invention of the "electrophorus." The year was 1796; George Washington had delivered his farewell address, revolution was fomenting on the continent, and two years were to pass before Thomas Malthus published his first "Essay on the Principle of Population." Volta's voltaic pile, the first electric cell ever constructed, was completed. Improved and demonstrated over the next 4 years, the battery provided a continuous flow of electricity using chemical energy—truly a major breakthrough in the search for an electric light. Sir Humphrey Davy, the eminent English chemical philosopher, provided a still greater step forward in 1809 and 1810 when he demonstrated the arc light before the Royal Institute. His electric spark, produced when two carbon rods were brought together momentarily and then separated one-fourth inch, generated tremendous luminescence.

Nevertheless, lighting remained little more than an expensive laboratory experiment until Davy's one-time 25-shilling-a-week laboratory assistant and protege, Michael Faraday, discovered the principle of the dynamo. Faraday studied the curious relation between magnetism and electricity; he wondered if magnetism could be turned into electricity. After struggling with the problem for 9 years, he found that if he moved a permanent magnet in and out of a coil of wire fast enough, the current generated could be measured on a galvanometer. This discovery, made in 1831, 16 years before the birth of Edison, provided the basis for the dynamo and the modern electric industry.

The power generated by a dynamo depends on the presence of a magnetic field, and particularly on changes in the strength of the field. This means that a loop of wire must be moved in and out of the field, or vice versa. The faster it is moved, or rotated, or the stronger the magnetic field, the more electricity is generated. The rotation, or spinning, in a magnetic field converts mechanical to electric energy, but the mechanical power must first be produced.

The greatest challenge to resolve was to make the magnet move past a coil of wire fast enough to produce a significant current. Secondly, an incentive was needed to find some use for the current generated. The primary incentive was to produce light. At the time, the arc light was already guiding ships through the Straits of Dover, and similar applications were being considered elsewhere, but some saw greater prospects in developing a practical incandescent lamp that might prove more versatile.

Four thousand years ago, oil lamps were buried with Egyptian kings to light their way to heaven; later the ancient Greeks used saucer lamps of bronze to extend the day and brighten the dark houses, but the luxury and brilliance of Greece and Rome were lost in the Dark Ages with a retrogression to ineffective means for illumination.

Gradually during the Middle Ages, burners for oil lamps using animal and vegetable oils were improved. The early use of mineral oil as an illuminant in 1853 gave impetus to still more powerful lamps. Gas also provided fuel for illumination. Late in the eighteenth century, William Murdock distilled coal in an iron retort, conducted the gas through copper tubes, and succeeded in lighting his home in Cornwall. Industry was quick to utilize coal gas in lighting factories and extending the working day; theatres soon used this means for lighting their stages at the expense of patron's lungs. Street lighting was demonstrated next, and in 1812, Parliament granted a charter to the Westminster Gas Light and Coke Company, the first public lighting company in the world. Many aroused leaders, including Napoleon, considered the proposal of "lighting the streets with smoke," *"une grand folie,"* but within the decade, the streets of London, Paris, and Baltimore were lit with gas. Inevitably, better, cleaner methods than "illuminating gas" were sought—methods that produced not only more light, but less foul smoke.

When Thomas Alva Edison produced the first successful electric lamp in 1879, he was besieged from all parts of the world to "light our cities." The young inventor, then thirty-two years old, drew on a background well-suited to utilizing his fertile genius. He had little formal education, and his thinking was not regimented to reason in the deep ruts of tradition. Typical of his day, education was largely in the home, plus what the student undertook independently.

Unhampered by tradition, Edison followed reason more than the established thinking of the day. Starting with the principles of Faraday, he recognized that the dynamo could only be effective when an engine was developed capable of turning at least 700 revolutions a minute. With Edison's support, such engines were built, and on September 4, 1882, at 257 Pearl Street in New York City, the first central generating station distributed current (Figure 11-4). The 100-kilowatt dynamos were driven by steam engines fueled by coal.

Power-generating plants burned the cheapest fuel available, and the

EXTERIOR OF THE PEARL STREET STATION
Edison's first generating plant.

Figure 11-4 The Pearl Street electric generating station which introduced electric power as a practical force. *(Courtesy of the General Electric Corporation.)*

pollution generated went almost unnoticed as a small price to pay for the newfound convenience and cleanliness of electricity.

Almost concurrently, other generators were made to run by hydroelectric power. The first modest water-powered dynamo appeared in Appleton, Wisconsin in 1882; shortly afterwards, 15,000 kilowatts of electricity were being harnessed from Niagara Falls.

Within 10 years, Edison's lights were illuminating homes and industries the world over. Electricity had become an everyday commodity, and new uses for it appeared each year. Edison's research demonstrated clearly that need provides the necessary stimulant to invention.

Electric streetlights were only the first achievement. They were followed within the decade by electric street railways, utilizing electricity during the day; soon a complete new industry of electric generators and motors emerged. Electric trains lofted people and goods up precipitous slopes in the Alps and the Andes bringing the farmers of remote mountain hamlets closer to civilization.

Electricity also has had a major impact on agriculture and food production, with electric motors replacing human, animal, wind, and water power. The pump began to play an important role in irrigating more land and increasing world food production.

THE INTERNAL COMBUSTION ENGINE

The internal combustion engine, dependent on the petroleum resource, came on the scene more recently. Abbe Hautefeuille, a French physicist, first conceived the idea of burning gunpowder in a chamber in 1678, but 2 centuries passed before Nicholas Otto made the engine a practical possibility. It was 1892 when Rudolph Diesel patented his first engine. That same year a single-cylinder engine was powering the first tractors. The efficiency of the new engine was quickly proved.

Popularity of the gasoline-driven vehicles increased rapidly. When Henry Ford developed the assembly-line production method to manufacture a "horseless" carriage, he brought costs down to where the public could afford to own their own Model T. The demand for "wheels" never slackened, and an entirely new way of life evolved. The 8000 cantankerous cars registered in 1900 were chiefly playthings of the wealthy; but by 1917, close to 5 million reasonably reliable vehicles were driven on the few existing streets and roads.

The development of cheap automobiles gave rise to numerous major new industries. The greatest of course was the petroleum industry, but the automobile proved a vast stimulus to the steel industry, rubber industry, and countless subsidiary manufacturers. Roads, gas stations, motels, and a multitude of services were still lacking. A whole new empire and way of life evolved to lessen the human burden and make life more "exciting and consumptive."

TECHNOLOGICAL MAN

Between the steam engine, electric power demands, and modern transportation, the per capita energy consumption of the technological age reached about 230,000 calories per day by 1970 (Figure 11-1); it continues to climb at a rate close to 4 percent each year. "Nonrenewable fossil-fuel resources currently provide 96 percent of the gross energy input into the U.S. economy," according to Dr. Earl Cook. How much longer can this and other energy resources last?

FOSSIL-FUEL RESOURCES

Energy from the fossil fuels—coal, petroleum, and natural gas—can occupy but a brief span in human history. Their supply is limited. But we have always operated on a philosophy of immediate expedience as opposed to long-term conservation.

Coal came into general use only as the forests of Europe were being consumed for fuel during the Middle Ages with no regard for what might be used when it was gone. Its use in America followed mostly after cultivable forest lands had been cleared and fuel wood became limited. The early settlers and pioneers sometimes utilized coal in preference to wood because of its greater warmth despite the more unpleasantly pungent smell, but the bulk of the coal resource has been consumed only since the industrial revolution, with its use in fueling engines, and with the advent of electricity and its use in turning the turbines of modern power-generating dynamos.

Gas and oil are said to have been used as early as 1000 B.C. by the Chinese who drilled for natural gas, piped it through hollowed bamboo stems, and used it for light and heat. Later application of petroleum as a lubricant and in lighting consumed slightly greater quantities, but such applications afforded little drain on the resource. It is only since the development of the internal combusion engine in the nineteenth century that any appreciable amounts of petroleum products have been consumed.

Fossil fuels are being depleted at a prodigious rate far exceeding the limited capacity of the earth to restore these resources. Plants still die and accumulate in bogs under anaerobic conditions wherein decomposition is minimal, but their accumulation is negligible. Our fossil-fuel resource must rely on plants buried in mud or sediment in the Cambrian Period some 500 million years ago, when the earth's climate was warm and moist, and plant growth was more rapid than their decomposition. Chemical changes over thousands or millions of years were required to transform these fossil plants to coal, oil, natural gas, lignite, tar, and asphalt.

The United States is the largest consumer of these reserves, each year producing some 685 quadrillion BTU of energy from the fossil fuels. S. Fred Singer, former Deputy Assistant Director of the United States Department of the Interior, reports that industry takes a third of this, mostly in the form of electricity. Another third goes to the nation's homes, mostly for space heating or cooling, lighting, and cooking, but energy is increasingly consumed to power a multitude of electrical gadgets of dubious "need."

Transportation consumes about 20 percent of the fuels, mainly gasoline for automobiles. Commercial establishments account for another 10 percent of the consumption. Agriculture consumes no more than 1 percent of the energy despite the wide use of fuel and power in mechanical equipment and pumps.

Each of these uses is expanding rapidly, far faster than the population. Industries keep growing, more people drive more cars, homes enjoy ever more electrical absurdities, as well as conveniences, and agriculture becomes increasingly mechanized—especially in more agrarian countries of the world. The amount of energy consumed doubles every 10 years.

If the material standard of living throughout the world is to improve, it will most likely do so at the expense of our energy resources. The standard of living is often measured by the gross national product per capita. This appears to provide a valid criterion for the material luxuries of life enjoyed by the population. When the gross national product is compared with energy consumption, we find a strong positive correlation. Such a correlation seems logical, since the more energy we have at our disposal to do our work, the less energy we would have to expend ourselves to provide for our needs.

The United States, with a GNP of nearly $3000 per capita leads with a yearly energy consumption of 180 million BTU per capita. Canada is next with just under $2000 per capita at the expense of 130 million BTU. Toward the bottom of the scale we find India, Brazil, and other less-industrialized countries, with a GNP of under $100 and 10 million BTU per capita.

When the depletion of energy resources is calculated, it is generally done at today's rate of consumption. More realistically the rate is likely to increase as more application for power is discovered, and the developing countries become more industrialized.

Economists and scientists often are heard to claim that an abundant supply of energy is essential to a civilized society. The historical record is clear though that highly civilized societies existed ages before electric or mechanical power was available. Even in modern societies it would be misleading to attempt drawing a correlation between how civilized a society was and the amount of power it consumed. Surely Europeans are not less civilized than Americans because they use less electricity. It depends on how we define *civilized* and *affluence,* and if the power goes largely for the home or for industry. The increased energy available and consumed by our technology is significant largely in enabling vastly more people to exist in a given area while retaining the same or better material standard of living. Continued growth depends to a great extent on the continued supply of energy and the fuels that sustain it.

With any resource, the significant question is not so much how long it will last, but rather over what period it can serve as a major source of supply. Long before the supply would be exhausted, its costs would rise prohibitively and its uses become limited to fulfilling the most critical or costly needs.

Coal

Formed in the tepid marshlands of the Cambrian period, under conditions that prevented complete oxidation, coal occurs as stratified deposits in sedimentary basins. Deposits commonly extend over large areas, frequently cropping out at the surface of the ground. Such a distribution makes it possible to estimate the coal resources with reasonable accuracy.

Paul Averitt of the United States Geological Survey estimated in 1969 that the world's initial supply of mineable coal amounted to 7.6 trillion tons. A more conservative estimate of 4.3 trillion tons was provided by geologist M. King Hubbert. Less than 2 percent of this supply has been consumed.

Of the initial resource, 65 percent is found in Asia and 27 percent in North America. Less than 5 percent lies in Africa, South and Central America, and Oceania combined. This uneven distribution might have a critical political impact on world affairs as the supply becomes exhausted.

According to Dr. Hubbert, if we use Averitt's estimate of an initial supply of 7.6 trillion metric tons and assume that consumption doesn't change markedly, peak production of coal will be reached between the years 2100 and 2150. Disregarding the time required to consume the first 10 percent and the last 10 percent, the time required to consume the middle 80 percent will be roughly the 400 year period from A.D. 2000 to 2400 (Figure 11-5). This assumes a constant rate of use; however, if the rate of coal use should continue to increase at the present rate of 3.6 percent each year, the coal reserves would be completely exhausted before 2100. Others, however, contend that the coal resource could provide energy for hundreds of years.

Petroleum

The outlook for petroleum products is even less encouraging. Petroleum can be divided into gaseous components, natural gas, the liquid compo-

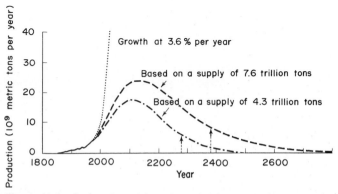

Figure 11-5 Cycle of world coal production assuming a continued increase per year in consumption and sustained at a constant 3.6 percent increase. Vertical arrows denote the point at which 80 percent of the reserves would be consumed. *(Based on M. King Hubbert, Energy resources, in Resources and Man.)*

nent, mostly crude oil, and the solid forms, the tars in tar sands and the solid hydrocarbons of oil shales.

It is generally agreed that petroleum is derived from plant and animal debris buried during the geologic past. Thus, oil is found in sedimentary basins in porous rocks or in randomly scattered pockets. The erratic distribution makes estimates of petroleum reserves highly speculative. In 1945, 26 wildcat wells had to be drilled to bring in a productive well. By 1963, the number had increased to 65. Dr. Hubbert believes that at least 75 percent of the ultimate amount of oil produced will come from fields discovered before 1965.

W. P. Ryman of the Standard Oil Company of New Jersey estimates that the total production of crude oil will amount to about 2100 billion barrels. More conservative estimates predict a reserve of 1350 billion barrels. New discoveries are constantly being made, but it is significant that the rate of proved discoveries has dropped since 1957, and the discovery rate is on the decline.

According to King Hubbert, the peak production period of oil appears to be the present. Using the 1350-billion-barrel figure, the time span required to produce the middle 80 percent of the total cumulative production would be the period between 1934 and 1999. More specifically, production figures showed that production of crude petroleum reached its peak in 1970 at 10 million barrels per day and had slowed to 9.1 million by 1973. If the 2100-billion-barrel figure were used for the total world production, peak consumption might not be reached until 2000, and the middle 80 percent might not be exhausted until about 2040 (Figure 11-6). These figures assume the present rate of consumption, although the rate of consumption is actually increasing at nearly 6 percent each year.

The substantial amounts of oil in tar sands and oil shales has not been considered. The large tar sand deposits of Alberta, Canada have about 300

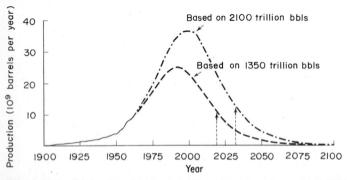

Figure 11-6 Cycle of world oil production plotted on the basis of 2100 trillion barrels and 1350 trillion barrels. Vertical arrows denote the point at which 80 percent of the reserves would be consumed. *(Based on M. King Hubbert, Energy resources, in Resources and Man.)*

billion barrels, and the oil shales roughly 190 billion barrels, of recoverable oil if refining problems can be solved. At the present rate of consumption, the world oil supply might be extended several decades. Improved technology to extract oil from shales lower in oil content than 25 gallons of oil per ton of shale might extend it even further. Development of oil shales has been delayed because of the high cost of extraction, but as the liquid petroleum sources diminish, or the price increases, use of oil shales becomes economically practical. Leases on oil shale lands that were declined in the 1960s sold to industrial conglomerates for over $100 million in 1974, but the problems of disposing of the 10 percent greater volume of shale that remains after the oil has been extracted and providing the large quantities of water needed for extraction remain to be solved.

Natural Gas

The peak for natural gas production is estimated to fall between 1975 and 1980, but this could easily be sooner if the rate of gas consumption continues to increase. Currently natural gas consumption is increasing at 6.3 percent per year. Gas is in great demand by industry and for electric power, especially in polluted urban areas, since it burns far cleaner than oil or coal. Furthermore, gas-fired power plants are less expensive to build and operate. On a short-term basis, natural gas could be replaced by gasifying coal. Coal liquefaction and gasification has been done on a commercial scale for many decades, but only recently, with the increased cost of crude oil, has it become economically expedient. Of course, this would reduce the coal reserves.

NUCLEAR POWER

If the fossil fuels continue to be used principally for their energy content, they are not likely to last more than a century or two. Any continued supply of energy must rely on other sources. Several options are available, none of which can presently compete economically with burning oil, gas, or coal, but the polluting nature of coal, and shortages of petroleum, have directed some emphasis towards finding alternate methods of power generation. Limiting petroleum consumption to its most vital uses might further encourage development of other means of power generation.

Energy from atomic reactors, based on the tremendous energy unleashed when an atom is split, has been utilized on a limited scale for many years. A reactor is fueled with a concentrated form of uranium stored in thin-walled tubes placed in the reactor's core. Of the several hundred naturally occurring atomic isotopes, only uranium 235 is spontaneously fissionable. The reactor tubes are separated by control rods that absorb neutrons and help regulate the flow of energy. When the rods are removed, the atomic reactions intensify, producing enormous quantities of heat. This heat is picked up by a coolant and transferred to water in a heat-exchange system that brings the water to a boil, producing very hot steam which is used to drive power-generating turbines.

There are two main types of fission reactors: burners and breeders. The burner reactor is most common but has some serious drawbacks. It burns only natural uranium 235, and this isotope constitutes less than 1 percent of the natural uranium supply. Practically all the reactors in use through 1970 were essentially of the burner type and dependent on this limited reserve. In 1968, Rafford L. Faulkner, Director of the Division of Raw Materials of the Atomic Energy Commission, estimated that the uranium supply would become critical within the next 2 decades if it were used exclusively in burner reactors.

However, by using a different reaction process in the "breeder" reactor, it is possible to convert both nonfissionable uranium 238, constituting over 99 percent of the natural uranium supply, and thorium 232, comprising essentially the whole of natural thorium, into isotopes that are fissionable. If nuclear reactors are to answer our energy needs, it is essential to develop the more costly breeder reactors right away.

The fast breeder seems to be a miraculous machine in that it produces slightly more fuel than it consumes. The original fuel, fissionable uranium 235, is surrounded by a "blanket" of nonfissionable uranium 238, which absorbs neutrons from the chain reaction in the core. These neutrons transmit the uranium 238 in the blanket into the highly toxic plutonium isotope, changing its structure so it can fuel another breeder. The breeder wastes less heat energy than any kind of power plant available today. While generating power, the breeder reactor also changes the original fuel into a new kind of fuel which can be used again, but sufficient uranium 235 must be available to start the process.

One large sodium-cooled, fast breeder reactor exists in the United States. It is the Enrico Fermi plant, built in Michigan in 1955 as an experimental unit, and largely shut down since an accident in 1966. New research has been limited. A liquid-metal cooled, fast breeder reactor (LMFBR) program is underway, but the initial power plant is not likely to be in operation before 1985. Another decade will pass before large commercial plants will be operating.

The ultimate energy source could come from fusion—the basic energy system of the stars, and specifically our sun. Theoretically, it is possible to fuse isotopes of hydrogen and deuterium into helium with the release of such tremendous energy as is in a hydrogen bomb explosion. The difficulty comes in heating up the isotopes several million degrees for a long enough time to start the reaction and in controlling this process. Progress is being made toward achieving controlled fusion by confining the highly ionized plasma in strong magnetic fields, but it is not at all certain that the process will ever become practical. The amount of energy that could become available, though, is truly astounding. In a deuterium reactor, just 1 percent of the deuterium in the ocean could provide about 500,000 times the amount of energy as in the world's initial supply of fossil fuels.

Certainly such reactors could provide the ultimate answer to the world's power needs, but since they are still a theoretical dream, let us look at some of the more immediately available energy sources.

WINDS AND WATER

The power in wind and water has been used for centuries. Wind has never been practical to harness on a large scale, but water power, harnessed in giant hydroelectric plants, has provided a major energy source since problems of large-scale electrical power transmission were solved at the beginning of the present century.

Using stream flow data from the United States Geological Survey and similar agencies around the world, it is possible to estimate the world's potential water-power capacity. M. King Hubbert gives this at just under 3 billion kilowatts, mostly in Africa and South America. This approximates the present total use of energy in industry according to Dr. Hubbert. "If the world's potential water-power capacity were eventually developed, it would be of a magnitude comparable to the world's total present rate of energy consumption."

Such calculations are obviously misleading. Damming all the world's rivers to achieve this power is not only impractical but undesirable. The objections are both esthetic and practical. Since all streams carry a certain amount of sediments, it would be a matter of time, perhaps only 50 to 100 years, before the new reservoirs were filled with silt. Obviously dams are a futile and destructive approach to providing energy.

Tidal power might be considered another type of water power. It has been used in small gristmills since about the twelfth century, and it is sometimes mentioned as a tremendous potential source of energy, but here too, the limits are finite. Tidal power is obtained from filling and emptying a bay or estuary that can be closed by a dam. The reservoir fills at high tide, and the water is released through turbines at low tide, generating electric power. Several promising sites exist where the tides are of sufficient magnitude to make generating stations practical. One tidal-electric power plant operates on the Rance estuary off the coast of France, generating 240 megawatts. Another small station operates near Murmansk, and the Russians plan more. The proposed plant at Passama-quoddy Bay on the United States–Canadian boundary off the Bay of Fundy has been discussed since the early 1930s and was once started. It was stopped by Congress and has never emerged from the snarl of politics. Few other sites hold any promise. When all sites are considered, the total potential tidal power amounts only to about 64 million kilowatts, or about 2 percent of the world's potential water power.

GEOTHERMAL POWER

Geothermal energy is generated by utilizing the steam from the natural super-heated underground water found in volcanic areas. Wells drilled into such reservoirs can conduct steam to the surface where it can be passed through conventional turbines. The first such operation of its kind has operated in the Larderello area of Italy since 1904. The geysers in Northern California and New Zealand are also being tapped, but the world potential is limited. Japan, Russia, and Iceland also have been using geothermal electric power; Icelanders have used their steam to heat homes and greenhouses since the turn of the century. A further potential for using the earth's heat for power exists if the hot layer of magma just beneath the earth's crust could be tapped. Research to exploit this source of energy is just beginning.

SOLAR ENERGY

Solar energy is inexhaustible and free from environmental hazards. So far it has been used only on a small scale for generating electricity for spacecraft by means of photovoltaic cells and in heating experimental buildings, but it could be practical in desert areas not more than 35 degrees north or south of the equator. Areas such as the Arabian peninsula, the Atacana desert in Chile, and the Sahara may receive 3000 to 4000 hours of sunshine each year. This energy can be converted to a usable electric form by using flat plates of voltaic cells, but the process has only an efficiency of about 10 percent, and the energy must be stored in batteries for nighttime use. More elaborate systems having efficiencies up to 30 percent have been proposed. If these were to become operative, about 4 square miles of desert would be needed for a 1000-megawatt plant, a typical modern size capable of supporting a city of 750,000 people. Dr. Hubbert estimates that the entire power capacity of the United States in 1970, about 350,000 megawatts, could be generated from an area somewhat less than a tenth that of Arizona. The physical knowledge and technological resources needed for this scale of operation, to say nothing of the costs, remain considerable.

At the present stage of technology, solar energy is far more expensive than conventional power. A recent evaluation of solar energy by the Atomic Energy Commission, however, suggests the technical and economic feasibility for its early development.

CONCLUSIONS

Ultimately other than fossil fuels must be harnessed if the energy era is to persist. J. S. McKetta, former Chairman of the President's Energy Policy Committee, reported in 1973 that the United States was operating on a 12 percent energy deficit with over a fourth of its oil imported. The United States supply of natural gas will be gone in the 1980s, and the global prospects are only slightly more encouraging. Only coal holds much long-range promise, yet mines are being closed for infringement of safety and pollution regulations. Fusion and solar energy on a practical scale are unlikely before 2000.

Energy from the world's fossil-fuel resources could best be prolonged by using each fuel where it was most efficient. Electric power would be generated exclusively from coal or nuclear sources rather than from oil or natural gas; oil would be used largely in engines, as a lubricant, or in the production of certain plastics where there is no substitute; and natural gas would be used only where there was nothing else to substitute, and even then gasified coal, though more costly, could be substituted. Meanwhile, the use of petroleum could be reduced by developing more efficient transportation systems. Energy resources also could be conserved by such practices as recycling metals, since the recycling refining

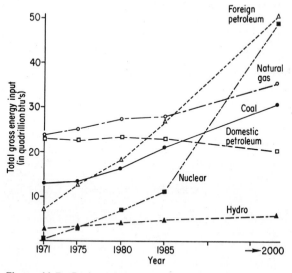

Figure 11-7 Projected energy needs in the U.S. to A.D. 2000. Data for this figure were compiled before the 1973 energy "crises" and projects an increasing dependency on foreign petroleum. Geothermal and solar power are not even cited. Social and political changes may alter the projections markedly at any time. Diminishing supplies of natural gas make the projection of utilizing this resource especially questionable. *(Based on Statistical Abstract of the United States, 1973.)*

uses only 20 percent as much energy as required to refine the original metal.

Should energy reserves continue to be depleted, causing a chronic energy shortage, a major readjustment would be imposed on western civilization. Higher prices for fossil fuels already have altered the life-styles of many and threaten to touch off a world depression.

Projections of future energy needs seem to inadequately consider, or even ignore, political and social interactions with energy sources and pending shortages of petroleum and natural gas (Figure 11-7).

For the first time in human history, we are able to foresee the disappearance of a natural resource and are in a technological position to resolve the problem. But our actions are subject to our social interactions, economics, and emotions. We may not be able to apply our knowledge and technology fast enough to avert a permanent energy crisis, although the information to do so is available.

SELECTED READINGS

Averitt, Paul. 1969. Coal resources of the United States, Jan. 1, 1967. U. S. Geological Survey Bulletin 1275.

Beddard, F. T. *A Book of Whales.* (New York: G. P. Putnam's Sons, 1900).

Cook, Earl. 1971. The flow of energy in an industrial society. *Scientific American,* vol. 224, no. 3, pp. 134–144.

Greenwood, Ernest. *Amber to Amperes.* (New York: Harper, 1931).

Guyol, N. B. *The World Electric Power Industry.* (Berkeley: University of California Press, 1969).

Hammond, A. L., W. D. Metz, and T. H. Maugh II. 1973. Energy and the future. AAAS, Washington, D.C.

Miller, F. T. 1931. *Thomas A. Edison.* (Philadelphia: Winston Co., 1931).

Putnam, P. C. *Energy in the Future.* (Princeton, N.J.: D. Van Norstrand, 1953).

Resources and Man: A Study and Recommendations. Committee on Resources and Man. (Chicago: W. H. Freeman, 1969).

Singer, S. Fred. Human energy production as a process in the biosphere. *The Biosphere.* (Chicago: W. H. Freeman, 1970).

Starr, Chauncey. 1971. Energy and power. *Scientific American,* vol. 225, no. 3, pp. 36–49.

Thirring, Hans. *Energy for Man. Windmills to Nuclear Power.* (Bloomington: Indiana University Press, 1958).

Weisberger, B. A. 1964. *The Life History of the United States: The Age of Steel and Steam.* (New York: Time, Inc., 1964).

White, Lynn, Jr. 1970. Medieval uses of air. *Scientific American,* vol. 223, no. 2, pp. 92–100.

Chapter 12

The Pollution Associated with Energy Production

The use of the sea and air is common to all.

Elizabeth, Queen of England, to the Spanish Ambassador, 1580

Many millions of years ago, anonymous hominids, probably lacking both names and language, first pulled some burning embers from a natural fire into their primitive shelter and started a revolutionary new era of utilizing energy. They used fire to keep warm, light their homes, and later to cook food. Together with the heat energy of fire, they introduced an unwelcome by-product, smoke, and with it, air pollution. Undoubtedly, they considered this an acceptable price to pay for a warmer environment. Eventually, openings in the ceiling and much later, chimneys, helped exhaust this early pollution, but smoky homes prevailed through countless millennia into recent times. To a cave-dwelling society, whose garbage, often including its own dead, was largely thrown out the front door, air pollution must have been a most insignificant aspect of life. Similarly in Roman times, when Juvenal described the fumes of lamps used in schoolrooms blackening the busts of Horace and Virgil, there were more important problems. Streetlighting remained several centuries away, although the early Romans lit their town centers and streets for festivals and other special occasions using pitch, resin, asphalt, resinous wood, or mixtures of all these. The gaiety must have been mixed with eye-irritating, coughing aggravation. None of the early energy sources were pollution-free.

Even medieval mills driven by wind and water power indirectly contributed pollutants to the environment. Domestic and industrial activities centered around the mills, creating urban environments and their inherent social and sewage problems, often to the detriment of streams and air alike, and fires from the homes fouled the urban atmosphere. Nevertheless, the material gains were considered to be well worth the environmental costs.

The steam engine added dramatically to the energy sources available to humans and materially to pollutants contributed to the environment. Engines of the eighteenth and early nineteenth centuries were relatively small; often they did little more than supplement water power to drive the pumps and mills of the day, and their environmental impact was relatively minor until the late 1800s.

POWER GENERATION

When the Holborn Viaduct Station of the Edison Company produced the first electric current to light the lamps of the New York Times building, a new era in pollution was imposed upon an already dirty environment. Coal-burning generating plants for incandescent lighting soon sprang up all over the United States and Europe to replace the more dangerously pungent and smelly gas and arc lights of the day. At first, electric power could not be transmitted more than a mile from the generator, but by 1885 George Westinghouse and others had developed transformers that could raise or lower the voltage of a circuit, making transmission over greater distances possible. The larger stations still had the problem of standing idle during the daylight hours. Only when Frank Sprague produced the first electric motor for commercial use in 1884 could the energy be fully utilized. From that day on, electrical energy consumption entered a dizzy cycle of new uses for electricity and more demand for the uses.

Even with transformers, long-distance transmission still presented obstacles difficult to surmount, and power stations of relatively small capacity continued well into the present century to be located close to where the power was consumed. Pollution generated by these small stations went essentially unnoticed; far greater quantities of smoke had been generated by gas lighting and were still generated in the thousands of fireplaces and furnaces used to heat the home.

An indirect influence of the power industry was its need for more copper for transmission lines. Smoke from smelters in Wales, Montana, and Michigan was already causing grave annoyance to the residents of the areas, and substantial damage to the vegetation, but smelter pollution was scarcely becoming recognized. The increase in iron and steel production, stimulated by the growing rail network of the nineteenth century, also contributed to air and water pollution. Power-plant emissions were ignored.

Working long hours in the factory or crowded workrooms, sleeping in stuffy, unventilated bedrooms lacking sanitary facilities, subsisting on vitamin- and protein-deficient starches, and subjected to all forms of disease and lice, it was small wonder that early nineteenth-century people had little concern for the environment save the most immediate surroundings. Even today, dwellers in tenements where mice run free and garbage litters the halls have little concern for the outdoor environment.

Concern for the environment came not so much with greater pollution as with greater prosperity, which allowed us time to be concerned about it. Environmental awareness develops only as more immediate problems are resolved. Also, while smelter pollution may have been obvious from the start, pollution from energy production was insidious in that it evolved slowly. Early power plants were small and scattered about the cities. Even when power spread to the country, per capita consumption remained modest, and pollution was slight and local. The luxury of electricity far outweighed any nuisance from pollution. Energy demands were divided between agricultural production, industry, transportation, and the home. Energy consumption rose with affluence; after the Second World War, electric power consumption lagged only slightly behind the prodigious acceleration of automobile use. World production of coal, oil, and gas increased markedly in the 1940s at a time when the world was far more concerned with employment and war than pollution.

The most dramatic increase in power consumption in the United States began early in the 1960s when, according to Dr. Earl Cook of Texas A & M, the rate of increase averaged 7 percent each year. This rose to 8.6 percent after 1965 and 9.25 percent by 1970. This demand for electric power was met by constructing power plants of immense proportions, each with generating capacities of over 1000 megawatts and typically burning over 20,000 tons of coal each day. By now the United States and many countries of Europe were sufficiently prosperous to take time to notice the quality of their air and water. They were taking industry and employment for granted and could afford to be critical.

Pollution from the new power plants began to receive serious attention in the United States with the passage of the Federal Clean Air

Act in 1967. This act grew largely out of concern about smog in such larger cities as Los Angeles and New York but encompassed all sources of air pollution. Power generation was but a small part of the total pollution concern.

SOURCES OF POLLUTION

Coal

Fossil fuels account for nearly all the energy input in the United States. The bulk of this, some 70 percent, comes from oil and natural gas, which are relatively clean-burning. Coal accounts for about 25 percent, and nuclear energy and hydropower contribute the remaining energy. As petroleum and gas resources diminish, coal and nuclear energy must assume more dominant roles. Both present potential threats to the environment.

Coal is only partially combustible. Of every ton of coal burned, 300 to 500 pounds of unburned wastes escape as fly ash. Coal consists of the same array of organic and inorganic chemicals found in living plants, including sulfur, mercury, and sometimes over 0.1 percent arsenic. Upon combustion, the sulfur combines with the oxygen of the atmosphere to form sulfur dioxide. The Environmental Protection Agency reported in 1970 that fossil-fueled electric plants discharge almost half of the sulfur oxide pollution and 25 percent of the particulate and nitrogen oxides emitted in the United States.

The trend is toward locating the generating stations away from large cities and close to a fuel source. This may be good for the urbanite but can be risky for the environment. The new stations are often located in forested mountains and fields lush with vegetation that is often sensitive to sulfur dioxide. Such is the case in the white pine forests of the Appalachian Mountains, the Norway spruce forests of the Ore Mountains of Bohemia, and the Scots pine forests of the Ruhr. Sulfur dioxide from power plants in these regions has destroyed thousands of acres of native forests.

In the Eastern United States and in much of Europe, where low-grade coal often contains 5 to 6 percent sulfur, a single large power station often wastes as much as 2000 tons of sulfur dioxide into the atmosphere each day. Fortunately, equipment to control these emissions is now being utilized in the United States despite high operational costs and problems. The costs of control are being internalized to be passed on to the consumer. Elsewhere, the major effort made to reduce ground-level concentrations still is to use stacks 1000 feet and more high.

Impact of Coal Emissions The sulfur dioxide ultimately settles to earth in lower but still sometimes toxic concentrations. Atmospheric sulfur dioxide wafted from European industrial areas of the Ruhr is reported to be acidifying the pristine lakes and streams of Sweden. New England streams have also been found to be increasingly acidified each year presumably because of sulfur or nitrogen oxides emanating from Pennsylvania and New York power plants. The full impact of this pollution remains uncertain.

The subtle consequences to the ecosystem are not always obvious. Careful measurements reveal that even where the highly sensitive conifers do not show the characteristic needle burning, their growth may be suppressed. Then there is the suspicion that the shrubs and weeds making up the understory of the forest may be damaged, or that reproduction might be impaired, but these possibilities have not been confirmed.

Residents near the mammoth electric plants want to know what effect breathing the sulfur dioxide, fly ash, nitrogen oxide, and assorted other chemicals has on them. The concentrations of sulfur dioxide near these stations are probably too low to cause any effects directly, but when mixed naturally with nitrogen oxides, or especially fly ash or other particulates, the toxic effects of sulfur dioxide are greatly accentuated. Most physicians agree that even the low concentrations demanded by modern air quality standards play a role in aggravating existing respiratory diseases.

Solid Wastes of Coal One might well wonder what becomes of the 4000 tons of fly ash left over each day from a 2000-megawatt power plant. Fortunately, control devices are available that can capture 99 percent of this waste on scrubbers and electrified plates. Unfortunately, that still leaves 40 tons per day to drift over the countryside, adding to the total atmospheric pollution burden. Then there is the problem of disposing of the 3960 tons of unburnable residue, or ash, collected daily. In a few situations, it can be packed into the mines from which the coal was removed. Too often it simply accumulates on the surface to be dispersed by the wind or wash into neighboring streams to produce acids and sludge.

Strip-Mining Coal for the giant stations must be mined on a grand scale. It is most economically mined when the beds lie close to the surface. Then the soil above it, the overburden, can be pushed aside by bulldozers or removed by huge draglines scooping out 40 or 50 cubic yards of earth with each pass. The scars left following such strip-mining are unmistakable (Figure 12-1). Naked bluffs and ridges of hardpan

Figure 12-1 Open-pit coal-mining operations in a subalpine forest region of northern Alberta, Canada, showing the destruction of forest and rangeland leaving bare lands and hills of overburden. *(Courtesy of H. M. Etter, Ecological Protection Biologist, Edmonton, Alb.)*

remain on about 1.5 million acres of the United States, and the ravines run red with orange and rust-colored, acid-tainted muck. Machines have chewed into hundreds of miles of cliffs in the Appalachians to mine 40 percent of the nation's coal. When the land is torn open to a depth of a hundred feet or more to get at a seam of coal, the devastation can take a millennium to heal. Modern controls require that such lands be reclaimed by grading and seeding, but there are few examples demonstrating the potential, although the 1974 costs added only 10 to 50 cents per ton of coal mined to the cost of obtaining coal. Mine owners have been forced by stricter laws to rehabilitate the scarred lands and have occasionally been successful, but gumbo subsoil and rock cliffs are not easily restored. Strip mining is not restricted to coal. Oil shale and uranium are also gouged from the land, leaving vertical-walled ravines.

Heat   The pollution of power generation does not end with the emissions, the unburnable residues, or the wasted lands. Power plants are not 100 percent efficient. About 60 percent of the heat from any fuel now goes to waste because of inefficient generating processes. Water is used to condense the steam once it has been used to drive the turbines. The water becomes heated in the process and heats the rivers and lakes when returned. Such thermal pollution can have a significant impact on aquatic life.

Water not returned to lakes, rivers, or the sea must cool before being used again. This is an expensive process adding to the cost of power; furthermore, the heat escaping wastes energy. Far more energy is wasted in transmission. In all, 2 out of every 3 tons of coal mined goes to waste through inefficient use of its energy.

Oil

Many of the pollution problems—air, land, and water—are solved by substituting oil or gas for coal. These fuels are often in short supply though, and will become more so in the future. Furthermore, they may contribute their own form of pollution.

Oil intended for the power plants of Japan, or shipped to the coasts of Europe or the United States, does not always arrive. Tankers can and do run aground or collide, spilling the oil at sea to drift into sensitive coastal shores. Day to day operation such as pumping out ships' bilges contributes more oil to the sea. Drilling platforms along coastal beaches leak and contaminate the oceans further. Still more is lost in dumping oily ballast waters, sloppy loading and unloading of tankers and barges, leaks from storage tanks and pipelines, and the disposal of used oil from filling stations and industry. More than 7500 major instances of oil pollution occur each year, with losses amounting to as much as 10 million tons annually.

Oil wastes are not new. In 1907, the seven-masted schooner Thomas W. Lawson sailing the North Sea lost 2 million gallons of crude oil. Puffins and other sea birds nesting on the shores numbered over 100,000 at the time. This and subsequent spills have reduced the population of these birds to about 100 in the same area today. During the intervening years, oil has decimated the bird populations off England, Europe, and America. Auks, guillemots, ducks, razorbills, and many more have been destroyed by oil. Evidence has been growing of oil's destructiveness to the marine environment. Oil can kill marine organisms by coating and suffocating them, or toxic components can sometimes kill on contact.

Marine explorer Jacques Piccard estimates that 5 to 10 million tons of petroleum products float on the seas' surfaces, much having settled out from the exhaust fumes of the atmosphere. The natural beauty of some of the most magnificent and popular beaches in the world has been marred by deposits of black tar.

As more oil is shipped, the threat increases. The shipping lanes have become crowded with tankers at sea, and the risks of collision become greater each year. During the past decade, 488 American tankers were involved in 553 collisions, 83 percent while ships were in or entering port—where the environmental hazards to the shore are greatest. However, oil wastes may now be salvaged. A new strain of the *Arthrobacter* bacteria, RAG-1, utilizes the energy in crude oil, leaving residues quickly broken down to carbon dioxide and water. So far, the bacteria has been tested only in removing oil from ship's bilges, but broader prospects appear promising.

Nuclear Energy

The ultimate, pollution-free energy some day will be taken directly from the sun or from the fusing of simple elements, but these sources are not likely to be harnessed economically in the twentieth century. Together with fossil fuel, nuclear energy from fission and breeder reactors will be increasingly important for many years. Nuclear reactors are not entirely clean. Heat, radioactivity, and the remote possibility of violent reactions must all be considered.

Nuclear reactors operate similarly to conventional power sources in producing steam to drive turbines, and the extent of thermal pollution is only slightly greater. The steam is condensed by passing through a water-cooled heat exchanger. The now warm cooling water is returned to the lakes, streams, or sea, altering the natural temperature to varying degrees depending on the volume of the water body. The Hanford, Washington reactors have discharged more waste heat into the Columbia River than any other reactors. Staff members state there has been no detrimental effect on aquatic life. The one-half degree average temperature increase of the river is only one-fourth that caused by the sun on a warm summer day. Thermal pollution of a larger body such as the ocean is even more negligible. The hazard is confined to smaller bodies. The heat, however, represents wasted energy. There are several ways this energy could be utilized. One of the most promising is in food production; water could be piped in coils to heat the ground and extend the growing season in nearby farmland. It could also be piped to heat greenhouses or homes. Another suggestion is to use the hot water in heating ponds for producing algae. The heated water might be particularly valuable if used in estuaries as a means of stimulating the growth of seafood animals such as oysters and clams.

Some hazard exists from chlorine used in cooling towers, where it is required to control fouling bacteria, and as the liquid evaporates, the concentration of the total dissolved solids is increased, but these problems are being minimized by diluting the primary effluent with enormous quantities of untreated water.

Another environmental hazard from atomic reactors is radioactivity, not just the threat of violent, massive releases of radioactivity in an explosion, but the constant slow seepage of harmful isotopes which have the potential for causing various types of cancer, leukemia, and genetic disorders. John H. Gibbons, director of the National Science Foundation environmental program, believes that nuclear power in this century is not expected to add more than 1/100 of the exposure we get from natural background radiation, which is less than a dose from a single chest x-ray. Radiation may be even less than that produced from burning coal in conventional plants. According to some authorities, though, small amounts escape even through a closed system and are released into the air or water at the reactor site. Although insignificant, radiation is selective and cumulative.

The greatest hazard may come from the unprecedented toxicity of plutonium. This is associated with the LMF breeder reactor and is a major reason for the delay in the development of such reactors.

Fusion, also, is not without environmental hazards. Problems are associated with recovering the tritium fuel, removing spent plasma, injecting new fuel, and assuring safe methods of repairing such complicated equipment as would be developed.

Another attendant risk is that radioactive trace elements accumulate and are concentrated in the ecosystem much as DDT is. Studies of wildlife in a pond receiving runoff from the Savannah River Plant in South Carolina revealed that algae had concentrated isotopic zinc 65 to 6000 times that in the water. The algae-feeding blue gill fish had concentrated the isotope 8200 times. Studies in the Columbia River disclosed a 15,000-fold buildup in fish and 40,000-fold buildup of radioactive isotopes in ducks. Radiation in young swallows that fed on insects near the river was 500,000 times greater than in the water.

The greatest danger exists when the reactors are being refueled. There is a hazard in every step of the tedious process of removing the fuel elements from the reactor to storing them. The wastes must be removed from the reactors and put into containers that will never rupture, or they must be reprocessed and concentrated and put back in the reactor, or removed to a burying site for permanent storage. The spent fuel, or isotopes, even though buried deep beneath the sea or in limestone caves, remain reactive and dangerous for hundreds of years. There is no known way to reduce their toxicity. So far the residue from power production is small, but the United States has accumulated large quantities of waste from the production of plutonium for nuclear weapons. The material is most commonly stored in large steel tanks shielded by earth and concrete, and a continuing hazard exists that radiation may leak from these tanks. New techniques are being studied to bind the most toxic wastes into cement or rock and burying the mixture in the sea or thousands of feet below the earth's surface. Even then, our descendants must contend with the potential hazard for half a million years. We and they must pay the price for our electric power.

CONCLUSIONS

We have always paid a price for energy to lighten our burdens and make life more comfortable; we have seen that we were always willing to pay the price—from smoke-filled caves to modern electric power production. At last technology has caught up with pollution. The fly ash from burning coal can be captured for a relatively small cost, and the gaseous wastes trapped for a somewhat greater cost. Scars left from strip mining can be restored for only a small added price to the consumer. Nuclear wastes present a further risk and cost, but these also can be minimized. There is no longer any need to pay a price in terms of pollution; only a much smaller price, that for pollution control, is necessary. Nevertheless, the ultimate answer to having clean energy is to utilize such pollution-free sources as the sun.

SELECTED READINGS

Cook, Earl. 1971. The flow of energy in an industrial society. *Scientific American,* vol. 224, no. 3, pp. 134–144.

Curtis, Richard, and Elizabeth Hogan. 1969. The myth of the peaceful atom. *Natural History,* March.

Dasmann, R. F., et al. 1971. *As We Live and Breathe: The Challenge of Our Environment.* (Washington, D.C.: National Geographic Society, 1971).

Energy Policy Staff. *Electric Power and the Environment.* (Washington, D.C.: Government Printing Office, 1970).

McCaull, Julian. 1969. The black tide. *Environment,* vol. 11, no. 9, pp. 2–16.

Zeldin, M. 1971. Oil pollution. *Audubon,* vol. 73, no. 3, pp. 99–120.

Chapter 13

Mineral Wealth and Waste

It was a town of machinery and tall chimneys out of which interminable serpents of smoke trailed themselves forever and ever, and never got uncoiled.

Charles Dickens
Hard Times

We have distinguished mineral ore from sterile stones from the earliest times. Our quest for mineral wealth has continued since antiquity, and the wealth of nations has risen and fallen with their abundance, mindless of pollution or the consequences to the human environment.

HISTORICAL SIGNIFICANCE

The wealth of ancient Egypt was based not alone on the fertile flood waters of the Nile, but on the vast gold deposits in the quartz mountains of Nubia. Here, where heat shimmered from the dead black earth, 10,000 slaves worked the mines with wedges and sledges, and small children followed the narrow twisting seams of gold-bearing rock into the belly of the earth. The unventilated corridors were lit by the light of burning bundles of sticks soaked in resin or fat that ultimately fouled the air to a degree that made breathing impossible; only then was the mine abandoned. Breathing the acrid air, parched and caked with dirt from crawling in the shafts, and subsisting on gruel cooked with dry locusts, the slaves who mined the riches rarely survived more than 2 years. The mineral wealth of Egypt, Greece, Rome, and other early civilizations was gained at the sacrifice of human beings.

Compassion was also lacking in the copper mines of Sumer in 3500 B.C., in the tin mines of Gaul, the silver mines of Spain, or the flint mines of Sussex.

Ores were smelted in sandstone furnaces or in crucibles made of mixtures of quartz, sand, and clay. The fuel was charcoal made from the wood of nearby forests and burned in alternate layers with the ore—a roasting process used into the present century. Green wood was often added because the large quantities of smoke and gases produced were thought to exert a favorable influence from the gods. On Cyprus, clay furnaces above ground were fueled the same way with air blown through from below using animal-skin bellows. The slag contained the copper or tin, and the sulfurous impurities were vaporized.

Tin had been used first in the Valley of Euphrates before 2000 B.C. and was more valuable than copper for tools, coins, weapons, and ornaments. Later it was used with lead to solder the lead pipes of Roman aqueducts. More important than copper or tin alone was the alloy composed of both—bronze—which possessed a greater firmness and hardness than either alone.

Lead provided another source of wealth. It was valued in waterpipes, roofing, cosmetics, in domestic utensils and vessels, and in medicines. The Spartans of 600 B.C. used pure lead to cast toy soldiers. The Romans exploited the lead works of Spain using 40,000 slaves. The mines were deadly from lead fumes, but the standard of living improved for the dominant minority who could afford the luxury of lead products. The environmental consequences were unforeseen, though, and it was this same group who suffered the impact of lead poisoning.

The first iron came from meteors, and its use was confined to ornaments; humans gradually learned to refine it from the rich ores of North Africa or India. Iron was smelted in clay-lined pits as early as 2200 B.C., and the often poisonous, sulfurous impurities of coal used in its smelting were vaporized, contributing to polluting the atmosphere.

Thousands of years passed before conditions in the mines showed much improvement. The few machines existing were developed more to improve production than to reduce human effort. There was no need for making work easier so long as the mines were burrowed by slaves and criminals, and there was always a surplus of slaves, especially after a successful military campaign.

ENVIRONMENTAL IMPACT

Sulfur Dioxide Air Pollution

Workers in the smelters possibly fared worse. No effort was made to control the sulfur, arsenic, zinc, and lead fumes belching copiously from the ancient furnaces of the Middle East, and no effort was made to control the smoke in Victorian England. The industrial revolution added to the demand for iron, copper, and other metals, and the improved technology hastened their exploitation, but there was little conscious concern for the welfare of the workers, the community, or the environment. The effects of chemicals on people were unknown, and the technology of control undiscovered. The foreign materials were removed from the ore by roasting them out and releasing them into the air. Sulfur was the most abundant impurity, composing 25 percent of some ores. More dangerous wastes were released making coke for iron smelting.

Smelters arose wherever there were minerals. In the nineteenth century, South Wales was the center of the world's copper industry. In the Swansea valley, an incredible 600 furnaces were smelting copper along the banks of the river Tawe (Figure 13-1). As the copper ores were depleted, emphasis shifted to activity in other ores and by-products. The sulfur reclaimed from the flue gases provided a base for an industry in heavy chemicals. But nothing saved the major industries of Swansea from ultimate extinction by 1921. Again, humans had exploited for immediate profit with no heed for the future.

In the United States, mining and smelting began on a major scale about the midnineteenth century. The area first developed was the Copper

Figure 13-1   Smelters in a characteristic valley in Wales.

Basin of Southeast Tennessee, where ore was roasted in open-hearth furnaces near the mines using techniques thousands of years old. Dense fumes constantly filled the sky. Trees that weren't felled for fuel were soon killed by the poisonous sulfur dioxide gases. White pine was especially sensitive and soon disappeared. Oaks, dogwood, walnut, and other trees of the southern Appalachian forests were next to go, then shrubs, and finally even the grasses nearest the furnaces could no longer survive. Before the turn of this century, 7000 acres were completely bare and 17,000 acres more were rendered suitable only for broomsedge. Without the native protective cover, the soil soon eroded, the topsoil was lost, and nearly a century has passed without the land recovering.

Rich discoveries of copper were made in the Rocky Mountain states around 1880, and small furnaces were built at the mines using charcoal as fuel. The ores contained arsenic, and as much as 25 percent sulfur, which was released in the heating with no effort to control the fumes.

The native conifer forests of the Rockies were even more sensitive to pollutants than the deciduous forests of the East. Smoke from one Montana smelter built near the turn of the century injured sensitive lodgepole pine trees 19 miles away and alpine fir 22 miles distant. Arsenic in the fumes settled out on the surrounding grass pastures, rendering them unsuitable for feed within 15 miles.

Sulfur dioxide has the same effect whether it is produced from mineral ores, coal, or petroleum. It is absorbed by plants until toxic concentrations accumulate in the leaves, damaging the cells. The specific mechanism of injury is not precisely understood, but essentially the sulfur dioxide upsets the ratio of reduced to oxidized sulfur so that critical enzyme systems are disrupted. Affected leaves become chlorotic, or yellowed, or they die and turn brown. When a sufficient amount of leaf tissue is destroyed, the entire plant dies. This mortality has been especially striking to native vegetation around smelters in the United States and Europe, and around power-generating industries where coal or high-sulfur oil is burned. As new smelters and power stations are constructed in Australia, Japan, and Africa, similar destruction is probable unless adequate pollution control equipment is utilized and new industrial plants are located with more concern for environmental risk than for resource availability and profits.

Smelter smoke is also hazardous to human health. The principal toxicant is sulfur dioxide, and in some cases arsenic, but the particulates and minor elements in the waste gases also interact, perhaps synergystically, being more toxic in combination than the additive effects could account for.

The smoke causes higher human death rates and, more insidiously, chronic respiratory ills such as emphysema and bronchitis. The concentrations necessary to damage health are not precisely known. Adverse health effects have not been clearly demonstrated around modern smelters where some control efforts have been made, although this might be argued by local residents. The greatest objection seems to be with the smoke and its foul odor and impairment of visibility. Where several smelters are located in close proximity, and their presence is aggravated by the atmospheric wastes of large populations and adverse meteorological conditions, the health risks may be considerably greater. With attendant risks from pollution, it was inevitable that efforts would ultimately be made to eliminate these wastes.

Fluoride Air Pollution

The pollutants from all smelters are not the same. Emissions from aluminum production, for instance, are free from sulfur, and sulfur dioxide presents no problem. Rather, the electrolytic reduction of the ores releases large amounts of gaseous and particulate fluoride.

The light weight and malleability of aluminum were not discovered until 1845, and 100 years passed before the pollution resulting from its production was understood. Aluminum production was so costly for many years that its use was confined to ornamental and luxury items. Large quantities of aluminum could not be produced until more economic electrolytic methods were discovered in 1887. Since then aluminum production has always depended on an abundance of electric power. The Neuhausen Falls on the Rhine in Switzerland provided power for the first electric aluminum reduction plant, and for many decades Switzerland was the main producer. Aluminum became widely used in utensils and for varied other purposes, but it was not until the 1940s, with the use of aluminum in airplane construction, that its production soared. The United States then became a major producer; it was not long before the aluminum industry became a major source of fluoride pollution.

Because of the tremendous electric power demand in making aluminum, about 20,000 kilowatts for each ton produced, plants are often built where hydroelectric power is abundant. Such areas are often in forests highly prone to damage, and the smelters are situated with little regard for the sensitive environment. Plant damage also is common near phosphate and ceramic operations because phosphate ores and clays are high in fluoride. Fluoride may also be released where it is used as a flux or in the petroleum industry, or in the manufacture of such products as freon.

Fluoride may settle out over pastures where it accumulates in the forage species. While a small amount is harmless, and even essential for normal tooth and bone development, too much is toxic. Toxic quantities ingested in the forage cause tooth mottling and stiffening of the animal's joints. The extremely high concentrations required to be toxic if inhaled, however, are rare, so the hazard to people is extremely slight.

Modern technology now makes it possible to control fluoride emissions below toxic thresholds, but in many areas damage has been sufficiently great that many decades must pass before the natural plant communities will restore themselves. New, chemical methods of aluminum extraction should eliminate future pollution from this source as well as eliminate the high power demand, but the high cost of construction will limit utilizing the new methods to new reduction plants, not in replacing the old.

Pollution Control

The greatest stimulus to pollution control in a free society has been provided by lawsuits arising from damage to agricultural crops. Where smelters have been built in agricultural areas, the farmers have initiated damage suits that have provided economic motivation for controlling emissions. Current air quality and emission standards, coupled with an increasing environmental awareness and social conscience, should further diminish future problems from industrial air pollution, at least in the United States.

The most common method of reducing the ground-level concentration of sulfur dioxide, whether from power-generating sources or smelters, is to release the smoke through tall stacks. This is sometimes erroneously referred to as a control, but is not, because the same amounts of sulfur dioxide still enter the global atmosphere.

Removing the sulfur dioxide from the smoke may solve an air pollution dilemma, but it poses a second problem of what to do with the sulfur. A large smelter may emit 1000 tons of sulfur each day. Where a market exists for sulfuric acid, some of this can be utilized, or if the smelter is located in an agricultural area where sulfur is needed for fertilizer, some might be utilized in this way. But for the most part, the sulfur simply accumulates and must be stored, adding to the cost of the metal. Until all the smelters of the world are compelled to invoke pollution controls, it will be tempting for industry to continue to expel their wastes in the cheapest possible way to remain competitive. Controls have already placed many United States industries at a competitive disadvantage.

Pollution of Aquatic Systems

Industrial wastes not escaping to the atmosphere are often disposed of into the nearest body of water. The first furnaces were built near streams from which water was taken to quench the hot metal and wash away the remaining impurities. This and the molten residue, or slag, was allowed to run back into the stream. Wastes from one small furnace may have made little impression on the aquatic life more than a few hundred feet downstream. But when a second furnace is built, and a third, soon the wastes from each become contiguous in an uninterrupted flow of industrial excrement. Acid and sulfur wastes from the coal mines, and runoff from the clay pits can and do drastically alter the aquatic environment sometimes beyond its capacity to recover.

Natural waters normally team with living organisms. Life in the freshwater rivers and lakes, like life in the sea, is dependent on the green algae and the energy they convert from the sun. Herbivorous fish and aquatic insects feed on this plankton. Anything injurious to the plankton, or any other biota in the food chain, disrupts the balance of the aquatic ecosystems. The stability or homeostasis is especially sensitive to changes in mineral composition, acidity, salts, sediment, or temperature in the water.

At first the great volumes of water, constantly flowing and swiftly replenished, must have seemed to provide an endless reservoir for diluting any wastes, but life in the smaller streams was quickly killed by the acids, arsenic, copper, and other contaminants. Life in the larger streams and lakes sometimes persisted for decades or centuries before any changes in the biota were noticed, but ultimately the environment and life in all these waters were altered.

To this day, manufacturing remains the leading source of controllable, manmade water pollution in the industrial countries. Domestic and agricultural wastes rank second and third. Production of primary metals, particularly steel and copper, makes the greatest contribution; chemical production, the petroleum industry, paper production, and food processing contribute somewhat less wastes to the world water supply.

Organic types of wastes are degraded, or oxidized, by the bacteria and fungi in the aquatic system, but this process requires a large amount of oxygen, consumed at the expense of the natural system. The quantity used is measured as the *biochemical oxygen demand* (BOD). The BOD is greatest for wastes of the chemical and paper product industries because of their organic, degradable nature. The heavy demand on the water's oxygen supply is exemplified by the paper industry. Older pulp mills generate about 200 tons of BOD for every ton of paper produced; the most modern plants have reduced this to 50 tons.

The dangers of wastes from metal, textiles, rubber, and petroleum production are largely of a different nature. The 3000 industrial plants along the Ohio River contribute much more: waste acids and ammonia from chemical plants, effluents from mines, sulfides from textile mills, and phenols, tars, cyanides, mercury, zinc, cadmium, and formaldehyde from a myriad of manufacturers. Some of the poisons are diluted, and bacteria break down some, but many wastes persist and may concentrate in the food chain of the surviving biota.

Much has been written concerning mercury from a variety of

sources. It occurs naturally in the ocean, in coal, oil, and cinnabar, and has always been present in the environment to some extent. Mercury is widely used in electric apparatuses in electrolytic preparation of chlorine and caustic soda and in paints. Smelting wastes 50,000 pounds of mercury into the atmosphere each year in the United States alone. Small amounts are used by agriculture. Once thought to sink to the bottom of the sea and become inert, mercury is now known to be converted by bacteria into a toxic form, methyl mercury, which may be picked up and carried through the aquatic food chain, ultimately to humans. Methyl mercury accumulates largely in the brain and kidneys, causing irritability, loss of hair, teeth, and nails, and ultimately brain damage, insanity, and death.

Many other waste chemicals exist in the world's waters and in the air. Lead, copper, vanadium, thallium, beryllium, cadmium, nickel, selenium, and arsenic are all present. Occasionally, some of these are reported to exist in quantities exceeding public health standards. Cadmium and lead may be especially dangerous since the body has no adequate mechanism to dispose of them, and they may readily accumulate in dangerous concentrations.

Cadmium is used largely in electroplating, in which it imparts an attractive, corrosion-resistant finish to ferrous metal. It is also important in pigments, plastics, stabilizers, alloys, and batteries; lesser amounts are used in alloys and pesticides. Virtually no cadmium escapes into the atmosphere during plating, although much may wash into the waste waters from plating baths. The real loss is in separating cadmium from the ore or in incinerating the plated metals, as in reclaiming scrap steel. Together they account for 90 percent of the nearly 5 million pounds of cadmium released into the United States skies.

Dr. Harold C. Petering of the University of Cincinnati indicates that people who smoke as few as 10 cigarettes per day are exposed to concentrations of cadmium 10 to 100 times greater than those in ambient air. Worse yet, smoke from the cigarettes of others contains as much cadmium.

The danger is greatest from cadmium getting into the drinking water. Ingestion causes an excruciatingly painful disease, osteomalacia, a skeletal disorder making bones so brittle they may fracture simply from coughing. In lesser amounts it causes shortness of breath and bronchitis; it is especially damaging to the kidneys, liver, spleen, and thyroid, where it concentrates. Cadmium may also cause cancer at very low concentrations. There is good reason to believe it contributes to high blood pressure and leads to hypertension frequently associated with kidney disease and shortened life.

The consequences of industrial water pollution may be more insidious than first suspected. The combined effects of two or more waste chemicals are especially poorly understood. Chemicals may act synergistically or antagonistically. For instance, zinc and nickel are far more toxic in combination than either alone. So are copper and zinc. Alone, copper is toxic to minnows at 0.2 ppm; when combined with trace amounts of zinc, it exhibits the same toxicity at 0.025 ppm.

Temperature also influences the degree of toxicity; high temperatures generally render a chemical most toxic. This is probably due to the increased rate of metabolism and the smaller amounts of dissolved oxygen. Also, the lower oxygen content alone accentuates the toxicity of any pollutant.

Pollutants are most toxic in acid or alkaline waters. Heavy metals are especially toxic in acid solutions such as the runoff waters of strip mines, which may well have an acidity in the pH 2 to 3 range. Salinity also affects toxicity, so the saline pulp mill wastes can be especially toxic when wasted into marine environments.

So many factors influence the toxicity of industrial wastes that isolating the effects of any one chemical is extremely complex. Evaluating their combined effects under the diverse range of environmental variables is even more difficult.

Lead is abundant in the atmosphere but originates mostly from automobile exhausts. The local contribution from smelters is generally negligible. Atmospheric nickel and vanadium also come mostly from automobile and diesel exhausts, although coal, with an average of 30 ppm nickel, also contributes. Further emissions are contributed by nickel refining and manufacturing stainless steel. Nickel refinery workers are prone to develop lung cancer; cancer of the nose and sinus are also common after several years' exposure. It is highly doubtful, though, that the general population is exposed to toxic concentrations. Refining, processing, and using the earth's mineral resources have resulted in a tremendous wasting of these materials. Residues from processing were discarded into the air or water—whatever was cheapest. The resulting pollution was accepted as a necessary by-product until recent times, when the hazards were recognized, but a more significant reason to curb the wastes and claiming every last vestige of a resource is evolving. This reason is the realization that the earth's supply of these resources is finite, and the remaining reserves are becoming exhausted.

MINERAL-RESOURCE DEPLETION

Egypt ran out of copper ore by 1600 B.C. Natural copper had been worked for nearly 3000 years by then and had provided Egypt and Mesopotamia with much of their early wealth. Copper, valued for daggers, lanceheads, and utensils was first worked from nearly pure ores; later it was smelted from the rich ores of Sinai, and later imported from Armenia and Cyprus. Ultimately, elaborate trade routes were established to bring copper ore from as far away as the British Isles and Scandinavia. Mines in the Caucasus and Spain were also once rich in copper and provided a basic source of wealth for these and other countries possessing the ores.

Tin ores provided further riches to the eastern Mediterranean countries, but gave out by 2000 B.C. Tin then had to be imported from Britain, "the Islands of Tin," and India. In the ensuing 4 millennia, the former wealth of Egypt and Mesopotamia has never been restored.

Mineral deposits can be a nation's most valuable but ephemeral economic possession. They provide a country's quick assets. Sooner or later the ores are gone and some other economic base must be found if prosperity is to endure. Three thousand years ago the Middle East was the center of the iron mining industry; now these nations barely subsist on a farming economy except where oil was fortuitously discovered. Ancient Greece was the center of lead and silver mining, but this great civilization largely died with the demise of their mineral ores. Britain successively provided most of the world's lead, copper, tin, iron, and coal. During the same period, it was the wealthiest nation on earth. In the 1970s, the petroleum resources of the Middle East and North Africa are providing these nations with great wealth and a position of increasing influence.

Nations prosper with the flush production of new resource discoveries and proliferation of smelters. Prosperity wanes with the subsequent decline in production as the resource is exhausted. The entire economy may fail as the nation becomes increasingly dependent on imports. This history of mineral exploitation has been observed in the Middle East, Greece, Spain, Great Britain, Belgium, France, and Peru. Disaster has been averted in the few instances where a nation has been able to turn successfully to other resources or to manufacturing. Germany, Switzerland, and Japan provide rare good examples.

Until recent times, nations depended on relatively few mineral resources—principally copper, iron, gold, lead, tin, and zinc. These resources are as vital as ever, but modern civilization now depends on many more. Nations possessing exportable surpluses of the basic resources should prosper only so long as they last. As the supply diminishes, dependence on external sources will increase, with economic and political consequences.

Disaster can be delayed by processing poor and poorer ores. The most accessible high-grade ores are the first to be mined; ultimately, lower quality ores must be tapped, despite the increased costs for capital, labor, transportation, and control of wastes. The higher cost of extracting metal from leaner ores provides a stimulus for technology to develop more effective and efficient means for utilizing such ores; as the costs of utilizing lower quality ores decrease, it becomes economically more feasible to mine these ores, especially if energy expenditures and environmental consequences are ignored.

The *A/G* Ratio

The possible increased availability of minable resources as the resource diminishes bears significantly on estimating the reserves of minable ore. There are far more reserves of low-quality than high-quality ore. Therefore, as technology makes it possible to mine low-grade ores profitably, the reserves should increase. S. G. Lasky of the United States Geologic Survey estimated in 1950 that an average deposit of porphyry copper would have about 60 million tons of 2 percent copper ore and more than 600 million tons of ore averaging about 0.6 percent copper. This and more extensive work led Lasky to a conclusion widely accepted by mineral economists. The premise was that "in many mineral deposits in which there is a gradation from relatively rich to relatively lean material, the tonnage increases at a constant geometric rate as the grade decreases." This is known as the *A/G* ratio, which refers to the principle that as the grade of the ore decreases arithmetically (*A*), its abundance will increase geometrically (*G*). Dr. Lasky qualified it by adding the proviso, "the geological evidence permitting." The principle is too often mistakenly applied with undue optimism. After all, the abundance of a mineral is still finite. While Lasky showed that the total tonnage of the ore in porphyry copper deposits increased with decreasing grade, it does not follow that the total amount of the metal in that ore increases.

Reserves of porphyry copper may increase with decreasing ore quality up to a point, but there is no reason to believe that this principle will hold up indefinitely, or that it applies to any other mineral resources. Each individual deposit is unique. Generalizations based on a half-dozen deposits will not apply even to the entire range of porphyry coppers, let alone different metals. However, the supply of manganese, aluminum, titanium, nickel, lead, and zinc does increase on a practical scale as the ore quality decreases when the decrease is gradual. The principle does not hold where the ore quality drops sharply. Ore deposits of gold, silver, zinc, lead, tungsten, antimony, and other elements do not show the *A/G* ratio. The *A/G* ratio may hold with a tenfold change in the grade of some copper ores, but there is no geologic reason to expect the geometric increase in tonnage with decrease in grade beyond certain well-defined limits. Even where it holds, the added required energy input may be prohibitive. The principle should not be used in estimating the unfound reserves of a nation. Geologist T. S. Lovering asserts that to extend the generalizations to deposits of different origin is "not only unwarranted, unscientific, and illogical, it is also downright dangerous in its psychological effects." One significant aspect of utilizing lower grade ores is the attendant disruption of greater amounts of land to recover the same amount of a mineral. This has enormous land-use implications. These environmental costs, and ethics, may be critical in projecting mineral reserves.

The Rate of Depletion

The national and world supply of minerals is clearly finite. The significant questions to be answered are how long will they last and where will the remaining supplies be. It is also necessary to consider the significance and impact of the different minerals. To answer these questions we must first know the potential future demand. This is a function of the population, the gross national product (GNP), and the particular type of culture. Presently most of the world's mineral resources, some 60 percent, is being used by a few industrial nations. The disparity is increasing each year.

Mineral-resource depletion should be calculated at the two extremes; one representing the present rate of depletion, the second representing the depletion rate as developing countries utilize more and more resources in catching up with the industrial countries. Although a few countries may wish to retain their present agricultural economy, by far the majority strive to achieve a material standard of living apparently not possible in an agrarian society. Despite any such aspirations, however, there are simply not enough minerals in the world to bring all the nations of the world up to the standard of living of the industrial nations. New steel demands for rails, copper for electricity, etc., would far exceed all known or inferred reserves.

As an example of the enormity of the demand, there are presently about 20 tons of steel in use for each person in the industrialized nations. Given a conservative eventual world population of 10 billion, and the same per capita steel inventory as now, some 200 billion tons more of iron would have to be extracted from the earth. This feat would take 400 years at the current rate of extraction. It would place enormous strains on the earth's resources and dangerous rivalries between nations seeking control of remaining ore deposits. Already the industrial nations have become dependent on the less-developed nations for their mineral resources. The United States, for instance, imports over 35 percent of its iron ore.

The consumption of all metals, as well as iron, and all aspects of economic growth, correlate reasonably well with per capita steel consumption. Use of some minerals, such as aluminum, has been increasing somewhat more, and others, such as tin, a bit less than the GNP; but on the whole, steel consumption still provides a useful index of growth. According to geochemist Harrison Brown of the California Institute of Technology, the worldwide rate of increase in per capita steel consumption from 1957 to 1967 was 44 percent compared with the United States rate of 12 percent and the Japanese rate of 270 percent. This points out the tremendous demand for steel of more recently industrialized countries. The world demand will continue to increase as more countries become industrialized, but the demand of already industrialized countries will tend to stabilize and be maintained more by the reuse of resources.

One must also consider the possible shifting rates of consumption which tend to slow as a resource becomes depleted. As iron becomes scarcer and more costly, other materials become competitive. Plastic will compete more and more. Aluminum already substitutes for copper in many roles. Copper and nickel have replaced silver in United States coinage. Prices also have a significant impact in that as prices and demand increase, the mining and refining of new sources become practical. These factors must be considered in making general estimates of resource reserves.

Interacting factors may have a significant bearing on a substitution. Silver, for instance, cost more to produce than the fixed price was worth. Thus, it became more profitable to melt silver coins than to mine silver, and mines could not be operated profitably.

Lifetime Reserves

Rough estimates of the possible lifetime reserves of various metals can be made based on the assumption that the utilization of metals will continue to increase with population growth and rising per capita demand. They also presume some new discoveries (Figure 13-2). However, estimates of resources include only the material that could be mined at today's prices and today's technology.

According to current projections, the world's supply of new lead, zinc, tin, gold, silver, and platinum will be gone by 1990. Manganese, nickel, and molybdenum will go about 2100. Aluminum will be gone about 2120, and the world iron and chromium supply will be exhausted about 2500. The United States already depends on imports from other countries for much of its minerals. Our own reserves of manganese, tin, and platinum are exhausted. Before 1978, our supply of chromium, nickel, aluminum, lead, gold, and silver will also be gone. Very likely though, as the supply of these resources diminishes, their recycling will become economically and technologically increasingly more feasible, thus prolonging their availability. Nevertheless, the sooner we recognize the ultimate demise of such resources, the greater will be the reusable quantities and potential for retaining a stable economy.

MINERAL RESERVES OF THE SEA

These predictions do not consider mineral reserves of the sea. The oceans and shallow offshore continental shelves have sometimes been viewed as

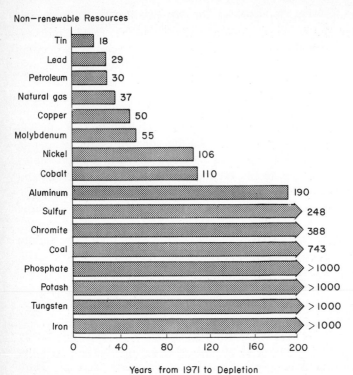

Non—renewable Resources

Tin	18
Lead	29
Petroleum	30
Natural gas	37
Copper	50
Molybdenum	55
Nickel	106
Cobalt	110
Aluminum	190
Sulfur	248
Chromite	388
Coal	743
Phosphate	>1000
Potash	>1000
Tungsten	>1000
Iron	>1000

Years from 1971 to Depletion

Figure 13-2   Lifetime reserves of major nonrenewable resources at the present rate of consumption. *(Based on U.S. Bureau of Mines Mineral Yearbook, 1972.)*

a mineral cornucopia. Significant quantities of sulfur, magnesium, bromine, and tin are already being produced from the sea, and 17 percent of the world's petroleum and natural gas comes from offshore drilling.

The quantity of mineral resources in the sea is tremendous, but the amount of sea water is huge. Often the percentages of most minerals are minute and the cost of extracting them enormous. Only 15 elements occur in concentrations greater than 1 pound per million gallons of sea water. A million gallons of sea water will contain only 0.09 pound aluminum and molybdenum, 0.03 pound uranium, and less than 0.0003 pound lead, mercury, or gold. Technology appears to be many years away from economically extracting minerals from the sea.

The continental rocks and sediment also offer little hope. Any offshore deposits would be covered with sediments from the land as well as the overlying water. Exploring and sampling are difficult enough; working any discoveries is even more remote. Furthermore, ocean floors generally consist of young, sparsely mineralized basaltic rocks. These are unlikely to be productive even if some day they were to become accessible. The mineral resources of the sea that are likely to be of practical interest in the next 50 years will probably be limited to those already being utilized.

CONCLUSIONS

The world's mineral resources have been utilized since the earliest civilizations, and waste products have been allowed to escape into the air and water, leaving a significant impact on the environment. Throughout most of human history, little concern was evident for the pollutants associated with mining and refining. Production was most critical, and air and water provided boundless dumps. Concern for the environment arose mostly in conjunction with affluence, after more "critical" problems had been resolved. Major advances in pollution control technology have been applied only in the most recent decades. Although these might be expected to reduce industrial pollution substantially in the next few years, the rapid expansion of more industries might override this prospect. A more serious constraint might be imposed by diminishing supplies of resources. Only recently has the finite nature of many resources been recognized. More and more, countries possessing the dwindling supply of mineral reserves should be able to name their own price. Keen competition for these resources will heighten among the industrial nations and among those nonindustrial nations seeking to improve their standard of living. The United States is already dependent on other nations for many critical elements. As affluence and populations increase, and technology improves in the developing nations, demands and shortages will intensify globally. No doubt economic and political pressures will play an increasingly significant role as tensions mount over the last of the earth's mineral resources.

SELECTED READINGS

American Chemical Society. 1969. Cleaning our environment: the chemical basis for action. Subcommittee on Environmental Improvement, Committee of Chemical and Public Affairs.

Brooks, D. B., and P. W. Andrews. 1974. Mineral resources, economic growth and world population. *Science,* vol. 185, pp. 13–19.

Brown, Harrison. 1970. Human materials production as a process in the biosphere. *Scientific American,* vol. 223, no. 3, pp. 194–208.

Cloud, Preston E., Jr. 1968. Realities of mineral distribution. *Texas Quarterly,* vol. 11, pp. 103–126.

Goldwater, L. J. 1971. Mercury in the environment. *Scientific American,* vol. 224, no. 5, pp. 15–21.

Lovering, T. S. 1968. Non-fuel mineral resources in the next century. *Texas Quarterly,* vol. II, pp. 127–147.

Malin, H. Martin. 1971. Metals focus shifts to cadmium. *Environmental Science and Technology,* vol. 5, pp. 754–755.

McCaull, Julian. 1971. Building a shorter life. *Environment,* vol. 13, no. 7, pp. 2–15.

Neuburger, Albert. *The Technical Arts and Sciences of the Ancients.* (New York: Macmillan, 1930).

Schroeder, H. A. 1971. Metals in the air. *Environment,* vol. 13, no. 8, pp. 18–32.

Singer, C., E. J. Holmyard, and A. R. Hall (eds.). *A History of Technology.* (Oxford: Clarendon, 1954).

Treshow, M. *Environment and Plant Response.* (New York: McGraw-Hill, 1970).

Wertime, T. A. 1973. The beginnings of metallurgy: A new look. *Science,* vol. 182, pp. 875–888.

Chapter 14

The Environment of the City

Building a good place to live is a process connecting man, nature and society— it is continuous.

Wolf von Eckardt
Place to Live

HISTORICAL BACKGROUND

The city was old at the dawn of recorded history. It was dirty, smelly, and crowded with congested streets and polluted air which might well make a twentieth-century time traveler feel right at home. The city was also a center of trade and a sanctuary providing security and convenience, order and stability (Figure 14-1).

Centering amidst garden plots and fields, the heap of mud or stick huts making the Neolithic village formed a new kind of settlement—a permanent association of a few families. The sparse populations yielded few enemies, food was generally abundant, and life was comfortable.

Figure 14-1 Mesopotamian city of antiquity showing the general plan and types of structures.

The village cultures had mostly to contend with each other and with nature. From earliest times, people have sought to tame and control nature. Always at the mercy of the elements, villagers had floods and drought as persistent enemies. Rains determined if the new seeds would emerge and if the plants would mature to yield a bounteous crop. The environment dictated success or failure, and its mysterious forces were feared. Since antiquity, every tribe or culture has had its medicine man or priest whose magic might intercept the mysterious forces of the environment—a person who could mediate with the gods to plead for human welfare and destiny. The city paid for these services by giving part of their crop to the priests and chiefs, who then controlled the surpluses created in good times.

Historian V. Gordon Childe points out that this surplus helped turn luxuries to necessities and transform villages to cities. The surpluses provided the chiefs with increasing wealth and power and funds to support specialists whose services were now in demand to produce the new necessities. At the same time, the market for services and goods was stimulated by the concentrations of the population seeking the services and material goods.

The advent of metal was especially significant in converting luxuries to necessities. The superiority of copper weapons over those of stone or bone was most decisive. The technology of mining and forging was too exacting to be combined with farming or hunting; specialists were required, and more surpluses were needed to support them. These could best be provided by pooling the resources of a larger number of people and villages, giving rise to the city.

Such pooling could best be achieved in subtropical countries where a small land area could support a large population, but even there specific factors were essential. The soil had to be rich, and productivity had to be reasonably constant from year to year. The necessary requisites were met in the valley of the Nile and in the Tigris-Euphrates delta, where each year flood waters carried down silt from the distant mountains—silt rich in the nutrients needed to replenish those removed by last year's crops.

The early farmers believed that successful crops depended upon the favor of deities, who were regarded as owners of the soil. To receive the favor of these deities, the farmers paid tribute to the priest in labor and crops. The revenues supported gigantic feasts for the gods and a corporation of priests who acted as their ministers. From this state it is easy to imagine the evolution of high priests, chiefs, or kings and a population often little more than slaves dependent on their whims.

The early city was a caste-managed society, organized for the benefit of a dominant minority. The chieftain acclaimed kingly powers and received supernatural sanction as mediator between heaven and earth.

People were created only to serve gods or their mediator. With this background of being stewards of someone else's land, civilization often emerged with a general lack of concern for pastoral or urban environment.

Life in the city prospered as it could nowhere else. There was spiritual communion, wide communication, trade, and a complex system of vocational cooperation. Most important, people were able to settle down in a relatively stable environment of their own making. They were no longer dependent on nature alone, but on the fruits of their own and other's labors.

Rivalries grew between cities as they had between tribes in an earlier era. Each city became the home of a powerful god, and religious competition emerged as a strong force in the struggle for mastery over the environment. War became a major reason for the cities' existence, and armed warriors formed a new professional caste. Enslavement, forced labor, and destruction evolved on a grand scale. Perhaps, as suggested by historian Lewis Mumford, natural selection worked for the evolution of urban adaptation. Perhaps, "in the course of five or six thousand years many of the milder, gentler, more cooperative stocks were killed off or discouraged from breeding, while the more aggressive bellicose types survived and flourished at the centers of civilization."

The city of antiquity provided a social structure and security from marauders. The city prospered in numbers, but new residents and their dwellings imposed new problems. Rubbish and excrement became a menace; wastes and sweepings were flung onto the streets so steadily that the street level gradually rose. New streets and homes were built on a foundation of trash, and the old living quarters became basements. Millennia passed before the urban environment improved; in many cities even today, pigs still provide a major sanitary agent of rubbish disposal, and wild dogs continue to hold down the rat population.

A small minority of the early city dwellers never knew this environment. The citadel of the ruler even 4000 years ago possessed drains, running water, baths, water closets, and private apartments all in fireproof buildings separated by paved streets. The pharaohs, priests, and kings enjoyed the luxury of sewer systems and had fresh drinking water from pipes of terra-cotta, and there was an aura of clean open space isolated amidst a rubble of congested dwellings. As with other animals, the distinction may have been essential to their power and dominant role, not mere luxury.

Whether cities were planned or simply evolved, the end result was often the same. The central citadel, surrounded by the homes of the priest class and their scribes and clerks or of government officials, formed the heart of the city. Around this luxury lived and worked the artisans, consigned by the rulers. Nearby were the doctors, magicians, and the marketplace. Then came the industrial and farming areas: the kilns to roast the bricks and clay pots; the furnaces to refine copper and later iron and 'tin; and finally the farms, sometimes partly enclosed within the town walls.

Water came from cisterns or springs, but sanitation and waste disposal were lacking. Streets served as public latrines, and dung beetles and pigs disposed of human waste and garbage. The richer cities piped water from mountain springs and enjoyed brick-lined gutters, tile sewers, and public baths, but these did little to allay a fetid atmosphere fouled by the acrid wastes of the kilns and smelters of the progress that provided their prosperity. Libanius, and Aristotle before him, wisely put the social function of the city above utilitarian needs. Environmental pollution had a low priority, and no one foresaw the consequences of a sustained growth economy dependent on resource depletion and energy consumption with their concomitant potential for instability.

The urban environment showed little physical or social improvement over the ensuing centuries. If anything, conditions got worse. In the tenement districts of Rome, domestic wastes were deposited in covered cisterns from which they were periodically removed by the dung-farmers and scavengers. Urine was often collected separately to be used in making cloth. Filth and odors, and dense swarms of flies and other insects abounded. The most basic precautions against disease were wanting, and a continuing succession of plagues helped keep down the population.

Yet the cities with their protective walls grew, perhaps partly because of human response to the sacking, burning, and slaying prevalent in the small medieval villages of Europe.

By A.D. 900, monastaries had become fortresses and villages small, walled strongholds. Life outside the walls was continually threatened by thieves and slave traders. Life within afforded security and protection from feudal gangleaders. Serfdom and congestion was the price paid for security. European life in the Middle Ages centered around the Church, and the main business of the community was the worship and glorification of God. Supported by tithes, the Church operated out of Rome with the uniformity, order, and authoritarian centralization of the ancient empire. Until the sixteenth century, kings ruled by divine authority usually at the discretion of the Pope. This fulfilled a basic human need to owe one's life to some superior being; no one down to the humblest peasant dared violate the king's rule for fear of the wrath of God. Education was the province of the Church and reemerged in Europe only after the absolute rule of Rome began to be questioned and truth was sought outside the Church.

THE URBAN ENVIRONMENT

The medieval urban environment was squalid by today's standards (Figure 14-2). Sanitary facilities were typically lacking, and gardens or fields cultivated behind the homes, or in the commons areas, provided the major waste disposal area. Such open spaces may have been adequate in some towns into the fourteenth or fifteenth centuries, but gradually the town malls filled with the sheds, shops, and housing of a growing population. The accumulating debris, along with the remains of the dead, were often buried several layers deep.

Gradually through the Middle Ages, sewers became available to run wastes into large fields at the outskirts of town or into the nearest river, but they could not keep pace with the growing population. Sanitary conditions grew increasingly obscure as the open spaces that served as disposal areas were built over. The occasional epidemics and plagues that once provided a natural homeostatic means to balance a population and its resources no longer held the population in check. The effects of overcrowding and poor sanitation increased late into the nineteenth century as industrial housing became increasingly more congested. The population suffered rickets due to lack of sunshine, malformation of the

Figure 14-2 The medieval urban environment.

Figure 14-3 Green belts of sixteenth-century Prague.

bones, skin diseases from lack of hygiene and polluted water, and tuberculosis from lack of sunshine and bad diet.

As recently as 1906, cities such as Gary, Indiana were built with little regard for anything but the location of the industrial plant. Factory agglomerations were often more crude than the feudal villages of the Middle Ages. The poor planning and sanitation were reflected in the open sewers. So long as towns retained their open spaces, or "green belts," that date back at least to sixteenth-century Prague (Figure 14-3), there must have been a fascinating blending of aromas of wastes with those of the widely cultivated flowers and herbs, the odor of flowering orchards in the spring, and the scent of new-mown hay.

Urban Air Pollution

Wood had provided the main fuel for heating since antiquity, but even by the tenth century the forests near larger cities had been felled and their wood consumed. On the tiny Mediterranean Isles of Malta, the wood supply was nearly exhausted by the thirteenth century, and wood was sold by the pound. Wild thistle and cow dung were the principal fuels. A far superior substitute had been discovered in England earlier. *Sea coale,* as it was called, or simply coal, glowed longer and with far more warmth than wood, but the Church viewed it as the fuel of the devil, direct from the hearths of Satan, and discouraged its use for more than a century. Though slow to become popular, little else was burned in England after the thirteenth century. The acrid smoke produced lingered in the air of such large cities as London and was to persist as a major input to the urban environment for centuries to come.

John Evelyn wrote that the "fuliginous and filthy vapour" made the city of London resemble "the Court of Vulcan, Stromboli, or the Suburbs of Hell." Writing in 1661, he accused particularly the brewers, dyers, lime burners, and soap boilers, "one of whose spiracles alone, does manifestly infect the aer, more than all the chimnies of London put together. This horrid Smoake which obscures our churches and makes our Palaces look old, which fouls our clothes and corrupts the waters . . . contaminates whatever is exposed to it." All this occurred before the steam engine and coking of coal.

He found it evident from the yearly Bill of Mortality that nearly half the children born and bred in London died under two years of age. The deaths of thousands of infants who were suffocated every year by smoke and stenches were accepted with small concern. Physicians affirmed the smoke to cause consumption and "indisposition of the lungs." Coughing and sniffling were more obvious.

Evelyn suggested that the smoke be controlled by using large fires to carry the smoke through taller chimneys. He further proposed research to divest coal "of its smoake yet leave it serviceable for many purposes." He advised planting such shrubs as yield the most fragrant and odoriferous flowers such as syringas, roses, rosemary, and many others, but the average Londoner was far more concerned with earning the price of a meal.

London's story of air pollution began still earlier, in 1273, when coal burning was prohibited in London, but the law was ineffective. Years later, Edward I tried again when he signed a Royal Proclamation to stop coal burning; this and a similar ruling by Elizabeth I were both ignored. Despite the offensive fumes of coal, wood was simply too costly, and there was no other substitute for warmth.

Urban air pollution worsened in the nineteenth century—both indoors and out—with the discovery of illuminating gas. The Napoleonic Wars had interfered with the supply of whale oil, and lighting had become terrifically costly. The gas formed by burning coal in a closed furnace was soon ducted through the cities in pipes of cast iron in London or wood in the United States.

The gas irritated both eyes and lungs. When Sam Clegg warned against the sickness and oppressive headaches from gas lighting in 1841, the public expressed little concern. Once again there were no alternatives, and the environmental consequences of illuminating gas were a price well worth paying for the convenience of light and heat. Furthermore, the soot and cinders of industry, often coupled with fog, were so dense that work would have stopped had it not been for illuminating gas.

Weak attempts to clean the air were ineffective for many decades, and it was 1876 before the first air pollution ordinance was passed in the

United States. The ordinance required only that factories raise their chimneys 20 feet above the adjacent buildings. Dense smoke was not regulated until 1881 when a Chicago ordinance declared it a nuisance punishable by a $5 to $50 fine.

Since that time many laws have been passed in Great Britain and the United States, but control efforts have been restricted to industrial sources. The dense clouds of black, brown, and orange smoke that marked the prosperous industrial cities of the East—Chicago, Pittsburgh, St. Louis and others—obscured the steady black pall of sulfurous fumes borne in the coals of the worker's hearths. Industrial and urban wastes mingled in the air sheds over every major city. Pollution became so bad in a few cities, particularly during periods of temperature inversions and air stagnation, that major air pollution episodes or disasters were recorded—Meuse Valley; Donora, Pennsylvania; and London. The filth of dirty air was not confined to those few classic, isolated instances; pollution was a daily problem intensified as more people moved with industry to the city.

It is difficult to imagine that air pollution went entirely unnoticed in the early twentieth century despite the limited reports about it. As with any problem, pollution must be viewed in the perspective of its priority. There are several reasons why air pollution, as well as other urban environmental problems, seemed to be largely ignored.

In the first place, nineteenth-century cities had not yet reached a critical size. According to demographer Kingsley Davis, before 1850 no society could be described as predominantly urbanized, and by 1900 only Great Britain could be so regarded. In 1850, New York, Chicago, and Los Angeles had populations of 515,547, 29,963, and 8,329 respectively. By 1900, New York had a population of 3,437,202; Chicago, 1,698,575; and Los Angeles, but 102,479 people. Cities were rapidly swelling with the increase in industrialization and available jobs. The jobs depended on industry, and a continuing plume of smoke was viewed as a sign of prosperity. In addition, technology was concerned with production, and had scarcely begun to attack the problem of pollution.

By 1920, pollution in a few instances was of sufficient concern to arouse at least minimum attention, but the nation was more concerned with recovering from World War I. Then the depression hit, and for the next decade, jobs were overwhelmingly more vital than pollution. World War II further obscured and delayed concern about air pollution. In some ways, air pollution began to show signs of lessening. For one thing, a prolonged strike among the coal miners in 1946 stimulated the use of oil and natural gas both in home and industry. Secondly, numerous lawsuits, public concern, and local ordinances had forced industry to clean up the most offensive pollutants. The black muck of particulate pollution was fairly inexpensively controlled and slowly diminished, but the gaseous sulfur oxides lingered on.

The horizon had barely begun to brighten over larger eastern cities when it became obscured by a new type of pollution. It crept first into the skies over the Los Angeles basin of California—an area once famous for its clean air. The air was no longer clear. The population had doubled in less than a decade, and the air was disproportionately soiled. A decade was spent pursuing traditional methods of pollution control such as prohibiting open burning and cleaning up industry. The sky continued to darken. This was not the usual kind of air pollution.

By 1960, it had become apparent that sulfur dioxide and particulates were not the main cause of this pollution. Rather, it was the acrid emissions from nearly 8 million cars, trucks, and buses in Los Angeles that were causing the eye irritation, aggravating respiratory ills, and causing crop damage.

Los Angeles was not unique. The condition was intensified there by a population and automobile buildup and a climate conducive to photo-chemical pollution, but automobile-related urban pollution during the 1960s became serious throughout the United States, Western Europe, and the larger cities of the world. In Santiago, a pall of smoke often obscures the snowy peaks of the towering Andes; the famous umbrella pines along the Appian Way in Rome are dying from dirty air; residents of Sydney, Australia complain of the rotten egg odor from the refineries; and smog from Kyoto, Kobe, and Tokyo is choking the Japanese. Urban pollution from home heating and industry, often involving sulfur dioxide, was there, but each year the automobile became a greater factor.

Infectious Disease

Life in the early industrial towns tolerated more than pollution. There was, for example, a high risk of epidemic disease compared with the country. Plague or Black Death, caused by a bacteria (*Bacillus pestis*) transmitted by fleas, exemplifies the interaction between disease and humans. The fleas are harbored by rats and other rodents, which thrive on human wastes. The rat was there first, having infested the houses of Europe throughout the Middle Ages. The fleas and the bacteria doubtless had existed through the ages with little impact. When people crowded together in unsanitary towns, however, the environment was modified in favor of the rat, the flea, and the bacteria. Humans became a chance target; as their numbers increased, chances of being hit increased proportionately. The potential existed for a spread of disease in epidemic proportions. A similar potential for the spread of a disease exists wherever people occupy an area where such a disease is endemic. These conditions exist throughout the world wherever the natural animal population harbors a disease to which people are susceptible.

In the Rocky Mountain states, rabies provides a good example. The disease occurs naturally in skunks, which are essentially unaffected, but when household pets are bitten, they in turn may transmit the disease to people. The risks of infection increase as humans continue their intrusion into the skunk's mountain environment.

Encephalitis provides another example. The disease is caused by a virus carried by a tick or mosquito. In the United States, the mosquito-borne virus is widespread. The mosquito prefers such large animals as horses. When the horses, once common in rural areas, are forced out by sprawling suburbs, the mosquito shifts to people. The virulence of the virus intensifies on people and may reach epidemic proportions with increased urbanization if the mosquitoes are not controlled; mosquito-control programs normally keep these pests in check, although pesticides are introduced into the environment to do so. Crowding enhances the chances of development of any virus epidemic whether a vector is necessary or it is spread by contact.

The fundamental basis for the existence of a disease vector is a continued presence of the disease and its ability to adjust as humans alter the environment, often with their own presence. The population of each animal species supports an assemblage of parasites, each of which favors a particular ecological habitat, or niche. If humans also provide a suitable niche, they become a likely host for any existing parasites. Often people have only chance encounters with the parasite, but as the urban population density increases and spreads into environments already occupied by the disease carriers, epidemics become more likely.

Even late in the nineteenth century so little was known about disease and epidemiology that the real threat from rats, fleas, mosquitoes, and poor sanitation was not recognized, nor was much known about the dangers of polluted water causing disease.

Urban Sewage and Treatment

Discoveries by Pasteur and Lister established that certain types of diseases, among them typhoid fever and cholera, were transmitted through polluted water. This provided the first real insight that discharging sewage into river water might be dangerous if this water were later consumed.

The discovery was most timely. Prior to the 1850s, urban populations had remained relatively small. Their sewage wastes dispersed into nearby waters were apparently diluted by large volumes of flowing water sufficient to avert wide-scale epidemics. Also, the death rate was already so high from other causes, and life expectancies so short, that a few more deaths from typhoid would scarcely have been noticed. Recall also that few sewers, other than to carry excess rainwater, existed in the nineteenth century. Sewers were usually natural watercourses or ditches inadequate to carry the bulk of the wastes into the main rivers from which culinary water was taken. The improved sanitary sewers by 1850 were more efficient in carrying wastes into the stream where they could contaminate the drinking water. In some ways, a good cesspool was safer, although disease germs sometimes leaked from these and caused epidemics.

Cesspools are still used for waste disposal in many urban and rural areas, but more and more, sewers are carrying urban wastes into nearby lakes, rivers, and the sea. Some 1400 United States cities still channel raw sewage into the closest river or stream. Sanitation sewage includes everything that goes down the drains of a city—human wastes; used water from tubs; garbage from sinks; washings from restaurants, hospitals, and mortuaries; and much more. Sewage may also include industrial wastes—acids, chemicals, oils, animal and vegetable processing wastes, etc.—but often these bypass the sewer and are dumped directly into the watercourse.

There are three main hazards of these urban wastes. First, there is the danger of spreading waterborne diseases—typhoid, cholera, dysentery, hepatitis, etc. Rivers, lakes, and even the ocean cannot provide an infinite dumping area. There is a limit to the ability of water to cleanse itself. Yet, some cities still depend on the age-old process of dilution and self-purification. The polluting effect of wastes is best averted by treating the sewage before it is released back to the watercourse.

In order to preserve the quality of water, the pathogenic bacteria must be removed. The number of bacteria in the water is generally expressed according to the numbers of a particular intestinal species, *Escherichia coli,* found in the water. This number provides a count or an index of pollution called a *coliform count.* Waters containing more than a background level of about 50 such bacteria per 100-milliliter sample are considered to have been contaminated and may carry waterborne disease germs. These can be removed or killed by sewage treatment, most commonly by introducing lethal quantities of chlorine or ozone. (See Appendix, "Water Quality Standards.")

Primary sewage treatment passes the sewage through a screen, which catches the large objects; it then generally flows through gravel and sand beds into a large settling tank. The solids settle out here as sludge, or rise to the top as scum. The water between these layers is drained off and treated with chlorine to kill any harmful bacteria. The scum and sludge are dried and can be used for fertilizer or soil conditioner. About 35 percent of the pollution load, but no nutrients or toxic agents, are removed in this way.

Sewage may then be passed through a secondary treatment plant. Here the waste water from the primary plant is sprayed on a bed of stones about 6 feet deep. As the liquid trickles through it, bacteria and algae that coat the stones absorb and ingest the suspended material and utilize it for food. The final effluent, which contains the inorganic breakdown products including nitrogen and phosphates, may then be treated with chlorine to kill any remaining bacteria or left untreated and returned to the watercourse.

This process may double or triple the cost of sewage treatment over that of primary treatment. The cost may be doubled again if tertiary treatment is provided, whereby phosphates, nitrate, and carbonates are precipitated and removed. The water is then returned to the streams, often in a more pure condition than when originally taken from them.

The second hazard of untreated sewage is to the aquatic biota. The microbial decomposition of organic matter, whether on land or in water, consumes oxygen. Large quantities of organic matter are contributed by food-processing plants, slaughterhouses, paper pulp mills, and other industries as discussed earlier, but major amounts come from sewage. Decomposition of excessive organic matter added to lakes and streams consumes much of the dissolved oxygen in the water. Aquatic life that depended on this oxygen dies. To decompose the wastes of a single person, 0.17 pounds of oxygen per day are required. When this is multiplied by the population of a large city, the oxygen demanded becomes huge.

Sewage also contains assorted chemicals such as pesticides from household and garden use that can be especially toxic. Some insecticides are toxic to aquatic insects at concentrations in the parts per billion range.

Silt from runoff can also destroy the natural biota. Covering the normal rocky or sandy streambeds, silt changes the habitat, often smothering aquatic life. Sludge worms and mosquitoes soon replace the mayflies, caddis flies, and stone flies, all of which are vital to the survival of desirable fish species. Finer particles cause turbidity, which reduces light penetration and impairs algal growth.

A third danger from urban sewage is to the body of water itself, in *eutrophication*. Eutrophication is a natural process; it means "well-nourished" and refers to the natural or artificial addition of nutrients to bodies of water and to the effects of the added nutrients. Eutrophication is also an aspect of aging—it increases the rate at which lakes get old and disappear.

Accelerated eutrophication causes a profusion of plant and animal growth. Blue-green algae and bacteria grow most profusely, interfering with the use of the water, detracting from the natural beauty, and threatening the destruction of water resources. The excessive growth chokes the open water with green decomposing slime, which fouls the air and consumes the oxygen vital for fish and other aquatic life.

Nitrogen and phosphates are occasionally added to waters intentionally to stimulate algal growth, which might make lakes more productive for fish. More often these nutrients are detrimental, largely because they stimulate the growth of bacteria and sewage fungi, which can form a dense gray slimy mat over the waters. Human sewage and washings, drainage from farmlands, and runoff from urban areas are the most significant sources of eutrophication-causing nutrients.

Cities, states, and the manufacturers themselves began about 1970 to phase out phosphates, only to learn that the alternatives were still more perilous. The most common phosphate substitute, nitrolotriacetic acid (NTA), cleaned well but combined chemically with heavy metals like mercury and cadmium in drinking water supplies. The combinations have been linked with birth defects in animals. Also, the nitrogen released possibly added to eutrophication as much as the phosphates it replaced.

Another class of widely used phosphate substitutes, caustic alkaline chemicals, can be dangerous if inhaled, swallowed, or brought in contact with the eyes. These examples indicate how knowledge of the total interaction of a "solution" on the ecosystem is vital to truly solving a problem.

Sewage pollution is not solely an urban dilemma. Organic wastes, like phosphates, are most significant where they are flushed into the relatively closed ecosystems of lakes. Eutrophication was first noticed where runoff from farms or nutrient-rich outcroppings drained into nearby lakes. Switzerland's Lake Zurich, for instance, drains a large number of rural farms, and the problem of eutrophication there goes back at least to 1896.

Rivers have a far greater ability to mix and aerate pollutants than lakes and so can far more effectively handle effluents that have a high BOD and nutrient content. A large stream might completely restore itself to normal within a few miles of a pollution source. Biological effects of pollution by sewage often extend only 5 miles or so downstream, although effects of more stable effluents may extend much further. The structure of the fish population is often modified for considerable distances, with many species being eliminated. Toxic chemicals, mostly from industrial wastes suspended in the bottom mud, may modify aquatic animal populations, especially where the normal invertebrate population has been destroyed. The low oxygen concentration, especially when the water temperature is high, is also a factor. While some fish species are tolerant of a low oxygen concentration and may thrive on the organic wastes of pollution, these rarely include desirable species.

In recent decades, pollution has encroached on thousands of mountain lakes which serve as cesspools for the surrounding campsites and cabin communities. The dilemma is not unique to the United States; recreation pollution infests every affluent nation. Often, where the human environment has been imposed on the natural environment, the sole water supply is from the same lakes or streams made murky by the algal bloom and wastes of pollution.

Solid Wastes

Less than a century ago, much of our garbage and other solid wastes were simply thrown out to the pigs. Only 30 years ago, urban wastes were burned in home incinerators, and wastes were minimal. Fruits and vegetables were often put in reusable glass bottles, fish was wrapped in newspapers, and meat came in waxed white paper. Plastic was unknown, and groceries were carried home in mesh bags, as they are today in much of the world, but superfluous packaging and waste follow affluence.

A European family rarely sets out more than a small can of wastes for collection each week. The total amount of solid wastes in the United States averages 100 pounds per capita each day. Of this, 7 pounds are household and municipal wastes, 4 pounds are federal and industrial, 15 are agricultural and crop wastes, 31 pounds are mineral wastes, and 43 pounds from animal wastes. Our gross national garbage includes some 50 billion cans, 8 million old television sets, 8 million autos, and 100 million old tires each year.

How can it be disposed of? Despite talk of sanitary landfills and recycling, 84 percent of all collected rubbish still goes into open dumps where it is often burned, or it is dumped into bays, lakes, or the ocean. Trash typically goes up in smoke, which contributes to air pollution. The ashes and noncombustible materials are buried or pushed into a convenient ravine, and the wet garbage is partly consumed by swarming populations of rats.

Incineration provides an effective means for reducing the waste volume. Properly burned, refuse can be used to produce electric power. A few European cities now burn waste to generate steam for power plants, and a few United States cities are experimenting with this possibility.

Smoke from burning urban trash can be dangerous depending on the material being burned. Polychlorinated biphenyls (PCBs), for instance, do not burn but are vaporized. Most of the PCBs in the environment enter through incineration. Some also enter in runoff from wastes and at the point of manufacture. Products containing PCBs, such as plastics, spent ballasts from fluorescent light fixtures, objects coated with PCB-formulated protective coatings, and sometimes epoxy paints, all find their way to the city dump or incinerator for burning. PCBs are also used as coolant-insulation fluids in transformers, for car bodies, and to increase the effectiveness of the chlorinated hydrocarbon pesticides.

Chemically, PCBs are similar to the chlorinated hydrocarbons and share many of their properties. They are even more persistent than DDT and are transferred in the food chain in the same way. PCBs have been found in fish, birds, and water throughout the world. By accumulating in the food chain, PCB has reached the level of 14,000 ppm in white-tailed eagles, and peregrine falcons off the coast of California have accumulated 2000 ppm. Shrimp exposed to 10-ppb Aroclor, the most common PCB, for 48 hours accumulated 1300 ppb, a thirtyfold increase. Oysters concentrated the chemical 33,000 times in 96 hours.

Dr. Joseph Street at Utah State University has shown that when PCBs accumulate in the liver, they stimulate metabolism of foreign compounds such as insecticides, which might otherwise remain inert. The chronic action of PCBs produces lesions in the liver and pigmentation of the skin. More acutely, they cause nausea, vomiting, loss of weight, and abdominal pain.

Pyrolysis has also been proposed to reduce the waste volume. This is a refinement of incineration in which air is excluded and heat is applied externally to burn the refuse. Trash is reacted with carbon monoxide at higher temperatures to produce crude oil from it. Wastes can thereby be used to generate electricity.

More and more cities, some 6 percent in 1970, are burying their wastes in trenches excavated below the ground surface or in natural draws. These sanitary landfills have the problem that wastes may leach into nearby water supplies and be a potential source of water pollution if the site is not carefully selected. Landfill has the advantage of serving to reclaim marginal or unacceptable land. If properly compacted, the fill will stabilize and provide sites for parks or industry. Children in Los Angeles and a few other cities now enjoy well-landscaped parks in areas where an earlier generation dumped their wastes.

A major problem with sanitary landfill in some areas is in finding a place to fill. Open land is scarce or nonexistent around many municipalities, and residents near prospective sites are intolerant of other people's garbage. To reduce the space needed, and New York City for instance uses about 200 acres per year, refuse could be better compacted. Modern balers can compress wastes to one-twentieth of their original volume.

Disposal methods might be refined by first removing all the reusable materials for recycling and, at the same time, utilizing rather than wasting the many valuable resources often buried in the garbage dump. During World War II, Los Angeles tried to salvage wastes by having homeowners separate paper wastes, cans, bottles, and garbage. This proved impractical and difficult at best. It could only be practical at the dumping site, and here it is a problem for two reasons: the cost of separating waste components, and the lack of a market for the products. The potential theoretical value of trash (Table 14-1) is irrelevent if no one wants it at any price. Virgin materials are often not only better but cheaper.

Separation is expensive, and conversion to usable forms is also expensive. It is cheaper to manufacture new bottles than reuse them.

Table 14-1   Potential Values of Trash

Component	% by weight	Dollar value per ton of component	Dollar value per ton of trash
Paper and paperboard	50	$100	$50
Ferrous material	9	20	2
Aluminum	11	200	2
Glass, ceramics*	10	10	1
Garbage, yardwaste	20	5 (as compost)	1
Miscellaneous—plastics	10	5 (as fuel)	0.50

*Glassphalt value at $3–4 per ton; scrap glass at $15 per ton.

Also, an affluent public prefers to throw things away. A reusable bottle once made over 20 trips; now 5 trips are unlikely. Only when materials become short in supply will values and attitudes be reoriented to where the resource value of "garbage" will be accepted.

CONCLUSIONS

During the long course of the cities' history, they have never been free from environmental depredation. One problem may be conquered only to be replaced by another. Generally, the hazards were ignored because life was manifest with far greater ills. Problems of disease, pollution, and wastes became increasingly intense with urban congestion and perhaps collectively reached a peak of repugnance in the nineteenth century. Only recently has technology begun to cope with the problems, but even where the technology exists, the motivation may be wanting. The price of clean air, water, and land may be more than society wishes to pay. Inner cities present the worst concentration of nearly every kind of environmental problem. The urban poor dwelling there breathe the worst air; the streets and vacant lots are littered with garbage; peeling paint exposes residents to lead poisoning; and obsolete, deteriorating sewer systems enhance the chances of disease.

Superhighways that speed the more affluent through city centers to parks, beaches, and mountains often cut off the innercity people from the outside, and all the while, the mounting acres of tar and cement paving aggravate an urban environment that has already been long void of meadows, fields, or any major unspoiled open space.

SELECTED READINGS

Childe, V. Gordon. Early forms of society. Chapter 2 in C. Singer, E. J. Holmyara, and A. R. Hull, *History of Technology,* vol. I. (London: Clarendon, 1954).

Davis, Kingsley. The urbanization of the human population. *In Man and the Ecosphere.* (San Francisco: W. H. Freeman, 1970).

Deevey, E. S., Jr. The human population. *In Man and the Ecosphere.* (San Francisco: W. H. Freeman, 1970).

Forbes, R. J. Power to 1850. In C. Singer, et al. *A History of Technology,* vol. V. (London: Clarendon, 1958).

Grinstead, R. R. 1971. No deposit, no return. *Environment,* vol. 11, no. 9, pp. 17–23.

Hynes, H. B. N. *The Biology of Polluted Waters.* (Liverpool: Liverpool University Press, 1970).

Kenahan, C. B. 1971. Solid waste, resources out of place. *Environmental Science and Technology,* vol. 5, no. 7, pp. 594–600.

Levine, N. D. (ed.). Natural nidality of diseases and questions of parasitology. Trans. by F. K. Plows from IV Cong. on the Natural Nidality of Disease. U.S.S.R. 1959. (Urbana: University of Illinois Press, 1968).

Lodge, J. P. (ed.). *The Smoake of London.* (Elmsford, N.Y.: Maxwell Reprint Co., 1969).

Mumford, Lewis. *The City in History.* (New York: Harcourt, Brace & World, 1961).

National Academy of Science. 1970. *Eutrophication: Causes, Consequences, Correctives.* (Washington D.C.: National Academy of Science, 1970).

Pavlovsky, E. N. *Natural Nidality of Transmissible Diseases: With Special Reference to the Landscape Epidemiology of Zooanthroponoses* (Trans. from Russian). (Urbana: University of Illinois Press, 1964).

Schoenberger, R. J. Solid waste—the third pollution, pp. 295–350. In: P. W. Purdom (ed.). *Environmental Health.* (New York: Academic, 1971).

Chapter 15

The Transportation
Spiral

What the few have, many want.

Alexis Tocqueville

It was a morning like every other morning. It was barely 6 A.M. and a well-meaning sun was attempting to sift through an impervious shroud of soot spilling from the city's countless chimneys. Rays of anemic light flickered dimly into a dusky veil of mist and rain as men and women filed from their monotonous tiers of dirty brick tenements and walked to jobs a few doors away.

One hundred years later, the monotonous tenements had been transformed to equally dull ticky tack tracts of suburban tedium. The workers still often woke before the morning sun had filtered through the gray vapor, but they no longer walked; they drove, often for an hour or more, to work, at the same time contributing to the expanding veil of exhaust fumes extending toward a murky horizon.

Life for each of the passing generations changed markedly between 1870 and 1970. For most, it changed for the better. Each generation saw progressively more rapid changes: electric lighting, indoor plumbing, improved sanitation, central heating, more privacy and space, better food and more of it, more leisure time, homes in the suburbs, and most of all, better, or at least potentially faster, transportation. To a great extent, the changes were made possible by a revolution in transportation—a succession of changes initiated by the discovery of new energy sources.

Life in 1870 moved slowly, and not very far. East and West were united by 3000 miles of rail, and many miles more linked the major cities of the East and connected much of Europe, but transportation within the cities remained limited to horse-driven carriages and foot.

As the industrial age unfolded in the 1800s, the size of the factory and the town were largely limited by walking distance. Factories and mills were built amidst existing homes where labor was abundant. New tenements were often sandwiched between the grim red-brick walls of the factory, and more tenements surrounded the factories. City planning concerned little more than compacting housing near the factory. Nothing could be done to relieve the congested existence of working families until transportation became available to reduce the density, and wages were sufficient to use any new conveyances.

The horse-driven coaches introduced in the sixteenth century were a rare and expensive luxury, and the roads in most cities were unsuited for wheeled carriages until late in the eighteenth century. Coal and other goods were transported on pack horses; people mostly walked. Ships and barges provided the major vehicles of transport, and rivers were the natural highways of inland commerce. The great centers of population arose at the most convenient ports, and it was natural for industry to develop at the same sites. Inland cities could become industrialized only when canals or rail made it possible to haul the raw materials and ship out finished products.

THE RAILWAY

James Watt patented the concept of "steam engines which are applied to give motion to wheel carriages," but several decades passed before George Stephenson and others made steam-driven rail travel a practical reality. Stephenson's engine, *The Locomotion,* traveled at 5 to 6 miles per hour on the level, and a commercial line, the Stockton and Darlington Railway Company, began carrying coal and passengers in 1825 (Figure 15-1). Five years later the Liverpool and Manchester railway proved the value of rail travel, and a new era in transport dawned. That same year, 1830, the South Carolina Railroad introduced steam locomotion to America.

New rail lines were started and soon formed a network over Europe

Figure 15-1   The opening day of the Stockton and Darlington Railway, September 27, 1825. *The Locomotion*, driven by George Stephenson, races a coach. *(From a painting by Terence Cuneo.)*

and America. By 1850, more than 9000 miles of track had been laid in the United States, and in 1869 the continent was linked by rail. Food and goods produced in the West could be easily shipped by rail to the eastern cities and then by ship to the ports of Europe.

New industries were no longer completely restricted to sites where coal or ores were abundant or where ships or barges could transport the finished products. The railway soon opened vast new areas to industrialization.

The large river valleys were most accessible, and such areas provided sites for many of the new industrial centers—sites where water was ample and coal and ores of all kinds could be carried by barge or rail. It was in these poorly ventilated valleys that the smoke of industry, railroad engines, and homes was most foul and decades later drew the world's attention to air pollution.

Locomotives with their black plume of sulfurous smoke trailing behind introduced a new blight upon the rural landscape; furthermore, unlike the tranquil waterways of canals winding through broad valleys, railbeds were slashed into the hills and mountains, leaving ugly scars. The immediate popularity and economic gains of the rail stimulated a rapid profusion of lines throughout every industrial country; railways soon crowded into the major cities from every direction, carrying noise and smoke. The dense smoke was of particular concern in the giant rail terminals, where it persisted to blend with the city's chimney and factory smoke to form a tenacious blanket clothing the area. The congestion surrounding the terminals provided a stimulus for improving transit within the cities which was to have permanent consequences on the urban environment. Immediate problems were resolved with little attention to the long-term environmental costs. In London, it led to the world's first underground rail system, opened in 1863, and to the more revolutionary deeper underground "tubes," opened between 1887 and 1890, which only coincidentally proved to be an excellent long-term solution. More people than ever before could work in the cities and live in the outskirts. The human environment improved largely with the advent of electricity.

Intercity travel was confined mostly to foot until the practicality of the electric railway was demonstrated at a Berlin exhibition in 1879. Shortly before then, in 1873, fixed electricity was used to turn cables and pull cable cars in San Francisco. Electricity soon replaced horse-drawn carriages and trams in the larger cities.

Electricity made travel within the city practical and inexpensive. Walking distances no longer limited the size of factories. Factories and mills could greatly increase in size, and workers were no longer confined to the squalid, soot-laden filth of the immediate factory environment.

As railways came to ring the metropolis, commuters had only to be concerned with the walking distance to the nearest railway station. By 1900, rail transit provided inexpensive and fast, if not comfortable, transportation extending many miles beyond the city's industrial heart.

Suburbs, or actually small new towns in themselves, were developed and spaced conveniently a few miles apart along the railroad lines. The workers were now able to move as far from the factory as they could afford into a cleaner, more pleasant environment.

The transit systems were often promoted by land speculators, electric power corporations, or transit magnates themselves. Perhaps the developers benefited the most, but for the right price, the workers could escape the sooty drabness of their tenements.

In southern California, the Pacific Electric Railway Company was highly effective in initially uniting the over 70 separate, mostly rural communities which once made up what is now essentially Los Angeles (Figure 15-2). Beginning at the turn of the twentieth century, the railway provided fast, inexpensive transportation that contributed substantially to

Figure 15-2 The Pacific Electric Railway, which provided fast, efficient transportation to the Los Angeles area. *(From* Ride the Big Cars, *by Spencer Crump. Photo courtesy of Spencer Crump.)*

the basin's initial settlement; similar railways operated effectively in Cleveland and many other larger cities.

The railway's success was short-lived. As early as 1919 the company's president, Paul Shoup, feared the inroads of the automobile when he referred to the "desperate situation of the electric lines in California." He complained bitterly that the rail lines were being taxed while the government was subsidizing the highways.

Once a patchwork of new cities emerged along the railroad landscape, it was not long before the expanding population began to ring the rail stations with ever denser numbers. Particularly in the already large, congested cities, the application of electricity to railways expedited the widening perimeter of the factory community and the ultimate fusion of once distant towns.

Barely into the twentieth century, the dizzy spiral of transportation and urban growth had begun. Land speculators needed the railroad to transport people to their new developments. The railroad needed land speculators to extend the city's boundaries to ensure sufficient passengers to support their investment. Customers were needed both for the land and the transportation. An expanding economy demanded an expanding population. Mumford cites the example of the philosophy of estimating the need for new subways in New York. All transit lines were laid to the objective point, Manhattan, to add to its real estate value. The value of Manhattan property would increase so long as the surrounding population increased. The same thing happened in London, whose subway was largely financed by land developers seeking material economic gain.

People have always relished a place in the country, even when there was some risk in going beyond the city walls. The railroad brought reality to such dreams when it made possible the suburb. The suburban dream was elusive from the start. As the city crept nearer the suburb, encroaching and ultimately engulfing it and destroying the rural flavor, the qualities that originally made the suburb attractive were lost. Urban congestion soon extended into the surroundings; but because of a lower population density, transportation became even more difficult. Soon the suburbs evolved their own suburbs as the industrial city spawned ring after ring of bedroom cities serving the initial core. Central city had stretched into the suburbs, and the residents had to migrate to even more distant bedrooms to escape, like a giant amoeba leaving behind its decaying remains. The railroad no longer kept pace.

The reasons for its failure are well known. Railroads found it more profitable to ship goods than people, and people found it more convenient and comfortable to travel by automobile. The transition was almost too fast to be noticed.

THE AUTOMOBILE

Development and Dependency

When Frank Duryea drove his first American car down the streets of Springfield, Massachusetts in 1893, no one foresaw the full consequences (Figure 15-3). But the same year, bicyclists in America induced Congress to appropriate $10,000 to start a Bureau of Road Inquiry to pursue the development of bicycle paths. The highway spiral began even before there were cars to use the roads.

From the nation's earliest days, Americans recognized the importance of roads in uniting the states and strengthening the union. The Philadelphia and Lancaster turnpike road, all 64 1/4 miles of it, completed in 1795, was the first long stretch of broken stone and gravel to surface the United States. A few years later, in 1808, Secretary of the Treasury Albert

Figure 15-3 The Duryea automobile that introduced a new means of practical transportation to the world. *(Automobile Manufacturers Assn., Detroit, Mich.)*

Gallatin issued a report urging "early and efficient aid of the Federal Government" in road building. The rationale of federal aid was based largely on the interests of national defense. Napoleon had used the same argument for promoting a modern network of roads in Europe between 1804 and 1814, and road promoters attempt to justify their goals the same way today.

With increased travel and transport on roads, the dust stirred up by horses, carts, and carriages became a serious nuisance. Dustless, concrete roads were introduced in Austria in 1850, and asphalt roads came into wide use in the 1860s to supplement the cobblestone streets of the larger cities and dirt roads of the country. Several states and counties were beginning to surface the dusty roads in the early 1800s, but when the railway boom hit in the 1840s, the effort waned. Much of the nation's gravel roads fell into disrepair after 1850, but highway programs were revived in the 1890s, just in time for the Duryea and many other automobiles that soon followed.

Now the dust became more than a nuisance. It was blinding and dangerous to drivers. At first protective clothing and dust palliatives were used, but as the number of car owners mounted, the dust was attacked with stone, brick, concrete, and other paving materials. Even by 1914 the nation had only 1500 miles of brick pavement, and insignificant amounts of wooden plank, concrete, or asphalt for the 1,800,000 motor vehicles in operation, although there were 71,376 miles of dirt and gravel roads. By 1964 this had grown to about 3,500,000 miles of road for 90 million registered automobiles.

With reasonable roads to drive on, the automobile population soared from some 4192 units in 1900 to 65,000 in 1908 and 187,000 in 1910. Everyone began manufacturing automobiles: bicycle and wagon makers (Studebaker); gas-engine manufacturers (R. E. Olds); plumbing manufacturers (David Buick); birdcage makers (Pierce-Arrow Company); machine-shop owners (Dodge); and many less successful entrepreneurs.

The tremendous stimulus to automobile production was fostered by the enthusiastic public demand for them. There was only the briefest period during which the automobile was exclusively a novelty for the wealthy. The dream of the low-priced car was realized in astonishingly short order. Two factors favored the rapid distribution of cars: a standard of living sufficiently high so many could afford a car, and the propensity among Americans in business to think in terms of a mass market—a concept unique to the United States.

Henry Ford with his "Tin Lizzie" in 1907 was the first to circumvent the expensive wooden, handcrafted framework prevalent at the time and succeed in producing a low-priced durable car. His assembly-line methods and use of steel enabled him to retail the Model T at $850 in 1908, when 5986 units were sold. He gradually lowered the price to $360 8 years later and achieved sales of 577,036 cars. In 1920, 2 million automobiles were produced. Automobiles had clearly arrived, and there was no turning back, whatever the demands upon resources were to become, or what the ultimate environmental consequences.

The popularity of the automobile, with the need for such ancillary activities as road building and petroleum production, had far-reaching consequences that led ultimately to dramatic social changes. The United States became gradually more dependent on the automobile, not just for transport but as a significant component of the economy. The automobile industry provided a major market for the nation's steel and rubber; shipment of raw materials and finished products constituted a substantial part of railway markets, and highway construction and maintenance now occupies 10 percent of the nation's labor force. Land speculators sometimes make more money from highways than do contractors. Chains of roadside restaurants and motels are linked to the future of the highway. Virtually every business uses trucks or cars. Automotive businesses alone account for 13 percent of the gross national product. When all the satellite industries are considered, about 1 out of every 5 people in the United States is directly economically dependent on the automobile—about the same number as engaged in producing the nation's food. From a symbol of affluence, the automobile had become the substance of the American economy and an integral component of the human environment.

America's love affair with the automobile has led to a distressingly unhealthy situation. Although it may provide a convenient means of transportation, the automobile is extremely inefficient in moving people. The American Transit Association estimates that the automobile can carry some 1575 passengers per hour on a single traffic lane. This compares with 9000 on buses, 40,000 on local subway trains, and 60,000 in express subways using the same amount of space.

Automobile-related Air Pollution

Meteorological Characteristics   One of the most conspicuous dangers of automobiles began permeating the eyes and lungs of Los Angeles urbanites during World War II. As it encroached over the entire region, pollution from the city's auto exhausts gradually shrouded the once clear atmosphere.

For many years, the notion prevailed that the situation was unique to Los Angeles. A gentle breeze almost continually blows off the Pacific Ocean, backing the smog-laden air against the mountains surrounding the basin. The condition is aggravated by frequent temperature inversions, where a layer of warm air settles over the lower, cooler air and prevents the smog from dispersing or escaping aloft. When the world's greatest agglomeration of automobiles and suburban traffic began spewing their exhaust wastes into this atmospheric deadend, disaster was imminent.

Circumstances in Los Angeles were highly conducive to air pollution, but many of the same conditions existed in other cities around the world, which soon were wrestling with the same problem. Like most fuels, gasoline does not burn completely. The unburned components include various hydrocarbons, aldehydes, particulate matter, and oxides, together with carbon monoxide and nitrogen oxides, which are formed by the high temperatures of combustion. These wastes pass into the atmosphere through crankcase vents, the exhaust system, or by simple evaporation.

Once in the atmosphere, many of the chemicals are acted upon by light energy, which initiates photochemical reactions that produce secondary pollutants. Most significantly, light energy breaks up the nitrogen oxides in the air to release an atom of oxygen that combines with molecular oxygen to produce ozone (O_3). The remaining nitrogen oxide combines with some of the hydrocarbons to form peroxyacetyl nitrate (PAN). This photochemical pollution is often more toxic than the better-known sulfur dioxide or particulate pollution largely associated with industry. Like other types of pollution, photochemical pollution adversely affects the health and welfare of people, property, and plants. The precise degree of this effect or the concentrations of a pollutant causing it are difficult to establish.

Human Health Effects   Considering first the effects on human health, the variables are enormous. Air pollution varies from day to day and place to place. It varies in concentration and duration of exposure. The combinations of pollutants vary, as do their additive or synergistic effects. The effects on individuals will vary with their sensitivity, which in turn will vary with their predisposition and physiology from day to day. A weak or asthmatic individual, or one with respiratory ills, will be more sensitive than a healthy individual. The very young or old are more sensitive than individuals over 6 and under 60. Also, some degree of resistance may develop with successive exposure. When evaluating the effects of air pollution on humans, all these factors should be considered.

Eye irritation is clearly the most perceptible effect of photochemical air pollution. Although no permanent eye injury has been attributed to air pollution, its stinging, eye-smarting annoyance is sufficient to warrant action. Formaldehyde and PAN in combination are largely responsible for eye irritation, but the exact chemical remains a mystery. Other parts of the body are unaffected by contact. The greatest impact is through inhalation.

We breathe in about 360 cubic feet of air every day, and with it all the contaminants of the air pass through our respiratory tract and into our lungs. Most of the particulate chemicals will be absorbed by the mucous coating and cilia; the soluble gases will be largely absorbed in the trachea. The gases not captured along the way pass into the air sacs, or alveoli, of the lungs (Figure 15-4). Much of this is expired out again, but enough of the pollutants can be captured to be dangerous.

Although no definite cause-and-effect relation has been demonstrated between an air pollutant and disease, some relation appears to exist. Lung cancer, for instance, has increased steadily over the past 50 years, and the incidence is greatest in the larger cities where pollution is most intense. Also, some of the pollutant components, such as the benzopyrenes, are known to be carcinogenic, and concentrated exhaust chemicals have been demonstrated to cause cancer in mice.

Chronic bronchitis and emphysema are also becoming more frequent. *Chronic bronchitis* is an inflammation of the lining of the bronchial

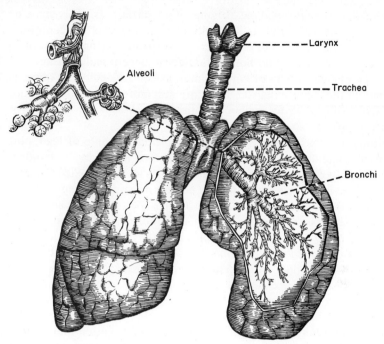

Figure 15-4 The human respiratory tract showing the alveoli, in which oxygen is exchanged for carbon dioxide in the blood.

tubes. When the bronchi are inflamed, air flow becomes difficult, sometimes putting a strain on the heart. The inflammation may be caused by bacteria, smoking, or climatic factors. Air pollutants probably do not cause diseases directly, but some, especially ozone, aggravate them.

Emphysema occurs when the fine membranes forming the walls of the alveoli in the lung break down. The reduced surface area available to absorb oxygen causes extreme difficulty in getting enough air to function normally. Breathing becomes more and more of an effort, sometimes putting a fatal stress on the heart. Emphysema is aggravated by ozone to such an extent that air pollution–control officials advise people with this malady to move out of Los Angeles or other areas where similar pollution conditions prevail.

Carbon monoxide (CO) is an acknowledged killer; it accounts for 47 percent of our air pollution by weight. At least 90 percent of it comes from the automobile. Once absorbed through the lung, carbon monoxide is preferred to oxygen by the red blood cells. Large doses are fatal, but the effects of small doses are not clear. Since carbon monoxide substitutes for oxygen in the hemoglobin, the heart must pump harder to provide the body with sufficient oxygen. The lower amount of oxygen dulls reactions and mental responses, making driving more hazardous. This may be caused by as little as 10 parts per million for 8 hours—a concentration common to almost any major city. Carbon monoxide concentrations of 50 parts per million for over an hour can affect judgment and hearing.

The combined effects of carbon monoxide, PAN, ozone, hydrocarbons, and all the other exhaust wastes are still more obscure, but major steps have been taken to reduce pollutant emissions while waiting for research to provide some of the answers.

Automobile exhausts also contain significant amounts of lead, plus nickel and vanadium. Lead is second only to iron as the most abundant single metallic pollutant of the atmosphere and is far more toxic than iron. It damages the liver, kidney, brain, and central nervous and reproductive systems. Dr. H. A. Schroeder finds that the life-span of mice is shortened when tissue lead concentrations are equal to those found in humans.

Lead is most abundant over such cities as Los Angeles and New York, which have high automobile densities. Motor vehicles that use tetraethyl lead contribute 50 to 75 percent of the lead to the atmosphere; in 35 cities the Public Health Service found a high correlation between lead levels in the air and gasoline consumption.

Vegetation Effects Damage to plants is much better understood. Bronzing and silvering of leaves on vegetable crops were first observed in the Los Angeles area in 1942 (Figure 15-5) and later recognized to have been related to automobile emissions. Leaf destruction rendered the affected crops unmarketable; even where there was no visible damage, growth was stunted on such sensitive plants as lettuce, spinach, endive, and chard. Susceptible crops could no longer be grown profitably. A single day of smog could destroy a season's crop. Ornamental plants such as petunias were also affected; the commercial cut-flower industry was hardest hit, especially the orchid growers who were among the first forced to move out of town. The smog turned the expanding flower buds yellow, and often they dropped before opening. If they opened, the flowers withered and collapsed after only a few days. Ethylene, a hydrocarbon in the exhaust fumes, was responsible for the disease and also caused blossom drop and premature defoliation of carnations, camelias, and roses.

Although ethylene and PAN are responsible for some of the damage to plants, ozone is the most destructive and abundant chemical. Ozone prevents normal plant growth even when the characteristic brown-flecking symptom is absent. Plants exposed to even low concentrations of ozone, such as occur daily in almost every large city, turn yellow and brown prematurely and become senescent earlier than normal. Affected plants are smaller than normal, appear weak, and often have poor color.

Figure 15-5 Air pollution injury to lettuce in the Los Angeles area.

During the 1960s, ozone was found to be responsible for such major plant diseases as grape stipple, weather fleck of tobacco, onion blight, and chlorotic mottle of pine trees.

The sensitivity of pine trees to smog presents a particularly serious dilemma in forested areas in every car-abusing industrial nation (Figure 15-6). Forests are highly sensitive to the sulfur dioxide and fluoride of industry, but they are at least as sensitive to ozone.

The pine-forested mountains rimming the Los Angeles basin to the north and east provide the clearest example of ecosystem disturbance. During the 1950s residents of the mountain communities noticed the older needles of ponderosa pine turning yellow and dropping in the middle of the summer; remaining needles were retained only a year or two rather than the normal 4 or 5 years. Each year the trees became more bronzed and the foliage sparser. By 1955, some 10,000 acres of pine trees were affected; by 1969 ponderosa and Jeffrey pines on over 260,000 acres, involving an estimated 1,298,000 trees, were damaged. No one knew the extent of more insidious injury, or damage to less-prominent species in the ecosystem, many of which might already have been killed by smog. A similar decline has been reported in the National Parks and the forests

Figure 15-6 Needle injury and decline of pine trees characterizing ozone injury.

east of the Central Valley in California where the number of automobiles triples each decade.

In the Eastern United States, still vaster areas are threatened by photochemical pollution. White pine trees, prevalent in the Appalachian Mountains, are highly sensitive to ozone; pine blight is widespread from Eastern Canada to North Carolina. Ozone kills the most sensitive trees or weakens them, which can permit the attack of fungus diseases. The more-tolerant trees survive, but growth is reduced to half or less of normal and the needles are often brown or chlorotic.

As the number of cars increases in Europe, photochemical pollutants threaten crops and forests from Italy to Sweden and Manchester to Moscow. Injury symptoms have been reported from every large city.

It is significant to note that in many areas, such as the Ruhr Valley, the damage to forests caused by sulfur dioxide from industry, power plants, or urbanization, is so severe as to mask any injury from ozone. Damage from one pollutant is sometimes evident only as the still more prominent pollutants are eliminated.

Controlling Automobile-related Air Pollution

The nuisance of air pollution, its adverse effects on health, crops, and forests, and mostly the economic losses it causes, both in terms of dollars and resources, have stimulated efforts to control it. Several measures must be taken to reduce the emissions from automobile exhaust. The first was the positive crankcase ventilation (PCV) system to trap unburned gases and recirculate them through the engine. Such devices, which eliminate 25 to 30 percent of the automotive pollutants, have been required on all cars sold in the United States since 1968.

Engine modifications such as lean carburation, spark retardation, improved engine construction tolerances, lowered compression ratios, and other improved engine design features have further reduced exhaust emissions. Tailpipe devices of either an afterburner or catalyst bed to burn the relatively low quantities of combustible products in the exhaust can reduce emissions still more. By 1970, the automotive industry had achieved an 80 percent reduction in hydrocarbons and a 70 percent cut in carbon monoxide emissions in the new cars compared with 1963 models. By 1977, an additional 90 percent reduction is anticipated. Nevertheless, the controls tend to lose their effectiveness if the engines are not properly maintained. Because pollution-controlling devices reduce the efficiency of engines, gas mileage per gallon is reduced 15 to 30 percent. Another limitation is the supply and expense of the platinum and palladium used in the most successful catalytic control devices.

Equally seriously, the catalytic converters required on 1975 models in the United States add roughly $200 to the cost of the car, and, although some of the pollutants are removed, some people fear that the sulfuric acid added from the operation of the pollution device may contribute more to pollution than it removes.

Such limitations illustrate the disadvantage of considering only short-term solutions to an environmental problem rather than viewing the total interaction in the human environment.

With the attendant costs required to clean up the internal combustion engine to an acceptable degree, it is not surprising that many other mobile means of transportation are being studied.

Electric vehicles almost predate the gas-driven automobile. Commerical production of these started in 1894 with Henry Morris and Pedro Salom's Electrobat. Salom pointed out in 1896 that electric motors had no odors whereas "gasoline motors belched forth from their exhaust pipe a continuous stream of partially unconsumed hydrocarbons in the form of a thick smoke with a highly noxious odor."

The principal roadblock to the popularity of electric power for automobiles was, and still is, the lack of a battery or fuel cell that provides both high power and high energy-storage capability. The vehicle range is too short. The tremendous power needed to recharge batteries might present a further problem if development ever reached that stage, but coal for power might be more available than petroleum.

Steam engines have also been offered as a substitute for internal combustion. The Stanley brothers started producing a stream-propelled vehicle in 1897 using a kerosene burner to heat the boiler, but they were expensive, boilers were prone to explode, and the steam car was given up in the 1920s. Stronger metals and improved technology are reviving the external combustion principle. Such systems emit few pollutants; fuels are burned at atmospheric pressure, minimizing the nitrogen oxide pollutants formed, to turn a fluid, not necessarily water, into a power-producing vapor. Engines are currently being mass-tested.

Gas turbine engines must also be mentioned. Although some are used in the heavy-duty commercial power field, and in racing, turbines operate at continuous high temperatures and thus require the use of heat-tolerant metals or alloys that are not only expensive but unavailable in quantity.

Use of cleaner-burning fuels than gasoline has also been considered. Hydrogen-burning engines may be promising, but large amounts of energy are required to produce the hydrogen. Alcohol might also be used, and recently developed methods to manufacture alcohol from cellulose wastes are bringing the costs down to within reason. This might seem to have the further advantage of being capable of using a renewable resource, that is timber—but unfortunately this resource is already in short supply.

Whatever method, or combination of methods, might be used to reduce emissions, auto pollution is not going to be completely eliminated. Despite a theoretical downtrend in pollution in the 1970s, the increased numbers of automobiles will begin to offset the hypothetical gains by 1985.

Congestion

Equally vital to transportation is the lack of space for all the vehicles. In 1956 the United States Congress failed to recognize the basic problems of transportation and passed a Federal-Aid Highway Act to finance road building. The fund pays 90 percent of major interstate highway construction costs. Many of the road segments go through cities where they are used by the bumper-to-bumper commuter traffic; they led only to ever-widening rings of suburbs around the cities. As the suburbs have grown, the number of cars has increased. This in turn has increased traffic and the demand, mostly by highway planners, for more roads. The added roads attract more commuters who use more cars. The new commuters need roads at a rate exceeding that at which roads can be provided for the former residents. This self-defeating highway cycle has already resulted in the conversion to street use of more than a third of the land in 53 United States cities.

Road congestion, and with it traffic congestion, has always been more critical in some regions than others. The worst is in Los Angeles, where fully two-thirds of the land is covered by freeways and roads and streets, parking lots, gasoline stations, automobile salesrooms, private garages, driveways, and other ancillaries to automobiling.

The environmental effect of taking land out of agriculture, paving potential park or recreation areas, or destroying irreplaceable open space, is more critical than is apparent. Further, urban freeways are an economic liability because they remove enormous acreages of business and industry from the tax rolls. This puts a greater tax burden on the remaining businesses, some of which then move out, contributing toward bankrupting the city. Another problem, which may ultimately prove the undoing of the internal combustion engine, and become, incidentally, the solution to its polluting effects, is the rapid depletion of the world's petroleum resources.

A recent survey posed the question of whether or not the automobile was worth the pollution, traffic congestion, 50,000 annual traffic deaths, and displacement of people and property that it cost. Eighty-five percent of the 5000 persons sampled said "yes." As Denis Hayes of the National Urban Coalition points out, "90 percent of all Americans who took vacations last year went by automobile." The advantages of the automobile were considered well worth the costs. In our quest for personal convenience, we remain oblivious to the long-range environmental costs.

Mass Transit

Abolition of the automobile and highways is undesirable and impractical, but more and more cities are looking toward alternatives, particularly mass transit for supplementing the automobile and providing the ultimate solution to practical transportation. The United States has what is perhaps the world's most poorly balanced transportation system. Public transportation is completely absent in many cities and more urban transport systems become bankrupt every year. Intercity rail travel is all but nonexistent in the United States. Only air travel, for those who can afford it, seems adequate, and even here the congestion at the airports of the larger cities and the surrounding traffic are incredible and getting worse.

A balanced system that provides adequate transportation for all the people in a community is desperately needed. Even if an ideal system were developed, however, the public would have to be reeducated to use it. Over the years, we have become slaves to the convenience of the automobile. It has liberated us by making us mobile, much as the railway did over 100 years ago, but in so doing it has created an unhealthy dependency. Few cities have an attitude responsive to commuter travel.

The Bay Area Rapid Transit system (BART) is a billion-dollar experiment in high-speed urban rail travel (Figure 15-7). A central

Figure 15-7 The BART system for rapid urban rail travel in the San Francisco Bay Area. *(BART, San Francsico.)*

computer monitors traffic and dispatches 80-mph trains to meet passenger demand. The trains travel smoothly and quietly. London, Paris, Moscow, and a few other cities have similar effective systems, and most of Europe is served by highly efficient railways, both inter- and intracity. Commuter trains should be economically feasible in areas having dense population corridors such as Washington D.C. to New York; Boston; Philadelphia; and Chicago. Prospects for success in such areas of dispersed populations as Los Angeles, which grew up with the automobile, are discouraging. Here the freeway will continue to play a vital role in transport until fuel resources are depleted or automobile use is discouraged by some form of taxation.

Benefits from the Automobile

Albeit the environmental, economic, and mental perturbations imposed by the automobile, the automobile also opened much of the environment to the people. Roads gave access to such vacation areas as the Adirondacks and the White Mountains, once the exclusive domain of the very rich; they opened the Great Smokies, known only to a few backwoodsmen; and they made Yellowstone Park, the Grand Canyon, and the Canyonlands available to everyone.

For better or worse, the automobile has weakened if not destroyed rural isolation and in so doing has brought a great unity and uniformity to large geographical areas. No community had to be left out of the mainstream of the national economy. It brought the amenities of city life to the country and opened the country to the urbanite.

By providing a substantial economic base, the automobile has contributed substantially to a high material standard of living. Its availability has facilitated the dispersal of populations far beyond the capacity of the railroad, and in so doing has added to the space and privacy individuals are able to enjoy. The automobile more than any other discovery, has added to the scope of the environment available to the average person, and thereby immeasurably enriched the quality of life. At the same time, the automobile has increased human dependency on this form of transport and contributed to the complexity of life. It has contributed markedly to the deterioration of the air we breathe, impairing our health and damaging crops and natural ecosystems. Although improving some aspects of the quality of life, the automobile has also done much toward destroying the quality of the human environment.

CONCLUSIONS

Throughout the ages, we have sought to improve our means of transport to trade and seek new lands. Early modes of horse or river travel had little impact on the environment, but the more recent rail and automotive travel, necessitating vast networks of railbeds and roads, left a lasting mark on the landscape. Transportation during the past century was developed for short-term gains as fast as technology and economics would permit; the total long-range interaction of different means of transport on the quality of the environment was not considered. This was clearly exemplified by the efforts made to control pollutants associated with the automobile by considering only the individual vehicle rather than the total transportation system. Occasional success in nonpolluting mass-transit systems was more coincidental than planned, but as the supply of fuels to power traditional conveyances diminishes, greater concern will likely be given more efficient, less disruptive means of transport.

Once-noted achievements as the 36,000-mile interstate highway system in the United States may become obsolete unless new means are developed to power vehicles. Conceivably, highways might ultimately serve as rights-of-way for more efficient transit systems. Society should consider such a possibility when planning new highways.

SELECTED READINGS

American Association of State Highway Officials. 1965. A story of the beginning, purposes, growth, activities and achievements of AASHO.

Ayres, Edward. *What's Good for GM.* (Nashville: Aurora, 1970).

Boulton, W. H. *The Pageant of Transport through the Ages.* (New York: Benjamin Blom, 1969).

Ellis, C. Hamilton. The Development of Railway Engineering. In C. Singer et al. (eds.). *A History of Technology V.* (Oxford: Clarendon Press, 1958).

Flink, James J. *America Adopts the Automobile. 1895–1910.* (Cambridge, Mass.: MIT Press, 1970).

Forbes, R. J. Roads to c. 1900. In C. Singer et al. (eds.). *A History of Technology V.* (Oxford: Clarendon Press, 1958).

Hayes, Denis. 1971 Can we bust the highway trust? *Saturday Review,* June 5, 1971, pp. 48–53.

National Geographic Society. 1971. As we live and breathe: The challenge of our environment.

Rae, J. *The American Automobile.* (Chicago: University of Chicago Press, 1965).

Schuck, Edward A. 1971. Did you know? *California Air Environment,* vol. 2, no 3, pp. 1–2.

Stone, Tabor R. *Beyond the Automobile.* (Englewood Cliffs: N.J.: Prentice-Hall, 1971).

Treshow, M. *Whatever Happened to Fresh Air?* (Salt Lake City: University of Utah Press, 1971).

Wilcox, D. F. *The Electric Railway Problem.* (New York: Afferton Press, 1921).

Part Three

The Price of Survival

Chapter 16

Happiness Is an Elusive Quality

That humanity at large will ever be able to dispense with artificial pleasures seems very unlikely.

A. Huxley

Much has been written about the quality of the environment, or what is wrong with it, or how it needs restoration, or how the quality of life has deteriorated; but what is this vague, arbitrary, and ambiguous value? What do we really mean by quality? Not only environmental quality, but the total quality of life? And for whom? According to our basic genetic instructions, does life provide less quality than it did 10 years ago? 100 years ago? And what is likely to be the quality of life in future decades with respect to human survival and increasing numbers? What place does quality have in the human environment of tomorrow?

MEASURES OF QUALITY

Biologists describe humans as homoiothermic, omnivorous, gregarious, and imaginative animals with no definite mating season. The implications of this can provide a basis for what we regard as quality. We are homoiothermic, that is, warm-blooded, so adequate shelter is important to our energy budget, and much of our pleasure is derived from the home. We are omnivorous and so can exploit a diversity of foods to provide this energy, and much of life's pleasures are associated with food. We are gregarious; we need social contact with others to achieve identity and security, and from this we derive pleasure. We are imaginative creatures to whom abstract symbolism and the arts provide further pleasure. We have no definite mating season, so we may continually associate with the opposite sex, and children are born at all seasons, which are powerful shaping forces for family, tribal, community, and national ties and life-styles. All contribute to the quality of life.

In attempting to measure quality of life, at least three major and basic groups of needs then must be met: physiological, material or physical, and psychic. We might subdivide the psychic to include such esthetic categories or personal motivating forces of the human psyche as social contact, security, creativity, status, achievement, identity, personal space, crowding, and pollution.

Physical Values

Food Needs   The quality of life depends to the greatest measure on obtaining the basic energy needs of sustenance, the food resources which have influenced the quality of life for most of the world's population from the time of earliest human beginnings. It is true for us and true for every other species in the animal kingdom. Other problems of quality can rationally be considered only after food needs have been met.

Shelter and Material Standard of Living   Once the food needs are met, shelter and the material standard of living might be considered as a second physical measure of quality. This includes largely the availability of material goods, and, together with food resources, is often measured by the gross national product (GNP). GNP, among other things, measures the amount of money spent on consumer goods and services. Despite its limitations, GNP does provide a fair index of the material standard of living. It reflects the production and consumption of such material goods as houses, automobiles, television sets, and clothing.

The GNP concept can be misleading if it is inferred to measure quality in more than a material sense. In a poor country, much of the GNP represents satisfaction of such basic wants as food, shelter, and clothing; but in richer nations, GNP reflects more trivial demands such as for automobiles and air conditioners. It does not measure comfort or happiness, but this concept fails to consider qualities more significant in determining contentment or satisfaction.

Harrison Brown points out that in the richer countries a human being's needs are no longer met by eating 2500 calories and 57 grams of proteins a day, providing simple shelter, clothing, and perhaps a small fire. Programmed genetic energy needs have long since been met and the demands are now learned or behavioral for much of the population, yet dissatisfaction is common. Today we must have tons of steel, copper, aluminum, lead, tin, zinc, and plastics to maintain our newly learned quality of life.

The quality of life might be far better without some of the criteria of the GNP. We might be happier with fewer cars and less roads provided alternatives were available. We might be pleased without the power-consuming neon signs dominating the urban landscape. We could do well without power mowers, motorcycles, and garbage trucks, to say nothing of trail bikes and snowmobiles. Is the pleasure they bring their owners offset by the nuisance afforded those who suffer their presence? As author Garrett de Bell points out: "The quality of our lives is improved by each power plant not constructed near our homes or recreation areas, by each dam not constructed on a river used for canoeing." To this brief list we might add other notes: Quality might be improved by every highway not gouged out of the side of a mountain, every power or transmission line not cutting off the landscape, every high-rise eyesore not erected, every snowmobile not roaring a swath across a once serene alpine meadow, ad infinitum.

The higher the degree of pleasurable experience evoked by a situation or given environment, the more favorable the quality of the environment. Here we run into trouble, however, for no two people will gain the same degree of satisfaction from a given situation. The fortunate achieve satisfaction from their work; others only in leisure. Then, too, psychologically, people vary in the intensity of their pleasure response. Some are satisfied with very little, others are impossible to please. Happiness is an elusive quality. Though we might ever seek happiness through gold, we would never have enough to purchase contentment. There are those who would fail to find happiness in Paradise.

But in many cases, the degree of pleasure achieved is related, perhaps inversely, to the material standard of living. The more we have, the more we want, and the more it takes to achieve some degree of satisfaction. Thus it would appear that our standard of quality as measured by pleasure is in a continual state of flux, rising with every improvement in the material standard of living. Our goals and expectations rise continually with every material gain or improvement. As our threshold of satisfaction rises, our baseline of quality becomes greater. Perhaps the desire for more, or more of what our neighbor has, is innate in us as inferred by the biblical admonition, "Thou shalt not covet thy neighbor's house, thou shalt not covet they neighbor's wife, nor his manservant, nor his maidservant, nor his ox, nor his ass, nor anything that is thy neighbor's."

On a material basis, we judge our own standard of living, often equated to the quality of life, largely in reference to our own group. We compare ourselves, or relate to those with similar backgrounds and incomes. By and large we are no better or worse off than those of comparable means. Yet there are those who devote their lives to accumulating wealth simply because this is what our culture appears to expect. In such a case, one's satisfaction then comes largely from the quest for material riches. Too often, luxury makes one harder to please; sooner or later the pleasures become a burden. Once we have seen the riches and material goods available to some, we develop an insatiable desire to possess them without realizing the negative qualities of attainment. True satisfaction or quality of life lies not in material gains but in the more fundamental psychological values achieved.

Psychological Values

In his book *The Social Contract,* Robert Ardrey discusses psychological values in terms of the hereditary need for certain qualities—not as an immediately inherited character, but as basic genetic factors evolved over the course of hundreds of thousands of years.

Identity, Security, and Stimulation   Ardrey suggests that there exists in all higher animals, including humans, certain basic or intrinsic needs: identity, security, and stimulation. For humans, identity must rank highest among the psychic needs. This would include recognition and achievement. We must know who we are, and others must know who we are. Identifying with a group is important to satisfaction, but identifying to oneself is vital. Both are indispensible though, because self-identity is often best found through a group. Consciously or unconsciously we all belong to some subcult and achieve some degree of identity, or at least recreation—bowling, skiing, tennis, bridge, boating   (Figure 16-1)— through it. This social call rewards us further with warmth, friendship, and approval.

Security is perhaps a less important psychic need, or at least the degree of security needed is most readily achieved. Security seems to rank high only so long as we live in a truly deprived environment not knowing where to sleep or where our next meal will come from. It also ranks high when we find ourselves in a truly alien or hostile environment lacking any familiar features or friends.

It is under such conditions of anxiety or stress that religion becomes particularly important. Religion has had vital security value since an-

Figure 16-1 Self-actuation, as achieving satisfaction and identity through the sport of river running. *(Courtesy of John Ogden.)*

tiquity. Religion reduces amibiguous information to which we are subjected, enabling us to devote our energy to problems more directly related to our survival. Our greatest anxiety has always been what happens after death. Religion explained this, and in doing so, provided a gargantuan measure of security. Religion also explained the wondrous forces of nature, most notably when there was a god for each natural force—rain, wind, fire, sun, etc. As these and other forces were explained more rationally, and life after death was questioned, our strongest security blanket was removed and religion assumed a more nebulous role. The loss of this religious security may leave a psychological gap not easily replaced.

Once we attain a modicum of security, and the modicum needed will differ greatly for every individual, we are quick to reach out for some stimulation to avoid boredom. Such might have been the response of our homonid ancestors eons ago when they reached out from Eden to explore the unknown and hostile African Savanna, and such is the case today when one climbs the treacherous east face of El Capitan or crosses the oceans on rafts of papyrus or balsa.

Recent research using encephalography provides exciting evidence of a need for frequent change in environment for achieving the greatest happiness. The more affluent and secure we become, the further we must reach to relieve boredom, but most basically and significantly, stimulation is the key that unlocks our genetic potential, providing the incentive for new discovery.

Environmental Concerns Environmental quality is sometimes gauged by the amount of pollution or crowding, but this seems to be largely a current suburban middle-class ethic imposed by a cultural "message." Many factors bear more heavily on the quality of life. We have already seen the importance of our most basic needs for food and shelter and the somewhat lesser relevance of material values. As these needs are met, new goals of quality arise.

Jay Forrester in his book *World Dynamics* discusses the quality of life as a function of material standard of living, food, crowding, and pollution. However, crowding and pollution have been imposed only in rather recent times and assume a dominant role only as more basic needs, or measures of quality, are met.

Although they represent but a small part of the total psychic need, Forrester considers that pollution or environmental degradation is most likely to make the greatest contribution in diminishing the quality of life. This need not be the case. It is not the case in the United States despite the smog still shrouding major cities. Reduced use of coal, and the greater pollution control demanded of industry to meet current air quality standards, has substantially reduced the sulfur dioxide and particulate pollution that once characterized every industrial area. There is every likelihood that controls on automobile emissions, and a rising popularity in mass transit, will reduce oxidant pollution in future years.

Rigid water quality standards should improve the condition of those streams and lakes still salvageable, although eutrophication of mountain lakes may persist until adequate technology is implemented.

Unfortunately, environmental concern is not universal, and pollution will no doubt continue to increase on a worldwide basis until the negative message of pollution becomes sufficiently strong to evoke positive action. The newly industrializing countries are far more concerned with production costs and profit than any environmental hazards. Similarly, East European countries and the Soviet Union utilize minimal pollution controls despite stringent air and water quality standards.

The greatest environmental disasters of tomorrow are less likely to spew from the stacks of industry or the exhausts of cars than from the dusts of overgrazed and cropped plains and prairies of the world as they did in the dust bowl of the 1930s (Figure 16-2). Land erosion throughout the ages has been far more serious than any recent pesticide threats and in all likelihood will continue to present a major environmental hazard. Soils the world over are apt to be increasingly overcropped and exhausted as

Figure 16-2   The dust bowl of the central plains of the United States during the 1930s following years of land abuse and draught. *(U.S. Soil Conservation Service.)*

more pressure for food is exerted. As tropical lands become denuded for agriculture, disaster there becomes more imminent.

The degree of crowding provides another psychic measure of quality. It seems that as the world gets more crowded, however, our capacity to tolerate or accept the new condition grows proportionately. Our seeming inherent preference to live in small semi-isolated groups seems readily outweighed by the learned behavior of adjusting to a crowded environment. The population along the northeastern seaboard from Washington, D.C. to Boston is now about 2000 persons per square mile, and many live quite comfortably. Hong Kong has a population density of 13,000 per square mile, yet the quality of life is considered adequate for most. What these figures fail to disclose is that where the populations are densest within these areas, life-styles may be far more dismal than in the more pleasant suburbs. We accept this density because there is no other choice. We live closer together in apartments, but we drive further into the country or hike higher into the mountains to avoid each other, but even here crowds mar the former isolation. As more people seek escape from urban congestion, the same crowd pressure is exerted on the mountains and deserts, and open spaces close fast around us. Thousands now hike the alpine trails in the Swiss Alps or the Canadian Rockies where only hundreds trod a dozen years ago.

If outdoor recreation is available in another decade, the crowds will certainly mar the quality, and the reservations needed will make it more cumbersome and destroy any spontaneity. But we will adapt. Nature has facilitated adjustment by leaving an open-ended information gap for learned behavior in the human DNA program. Our DNA allows greater behavioral flexibility in developmental, or ontogenetic, learning than for any other organism.

Crowding may also be expressed as the amount of geographical space available. This is related to housing density in the city or availability of open or natural areas in the country. Crowding, of course, is also related to the birth and death rate. If no limits are imposed on births, crowding will intensify to impose obvious physical stresses on our resources and psychological stresses influencing the quality of our lives. Possibly crowding would lead to international conflict and nuclear war, but it could just as readily lead to epidemics of disease and frustration in life, as well as the more direct effects of the larger population on depleting food supplies and causing pollution.

Leisure   Studies by psychologist H. F. Harlow with rhesus monkeys show that play in youth is essential to normal development. Studies with other animals show that play is a normal part of the learning process, and the need for it may well be part of our innate heritage. This need may carry over to the adult's need for leisure and recreation, and the availability of these things provides some measure of quality once the more fundamentally inherent requisites have been met. Nevertheless, play cannot be completely equated to happiness, since too much can become an obsession or even a bore. Pleasurable pastimes or experiences to relieve the monotony of routine jobs have become almost a fetish in modern societies in both Europe and America, yet these societies are no happier than others.

Music and art per se are a heritage of the earliest cultures dating from the petroglyphs or pictographs on the walls of primitive cave dwellings. We look to the arts to enhance the enjoyment of the world around us; they remain a vital part of our lives and appear to be part of our genetic makeup, but they seemingly fail to fill our leisure hours.

Snowmobiles, trail bikes, campers, camping, sailing, bowling, and a multitude more activities now fill our leisure hours. Sports such as football and baseball have also become an obsession with many, as has television. Even these are not enough for some who seek escape (or purpose) in alcohol or drugs. Surely it seems that the more opportunities a culture has, the more it must reach out for quality and escape from tedium.

Social Justice

We have seen how the quality of life is determined by basic physiologic needs for food, physical need for shelter, and psychological need for identity, security, and stimulation.

Forrester's criteria of quality plus Ardrey's psychological criteria at first appear to be reasonably inclusive, but as the goals are realized, new dimensions of quality, once never dreamed of, or taken for granted, emerge. Personal freedom is the most vital of these. We have come a long way in determining our own destiny from the early days of universal slavery and more recent era of divine authority. Yet even today, much of the world's population has little choice over its own destiny.

Economist and philosopher Kenneth Boulding calls it *social justice*, the need for personal freedom and justice—the utopian dream where everyone is happy with society. Social justice infers not only that everyone be satisfied, but that wealth be distributed equally. How this might be achieved is beyond the scope of this chapter, but the question should be raised whether or not such "justice" is worth achieving. To what extent does social justice measure quality of life?

Picture a life in which everyone shared the same monetary and social resources regardless of profession or talents, and in which all dwelled in similar standardized apartments furnished almost identically. With everyone having nearly the same income there would be little need for manufacturing a wide range of furniture types, or houses, or providing a wide selection of foods. Our physical surroundings would be monotonous and our life dull. With food and space uniformly shared, the average quality of life might improve, but with no motivation for betterment, there would be no hope for a better than dismal quality of life for anyone. Life for everyone would be raised or lowered to a standard of mediocrity. Such a situation might provide stability and security, but the individual would lack identity and stimulus; very likely no one would be happy. Perhaps an inherent need would be unfulfilled. Some material improvement might be realized in the poorest countries, but the material quality of life would be reduced for many in the richer nations.

Rather, the challenge should be for the poor to achieve greater material gain with no loss in psychic needs, and at no social costs to the richer countries. But it would seem that the more we try to please everyone, the less we please anyone. Social justice must be sought by means other than uniform sharing of resources if we hope to achieve quality in terms of other psychological needs. In order to be happy, we must be able to live and pursue and achieve the values of our choice. Our lives must belong to ourselves.

While striving for universal equality, we achieve only universal frustration. In attempting to unify quality in social justice, we might too easily sacrifice the two most vital psychic needs—identity and stimulation—for security, and the strength and durability of that security might be seriously questioned. We might fight to correct the dullness of inopportunity as readily as the injustice of social inequality.

It looks then as though social justice would inevitably end in personal discontent which in turn might well lead to social injustice. If this were true, the quality of life could never reach a level to satisfy everyone.

Boulding suggests that a competitive relationship exists between justice and freedom. Institution of justice inevitably limits some freedoms to preserve greater freedoms for all. The challenge is to achieve a balance between limited freedom and a degree of social justice, but this becomes increasingly difficult as populations increase in size and complexity.

CONCLUSIONS

Two basic principles emerge. First, as with any group of psychological parameters, the criteria we value highest are those that are most limited. Secondly, the values of quality will differ depending on the stage of social, cultural, and technological evolution of the society. Quality, while perhaps founded on a genetic base, is an intangible, highly subjective value, determined largely by culture. The criteria for judging it will vary with every society as well as among the individuals within the society. Only the most basic needs, such as for food, will be shared universally.

The more advanced or developed the culture, the more of these criteria for quality must be considered. Values unknown to a society can hardly be considered in assessing quality. A primitive society living in an uncrowded environment will be content materially with much less than the modern urbanite, partly because many of the values of modern society are unknown to it.

Only a society possessing social justice, unfettered in pollution, with opportunity for identity and stimulation and ample leisure time, will finally be in a position where we can achieve full satisfaction from life and begin to understand our role in it as an integral part of the environment and the total ecosystem.

SELECTED READINGS

Boulding, Kenneth E. Environment and Economics. In W. W. Murdoch (ed.). *Environment*. (Stanford, Conn.: Sinauer, 1971).

————. *Beyond Economics.* (Ann Arbor: University of Michigan Press, 1968).

Brown, Harrison. 1971 After the population explosion. *Saturday Review,* June 26, pp. 11–13, 29.

Daly, H. E. Towards a stationary state economy. In J. Hart and R. H. Socolow (eds.). *Patient Earth.* (New York: Holt, Rinehart & Winston, 1971).

Forrester, Jay W. *World Dynamics.* (Cambridge, Mass.: Wright-Allen Press, Inc., 1971).

Johnson, Warren A., and John Hardesty (eds.). *Economic Growth vs. the Environment.* (Belmont, Calif.: Wadsworth, 1971).

Marsh, George P. *Man and Nature.* (New York: Charles Scribner, 1864). (Reissued by Harvard University Press. 1965).

Passell, Peter, and Leonard Ross. New York Times Magazine. *In Salt Lake Tribune,* March 12, 1972.

Richter, Peyton E. (ed). *Utopias, Social Ideals and Communal Experiments.* (Boston: Holbrook Press, 1971).

Toffler, Alvin. *Future Shock.* (New York: Random House, 1970).

Chapter 17

The Economics of Growth

So long as unlimited multiplication goes on, no social organization which has ever been devised, no fiddle-faddling with the distribution of wealth, will ever deliver society from the tendency to be destroyed by the reproduction within itself.

Thomas H. Huxley
The Struggle for Existence in Human Society, 1888

The year was 1518. Hernán Cortés set sail from Baracoa, Spain in search of El Dorado to trade and to undertake serving the spiritual welfare of the natives. Incessant wars and a backward agriculture made it imperative for King Charles to take all the riches American could offer. But the actual economic response was unpredictable. An unreliable flow of gold proved no panacea for Spain's financial ills; rather it led to higher taxes and a disastrous inflation. Gold failed to bolster either the economy or the living conditions.

The early participants in the conquest of Latin America had the taste for gold and an adventurous, greedy incentive of promised feudal holdings to drive them. The Spaniard nobles leading the expeditions brought with them the Spanish culture and the royal protocol of the court of Spain. From the very beginning a rigidly class-structured society born of nobility became firmly entrenched in the new land; it was structured first by birth and then by right. The Spanish conquest laid the groundwork for abuse and exploitation in accord with the designs of the Spanish court. The structure of the newly founded society, and the religious beliefs espoused by the Spaniards and imposed upon the native Indians, contributed to the life-styles and economies for future centuries.

ECONOMIC DEPENDENCE

The aristocratic culture of stately splendor and protocol was imposed upon established and homeostatic cultures in the New World with no adjustment for making the new social environment of the Colonies self-sufficient. Resources and wealth of the conquered were stolen, which created an era of economic dependence that limited the quality of life for the vanquished. Subsequent independence severed the alliance with Spain but gained no appreciable change in the social structures. Only the titles of the dominant minority changed. Landlords had to contrive other means for holding the loyalty of persons once subject to them by "right"; economic dependence was a viable method. Economic dependence is as effective today as it was then and continues to be practiced by governments that bind the people through welfare programs, grants, and other financial-assistance mechanisms.

The new nations established throughout America, Africa, and Asia at the expense of the ancient conquered cultures became dependent on the policies and support of Europe. Dependency was achieved when influential interests in the "mother" countries established businesses in the undeveloped country (UDC). (*Less industrialized countries* might be a better term, since the UDC might be better "developed" by some definitions than the DC, or developed country.) Wages paid local labor were minimal. Most of the production was exported because the UDC could not afford to buy much for its own use. The profits might be reinvested in expansion or taken out of the country, but the natural resources were drained from the host country. No capital was accumulated for future growth, and the only profit was temporary, lying in the meager wages paid the workers.

The huge monopolies created by industrialized countries were so big that they continue to dominate the course of economics for the entire country. Exploitation of this type continues to widen the economic gap between the industrialized and nonindustrialized countries. Through this mechanism of economic dependence, 15 percent of the world's population controls 55 percent of the world income.

The dominant religion of Latin America, established by zealous missionaries, contributes further by reinforcing the capacity to believe, teaching the virtue of suffering as a purifying fire to which humans must be subjected as a sign of their abnegation before God; it imbues the people with the value of resigning themselves to whatever life happens to concede—a carryover from the early civilizations of Mesopotamia.

The same principles apply to many of the nonindustrial countries (UDCs) throughout the world. In some, exploitation both from within and without is even more flagrant. In the Philippines, 2.5 percent of the families control 85 percent of the nation's wealth. In Southeast Asia, the French and Dutch controlled virtually all the wealth until recent times, and a minority of their native proteges subsequently have "inherited" the land and wealth.

One is awestruck at the contrast between the "haves" and "have-nots" even within the Latin American countries. The elegant conveniences of the rich neighborhoods stand in shocking contrast to the primitive poverty of the surrounding slums, and leaders have made little effort to improve the real incomes of the people. The preeminent social and economic positions of the wealthy remain almost unquestioned.

Foreign aid by the industrial nations has done little to alleviate the situation. Instead of being directed toward the redistribution of wealth, money is lavishly bestowed on military aid to build armaments in the satellite countries of the underdeveloped world. Money channeled into the domestic economy remains in the dominant hands of the wealthy ruling minority. There is no transfer of wealth from the rich to the poor. Such unequal distribution of wealth, and lack of any mechanism for change, underlies the hopeless quality of life for most of the world.

THE BASES FOR ECONOMIC SYSTEMS

The economic dependency and dilemmas of today go back much further than the Middle Ages. They are basically rooted in changes perhaps 25,000 years old. In those early days, when human numbers scarcely exceeded 100,000, they subsisted on a basic gathering and hunting economy. According to anthropologists Tiger and Fox, humans evolved as hunting animals, and all economic and social values are tied to this heritage: "Tools and deals are the bedrock of human economic behavior." Dealing and exchange, originating with a hunting economy, are sometimes considered as basic part of human nature and part of its uniqueness. Humans needed spears, clubs, or arrows for the hunt and tools to prepare the prey. Some people were far better toolmakers than others, some were most skilled at making weapons, others excelled in tracking, and others were superior hunters. To take advantage of this inherent variation of talents, some mechanism of exchanging services was necessary, and a social organization was needed to effect it.

All early economies developed by sharing, and by taking advantage of the services of others. Men were provided for by women, essentially in exchange for sex, protection, and certain material needs. Women helped each other in gathering herbs, preparing skins and food, and caring for the children. Men helped each other in the hunt and in defense against enemies.

All this sharing and exchange of responsibility involved bargaining, calculations, assessment of odds, speculation, making deals, controlling distribution, making investments, and accumulating capital—the bases for any economic system.

In hunting and gathering societies, everyone had a job but also ample hours of leisure. But humans became increasingly efficient. They learned how to domesticate animals, raise crops, and congregate in larger numbers to enjoy the advantages of companionship, but with agriculture and urbanization came unemployment, unknown among hunters. Wealth became concentrated in the hands of a ruling class to a far greater degree than was ever known in a hunting or gathering society. Centuries later, when industrial society was superimposed on agriculture, leadership passed to the industrialists, and wealth became concentrated in the hands of still fewer. A hunting and gathering ancestry may have predisposed us to expect satisfaction from collecting food, and now only a few could realize this goal. The societies that developed subsequent to these early types have retained their counterparts, but the jobs available in modern economic systems may be remote from natural inherent human needs, and inadequately sublimate for them. True satisfaction from work, or goal realization, is then not realized. Indeed, satisfaction is rarely considered as a major value in modern economics.

ECONOMIC GROWTH

Civilizations have largely equated growth and prosperity for so long that it is difficult to envision a favorable quality of life without economic growth. Growth is deeply entrenched in our economic thinking. When the United States was sparsely populated, growth made sense. It permitted exploitation of the vast resources, provided a phenomenal increase in wealth, and facilitated a reasonably equitable distribution of wealth, but in a crowded environment of diminishing resources, growth has critical side effects, and an increasing portion of what passes for progress is illusory. Our fundamental philosophy of growth for growth's sake, with its growing consumption, must be reevaluated. Mumford calls it techno-logical compulsiveness, where we submit meekly to every new technological advance without questioning. Instead of accelerated consumption and the production of more and more inferior and disposable merchandise to burden the growing piles of junk, society might concentrate on achieving psychological satisfaction; in other words, improving the total quality of life.

The growth incentive persists in virtually every modern society. Socialism, communism, and capitalism all are obsessed in their quest for more material commodities for more people. All equate growth and prosperity with quality. China might provide an exception, since subsistence needs have not been completely achieved.

A typical growth pattern, whether organismal or economic, starts slowly then gradually accelerates, eventually slowing as limiting factors build up. These limitations can include crowding or poisoning from the accumulation of wastes, lack of space, saturation of the market, or the exhaustion of materials needed for growth. They can limit economic growth as well as the growth of natural biological systems. The growth curve is especially apparent in the United States, where economic growth exploded rapidly following the initial settlement from Europe. The same pattern was followed by virtually all earlier civilizations. Although it is still debatable, there are signs that we have reached the crest of the sigmoid curve of economic growth.

Several factors have contributed to slowing economic growth in the United States. One of the strongest has been the competition from abroad to which a number of internal problems contribute. Economist R. L. Heilbroner lists three other factors: the dependency on defense expenditures to maintain growth; the inherent instability of capitalism; and the third, the accelerating government expenditures required to maintain growth.

Mumford espouses in his *Pentagon of Power* how the economies of both capitalist and communist countries have been bolstered artificially by the effective device of keeping the overproductive technology in full operation.

Diminishing resources, energy, and the expensive technology required for pollution control have begun to slow the economy in some parts of the United States, but not in other countries where a higher priority is given economic growth. Economist John Fisher finds that "the competitive free enterprise system apparently has gone dead on us." In the future, the greatest economic and organizational slowdown will come when the complexities of an overpopulous society overwhelm the political machinery, and society has become so interdependent that failure at any point could trigger total collapse as in any other biological system. Economic input is a vital part of the total ecosystem information grid, and a faulty "message" is entirely capable of disrupting it.

GROSS NATIONAL PRODUCT

Economic growth has become the standard measurement for progress, a benefit for which to strive that warrants any social cost. The gross national product (GNP), representing the value of everything produced, is a reasonably easy way to quantify and measure growth, yet the criteria are often erroneous.

Specifically, GNP is the sum of personal and government expenditure on goods and services (whether the environmental impact is beneficial or harmful) plus savings and expenditure on investment. The composition of GNP is not fixed. In other words, the components of GNP may vary. Services, and goods with reduced material content, may replace highly consumptive goods. A stable economy requires that savings must equal investment. Since there must be a profit on the investment, the GNP must grow commensurate with the profit required to justify investment; although if government assumed full control of investment and did not require a profit, perhaps the GNP could remain stable without profit.

Growth of both population and the material standard of living appear vital to a growing GNP. In order for GNP to grow, the consumption must increase, often through an increase in population. If the population fails to increase, then a stable GNP can be maintained primarily by an increase in consumption or demand. Presently, about 2 percent of the growth in the United States is caused by population increases and 1 percent by the increased consumption for an "improved" standard of living.

The common use of GNP as a measure of prosperity is misleading; the annual product, that is, the ratio of GNP to total population (GNP/P) has the same inherent faults. This value, or income, depends largely on the population (P). If the population is growing faster than the GNP, the economy is actually declining, with more people getting poorer each year. Human reproduction in poor nations is roughly twice that of rich nations. As the death rate in the nonindustrial countries is reduced, these nations will continue to get poorer, with little hope of raising their standard of living, at least as measured by GNP. Even though the GNP may be growing at roughly 4 to 5 percent annually in rich and poor countries alike, the rapid population growth rate in the latter means that the per capita income is growing slowly or not at all, and the gap between rich and poor countries widens (Figure 17-1).

The gap may once have passed unnoticed, but modern communication technology has now lent knowledge to millions of the more luxurious material quality of life existing in the United States and Europe. Naturally the long-deprived and unaware majority of the world population now want more—a "better" life which can be achieved only by

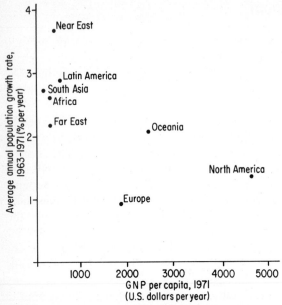

Figure 17-1 Comparison of the population growth rate with material wealth (as measured by GNP) of industrial and nonindustrial countries showing the lower per capita countries having the higher rate of population growth *(Based on U.S. Arms and Disarmament Agency World Military Expenditure, 1971).*

economic growth. In their emulation, why should the less industrialized countries accept the physical and ecological impossibility of trying to catch up? Rich and poor nations alike are reluctant to accept the finite nature of growth.

One solution to raising per capita incomes in many of the less developed countries lies in lowering birth rates. Money spent toward this end have been shown by economist Stephen Enke to provide by far the greatest return on investment of any course of action. The reason is simply that it costs fewer resources to prevent a birth than to produce a person's share as a consumer in a national output.

Governments might well develop programs to provide information on birth control, make the necessary devices available at clinics, and even subsidize retail sale of contraceptives. They can also educate through the advertising media to modify attitudes. However, social pressures in many nonindustrial countries are often so strong in favor of having large families that even an active campaign will not change existing attitudes. Also, governments unwittingly often encourage larger families through antiabortion laws, free schooling, public housing, and tax incentives. Economic incentives would provide the greatest stimulus for limiting populations and raising the per capita wealth.

Shortcomings of GNP as a Measure

It is important to recognize that the composition of GNP can be far more significant than the GNP per se. Growth is not always adversely related to the environment. If GNP were largely composed of services and environmental improvement costs, such as money spent for reforestation or parks, a high GNP could be desirable. Similarly, money spent for pollution control represents an environmental gain. To achieve this, values must be shifted from desirability of material to esthetic gain as a measure of quality. Perhaps a new term might be coined to denote that part of the GNP that represents gross environmental improvement (GEI).

While the GNP measures many things, it fails to measure many others. It measures the amount of money spent on consumer goods and services; investment goods including producers' plant and equipment, housing, changes in business inventories; expenditures by governments at all levels; and net exports. But it is not a measure of personal freedom, nor a measure of the health of a nation. It measures the rate of natural resource depletion but does not reflect what is left. It does not reflect the esthetic or psychic values or satisfaction. As biologist author Paul Ehrlich points out, it "does not measure the stability of the environment system upon which life depends." Nor does GNP measure its interaction or dependency on the ecosystem information grid as discussed in Chapter 2. In no way does it measure the quality of life though it may reflect material gains (or losses). It has no bearing on the social gains of a society.

GNP does provide a general measure of the amount of production and consumption. This can be considered the "throughput" because it represents the amount of materials passing through the economy and is derived partly from production of goods from reservoirs of raw materials.

Throughput, or GNP, has been classically considered as desirable and to provide a valid means of measuring the success of an economy; yet it more accurately measures the cost of maintaining the capital stock. GNP reflects the rate of resource consumption or depletion, and should be minimized, not lauded. Kenneth Boulding suggests calling the GNP the "gross national cost."

The greater the economy, the more it costs to support it. There is more to decay, so more must be produced simply to maintain it. Therefore, the rate of increase of GNP would be expected to decline as the actual per capita GNP increased. Boulding shows this when he plots the logarithm of the rate of increase of per capita GNP for the period 1900–1960 against the actual GNP itself. The countries fall into two main groups: poor and rich. The poor group of countries are not growing in per capita wealth as fast as the rich countries. In fact, they are not going anywhere. On a per capita basis, their GNP is declining.

Although growth in GNP may still be a good thing in poor countries, it may be bad for the rich nations. Extra GNP in a poor country, assuming it is equitably distributed over the population and not solely to the rich, represents satisfaction of such basic wants as food, clothing, and shelter. A rich country is saturated with material goods, and extra GNP represents satisfaction of more trivial wants. As ever more trivial wants are fulfilled, an extra unit of GNP costs more than it is worth.

In more-developed countries, the richer a country is, the slower it grows economically. According to Boulding, if the trend were to continue, it appears that "all these countries would stop economic growth when they are two or three times richer per capita than the United States is now."

The GNP in the United States has gone up 40 percent since 1958, but are we any more comfortable or happy? Growth has improved income but not happiness of either rich or poor. Boats, campers, and vacations abroad do not guarantee happiness, nor do they assure satisfaction of basic psychosocial needs.

The Linkage of GNP to Environmental Destruction

It is the material content of GNP that can be the most important to environmental destruction. Economist John Hardesty shows how given our present technology and social systems, most components of GNP are in some way linked to environmental destruction, a fact that should give further impetus to recognition of programs that would decrease the GNP. Because a high GNP reflects a high rate of resource depletion and pollution, it would seem obvious that we should demand a low or even zero GNP growth. Automobile production, for example, possibly accounts for 10 percent of the GNP. It provides a prime example of the pollution that may be thought to represent the GNP. The more auto production (and the higher the GNP) the more smokey wastes are released from steel production and the more toxic gases that are exhausted from the completed product. Still more pollution and environmental degradation result from the traffic on the highways and building of highways into the landscape. Finally, discarded automobiles provide a disposal problem which contributes further to pollution.

STEADY-STATE ECONOMY

To minimize consumption, it would be most desirable to maintain the GNP at a steady state where the throughput is constant and as low as possible. A *steady state* implies a theoretical condition in which growth in wealth and population will have ceased. Although the real worth may be moving toward a steady state, it could never be fully realized, since people die and materials wear out. Consequently, stocks (i.e., inventories) must be maintained by a continuing production, and births must be equal to deaths and consumption. Nevertheless, to move toward a steady state would require that goods have a greater life expectancy or durability and that production of new goods be minimized. Production inputs, of course, are taken from the environment at the expense of nonrenewable natural resources. At the other end, an equal amount of matter and energy is returned to the environment as waste. The slower the cycle, and the more that can be recycled, the longer the resources will last and a favorable standard of living maintained.

The world is finite and the ecosystem is a steady state. Since the human economy is a subsystem of the total ecosystem, it follows that ultimately the subsystem must also achieve a steady state. Even if the disadvantages of accelerating material growth were recognized and accepted, the formidable problem of slowing it down would still remain. Although the GNP growth is already slowing in a few of the most affluent countries, it continues to accelerate in others, and all nations strive for economic expansion. If the economy is to slow further, the underlying factors contributing to economic growth must be understood, and society must recognize the advantages of a stable GNP.

The stationary state would put less pressure on the environmental resources and more on the moral and psychic resources. Economic growth would then be in nonmaterial goods such as leisure and services.

Existing economies now have the reverse of stabilization, which means the flow of production is maximized and services are minimal. Goods are made to wear out faster because of a policy of planned obsolescence. Such a policy is equivalent to a policy of maximizing depletion and pollution.

As Kenneth Boulding has been pointing out since 1949, the central concept should not only be the flow of wealth or production, but the stock of wealth, or capital. The important issue then becomes the distribution of wealth, not the production.

Distribution of Wealth

Two types of wealth distribution must be considered: the disparity of wealth among the people of a nation, and the disparity between the industrial (rich) and nonindustrial (poor) countries. Wealth always has been inequitably apportioned in the advanced societies. Inequities are only slightly less in more primitive societies.

In an evolutionary or biological sense, wealth might be considered a measure of success, or a better adaptation for survival. The richer, or more "advanced," segments of a society are in a better position to occupy the niches of the species. They can better compete and better exploit the environment.

As affluence is gained, however, an increasing concern seems to arise for less-fortunate, or less-adapted, members of society. There is increasing concern for other members of the species. Pragmatically, a few of the most materially successful nations have now reached a sufficient degree of affluence to reflect some concern for less-industrialized countries. Though they might be willing to share the wealth even if it meant reducing their own standard of living, they would more reasonably hope to improve conditions in the less-developed countries (UDCs) without decreasing their own wealth noticeably.

It has been suggested that the first step should be to slow down our own economy. This is taking place unwittingly as the reserves of natural resources diminish regardless of overt efforts to avoid it. The desirability of such a slowdown has been questioned because it is contended that the UDCs need our technology to improve their own circumstances. A second argument against limiting growth is that there is no indication that restricting growth in some nations would benefit others. The only benefit might be derived as the waning industries of the DCs were replaced by prosperous new mills of the developing nations whose exports might bring to them new dollars. Limiting economic growth in the DCs might more rationally be justified to prolong our supply of resources and enhancing our chances for economic and ecological survival.

Global economic equity might appear to be best achieved by increasing direct financial aid to the poor countries, for example by the developed nations giving up 10 to 20 percent of their GNP to the developing countries as suggested by Lord C. P. Snow of England and academician Andrei D. Sakharov of the U.S.S.R. Yet this is impractical logistically and administratively; further, the numbers of people in the UDCs are so great that the world's wealth would not go far.

Nevertheless, a major shift in the world's wealth is already taking place from the oil-consuming nations—whether rich or poor—to the oil producers. Nations having to spend more money for oil have less for other needs or luxuries. Although this may not be critical in the richer countries, it may mean starvation or even bankruptcy to poor nations lacking sufficient salable commodities.

Many of the UDCs possess the potential for great wealth in their untapped natural resources. Equitable payment for these resources might greatly improve the balance of wealth among nations. Heavy taxation against the resource consumers would be especially effective in distributing wealth and more significantly slowing the resource consumption consistent with ecological harmony. Yet it would not necessarily improve the balance of wealth within the nation. As is well known, the wealth in many of the poor countries is frequently concentrated in the hands of a few. Past experience shows that those controlling it are more likely to enrich their own holdings than help the more needy.

Leisure

The real wealth of a nation or a people is the time of its members. Time may be used to produce wealth or it may be used in esthetic or educational pursuits, or leisure. Western civilization often regards wealth as the result of productive work and leisure as inefficiency because it does not contribute to the stock of capital goods in the usual context. But leisure connotes purposefulness of choice; it certainly includes recreation, but it may also include constructive effort. It means expanded choices for such time-intensive activities as friendships and reflection. Leisure may therefore also contribute to the quality of the human environment by substituting time activities for material-intensive activities.

Leisure time and activities are increasing, but not always to the benefit of the environment. Frequently, leisure utilizes material goods such as trail bikes, snowmobiles, boats, autos, airplanes, etc., which are highly consumptive and often directly damaging to the environment. Consumptive costs are minimized when leisure time is used in activities such as reading, conversation, or listening to music, or hiking, fishing and swimming—but even here, large amounts of land and water are often utilized, and enough feet in limited areas can be as disruptive of the land as a bulldozer.

Replacement of Goods

Ezra Mishan of the London School of Economics argues that advertising is a major contributor to the GNP because advertising, and money spent for it, is used primarily to create wants and dissatisfaction rather than to satisfy existing wants. Advertising maintains excessive levels of demand by creating ever-expanding markets. It also perpetuates behavior inconsistent with ecological balance.

Advertising contributes to replacement of products in stimulating renewal even before things wear out. The undesirability and cost of using poor quality as a basis for stimulating the need for new replacements are obvious.

It has geen suggested that a system of monetary incentives and disincentives (i.e., penalties) might be used to put a premium on durability and a penalty on disposability, thereby reducing the throughput of materials. This could be accomplished through taxes inversely proportionate to the estimated life of the product.

Money spent continuously on replacement luxuries, or new products promoted to achieve status, could better be directed toward leisure, savings, or investment. Money could be directed toward pollution control, recycling diminishing resources, services, and arts. All would reduce consumption of resources while at the same time promoting economic growth and a gross national product measured in environmental protection rather than costs.

Consumption of new products, with any attendant resource depletion, is in the hands of the producer, who determines the range of market goods produced and from which the consumer must choose. In an affluent society, consumption is dictated by a want-creating mechanism promoted by advertising. Advertising points out the goods we lack, stressing or implying the "need" of ownership or achieve status, to keep armpits dry, have a sexy smile, absorb the gas in the stomach, or in essence keep up with the neighbors.

Consumption is further aggravated by our innate quest for identity or status. Wants are rarely met to the extent they are created. The consumers whose wants are out of phase with production buy something they do not want. Affluent people have little choice but to adapt to the prevailing style that is being promoted. Were it not for the producers' ingrained quest for profit and to achieve the growth seemingly demanded by society, there would be no need for continued replacement of goods. Every kind of item could be built to last a reasonable length of time for that item and the kind of consumer it has. No one expects a child to be able to keep a small toy indefinitely, say a water pistol—it will be lost if it isn't cracked open with a brick—but it could still be made to last, and work, for at least a year or two. It shouldn't be deliberately engineered to fail on the fourth filling or the thirtieth trigger pull. Quality could be built into automobiles, appliances, clothing, and most other consumer products, but to do so would suppress continued new sales. Ultimately, product quality will become essential to sustaining our supply of nonrenewable resources.

Psychological Fulfillment as a Substitute for Growth

In wealthy nations, affluence is measured by the welfare of the individual, but it is the relative income that is important to human identity and status, not the actual affluence. Status values come from having something others do not have. This relative income hypothesis stipulates that what matters most is not a person's absolute real income, but position relative to the income structure of society. Our relative status outweighs the value of our purchasing power; we are happy with little so long as our neighbors have less.

Economist Warren Johnson of San Diego State University suggests that slowing economic output or redirecting it to provide greater equity might best be accomplished by encouraging uneconomic but gratifying forms of work that are now largely lacking in industrial societies. This could mean expanding opportunities for public service. A guaranteed income might foster a movement back to rural areas because of the prospects of independence and a more restful life-style. Johnson believes that a guaranteed annual income could be used to encourage people to abandon traditionally high-paying or emotionally unsatisfactory jobs and spend their time at more rewarding jobs that give them more satisfaction than money. Presumably this would foster less consumptive life-styles. If everyone did not regard economic gain as the only measure of success, and the basic competitive need for identity were not based on possessing something others lacked, consumption could be slowed. If higher values were placed on satisfaction or a quality life-style, as measured by free time, expanded personal relations, or the absence of social pressure, the impetus might be greater for a shift in consumption. Of course, an obvious problem arises in finding people to do unpleasant, but still essential, types of work.

Western civilization assumes that everyone must be employed or occupied in some useful capacity, that we have an inherent need to achieve self-gratification through work. The universality of this "need" might be questioned, as in Polynesian cultures whose members seek only food and relaxation. It is also false in Western societies where many would be satisfied in doing nothing and live contentedly on a guaranteed wage. Although they might theoretically be employed in useful activity— social programs, environmental improvement, etc.—they might also choose to do nothing. A few such people have probably always existed, but the attitude that the world owes them a living has been especially encouraged in the United States since the social welfare days following the Depression. Nevertheless, everyone's needs will differ to some degree depending on early experiences and learning.

In order to provide for a guaranteed wage, as well as all other government programs, someone must work. In order for production to keep up with consumption, some employment would be necessary, although not to the extent required when consumption continues to be stimulated, as through advertising.

There may be advantages in fewer people working. Overproduction and underemployment, major problems of technology, could theoretically be overcome if everyone worked less. This could come about by more people working fewer hours or fewer people working at all. The shorter work week, which could solve overproduction, has been rejected because those who could take advantage of it simply work two jobs. Compulsive workers have the need to fully occupy their time. Equally or more important, they feel they need the extra money to purchase the material goods the producers insist they need to improve their relative social status.

To have a guaranteed annual wage and allow people to spend their time at their own discretion, tax revenues are needed; the only way to get them would seem to be through rapid economic growth that only a higher GNP will generate. Thus the environmental advantages of an economic slowdown would appear to be diametrically opposed to the welfare of the economy and a favorable quality of life.

Consequences of a Slowdown

The classically purported consequences of slowing down economic growth are well known. First, 50 percent reduction would eliminate the majority of existing firms, with the largest the hardest hit. These are the same petroleum, automobile, and defense industries that wield the bulk of political power, a situation that makes any such change as unlikely as South American landholders voluntarily disbursing their land. The alternates to economic growth are generally seen as unemployment, recession, and eventually depression.

Reduction in growth would leave industry in fewer and fewer hands; only the most successful could survive. Wealth would thus tend more to concentrate in the hands of a privileged minority.

Hardesty concludes that despite its negative qualities, zero GNP will ultimately be attained either through cultural-political revolution or through complete depletion and destruction of the environment. Ultimate conservation of resources necessitates a major consideration of the market systems. Voluntary conservation is unrealistic in a completely open capitalistic economy; resource conservation is most likely to be forced by depletion. The classical economists, particularly Malthus, Ricardo, and Mills, all predicted that scarcity of natural resources would eventually lead to cessation of economic growth.

Limitations of resources inevitably have an inflationary influence that provides a third factor restraining a rising GNP. This is inflation. As goods become more expensive, and wants remain relatively stationary, the same amount of money buys less. Thus, the real GNP decreases.

Furthermore, higher prices for necessary items mean less money free for buying luxury items. Inflation has been playing a particularly strong role in slowing economic growth in terms of GNP. Inflation is caused in part by too many people with affluence buying and competing for goods. A second factor seems to be our reluctance to accept any arbitrary limit on our own income. Competitive need seems to exist to be as good or better than anyone else and to be rewarded by monetary gain. In order to meet such continued demands for higher wages, the number of employees must be reduced to maintain the stability and viability of a business or system. This leaves more people unemployed who must be

Table 17-1 World Inflation Rates for 1973, in percent *

Greece	30.6	Switzerland	11.9
Iceland	28.4	United Kingdom	10.6
Turkey	19.9	Canada	9.1
Japan	19.1	United States	8.8
Finland	15.6	France	8.5
Spain	14.3	West Germany	7.8
Australia	13.2	Sweden	7.5
Denmark	12.6	Belgium	7.3

Source: Based on the Organization for Economic Cooperation and Development.
*These figures represent the decreases in buying power in the respective nations.

supported by those still working, thus cutting back on surplus funds to improve the standard of living.

Voluntary pay limits, or profit limits, would stop the spiral, but everyone feels underpaid compared to one's neighbor who is paid more for "work requiring less effort or ability."

The disposable income may still be gaining each year, but the real income, in terms of what a dollar will buy, is clearly decreasing; thus reducing the standard of living as well as savings.

In real terms then, the consequence of a slowdown as is currently being experienced is a depression where the inflation rate is higher than the rate the GNP increases. This is a global situation of considerable magnitude and perhaps lasting impact (Table 17-1).

CONCLUSIONS

Classic concepts of economic principles regarding growth may no longer be valid. As in any field, knowledge of economic theory and practice grows with time and study, and economic thought evolves just as attitudes regarding the environment change. As technology and population expand, there is no reason why economic responses should remain stagnant. Natural systems are constantly changing, and economic succession may parallel ecological succession.

The fundamental tenets that regarded humans as a measure of all things, and that the universe existed for their ends, are being questioned by economists as well as by biologists and all concerned society. Thus the idea of material gain as a measure of success is being reevaluated and replaced in some minds by the values of esthetic and social gain. Economic thought is becoming less human-centered and more environment-centered; it is beginning to recognize the finite reservoir of nature. It is time to view the information input of economics and its interplay as part of the total ecosystem.

The continued quality of life and our material standard of living require conserving the resources and other values that provide this quality, but does quality depend on continued economic growth, or can a change in the composition of the GNP alter its adverse consequences? An economic slowdown need not inevitably result in economic stagnation. A slowdown in growth should be compatible with a prosperous economy if the makeup of the GNP were shifted toward services and leisure so long as the people initially have a comfortable degree of affluence. Higher values must be placed on quality and esthetic satisfaction as opposed to material gain if the human environment is to achieve quality and permanence.

In the final analysis, neither material economic growth nor a no-growth economy may prove the most desirable social goal. The outcome of either program is unknown. The question to be resolved is how best to channel economic output to best serve humanity. It may be argued that we are largely ignorant about both the negative and positive developments that may accompany growth; and it is not obvious, especially to the less affluent societies, striving to "catch up," that it is most prudent to conserve resources for future generations. We remain ignorant of technological breakthroughs that may bring vast improvements. The real course of action lies in solving the immediate problems that face us and projecting their ultimate consequences.

Economies that fail to recognize the kind of animal we are and the kind of social relationship with which we developed—be they capitalist or socialist—will flounder if they fail to deliver the psychosocial values basic to human needs. It is not sufficient to evaluate economies on the flow of material values provided, or even on the capital stock of wealth. In the final analysis, the true measure of success is the degree of fulfillment provided the members. Satisfaction generated is as important to the quality of life as the material wealth of a society. Modern economics may be looking too myopically at the wealth-generating capability of a system and ignoring innate human needs for satisfaction and achievement.

Perhaps economies might be developed to better fit the people, instead of people having to fit economies. Economies must fit into the needs of the human environment and become a comfortable component of the total information grid of the human ecosystem.

SELECTED READINGS

Boulding, Kenneth E. Economics and ecology. In F. F. Darling and J. P. Milton (eds.). *Future Environments of North American.* (Garden City, N.Y.: Natural History Press, 1966).

Boulding, K. E. *The Meaning of the 20th Century.* (New York: Harper & Row, 1964).

Clawson, Marion. 1966. Economics and environmental impact of increasing leisure activities. pp. 246–260. In F. F. Darling and J. P. Milton (eds.). *Future Environment of North America* (Garden City, N.Y.: Natural History Press, 1966.)

Daly, H. E. *Toward a Steady-State Economy.* (San Francisco: W. H. Freeman, 1973).

Enke, S. Birth control for economic development. *Science,* vol. 164, pp. 798–802.

Fisher, John. 1971. The easy chair. *Harpers,* vol. 243, pp. 19–23.

Heilbroner, R. L. *The Future as History.* (New York: Grove Press, 1959).

Johnson, W. A. and John Hardesty (eds.). *Economic Growth vs. the Environment.* (Belmont, Calif.: Wadsworth, 1971).

Mishan, E. J. *The Costs of Economic Growth.* (New York: Praeger, 1967).

Ridker, R. G. 1973. Grow or not to grow: That's not the relevant question. *Science,* vol. 182, pp. 1315–1318.

Tiger, L., and Robin Fox. *The Imperial Animal.* (New York: Holt, Rinehart and Winston, 1971).

Wagar, J. Alan. Growth versus the quality of life. *Science,* vol. 168, pp. 179–1184.

Chapter 18

Quality of Life in the City

Each form of organization has an upper limit of size, beyond which it will not function.

D'Arcy Thompson, 1942

The large city is filled with crowds and congestion; opulence, elegance, and ugliness; noise and emptiness; excitement, stimulation, and culture. Obscured in the densest crowds, some still feel alone. Lost is the identity and self-esteem of confidence; replacing it is the futility of apathy and moral emptiness. The humanity of life is compromised as one becomes a mechanical component of a plastic environment. It is an environment alien to our genetic endowment, but vital to our economic success, and especially to our growing numbers.

THE CHARACTER OF THE CITY

The basic character and esthetic quality of the city are partly provided by the physical features of its architecture and landscape. Even in the smaller communities, new buildings rise each year to house more businesses and offices, altering the city's character. Classic old buildings are demolished to make way for the new (Figure 18-1). Other old buildings deteriorate, and rehabilitating them is too expensive.

Structures often contribute less to the urban character than their surroundings—the seas of asphalt surrounding sprawling shopping meccas, obsolete freight-yards, rubbish-strewn vacant lots, high-tension lines with their stark, bare poles, the peeling billboards, and most offensive of all, the harsh, glaring neon signs. And there is the car cemetery and what landscape planner Ian McHarg calls "that most complete conjunction of land rapacity and human disillusion, the subdivision." Their disharmonious contrasts create a dehumanizing atmosphere of frustration and turmoil. The blanketing of this muddle beneath broad bands of airy freeways has somehow made the city less real, even more mechanical and remote from the bewildered dweller. Here, continues McHarg, live "race and hate, disease, poverty and despair, and the remains of a despoiled park in memory of better days."

The impersonal effect of this disarray gives more than an ugly physical image to the city. The physical character is transcended by its

Figure 18-1 Demolition of a classic old building, taking with it part of the atmosphere that was once part of the desirable character of the city. *(Courtesy of John Milhaupt.)*

cultural and social amenities which give the city its purpose and determine in a large measure its esthetic and psychic quality.

The character of a city is reflected by its total environment, from the
approach to the heart of its inner core. If the approach is open with
spacious lawns, and the streets are lined with trees, the character is one of
relaxation and happiness. If the approach is cluttered with poles and
signs, and lined with dumps and dying cars, the character is one of tense
confusion. If the core is paved with parks and vistas, the character
portrays an image of satisfaction, pride, and security. If the core is paved
with debris and the murky shadows of degenerate buildings, the character
is one of fear and insecurity. The most despondent character is imposed
by the abandoned dwelling units—100,000 in New York City, 30,000 in
Philadelphia, and over 10,000 in St. Louis. There remain a few ghosts of
our heritage—the great statehouses, city halls, and museums; universi-
ties; and churches; the great urban park systems of the last century. In
most cities there remain a few generous and spacious suburbs shaded by
old trees and warmed by neighborliness.

The environment, whether urban or natural, exerts considerable
influence on the psyche—the emotional welfare, or happiness—of the
individual. In a large measure, the esthetic values of the city are inherent
in its architecture and landscape; they influence our response to it and
how we treat or abuse it.

URBAN LIMITATIONS

Structures

Perhaps it is not the structures alone that create a disturbing atmosphere
and urban blight so much as their extraneous appendages. Cold, unnatural
advertising signs and wastes contribute greatly to an impersonal atmosphere alien to everyone. Abandonment of houses, crime, and slums are
fostered partly by the absence of community pride, but this is a difficult
character to retain or establish when an area is shared by so many. The
same degrading and offensive impact is created by strip zoning, that
inconsistent splitting up of land for a multiplicity of uses, which creates
areas where nothing appears to belong, where nothing is in harmony with
its surroundings, for example, gas stations next to grocery stores, and
stores interspersed with bars, a liquor store, and the remnants of a house
or apartment.

As we travel the same streets each day, even in the "worst" parts of
town, we adjust to the urban landscape. For better or worse we come to
accept it. We become anesthetized to many things we might first find
irritating, unpleasant, or obnoxious. Consciously we become overfamiliar

with the landscape we once found objectionable and would again if we viewed it more critically. We adapt behaviorally, but the same annoyances unconsciously may continue to aggravate the inner person.

The urban poor in the innercity are beginning to accept the misery of the slums, drug addiction, rampant crime, chronic sickness, and rat bites as normal aspects of city life. The tremendous human capacity for adjusting through ontogenetic learning is supplementing the genetic heritage to barely accomodate survival in a hostile environment.

Even the most congested urban areas can be made to appear spacious if the suitable illusions are created. More amenable use of the available urban land, creating small parks, planting strips, and open spaces and walking malls can go far toward creating a character of pleasure and pride—a pride going far toward deterring littering, abandoning buildings, and crime.

Population Density

The maximum or optimum number of inhabitants a city can accommodate and still retain a desirable quality depends on its character, both physical and psychic. If the urban attitude or atmosphere is one of sharing and cooperation, large numbers of people can be accomodated. If the attitude is one of competition, suspicion, and selfishness, few can be tolerated. Too often these negative characters increase with the population density and provide one of the major urban dilemmas.

The classic experiments of psychologist John Calhoun show that the only mice that survive overcrowding are those that remain completely unstressed. The stressed, overcrowded mice built no nests, never fought, never foraged, reared no young, and neither copulated nor conceived. They simply ate, drank, and slept. They ceased to be mice just as some people cease to be human under similar but extreme circumstances. The loss of incentive, the loss of any desire to work and achieve, may be symptomatic of this, but it would be going too far to say that social ills are a reflection of overcrowding. Crowding may intensify a bad situation, but is not a causal agent per se. Social ills are more deep-seated.

Calhoun concludes that as density increases, so do pressures that manifest themselves in stress diseases. Behavioral changes were also observed in a number of other extensive animal experiments. The predominant heart and kidney diseases increased in the descending order of social rank. In the upper ranks, disease was mainly physical, and neurosis, psychosomatic diseases, or social deviation increased with decline in social rank.

The primary effects of population increases, and of the overcrowding and social pressure that result, are reduction in guarded activity and increased mortality in the young. Calhoun is convinced that the effects observed also hold for people, although proof of similar responses in human populations is still lacking.

Overcrowding is often thought to underly the adverse social behavior most prevelant among the poor—for example escape from pressure through drugs or crime—although possibly changing attitudes are more to blame, and crowding is merely coincidental. In Tokyo and Hong Kong, two of the most congested areas, crime is not as rampant as in less-crowded Manhatten, but the attitudes are more of cooperation. Crime in the world's largest city, Shanghai, is almost unknown. The answer for this lies partly in the laws, and their enforcement, and partly in the urban environment itself, but it may also lie in the ability of a culture to adapt to close contact. The Kung culture maintains extraordinarily close social distance, often with constant bodily contact in their settlements, even though ample space is available.

Loss of Interaction

Although urban blight and crowding may be the cause of much of the social unrest that goes with urbanity, and may further aggravate the problem, these are but symptoms of a deeper stress. Underlying all the superficial ills lie more fundamental weaknesses. One is the growth of cities to such a degree that the people living in them are isolated from each other, from the total community, and from their local government. We have lost our ability to interact with the city. When the spirit of self-government is lost, human direction and destiny in the city become lost, and all responsibility is shifted to a multitude of agencies. The linkage between these agencies becomes more remote as their individual areas of responsibility grow. Further, the agencies tend to become so deeply engulfed in their own activities they fail to see themselves as part of the total system; they become separated from the community they are supposed to serve. The stranglehold of bureaucracy can only be broken by developing a new or better organized set of systems in the city with communicable linkages or interlocking mechanisms between the agencies. In any biological system, the components of the system must be able to communicate and interact if it is to remain viable.

Economic Limitations

The problems of the city are more than cultural, social, or environmental; they are economic. The bigger a city gets, the more it costs to run it. More welfare funds are needed, more hospitals, courts, jails, fire engines, and police. The cost of water to an individual goes up many times as the distance it must be drawn from increases. Here in the crowds, the pickpocket, the thief, the rapist can lose themselves in obscurity. Yet all this is part of the human environment and has its place in the total ecosystem.

As more people migrate to the city, the urban environment becomes an increasingly important segment of the human environment. The city becomes a natural outgrowth of human evolution, and as such, part of the ecosystem.

Farm workers have been moving to industrial cities for generations seeking higher salaries. Many were forced off their farms, having sold them to corporate interests; others were replaced by mechanization. Many were unskilled, uneducated, or otherwise ill-fitted for permanent employment in a rapidly automating world. Instead, they were forced to join the welfare rolls.

The rural dweller left behind is often economically more distressed than the urban counterpart. Large numbers subsist on below-poverty incomes, and agencies to help this plight are lacking. Old rural neighborhoods suffer the same physical deterioration as in the city, and the social structure may be equally disorganized. Money to alleviate rural poverty is lacking even more than in the city.

Meanwhile the more successful and wealthier urbanite has abandoned the city for the suburbs, leaving behind a greater tax burden and vacuum that soon became filled with welfare recipients. Since 1950, state and local expenses have multiplied 12 times while revenues have increased only 6 times. The increase in welfare costs alone has been disastrous to such major cities as New York City. Other costs have included increasing salaries to city employees, early pensions, and larger payrolls that have resulted from increasing demands for services. Jamming of more people has aggravated costs in every area. Inflation has placed a further stress on city budgets. Expenses not of local origin still must be paid locally, adding to the costs.

SOLUTIONS

Developing new cities complete with industry may provide a partial solution by having the beneficial effect of encouraging industry to settle there, with the attendant migration of the unskilled worker from the old city. But what becomes of the old city, which has little autonomy to direct its own destiny?

At least one city, San Francisco, has started a program of buying old and notable, though often tax-delinquent, homes and selling them at modest prices under protective covenents to preserve them.

The basic local government in the United States was designed for a rural, agricultural society whose inhabitants had a general distrust of large central governments. Cities have few self-ordained rights, being merely municipal corporations created and limited by the state and able to tax only at the state's descretion. Provincial attitudes of city councils have also imposed problems. Elected officials, who are usually untrained in city government or finances, handle budgets of millions of dollars. In the early United States Colonies, the concept of states grew out of land grants to a number of rich merchants and financiers, each group wanting a colony of its own. Government was not, and still is not, based on human settlements or metropolitan areas; it has not accepted its position in the total environment.

Employment

The solution to improving the quality of life in the city lies in meeting the physical and psychological needs for each individual. This can only be done by employment. Unemployment and poverty developed with the city. When cultural taboos, infanticide, disease, and war ceased to effectively restrict populations, more people moved to the cities. When agricultural improvements displaced the workers from the farms of Europe, they fled to the cities for jobs, adding to the population of beggars. Their numbers in fifteenth-century Paris were estimated at 80,000; a full third of Cologne's seventeenth-century population of 60,000 were beggars. Even by 1888 a fourth or more of London's population was impoverished.

The same destitute poverty lingers today from Calcutta and Baghdad, to Lima and Panama City. Conditions have changed little, but millions more now endure them in a living realization of Boulding's utterly dismal theorem. To a lesser degree, the same conditions persist in the industrial countries wherever industry and employment have failed to keep pace with rural migration and increased populations.

Unemployment is at the heart of urban poverty. In Harlem, for instance, unemployment is double that elsewhere in New York City—one out of every four people is out of work. Half of Harlem's children live in broken homes. A quarter of a million people are crowded into $3^{1}/_{2}$ square miles. Jobs must somehow be created for the unemployed; where necessary, education must be provided to train and qualify the unemployable for more available jobs. Newark, for instance, lost 20,000 manufacturing jobs in the last 15 years. In this training camp for the poor, one of every three receives some form of welfare. More employment would mean more taxable revenue, but equally important, fewer funds would be needed for welfare programs.

City Planning

Before we can solve the problems of the cities, we must first understand what caused them. For one thing, modern technology and cities with it have grown too fast for social methods to keep pace. There was not enough time to plan their accelerated growth. With the aid of rail and road, the population rapidly diffused from the central city. The occasional zoning laws were inadequate, and the city planning commissions suffered from lack of authority and political control. They were further ineffective from their lack of foresight. City planning must regard the concern of the public and ignore political pressure.

Sensible city plans have been proposed for eons, beginning with the Greeks, but no one really paid much attention. One contemporary plan was the garden city concept Ebenezer Howard proposed in 1898. Howard assumed first that industry and population had begun to disperse. His city population would be held to a maximum of 30,000 people; a central 5 acres would contain the civic buildings, library, theatre, and shops. Around this would be the homes, churches, schools, and parks. The outer ring would contain the industry fronting on the railroad. Six main boulevards would radiate from the center 1000 acres, providing quick access to any part of the city. Surrounding it all was 5000 acres of unviolable greenbelt of natural landscape, trees, and rivers solely for purposes of recreation—fishing, boating, running, lovemaking, etc. Surrounding this was the agricultural belt forming an added buffer to urban sprawl. The city cooperative corporation would own all the land, leasing it for specific purposes for a lifetime. The economic base would be spread over several basic industries.

Greenbelt towns were created in the United States through the New Deal legislation of the 1930s. The idea was to establish towns to provide work and housing for people of modest income. The essential shape of the greenbelt town was dictated by nature, and it was the planners' job to discover and develop the most harmonious relation with the natural environment.

The four greenbelt communities developed in this era—Greenbelt, Maryland; Greenhills, Ohio; Greenbrook, New Jersey; and Greendale, Wisconsin—all provided for a healthy, community way of living closely allied with nature. Unfortunately, the communities were beset with typical urban problems of unplanned growth and sprawl and lack of nearby employment. McHarg calls them "greedbelts," "where the farmer sells land rather than crops, where the developer takes the public resources of the city's hinterland and subdivides to create a private profit at a public cost."

Much of the urban dilemma can be blamed, at least indirectly, on too many people for the limited housing. Frequently, central city areas may have a population density of 1000 to 10,000 or more per square mile. This is usually in the oldest part of town which has grown up amidst factories and tenements.

The dilapidated housing in slum areas may be old or new but is always in need of repair and short of services. The rent is high proportionate to the meager income of the inhabitants, but no housing is available for less. The shortage of housing may easily become more critical in the future in country and city alike if populations increase faster than our capacity to build new homes or apartments. Slums and ghettos are common all over the world and share many problems. The people living there are unemployed, have no money, and cannot afford to live elsewhere. Their degree of strife varies with the economic condition of the country.

Architecture and planning cannot provide the needed urban houses. Attempts to replace slums with low-rent housing in the 1950s have failed. The high density of high-rise buildings is unnatural to people, being too vast to allow them a sense of identity or territoriality; they are soon transformed into vertical slums. The Pruitt-Igoe project attempted to replace 57 acres of central St. Louis slum with 33 modern, well-designed buildings. Many of the early tenants were drawn from high crime areas and brought their problems with them. Working-class families soon moved out to be replaced by welfare cases. The proportion of welfare recipients grew until they made up the majority of the project's population. The children of these families formed street gangs that terrorized tenants and vandalized buildings. A large segment of the tenants earned no money and could not pay the existing rents. Rents were lowered and became inadequate to maintain the buildings; the city had to skimp on services, and the facilities literally began to fall apart. Within 16 years of its construction, three-fourths of the 2800 apartments stood empty. By 1972, St. Louis began tearing down the trash-littered abandoned remains of the structures to start fresh. Less-monumental disasters are characteristic almost wherever they have been attempted. New buildings to live in do not guarantee new patterns of behavior for the inhabitants.

One trouble with big housing projects is they tend to look like big housing projects. They have the stark, distant appearance whether in St. Louis or Copenhagen, Finland or England. Vertical ghettos have broken down in Caracas and in England. Foreboding, monotonous, high-rise concrete slabs now characterize nearly every city in Eastern Europe.

Urban planners now realize that public housing cannot be used as a dumping ground for welfare cases. Low-rent projects must be diluted and scattered throughout the urban areas. The solution also rests in education and changing attitudes, concern and respect for the rights and property of others, and pride of ownership or possession, which is basic to maintaining a favorable quality of any environment. Disregard of others is an acquired character learned in the home and community. It afflicts rich and poor alike.

Urban and suburban growth is still viewed as a mandate, as inevitable; the populace is here and must have a place to live. Just west of Baltimore lie the green hills and swales of Green Spring and Worthington

Valleys. The next 30 years will see the population rise from 17,000 to over 100,000 in this area.

This growth seems inevitable and cannot be halted or diverted. It is considered essential to the growth of the Baltimore region. The only consideration appears to be the best way to develop. The question, "should it be developed?" is rarely raised. Proper planning is obviously better than no planning, but perhaps a still broader planning commission, with far-reaching powers, should dictate that an area should remain entirely undeveloped, or that a population limit should be established. Such policies are now being considered in a few areas. Freezing of land values and zoning could keep much of our land in its present state. Areas more suitable for development of new industry as well as homes could then be properly developed. A federal urban land policy has been urged but not necessarily accompanied by compulsive federal ownership. This is not the American way. It violates our private rights to do as we wish with our land. At least one judge recently ruled that limiting growth of an area violates the individual's right to live where he or she pleases, but with so many people to be housed, and the diminishing of our land resources, many of our earlier "rights" may have to be abrogated for the greater good of the larger number. Even carefully selecting the most appropriate sites for housing and every other function would require strictly enforced zoning for the greatest benefit of the community. Again, we see strictly individual sacrifices for the welfare of the species. As in any biological system, all organisms living together must concede some part of their autonomy toward the ends of sustaining the system and achieving the best environmental quality for the greatest number.

This proposition also can be applied to a human, an organism composed of some 30 billion billion cells. The original cells are unspecialized and evolve to occupy specialist tissue such as bone or blood. The organism exists only because these cells assume interdependent roles within the total single organism. When first formed, each cell is independent, but as more develop, and metabolism becomes more complex, each concedes some part of its freedom and assumes a cooperative role to ensure the survival of the single organism. The intercellular communication or information exchange so vital to the organism is equally vital to a viable population living together in the city.

Two major areas of concern stand out—reclaiming existing cities and preventing the decimation of outlying areas. They are not separate problems; like all ecosystem components, they are linked and must be considered together. Neither proposition can be achieved without strong authoritarian planning commissions free from political pressures and independent of existing bureaucratic machinery. Citizens free from any vested interests must sit on these commissions to deal with the total human environment, not bits and pieces of housing, business, or industry, but the total urban scene as well as the natural environment.

The Nuclear City

Dr. Richard E. Farson, psychologist at the Western Behavioral Sciences Institute, says that the city is an almost total failure as a place for humans. It has outgrown the reasons for its existence and no longer fulfills the functions that brought it into being. Urban planner Eugene Raskin suggests the city is becoming obsolete and we are entering a posturban era.

If this is true, urban populations should soon decline, contrary to predictions of their doubling in the next few decades. Already cities have grown too large for the diminishing number of functions they can successfully perform. Rather than perpetuate cities through urban renewal programs, it might be more rational to rebuild appropriate rural areas and replace the dying ghettos with open spaces.

Vast areas of St. Louis already have been abandoned. It is clear that much of the South Bronx must be razed. Parts of Newark are doomed. Why not develop adequate housing in the country for the few lingering inhabitants and replace the disheveled, broken urban structures and asphalt with parks, or return the land to agriculture and nature?

Urban overpopulation and central city despair is not exclusively a Western problem. Political and cultural centers—Bangkok, Mecca, Nara, and Mandalay—have been crowded since antiquity. So have the outposts of European empires—Bombay, Calcutta, Rangoon, Hong Kong, and Mexico City. Their populations continue to swell despite their degenerating quality. In Java, where the population density exceeds 1100 per square mile, 500 families a day were moving into Djakarta from the surrounding fields. Half this number were moving into Bangkok and Rangoon each day in the 1960s.

The city provides the opportunity to concentrate populations efficiently to achieve the maximum benefits in sharing their resources and industry, but there seems to be a limit to the functional size or complexity of the city beyond which it becomes incoherent and inefficient. Decentralization is imperative. Industry and business no longer need be close to the consumer. It is economically feasible for many corporations to begin dismantling their giant central organizations and spreading out. The breakdown of conglomerate operations would help the city's economy to spread employment into new areas.

This is not to abandon cities, only to reduce the urban populations and acres of rat-infested ghettos no longer needed. As Eugene Raskin and others suggest, exposition grounds, cultural trade and exhibition centers, and transport and shipping facilities that require central rail and sea access would still remain in the urban nucleus. Cable television and telephones now make personal communication technically unecessary in business; we are free to live where we choose. Two kinds of residential structures would support the nucleus. One would be for the permanent residents working at the remaining exhibition, hotel, travel, and government facilities. These would be the high-rise luxury flats like those now found along the East River and Fifth Avenue in New York or the new luxury blocks in London.

The second type of housing would be for the visitors who come for the conventions, exhibitions, or business. These would be hotels with ancillary shops and restaurants. The numerous employees could live in the same area or commute to the suburbs or satellite cities over clean, convenient monorails. The "Exposition City," as Mr. Raskin calls it, would solve the problems of traffic, pollution, municipal solvency, crime, racial, and ghetto ills, and the basic dilemma—crowding and indifference.

The city of the future must be designed for the residents of the future—for people working 4 days a week or less with ample time to enjoy their surroundings. Open areas and recreation facilities should abound. A few cities already portend of the future. Reston and Columbia are best known in the United States; Taliona in Finland. Outside of Stockholm, heating is a public utility produced centrally and distributed through pipes beneath sidewalks thus made free from snow. Subways serve the central city, and shopping centers are sited for easy access by elevators and walking. Eventually power may be generated near every city and waste heat used to heat the home and clear the walks of snow. People of mixed incomes and backgrounds would live in the same varied and architecturally stimulating developments amidst expanses of green.

THE STABILITY OF THE CITY

Though environmental quality may not always be among them, there are definite advantages to the city—too many for their complete abandonment. There are the obvious advantages of greater political and economic stability as well as the diversity of industry and opportunity both in culture and employment. Increased diversity or randomness tends to be an outgrowth of any biological system in which energy is dissipated, including the city.

The city is a product of people and thus subject to the same biological principles that govern their behavior. One of these principles is that the stability of an ecological system tends to increase with its diversity or complexity, at least up to a point. The stability of a plant and animal community tends to increase with the diversity of niches occupied, at least up to a point, beyond which it begins to break down. The same might be said of a city whose stability is enhanced by numbers up to a point beyond which disintegration begins. Stability, or permanence, must be regarded in perspective to its duration. A forest is stable in terms of a person's life-span but not in geological time. A community of herbaceous plants, though, has a more rapid turnover rate and could become unstable even in perspective of a few years.

Similarly, a city is unstable during its growth period until it gradually reaches the stability of maturity, but then, as it exceeds a critical mass or energy demand, it may again become unstable and fall apart in a short time. If we view the evolutionary stages of the city in historical context rather than only in terms of the present, we might be able to predict its future, and rate of degeneration, and thereby control its destiny. By far the majority of cities have not yet reached the critical stage of decline and could circumvent it if corrective measures were taken in time. Sociologists have devised methods to measure the status of decline. Basically they involve the preparation of annual reports on the status of the metropolis that account to the citizens and agencies. Included therein could be inventories of the number of people able to support themselves and the numbers dependent on public support. The economic growth, status of social services and revenues, etc., also would be included.

Once a critical mass or degree of complexity capable of precipitating decline was approached, counter measures could be taken. A population limit could be set, or the city could be diversified by subdividing government units, or industries could be decentralized. With individuals as complex as we are, and a system as complex as the city, no specific number can be set which would comprise a critical mass; but there should be some type of planned optimum. This will vary to the greatest extent with cultural and social attitudes, and the physical surroundings, but some other related measure could provide an index of deterioration.

The underlying advantage of the city lies in the greater stability through diversity—diversity of labor and services, of interests, of economic bases (business and industry), of cultures, and of opportunity. Such diversity must be maintained and not allowed to conglomerate. As in any ecological system, the greater the diversity, the greater are the healing properties of the system and the greater are its stability and permanence. The city provides a natural stage in human evolution as a social animal with each stage enhancing our permanence and dominance in the biosphere.

The end of this stage of evolution is in sight. It has been reached in some of the larger cities. Since evolution, or change, is a continuing process, it is time to anticipate the next stage. We can see several stages in progress, depending on where we turn. In the larger cities the stage is one of emigration and abandonment, leaving the rotted hollow core of a former stage; the urban population then becomes one of commuters.

Amidst the urban cores of Europe and America remains a new network of superstructures—hotels, convention centers, office buildings—and a feeble effort toward plazas and parks borne on the cleared remains of a former era. It has taken centuries to pass through the early stages of transition, but with sufficient foresight, we might enter the next stage in decades.

Problems have arisen with each stage of urban evolution, but gradually they are being solved. It never seems they are, but our standards of values continue to improve. We are now concerned with 10 percent unemployment, while a century earlier 20 percent was a norm. We are now shocked by air that was considered pure by people of 30 years ago. Garbage and debris are removed in all but the worst ghettos. As each problem evolved it was solved in part in the course of social evolution when the shock was sufficient to demand action.

CONCLUSIONS

Quality of life in the city should be improving each year; superficially it seems to be degenerating. So much is said of the sorry state of the city that we often take its decline for granted, but conversation with long-time residents of almost any city suggests that with some exceptions, many things are better. Worse times are easily recalled. Conditions are certainly better in cities with populations under a million. The most insurmountable problems are still confined to the larger cities of over at least half a million. In cities under this size, the agency linkage mechanisms still work. In larger cities, the system breaks down; the crime and neglect that result are symptoms.

New structures and landscape improvements are helpful (Figure 18-2), but the old buildings are decaying faster than they can be replaced. The stresses of crowding in the larger cities are telling on the inhabitants in the form of crime and drugs, which accelerate the decay. As industries move out, unemployment and poverty increase in the abandoned area. Like an old tree, the large city rots from within at a rate scarcely behind the new growth.

Technologically, and perhaps economically, urban rot could be resolved, but sociologically, prospects are less encouraging. The radical new approach and departure from tradition, coupled with the rigid government controls needed, would be unacceptable. Solutions lie in understanding humans and the city's place in the total ecosystem.

Robert F. Kennedy summarized it: "The cities are centers of cultures, fashion, finance, and industry—of sports and communication for us all—and thus the center of possibilities of urban life. They are also the center of the problems of American life: poverty, and race hatred, scanty education and stunted lives, and other ills of the new urban nation—

Figure 18-2 Landscape improvements enriching the character of a renewed section of London.

congestion and filth, danger, and purposelessness, which afflict all but the very lucky, and some of the very rich."

SELECTED READINGS

Blumenfeld, H., and P. Spreiregen (eds.). *The Modern Metropolis: Its Origins, Growth, Characteristics and Planning.* (Cambridge, Mass.: MIT Press, 1967).

Boskin, Joseph. *Urban Racial Violence in the Twentieth Century.* (New York: Glencoe Press, 1969).

Calhoun, J. B. Population density and social pathology. *Scientific American,* vol. 206, pp. 139–148.

Glaab, C. N., and A. T. Brown. *A History of Urban American.* (New York: Macmillan, 1967).

Hawley, Amos H. *Urban Society. An Ecological Approach.* (New York: Ronald, 1971).

Holden, L. K., L. H. Moscotti, C. J. Larson (eds.). *Metropolis in Crisis.* (Illinois: F. E. Peacock, 1967).

Hughes, Helen MacGill. *Cities and City Life.* (Boston: American Sociological Association, 1970).

Kryter, K. *Effect of Noise on Man* (New York: Academic, 1970).

Moynihan, David P. (ed.). *On Understanding Poverty,* (New York: Basic Books, 1969).

Page, John. A protest of urban environment. *The Political Quarterly.* October 1969, pp. 436–447.

Raskin, Eugene. *Sequel to Cities.* (London: The Rebel Press, 1969).

Rockefeller, Nelson A. *Our Environment Can Be Saved.* (Garden City, N.Y.: Doubleday, 1970).

Short, James F., Jr. (ed.). *The Social Fabric of the Metropolis.* (Chicago: University of Chicago Press, 1971).

Starr, Roger. *The Living End. The City and Its Critics.* (New York: Coward-McCann, 1966).

Thomlinson, Ralph. *Urban Structure.* (New York: Random House, 1969).

Tretton, R. W. *Cities in Crises.* (Englewood Cliffs, N.J.: Prentice-Hall, 1970).

Weaver, R. C. *Dilemma of Urban America.* (Cambridge, Mass.: Harvard, 1965).

Whikehart, W. R. Public housing projects. *The Plain Truth.* vol. 37, 1972, pp. 16–18.

Whyte, W. H. *The Last Landscape* (Garden City, N.Y.: Doubleday, 1968).

Wynn-Edward, V. C. *Animal Dispersion in Relation to Social Behavior.* (New York: Hafner, 1962).

Chapter 19

The Need for Nature

In wilderness is the preservation of the world.

Henry D. Thoreau

Wilderness is where the earth and its community of life are untrammeled by humans, where we are visitors who do not remain; where no permanent human habitations exist. The dictionary defines *wilderness* as "an uncultivated, uninhabited region; waste, wild," and *waste* is given as a synonym. Wilderness is a window into the natural order of which we must realize we are but a part. Yet as Ian McHarg writes, "anthropocentric man seeks not unity with nature but conquest." Our instincts prompt us to compete for our share of the total ecosystem.

BIOLOGICAL NEED

Nature in our daily lives may well be an inherent biological necessity, not a luxury. Millions of years of inheritance and culture have programmed us to a natural habitat of fresh air and a varied wild landscape unspoiled by the perturbations of civilization. We are genetically adapted to a nomadic life, characterized by our living largely in family groups and associating mostly only with the limited members of the tribe. For a million and more years, contacts with larger groups were rare. The gradual confrontation in larger groups has in part psychologically adapted us to increasing crowds, but physiological inheritance has not kept pace. Crowding, which has evolved with the city over the past 5000 years, is still a relatively recent trauma. There are those whose early experiences profoundly influenced their later attitudes and wittingly or unwittingly adjusted them to the congested jungles of asphalt and concrete to varying degrees. But 200 generations of city dwelling by a segment of the population have freed few from the need for open space. It is the urbanite who most needs to escape from this artificial world, but not every one has the resources to escape from the city for even the briefest periods. Lewis Mumford writes that our capacity for growth is the primal gift of life that flourishes best when living creatures are present. A day without "emotional stirrings— responses to the perfume of a flower or an herb, to the flight or the song of a bird, to the flash of a human smile or the warm touch of the human hand . . . , is a day empty of organic contents and human rewards."

Though these are more rare in the city, do people really need wilderness? Wild nature seldom provides an ideal environment. Those who live in primitive societies suffer from uncontrollable disease, starvation, and a short life. They live in fear and superstition. Western civilization was founded on the banality of nature. Earth and nature were carnal, and only humans could conquer them and make the desert bloom. Until recent times, contrary views were expressed by only a few, such as Duns Scotus and Evigena, who sought to show nature to be a manifestation of God; and Francis of Assisi, who sought to love nature rather than conquer it and preached human partnership with all living things.

Explorer Bob Marshall considered that the singular aspect of the wilderness was its gratification of every one of the senses. "Adventure, whether physical or mental, implies breaking into unpenetrated ground, venturing beyond boundaries of normal aptitude, extending oneself to the limit of capacity . . . .Life without the chance for such exertion would be for many persons a dreary game, scarcely bearable in its horrible banality. Wilderness provides the ultimate delight because it combines the thrills of jeopardy and beauty." It is the perfect esthetic experience fulfilling all the senses.

THE CONQUEST OF NATURE

Since antiquity we have done our utmost to eliminate natural habitats and conquer its wild inhabitants, notably predacious species—the wolf, bear, and lions which only a few centuries ago roamed freely over Europe and

North America. Bounties on the wolf and cougar date back to the year 1600. We have eliminated the 30 million buffalo as a basic food animal and controlled the population of deer to numbers suitable for closely regulated game management. Our success as pioneers depended on our ability to fight the wilderness and win. Wilderness was to be conquered. Animals were to kill—for food, for sport, and to prove a man's virility. As stated by one early writer, wilderness was that "dismal place where all manner of beasts dash about uncooked."

Wildlife

Wildlife has become scarce throughout the populated world and entirely displaced in all the more populous areas. Many never miss it, but there are those for whom the sight of a lumbering porcupine or a silent deer standing motionless in the woods hastens the pulse and gives an indescribable glow of pleasure. Years or an entire lifetime may pass seeing wildlife only in zoos or preserves, or not at all. Those able to hike into the wilderness areas may fleetingly glimpse a deer retreating through the aspen, a curious pica peering around a rocky crag, or a kit fox vanishing into the desert sage.

Occasional associations with wildlife may measure the quality of life for some, but they seem hardly essential. We have spent too many centuries doing our best to destroy the hostile species that once preyed on the children and herds and, according to some, still continue to prey on the sheep. We have progressed too far in the destruction of competing species in making way for agriculture and the city. Only the most tenacious species endure over much of the world. Almost without exception, wherever wildlife has abounded we have exploited it for profit or pleasure, or to make room for our expanding numbers. Some species have been especially vulnerable so that their demise was inevitable and almost incidental to human population growth. Such was the case with the passenger pigeon, Carolina paroquet, ivory-billed woodpecker, peregrine falcon, tule elk, Atlantic salmon, and many more, from the aye-aye to the vicuna. Others, such as the trumpeter swan and whooping crane, were large, conspicuous, and edible—obvious targets for unbridled gunnery. The woods no longer abound with the black bear, wolverine, pine marten, or lynx. Since 1600, approximately 250 different species of animals have become extinct. An additional 817 varieties of birds and animals are threatened by illegal hunting, growth of industry, spreading of urbanization, and other development. Protective legislation and the formation of wildlife sanctuaries have made possible the return of some threatened species in increasing numbers. The presence of these and other protected species—the alligator, bison, eagles, the wolf in Minnesota—has a definite recreational and esthetic value. Many, as the Gambel quail, pronghorn antelope, elk, and deer, are valued game animals. Still, the list of vanishing species lengthens each day and the number of endangered species grows even faster. Once a species of life is lost, it can never again appear. There is some question whether some species should be saved. Such is the case with the grizzly bear. They are protected in National Forests and Parks, but their presence is often incompatible with humans. The few instances of grizzlies mauling and even killing a few tourists have raised the question of whether there is room for both human and grizzly. In such places as Alaska, they are still a menace to the hiker and fisherman.

Wildlife and humans might both be accommodated with proper management, particularly if the animal does not pose a threat to people. Animal ecologist Norman Myers shows how present populations of herbivores could be maintained within the carrying capacity of the land and harvested on a sustained-yield basis. Elephants, hippopotomi, buffalo, and numerous antelope species could all be "cropped" probably more profitably and productively than cattle, and the land left untrammeled.

All species are not disappearing. Game species such as deer and elk are carefully managed, like so many cattle, and their predators are destroyed; they have never been more numerous. Mountain goat, moose, and other species are being introduced into new habitats. Quail, pheasants, and partridge are continually introduced to new areas where they thrive for human benefit, possibly to the detriment of the existing fauna. Antelope feeding on alfalfa in the farmlands of the Wind River Mountains are thriving. Cottontail rabbits, gophers, and the Columbia ground squirrel are a constant farm nuisance in the West and benefit from agriculture. Protected birds may damage crops, and their esthetic value must be weighed against the losses they cause. The house finch feeds on fruit buds and cherries, the band-tailed pigeons damage orchards and truck crops, and the horned lark destroys lettuce. The brown bear of Kodiak Island, occasionally preying upon the introduced cattle, is a menace with which the local ranchers must contend. As leopards are killed in Africa, the baboon population they once kept in check becomes a menace to farmers.

Rats, cats, dogs, and a myriad of pets and scavengers thrive in the city, while in the country, rodents and rabbits prosper due to our elimination of predacious coyotes, wolves, lynx, lions, and snakes, eagles, and hawks, which once kept their populations in balance. Now they multiply freely competing for forage with cattle and sheep. In the subalpine parklands of the Rocky Mountains, the northern pocket gopher and montane vole were found to eat one-fourth of all the natural herbage produced. Ranchers are surprisingly slow to realize that the predators they continue to eliminate are their friends.

Flora

We do not seek nature for the animal life alone but for the beauty of the wildflowers and forests that provide their shelter and food and give nature its quality. In Emerson's words, "the beauty that shimmers in the yellow afternoons of October, who could ever clutch it?" Each year more people enjoy the brightly colored mushrooms, the minerals, the birds, insect life, and striking flowers of the wild—but not unobtrusively.

Wildflowers are especially abused. For centuries those who enjoyed them most picked them, held them, and watched them wither. The sparse populations of a hundred years ago had little impact, but today's crowds would soon decimate the flora were it not for restrictions. The problem is especially acute near the city but is becoming critical wherever populations invade the mountains and deserts.

The poppy and lupine fields of Southern California have all but disappeared over the past 20 years. The wildflower fields of the Rockies have been reduced in the foothills and trampled by horses, cattle, and people even in the lush alpine meadows. Their demise has been gradual, obvious over the years only to the naturalist; but the wildflowers are disappearing in America just as they have over much of Europe where obscure, protective laws have long been ignored.

The virgin forests of Ohio and the Midwest are gone except in the records. Apparently the relic wilderness was worth little. Over the years, far more money has been spent on statues, monuments, and memorials than to salvage a few acres of natural vegetation. The pioneer attitude of conquering the wilderness and gaining cropland spared little of the original cover, or the dependent fauna. The most accessible virgin forests of the Northwest were scalped before 1900 with no regard for the future. The same attitude prevailed in Europe except that there the early feudal kings and wealthy landholders retained substantial land for their private hunting preserves. Today these forests remain in a near natural state for the public to enjoy.

Along the Pacific Coast of the United States, the primeval redwood forests, towering over 350 feet high, continue to be logged. The oldest trees matured with the Roman Empire, and a few such groves with their dense thickets of undergrowth are being preserved, but most of the redwood range consists of young, second-growth stands. Over three-fourths of the roughly 300,000 acres of virgin redwoods left in the world are owned by lumber companies who must weigh the private economics of logging against the public gain from not logging.

The scarcer forested lands become, the more they seem to be appreciated. Thus, in the older most mature cultures, a genuine appreciation for nature is aroused. Such an appreciation was stimulated as early as the third century B.C. following the deforestation of so much of northern China. Even by then, the expansion of agriculture and the building of cities had taken their toll. An ancient custom of burning forests to deprive dangerous animals and bandits of their hiding places, and slowing horse-riding barbarians, recorded in the fourth century B.C., had almost eliminated the forests. Ultimately, the loss was countered by the employment of conservation officials who strictly regulated the cutting of trees, but by then most of the rich topsoil had been washed away.

Similarly, by the time of Shakespeare, when the forests of England were all but gone, hedgerows were planted along the rural lanes and property lines. These mixtures of trees, shrubs, and other flowering plants are possibly the most memorable feature of the British countryside and provide a shady sanctuary for birds, animals, and hikers.

The closest approximations in the United States are the 18,000 miles of windbreaks started by the Forest Service between 1934 and 1941. Fenced strips along the nation's railways and highways also provide a natural area and refuge for native fauna if left undisturbed.

Birds

When gone, forests with their diverse undercover of shrubs and wildflowers are not the only loss; in destroying many of these species, the song and game birds they support, such as the finch, quail, and warbler, also disappear. When the home or community is destroyed, the species can no longer reproduce and is soon eliminated.

Diverse habitats provide for numerous ecological niches where a large number of species may thrive, but habitats have been destroyed or their area diminished, proportionately limiting the number of wild dwellers. Between encroachment and hunting, the Labrador duck, heath hen, Carolina paroquet, and many more species have become extinct; the whooping crane, trumpeter swan, California condor, and Eskimo curlew, nearly so. Some species, such as the ivory-billed woodpecker that formerly inhabited the swampy forests of the Southeastern United States, have very specialized habitat requirements. They feed on insects in large, dying trees. These occur mostly in old virgin timber stands—the prime target of the lumber companies. The single-species tree farms that replace the virgin stands are free from the insects and cannot support the ivory-bill.

Habitat

Wildlife is threatened not only directly by wanton killing, but by the decimation or usurpation of their natural habitat as we continue to broaden our occupation of the environment. Wildlife species over nearly a billion acres of America's public lands must share their habitat. Cattle have displaced the bison and elk that once abounded across the grass prairies of the Midwest and the wild mustangs that freely roamed the western deserts. Herded sheep now range on land once the exclusive domain of the bighorn sheep. Short-sighted stockmen continue to graze more stock than the land can carry. The same land was coveted by early settlers, who soon put the fertile lands to agriculture, factories, and highways. The less adaptive wild species were soon replaced, and the more durable slaughtered by people. Diminution of habitat from encroaching populations and the draining of marshlands will limit numbers still further. The remaining habitat is fast disappearing as each year a million acres of forest lands are eliminated by road, power, and pipeline construction and community growth. Each day, wildlife habitat is reduced. Valleys are inundated into reservoirs, and cities leashed together by tentacles of highways spreading relentlessly across the landscape. Every piece of accessible land, public or private, within 50 to 100 miles of all major cities is considered to be in danger of being "developed" by 1985.

Traditionally, the decision to develop an area was determined by a cost/benefit analysis in which the simple measure of values was the monetary gain. Dollars served as the determining criteria of whether an area should or should not be developed. Economic value of leaving an area alone must also be considered; dollar gain must be balanced against esthetic loss. Since this is a more difficult value to measure, it has been ignored. Esthetic values are no longer ignored, but rather provide a major incentive for development. Mountain or desert areas are now being prodigiously exploited for their beauty and solace. Yet the same developments too often destroy their "raison d'etre" as development lays to ruin the natural assets of an area.

Real estate developers who advertise skiing, hiking, fishing, and clean air are doing their best to relocate urban refugees in the untrammeled remnants of open space. "Own a piece of Colorado" they cry. In that state alone, bulldozers are grading over a million acres of mountain habitat for subdivision. The steep slopes hold little water, and the sensitive alpine vegetation is readily disrupted. Neighbors foul each others' property with the outflow from shallow septic tanks, and the raw sewage seeps into the limited underground water, streams, and lakes. Raw land is scarce in the West, scarcer in the East, and the great forest and meadowlands of the Rocky Mountains and New England are rapidly being exploited. The same fate threatens Idaho, Montana, Arizona, Utah, and Alaska—wherever virgin land remains. Wilderness is melting away like the last remains of a snowbank in the hot sun of an afternoon in June.

In Africa, expanding populations continue their advance on nature. In Murchison Falls Park in Uganda, the Falls are being harnessed for power, and the remaining 1500 crocodiles are threatened by fluctuating waters. Already humans occupy almost every stretch of the sloping shores favored as a habitat by crocodiles.

A continuous change or turnover in species and numbers is normal. But we have accelerated the change, largely by destroying habitats, through our activities of draining swamps, logging, irresponsible shooting, land "reclamation," monoculture, indiscriminate poisoning, and worst of all, urban sprawl and pollution.

As open space becomes more limited and our lives become more confined, we slowly begin to appreciate the esthetic value of nature and we wonder about its ability to fulfill an inherent sense. Often the recognition comes too late, as when desirable natural features got in the way of developing cities. Vast sectors of preservable land are in private hands, and too few funds are available for the government to purchase sufficient acreage to support natural ecosystems, and even when land is set aside for wilderness or subjected to control, there are objections. When the New York State Legislature, in 1973, passed a bill to control land use on 3,700,000 acres of Adirondack valleys, lakes, and mountains, many of the region's residents were aghast at the presumed loss of potential tax revenues and dreamed-of riches in land sales.

Such irreplaceable resources, from the redwood forests of California to the cypress swamps of southern Florida, are succumbing to development. Even where land is held by the Forest Service, it continues to be subjected to multiple abuse—logging, livestock grazing, mining, skiing, and cabin building, trailer camping, trailbike riding, and snowmobiling. Management continues to be directed more toward monetary gain than esthetic profit or ecosystem harmony. Perhaps segments of "ultimate" wilderness area should be set aside for future generations; blocks of land where even access by people is prohibited.

Such drastic measures are, of course, absurd, but an environmental awareness is arising toward a land-use ethic as illustrated by the passing in 1973 of the National Land Use Policy and Planning Assistance Act to provide financial aid to states implementing planning programs. Nevertheless, efforts to correct blatant misuse of the land often are adamantly opposed by ranchers, lumbermen, farmers, and land developers who fear controls will be taken out of the hands of local governments. As more people vie for the same amount of land, sagacious development becomes ever more critical.

Coastlines and estuaries have been seriously threatened with exploitation along both Pacific and Atlantic shores. Land-use policies have had the best success on the West Coast, where bulldozers, dredges, and drilling rigs have all been stalled by planning commissions that now regulate development up to a thousand yards in from the shore.

An unwanted side effect of land-use regulation yet to be coped with is that as less land remains available for development, the more expensive it becomes. The available shorelands not left in public domain may soon be available only to the very wealthy.

FURTHER DISRUPTION

Winter is a beautiful season. Beneath a mantle of snow, for many it is solitude and silence, serenity and solace. Winter makes nature more vibrant, the wilderness more wild. But even in the still of winter, wilderness is threatened both directly and indirectly by human activities.

In recent years, the sublimity of winter wilderness has been shattered by the vibration and roar of the snowmobile—50,000 of them in 1965; over 7 million only 5 years later. The objection to snowmobiles is not limited to noise. The impact on wildlife and habitat may be more serious. Spooked by the roar of unmuffled engines and run down by throttle-happy drivers, frightened animals soon exhaust their limited energy reserves in flight from a loathsome enemy. Some die of exhaustion; a few survive to be pursued again; the unborn young of a pregnant doe may never leave the womb alive.

Remote areas once reached only by days of backpacking or hours of canoeing and portage are now inundated by snowmobiles and a layer of trash left by their drivers for the summer hiker to bury, along with human wastes that contaminate the spring runoff.

Empty cans and plastic wrappers are not the sole domain of the motorized despot. Horse packers and backpackers are also guilty of littering the land. Their increasing numbers demand acute propriety in the disposal of everything carried in lest the scant remains of nature assume the character of an abandoned vacant lot.

Desecration of the environment and a heritage of petroliths, pictographs, and artifacts provide a further threat. Each year, as more people tread the wilderness paths, once-remote sites fall prey to the vandal (Figure 19-1).

The warm solitude of the summer trail is also shattered by the roar of the internal combustion engine of trail bikes and other recreation vehicles. A single track across the desert or tundra may never heal.

The loss of wilderness is further reflected in the diminishing miles of natural rivers throughout the world. A river dammed to impound a rising and receding lake is forever ruined as a primitive retreat. Dams, farms, cities, industry, pollution, and crowds have all taken their toll. Even the rare stretches of river passing through National Parks are no longer

Figure 19-1 Defacing of early Indian petroliths.

pristine. Power boats and daily incursions of thousands of river runners have left their wastes and refuse to foul the land or be flooded into the nearest downstream reservoir. No longer can escape be gained on the waters of the more popular stretches of the Colorado, Snake, Madison, or Green Rivers. Furthermore, the shores remain filthy because dams eliminate spring floods that normally cleanse the sandy beaches.

River systems may not be essential to humans other than for the water they carry, but they provide a recreational retreat and relaxation somehow basic to our well-being. As the pressures of advancing populations impose on the world's remaining streams humans will have to share them, sacrificing further the quality of life. Residents still stroll along the quiet tree-lined banks of the Seine, Thames, and Danube, but their reflections are shared by a thousand others.

The United States Congress recognized our need for nature when it established the National Park System in 1872. Railroads had linked the country only 3 years earlier and smelter smoke was scarcely known in America, but already the need for protecting areas of unique beauty was foreseen. At the time, Yellowstone Park, for instance, was scarcely accessible. The population centers were over 2000 miles distant, and the few visitors had to travel by trains and stagecoach at a cost only the very rich could afford. Even by 1917, only 5000 cars had ventured into the park. Within a hundred years of their inception, automobiles in an endless procession were conducting over 2 million visitors through the park during the brief summer, and 15 million more through the Great Smokies. Some 200 million tourists visited the National Parks in 1972. Mass transit in the parks is projected for the future. Accommodations must be reserved months in advance, and roadside camping space is as congested as in many an urban ghetto.

CONCLUSIONS

Can we really afford nature? Wilderness in biblical days was viewed as a desolate, unusable desert or wasteland to be avoided. Many still feel this way, but the number who value wilderness seems to be growing as this irreplaceable resource disappears.

Although an individual's definition of nature is learned, nature in our daily lives must be recognized as a biological need, part of our genetic message. Borne over a million years of genetic input, perhaps the undisturbed forest or field is essential to the well-being and quality of life. Comprehension of the relationship of wilderness to our happiness and peace of mind seems to be growing.

As western civilization matures, we begin to view wilderness not as savages, nor as pioneer exploiters, but more with the enlightenment of people understanding and appreciating its real meaning and value. In less than 200 years, the United States has moved from being a nation of endless hostile wilderness to one where nature is a diminishing resource. Europe reached the same stage a thousand years sooner.

Problems of congestion are intensified and become more critical in the wilderness. What becomes of the garbage and human wastes? Where is water available? How can the atmosphere or values of wilderness be retained and yet accommodate a transient population of millions? They cannot! More people are crowding into less remaining wild land to turn the more popular and populous parks into wilderness slums. The crowding is entirely out of proportion to the growing population because more people now have a greater awareness of nature and value it more. Furthermore, they have greater affluence and leisure time. To accommodate the increasing population, more natural areas must be preserved and further intrusion by development must cease or be more closely regulated, a feat that might readily be accomplished through tax penalties (disincentives) on natural area property.

In destroying nature, humans may be destroying themselves. With each permanent intrusion of the wild, we are lessening the land where we can escape from our own turmoil. We are enclosing ourselves into an ever narrowing corner. The more we exclude ourselves from nature, the more adjusted, yet frustrated, we become to its absence, and the more irreversible becomes our course.

We are part of nature and at the same time apart from nature in our awareness of it and our ability to analyze and control it. We must utilize this capability to control our natural environment for stability and permanence so that future generations will also know it. If not, we will lose the traits of perception and appreciation that go far toward making us what we now consider human.

SELECTED READINGS

Baldwin, M. F. Snowmobiles and environmental quality. *Living Wilderness*, vol. 32, pp. 14–17, winter, 1968.

Bates, Marston. *Man in Nature* (2d ed.). (Englewood Cliffs, N.J.: Prentice-Hall, 1964).

Bloomfield, H. V. Snowmobiles: Boon or ban. *American Forestry*, vol. 75, pp. 4–5, May 1969.

Knobloch, I. W. (ed.). *Selected Botanical Papers*. (Englewood Cliffs, N.J.: Prentice-Hall, 1963).

Marsh, George P. *Man and Nature*. (New York: Scribner, 1964).

Marshall, Robert. 1970. *Alaska Wilderness* (2d ed.). (Berkeley: University of California Press, 1970).

Mathiessen, Peter. *Wildlife in America*. (New York: Viking Press, 1959).

Myers, Norman. Wildlife and development in Uganda. *Bioscience*, vol. 21, no. 21, pp. 1071–1075.

Nash, Roderick. *Wilderness and the American Mind*. (New Haven: Yale, 1967).

National Research Council. Committee on Agricultural Land Use and Wildlife Resources. 1970. Land Use and Wildlife Resources. *National Academy of Sciences*.

Shephard, Paul. *Man in the Landscape: A Historic View of the Esthetics of Nature*. (New York: Knopf, 1967).

Ziswiler, Vinzenz. (Trans by Fred Bunnell and Pille Bunnell) *Extinct and Vanishing Animals*. (New York: Springer-Verlag, 1967).

Chapter 20

The Utopian Dream

There is nothing more difficult to carry out nor more doubtful of success, nor more dangerous to handle, than to initiate a new order of things.

Niccolo Machiavelli
The Prince

And God said, "Let us make man in our image, after our likeness: and let them have dominion over the fish of the sea, and over the fowl of the air, and over the cattle, and over all the earth. . . ." And for a time Adam and Eve had things much their own way. Then Eve conceived and bore Cain, and before long Cain's wife bore Enoch, and to Enoch was born Irad, and Irad was the father of Mehujael, etc.

Anyone reading further in the Bible realizes that even this small society could scarcely be considered utopian. If one family is unable to find an ideal social order, what hope is there for a dozen families, or a billion? Certainly the problem of harmonious relations and of personal freedom increases geometrically with numbers of individuals. Society has evolved in response to increasing human numbers and has had to become proportionately more structured and regulated with each increase in size to retain any degree of order and harmony. In our quest for happiness, we have always sought the ideal society, and utopian philosophy has formed the basis of the most influential movements in history—Judaism, Christianity, Confusianism, Islam, socialism, and communism. Utopia has been the vision of philosophers from Plato to Rousseau to Skinner.

Physical and psychological needs influence the quality of life, and quality is determined to a large measure by our ability to achieve security, identity, and stimulation. All of these affect our relation to and interaction with ourselves and the human environment. Ideally we should be able to interact comfortably with both to the benefit of all. This cooperation is vital to the survival of the environment and humanity.

SPIRIT OF COOPERATION

The spirit of cooperation may be ingrained to some degree in human inheritance through having shared a common evolutionary origin. As suggested by William Glasser, primitive man "suffered from lack of food, lack of shelter, lack of ability to make tools and materials to survive, but he got along with his fellow man." As humans met their basic needs, populations grew, and we demonstrated an outstanding ability to use the resources of the environment to our own advantage, but failed to get along with our fellows beyond the band. The common bond of survival also diminished. The need for defense against environment has diminished as we have conquered it; vestiges of a cooperative nature are strongest when we are exposed to some stress situation—flood, fire, war, or some other mutually shared crises that provide a common identity.

The attitude of cooperation, and our relation to ourselves in society, is idealized in the history of civilization and in the social thinking of utopian philosophy. It also provides a background from which to judge the direction which society might be taking and the future role of humans in it.

Utopian thought is often said to reflect the social and political conditions of the times. Utopian thought also gives insight into the environmental as well as social attitudes of the day, and changes in human thought. Attitudes and social patterns are reflected in the minds of the poets, philosophers, and artists of the day. They are discussed by political idealists and dreamers, but often with little consideration of basic human nature. The biological limitations of any utopia are mostly ignored. A genetic character imprinted by a million years of human dominion on earth is not easily altered by a few generations of wishful thinking or modification by behavioral learning.

In some primeval forest there once dwelled troops of ancestral prosimians. At their psychological extremes we might hypothetically place a giant, muscular, but docile and pleasant creature that evolved to become the modern gorilla—an animal now all but extinct. At the other extreme we find a self-reliant, aggressive, perhaps a bit obnoxious hominid that evolved into a human. According to anatomy professor Raymond Dart of the University of Witwatersrand in Johannesburg, the early success of the genus *Homo* can be attributed to aggressive behavior, which caused the genus to destroy other closely related animals including the more docile prehominids.

This is not to say that aggressiveness was the most successful strategy in all environments, nor does it infer that a species is either all aggressive or all altruistic. Undoubtedly, there are innate degrees or combinations of both. The most successful species is the one that has evolved the optimum degree of aggressiveness for a particular environment.

The character of any social system can be no better than that of the people who compose it. In other words, our basic nature must be the limiting factor to the excellence of any society. The inherent nature of humans as discussed in *The Naked Ape, The Imperial Animal, The Social Contract*, and similar volumes on animal behavior suggests that we are a selfish, aggressive, and perhaps territorial animal. These very traits that contribute to our competitive success as an animal hinder our ability to live in harmony in large groups. Societies have been reasonably successful in developing cultural or social adaptations to tame individual aggressiveness and to teach the young how to sublimate their presumed primitive impulses. Through tribal religion and governmental law, prescribed by behavioral adaptation, we have survived. But we remain the product of our inheritance.

The basic biological nature of people is ignored by utopian thinkers conceiving the idyllic society. Rousseau's utopia, for instance, was based on the essential goodness of humans, our original freedom and equality, and the possession of inherent political rights. Further, utopias presume with modern behaviorists, that human character can be changed.

A society can only be successful if basic human needs are met. These needs are not limited solely to the physical wants of food and shelter. They include our need for identity, stimulation, and other values we may hold in esteem. As Plato submitted 2000 years ago, because individuals are created unequal, a society utopian to all could never become a reality. Some individuals would constantly be struggling for the superior position.

UTOPIAN THINKING

Any utopian society is based on several premises regarding human nature. First, the plasticity of a human is assumed. Behavioral psychologists argue that the human mind can be molded to the best interests of the total society. Taken at birth, it should be possible to condition the child's behavior to regard consideration for others above all else—to value society more than oneself and to work for the good of all.

Secondly, utopian thinking assumes that rulers can be found who will rule justly and selflessly with no thoughts toward personal gain, or that people might be selected and trained to rule justly. Somehow it does not work this way. Our seemingly inherent aggressiveness and competitive attitude or need for identity, to say nothing of our selfishness, often drives those in a position of power, or dominance, to seek more. Such a situation exists with every form of government, except that it diminishes in proportion to the longevity or tenure of the government and the extent of government control. Thus, the expression of human nature might best be averted with a minimum of governmental control, which should be as broadly dispersed as possible, and have as rapid a turnover in leaders as commensurate with order. This principle seems to be incorporated in the Constitution of the United States which recognizes this in its periods of tenure for elected officials plus its system of checks and balances.

The animal heritage of humans was recognized in early Greece. Evolving from a military-religious civilization, Athens learned to appreciate unlikemindedness. It came to value individual initiative and voluntary organization. Recognizing that criticism of or by the progressing individual constituted the lifeblood of human progress, the Athenian democracy supplanted the divine right of kings with a constitutional government and freedom of thought and action. Minimal government control and direct and immediate participation in politics by all the citizens were afforded by the small city-state. It provided a freedom and raison d'être rarely achieved since.

The golden era of Hellenic Greece and Imperial Rome was not destined to endure, and it was our heritage of selfishness that destroyed it. As Barnes states, "Rome developed the attitudes and policies of the parasite and spendthrift . . . .The provinces on which Rome depended were sucked dry by administrative grafters." The era of small, peasant landholders was largely replaced by a system of great landlords and slaves.

THE SUPERNATURAL AS A GOVERNING FORCE

Since our beginnings, we have sought to understand nature in terms of the supernatural. We offered sacrifices to appease the gods which controlled the elements of our fate; we submitted ourselves or our tribe to the sacrificial altar. Later we substituted animals, grain, or other possessions, but the principle persisted that we owed our right to exist to a supernatural force. This mysticism of owing one's existence to a superior force gave birth to the principle of altruism, which, as defined by August Comte in the nineteenth century, held that one must make the welfare of others a primary moral concern and place their interests above his or her own. No one had the right to exist for his own sake. We have twisted ourselves to sacrifical service and assumed we owed everything to some higher agency. We owed our existence to God, or the pharaoh, or emperor, or the Reich, or the state, etc. This allegiance relieved the stress of the unknown and gave us security, but it has provided the basis of every dictatorship since the early God-Kings of Egypt. Humans have always been the victim when commanded to be "unselfish" and serve some allegedly higher value. Yet our selfishness may be essential for the welfare of the species.

Mysticism persisted throughout most of human dominion, reaching its height of stagnation and brutality during the Dark and Middle Ages, when there existed a rigid society of status, tortures of the inquisition, cruel punishments, prohibition of inquiry, and limited trade and production. Little free thought filtered through the veil of religious authority until the human mind gradually escaped and we began to understand our place in nature.

EMERGENCE OF FREE THOUGHT

Emergence of free thought allowed some expression of ideology. Roger Bacon in the thirteenth century was the outstanding personality instrumental in the transition of medieval thought. Bacon assailed magic as a delusion and denounced reliance on authority; but he was a clergyman writing for the church and his main desire was to elevate religion. He called for improvements in science and scholarship primarily for holy purposes, but his thinking fostered the intellectual movement that revolutionized civilization and reopened the way for utopian thought together with the foment of later revolution.

The Utopia of Thomas More

A society open to free thought was slow to replace the medievalism of western civilization. By the sixteenth century, writers prompted by the new spirit of inquiry began to envision conditions that might eliminate the evils of their age. The work of Sir Thomas More in 1516 was first to bear the title *Utopia* and first to present the lofty ideals of the Oxford reformers. More severely indicted the disorders attending the great social and economic transformation from an agricultural to an industrial and commercial state. Even in these early years, serfdom was breaking down and the manorial system was disintegrating under the rise of commerce. Most important were the changes in agriculture. Landlords were discovering that farming was most profitable on a large scale, and that sheep raising brought larger returns than cropping. Arable lands were turned into pasture, thus depopulating the old villages and setting the tenants adrift to find work where they could. One shepherd could look after a flock, which stocked an extent of ground that once required many hands to plow and reap. The reduced amount of cropping caused the price of corn and small grains to rise; the poor and numerous dispossessed families were reduced to beg or rob. The Commonwealth island of More's utopia pictured an ideal community where the misery and distress of the displaced populace were corrected (Figure 20-1).

More sought to achieve utopia partly by limiting the population. Further, he would get rid of the sheep and restore cropping as a means of employment. Such a philosophy would also have been appropriate in the Western United States before sheep had destroyed the rangeland.

As for government, More's thinking reflected that of his time, namely the concept of a monarchy, but with a minimum of control. More's island would be governed by senate representatives sent from the cities and chosen by the people. The leader was a Prince chosen for life by the council unless he was removed for suspicion of some design to enslave the people. Each city was limited to 6000 families, each with no less than 10 and no more than 16 persons in it. Numbers within both families and cities were kept constant by relocating both children and families.

Concern for the environment was expressed in policies that called for butchering cattle only outside of town near running water; nothing unclean or foul was to be brought within the towns lest "the air should be infested by ill smells which might prejudice their health."

Medieval thought was still reflected in reverence for a Divine Majesty "to whom we owe both all that we have, and all that we can ever hope for." Humans were still not ready to accept their free agency. They were still far from accepting their place in the human environment.

Francis Bacon

Francis Bacon's Elizabethan era utopia was ruled by a divine but benevolent king. Bacon's *Novus Atlantis*, published in 1627, concerned mostly politics and philosophy but also made brief mention of "parks, and inclosures of all sorts," possibly reflecting the crowded urban condition of the day. In general, utopian thought has largely ignored environmental issues, expressing more concern even about marriage and sex. This tells us much about the major problems or concerns of the period.

Figure 20-1 More's Utopia.

Rousseau's Social Contract

By the eighteenth century, the divine right by which kings ruled had been seriously questioned in Europe, and more freedoms were being gained by the people. The voice of Rousseau was particularly strong and effective in advocating a free or republican form of government. With such a form "the public hardly ever raises to the highest posts any but enlightened and capable men, who fill them honorably."

More than an elected government, Rousseau advocated a social contract between the people in which "each of us puts in common his person and his whole power under the supreme direction of the general will; and in return we receive every member as an indivisible part of the whole." Absolute authority of the people was his central theme. He held that government was the result of a social compact, a common agreement between individuals who voluntarily yielded themselves to the common will. Institutions had no more right to exist than private property or inheritance.

Rousseau's utopia appealed to the masses, especially in France and America, both ripe for revolution. The French Revolution was a great victory of the third estate—the great masses who worked in production over the privileged idle classes of nobles and priests. Nevertheless, France was soon taken over by another small but aggressive minority who were quick to assume the social privilege. What began as a class struggle between nobility and the bourgeoisie became more of a battle between the nonpossessors and the possessors. Thus, in truth, the nobility and bourgeoisie were really on the same side. Even today the battle is not so much between industrialists and workers but between people who earn values and people who seek the unearned.

The French constitution of 1793, founded on the ideals of Rousseau, Mably, Marset, Robespierre, and others, was an attempt to form a society of equals. But humans are not equal. The laws of genetics attest that every individual is different from every other individual, be it plant or animal, and we are genetically no exception. In any sexually reproducing species, equality of individuals is a natural impossibility. Inequality must be regarded as the first law of social materials. Equality of opportunity might be regarded as a second law, or ideal. Though ideally possessed of equal opportunities, everyone differs in ability, initiative, motivation, needs, and every other character. Legislation cannot change this biological fact.

Laissez Faire

Possessed of differences in ability and leadership, it was only natural that once the lineal monarchies were overthrown, the most aggressive and charismatic leaders would rise to the top. Such leaders were not always

the most idealistic social philosophers, but too often were selfish individuals out for their own gain with little knowledge or concern for the human
welfare or environment.

The free agency that evolved even within the framework of monarchies afforded opportunity for people of ambition and creative mind to
discover science and political freedom. The freedom of thought in this era
led to the industrial revolution and the emergence of the laissez faire
economics of capitalism, which favored the success of the most productive people by leaving everyone free to choose the work they favored and
to go as far on the road of achievement as their ability and ambition would
carry them.

People were free to think, to act on their own judgment, to explore, to
create, to attempt to be unprecedented, and to earn their reward. The
result of this freedom of thought and production was that after centuries
of stagnation and poverty, we suddenly found a stream of abundance
never before known. Once we were free to act, the rise of capitalism and a
free-market society lifted us to a standard of living formerly not even
envisioned by the feudal barons. Productive work replaced inherited
position and conquest.

Unfortunately the abundance and achievement were not for all and
were too often gained at the expense of others. Friedrich Engels points
out how the industrial revolution in England rapidly split society into
categories of capitalist and worker. Social abuses accompanied production—deplorable working and living conditions, patriarchal subordina-
tion, and overwork. Worst perhaps was the unstable insecurity of the
workers not knowing from one day to the next if they had a job. The
critics purported one basic evil of capitalism that was seemingly inherent
in the system, and possibly inherent in human nature. Capitalism was said
to represent institutionalized selfishness.

Exploitation, and even individualism, gave rise to opposition from
medievalists and socialists alike. The medievalists found the pursuit of
profit spiritually repugnant. This was easy for them because their needs
were already well-filled. They considered the concept of individual rights
vulgar. Clinging to the creed of sacrifice, medievalists still believed their
life belonged to a higher being. John Ruskin proclaimed that "commerce
or business of any kind may be the invention of the devil." Both
opponents of capitalism viewed the factory to be dehumanizing because it
alienated humans from nature.

The socialists, on the other hand, wished to take over production for
their own gain. Engels had regarded the small preindustrial domestic
manufacturing era as the Golden Age of the working classes.

Karl Marx and the socialists saw bright prospects for the worker only
when the rights of the individual, together with the profit motive, were

abolished. The Marxian socialists believed the human mind and its content were determined by the material factors of production (dialectic materialism); also that historical providence had ordained the inevitable coming of socialism. Marx reintroduced the old slogan: "From each according to his abilities, to each according to his needs." Society's needs would be filled by the sacrifice of the individual to the collective.

Medievalists and socialists alike shared a longing for a society in which a person's existence would be automatically guaranteed, a life in which one would not have to bear the responsibility or decisions for their own survival, a life characterized by freedom from challenge or competition, and a society where everyone contributed to the well-being of the whole. Security would replace identity and stimulation. Order would supplant disorder.

SHARING THE PROFITS OF TECHNOLOGY

Robert Owen's Communal Plan

Robert Owen directed a cotton mill in Scotland for over a quarter of a century during the worst times of the industrial revolution—1800 to 1829. He quickly realized the needless plight of the workers and their dependency on the whims of the mill owners and managers. He responded by turning his mill into a model colony of 2500 workers. He founded schools for the children over two years of age and shortened the workday from 14 to 10 1/2 hours. He also realized the values of the new production methods. A century earlier, 600,000 workers would have been needed to create the same goods. The difference in wealth generated by utilizing the new machines was used to pay huge profits to the proprietors on their capital. Owen felt much of the profit should be returned to the workers, and expedited this concept, thus demonstrating that the profits of capitalism need not be achieved at the expense of the workers. Rather, the workers shared and benefited commensurate with their ability and productivity.

Owen expanded his ideals by establishing a communal plan of colonies in Ireland, and New Harmony, Indiana (Figure 20-2). Here the "Father of English Socialism" tried to establish a new moral world. He believed the character of humans was formed in the early years and that if properly educated, people could live in a world where everyone was happy. Private property could be gradually abolished for the eventual establishment of true communism.

Toward this goal he purchased a complete village in Indiana in 1825, but within 2 years it became obvious the system would not work. The failure was partly due to administrative bungling but largely also because Owen did not select the population carefully.   Also, he encouraged

Figure 20-2   New Harmony, Indiana, Robert Owen's conceptualized Utopia. *(Indiana Historical Society.)*

diversity when he should have insisted on unity. Most left the colony, and those who did not followed the normal course of returning to individualism. Owen wanted honesty, temperance, and industry but got the reverse; especially idleness.

Religious Ideals

Of all the modern voluntary communal societies attempted, only the theocracies founded on religious ideals have had even a modicum of success. The "Millenial Church" of the Shakers, bounded together by a common way of life, common covenant, and a common source of authority, provides an example. They gave all their possessions to their church for equal dispersal, thus enjoying an environment of security and comfort, but the price of unquestioned reliance on external authority was too high, and the system broke down under selfish leadership.

The theocratic story of Mormon communism was much the same, as eloquently told by Maurine Whipple in *The Giant Joshua*. All possessions and monies were submitted to the common stores of the church for dispersal largely according to need. Although the original faithful abided by this policy for some years, the next generation reverted to their inherent individualistic greed, contrary to their childhood teachings, and the system broke down despite the accepted divine sanction of the hierarchy. Strict controls evoked by the religious leaders created order, for a time, but it was not human nature to perpetuate the cooperative sharing. The church was kept viable only by modifying such practices in substituting tithing and allowing individualistic initiative.

Some insight on the uncooperative nature of people might also be gained from Oneida, founded by John Noyes in the 1870s as a Bible commune on the Christian tenet "all mine thine, all thine mine." Common possession extended even to the women and children. A multiple marriage plan and loving en masse even failed to hold the colony together for long. Mutual criticism to correct each other's faults also helped little.

Failure was attributed mainly to the imperfection of human nature, a flaw universal in any society. Other failures, common to such societies, included the loss of a charismatic leader and unexpected disaster. Also ranking high was the failure to select members with appropriate financial, physical, intellectual, and moral attributes. One wonders with what rigid care the participants must be selected to ensure the success of utopian society.

CONFLICT BETWEEN THE INDIVIDUAL AND THE SPECIES

Social utopias attempt to guarantee human security and survival, but in doing so they deny us the right to exist for ourselves. Ideally, we should retain the responsibility for our own survival and make our own decisions on matters affecting our lives. Biologically, we must exist for our own sake. We are an end in ourselves, not a means to the ends of others. Our nature as a living being must be considered, and altruistic traits may well be incompatible with the success of *Homo sapiens* beyond the tribal level of organization.

Our purported basic selfish nature places a severe strain on any social system, but especially on any socialistic system wherein sharing and cooperation are the central concepts. In a capitalistic society, selfishness and competition for material values are almost institutionalized. In a way, this competition is related to a profit motive, with the individual profit as a major goal or incentive. Similarly, the profit motive is rampant in socialistic societies, except that the profit goes to the government and its leaders rather than to the workers and industry.

The greatest negative quality of either system, so far as the environment is concerned, is not the universally shared profit motive but production and the depletion of resources accompanying it. Profit is only the incentive that drives production, whether for individual or state gain.

The utopian society of Henry David Thoreau was simple and natural. Thoreau considered nineteenth-century man to be living in needless luxury. Thoreau would live the life of the Indian in a natural shelter and eat the local fruits. All his needs for body and mind could be satisfied in the woods. Such an idyllic life was fine for one, or perhaps a dozen, or a hundred dozen. But when the woods are filled with a million and more, the land collapses beneath their mass. The woods of Europe collapsed from overpopulation by 1850, and it was only by turning from an agrarian to an industrial economy that more could be supported. Only by turning back the population clock and reducing the numbers to a nineteenth-century figure could Thoreau's idealized agrarian life be permitted.

Society must develop a system that respects its environment and can exist within the framework of its limitations. Humans have been extravagant in their abuse of this environment, especially with regard to what might be called the four "p's": Population, Production, Power, and Pollution.

These stresses on the environment have been allowed to swell without regard for the consequences. Cultural population checks, prevalent in primitive societies, have long since been abandoned; production has soared above demand without regard for the limitations of resources; power demands have risen proportionately; and pollution is still increasing in most industrial societies. Nonindustrial nations aspire covetously toward the same productivity as developed nations have, with the same disregard for the consequences. Rich and poor countries alike strive to become richer, the only difference being the greater capacity of the rich countries to further exploit the world's resources.

Unfortunately, our primate nature, or at least behavior, suggests that every society is going to use all the resources it can get with little regard for the other societies. Cultures that already possess and utilize these resources are unlikely to use less if they can avoid it. Rather, they will persist in their disproportionate rate of consumption so long as possible. Yet if our resources are to be available to future generations, they must be managed sagaciously on a global basis.

SOLUTIONS

Utopian though this might be, the industrial societies are not likely to reduce their material standard of living willingly. We are not likely to conserve any resources for posterity if there is any choice, even when the end of a resource appears imminent. The only hope of preserving a resource is through careful management, recycling it, or substituting some other material for it. As a resource supply wanes, alternate materials sometimes become competitive in cost, and substitutes may enter the economy faster than the supplies become exhausted.

Accelerated power consumption accompanies industrialization and affluence. For better or worse, every society is striving toward both of these goals. The only question is whether or not they will attain them at the expense of the environment. This depends on the attitude of governments more than the attitude or concern of the public. An open society responsive to public concern or pressure is most likely to manage its resources and wastes in the best interests of the environment. A government run by a committee is in a favorable position to manage its resources for the common good, but in reality is more likely to run it for immediate gain (e.g., of "vested interests") regardless of environmental disharmony.

Human Genetic Nature

Can a society of today be utopian and still persist to the benefit of future generations and the preservation of the species? Morally it should, but realistically can it? We may give lip service to the preservation of the environment and the perpetuation of the species, but does our genetic nature allow us to be concerned for even the next generation if it will cost anything? Some altruistic message in the human genetic code seems to encourage sharing within every social group. Self-sacrifice of parents for their children in the face of danger is an instinctive and powerful force in people, but it is also argued that evolution must have been selective for egoism. In the words of biologist Robert MacArthur, "an altruistic individual who endangers his own life to save others not related to him must be less fit, and his type will be eliminated by natural selection."

The principle might easily extend to the sacrifice of material values. We are not likely to sacrifice today's conveniences or even luxuries for tomorrow's survival. If we are to be concerned for the future, it is most likely to be for the future of the present generation. If we are to act toward achieving and preserving a quality environment in terms of open spaces, ample resources, absence from pollution, etc., action must be taken that will be beneficial now, but measures could well be taken that also would have long-term benefits.

An example of this might be development of mass transit systems as opposed to more highways. This would benefit today's world in terms of convenience and economy, but it would incidentally help tomorrow's world in terms of conserved resources and land areas not decimated by highways.

Although we are unlikely to sacrifice for the future of other than our own descendents, the future may be protected inadvertently by our rapidly advancing technology. If technology advances at a faster rate than problems become critical or unresolvable, then the species might persist indefinitely.

One example in which technology might not be able to keep pace with environmental degradation is that involving some stress situation with consequences that are unrecognized until it is too late. The release of DDT and PCBs into the environment may provide examples. These and related chemicals were allowed to flow freely into the environment long after the hazards were realized. Even now when the hazards and stability of the chemicals are known, they continue to be widely used, but their use is a social and economic problem, not a technological one.

The social or economic restraints on applying known technology are more apt to become limiting. Even today when the technology exists for controlling pollution and recycling resources, the knowledge is rarely applied without some economic or legislative incentives, and politicians are not always the most knowledgeable concerning human needs.

Behavioral Constraints

Behavioral scientists might hold more hope for our regard for future humans. We are already "conditioned" by heredity or our childhood environment to be concerned for our immediate family. At the most fundamental level, our behavior is determined basically by a genetic endowment traceable in evolutionary history, but upon this is superimposed behavior and learning conditioned by the environment to which the individual has been exposed. Perhaps a social environment could be provided, as proposed by behaviorists, that would induce us to behave for the good of others. This should be possible if the suitable values, or personal reinforcers as Skinner calls them, were provided. The cultural designer seeks to develop practices that will incorporate these values into society. Desired behavior would be rewarded and deviant behavior punished. Individual control is denied. There would be no sense of individual responsibility or guilt because these traits would have been abolished or given up to a power elite made up of the technicians or engineers of behavior.

As populations grow, cultural practices and attitudes become highly significant. They are significant to the rate of depletion of resources, pollution, population, and every other environmental stress. For example, a universal cultural practice of late marriages and late childbearing would go far to eliminate problems of overpopulation. A concerned attitude toward resource depletion could avert a problem in that area. Pride in workmanship could also prolong the use of resources. It is conceivable that with the suitable conditioning based on our inherent capacity for ontogenetic learning, we might psychologically be trained to be equally concerned for the well-being of all others and the environment—present and future.

Such conditioning might be considered an infringement on one's freedom, and if imposed must be done voluntarily. B. F. Skinner allows that our genetic endowment may include a need for freedom. "When treated aversively people tend to act aggressively or to be reinforced by signs of having worked aggressive damage." If freedoms are knowingly deprived, we seek escape and will rebel. Yet if restrictions are gradually or voluntarily imposed, they may be willingly accepted. Skinner points out how "many people have submitted to the most obvious religious, governmental, and economic controls for centuries, striking for freedom only sporadically, if at all."

CONCLUSIONS

Now we have reached a stage in social evolution where some cultures are able to question the human role, its impact on the environment, its interrelations, and its place in the ecosystem. We question our egoistic social system, and the inequality of opportunity for many. At the same time, a majority of cultures have not evolved to a stage of questioning. They have only recently broken from feudalistic authority and transferred their authority from emperors or czars to the people's representatives. While theoretically altruistic, and with more opportunity than before, they still lack the opportunity for the egoistic expression of the human psyche.

Somewhere between these dominant forms of government, there must lie a utopian haven of Atlantis, where all people could fulfill their physical and psychological needs unfettered by restriction and free from the incursions of others. Utopia cannot be produced by expanding economy or material wealth. Rather, it requires maximum interaction and understanding of the environment to which we are intimately bound. Most important, we must have social interaction in groups of a manageable size consistent with human inheritance. Cultural adaptation is the basis of human success as a gregarious social animal, but it must progress more rapidly if it is to keep pace with the accelerating complexity of society. Utopia is technologically possible, but it is sociologically unlikely and biologically perhaps even impossible.

SELECTED READINGS

Andrews, Charles M. *Ideal Empires and Republics.* (New York: M. Walter Dunne, 1901).
Branden, Nathanial. *Who is Ayn Rand?* (New York: Paperback Library, 1962).
Glasser, William. The civilized identity society. *Saturday Review*, Feb. 19, 1972, pp. 26–31.
Iltis, H. H., U. L. Loucks, and P. Andrews. Criteria for an optimum human

    environment. In J. P. Holdren and P. R. Ehrlich (eds.). *Global Ecology.* (New
    York: Harcourt, Brace, Jovanovich, 1970).
Kateb, George (ed.). *Utopia.* (New York: Atherton, 1971).
Richter, Peyton E. (ed.). *Utopias: Social Ideals and Communal Experiments.*
    (Boston: Holbrook Press, 1971).
Skinner, B. F. *Beyond Freedom and Dignity.* (New York: Knopf, 1971).
Thoreau, Henry D. *Walden.* (Boston: Houghton Mifflin, 1854).

Chapter 21

Our Genetic Future

All men plume themselves on the improvement of society, and no man improves.

Ralph Waldo Emerson

Quality of life is measured by more than harmony with the environment, and it is more than experiencing pleasure or finding happiness. Quality is measured by the total fulfillment of basic physical and psychological needs. This must be kept in mind as one considers the potential for improving the human race through genetic or behavioral engineering. That is, what is the real, underlying motivation for trying to improve human society?

THE GENE POOL

Genetically, human evolution may be conceived as occurring through changes in the frequency of particular genes in the human gene pool. The gene pool, coupled with human ability to learn and adjust, must, and likely will, keep pace with any environmental changes; if it does not, the species will perish. A gene considered bad now may become essential to survival at some later date. Conversely, a trait desirable today may be useless or even harmful tomorrow. Our biological evolution has selected us for fitness in a "natural" world. Both people and the natural world are constantly changing. Social and medical progress in recent decades has fostered the preservation of deleterious genes in the gene pool that may possibly unbalance it. Genes fostering diabetes provide one example. Human manipulation of nature in terms of injecting air and water pollutants might further alter our inheritance by favoring pollutant-tolerant characteristics. The original environment has been modified, and much of its initial attributes, for which humans became selected, have been exhausted.

It has been said that our egocentric nature makes our survival unlikely; perhaps in seeking material gain through an ever-growing standard of living we may destroy ourselves along with our environment. We may be changing our physical and social environment faster than our genetic ability to keep pace with the change. If it is human genetic nature to take all we can, human nature must change if we are to survive. Our possible basic need for nature, for instance, may be essential. Yet, nature may be disappearing at a faster rate than human ability to adjust to its absence. The complexities of cities and government are accelerating out of proportion to our sagacity in resolving the problems that develop. Solution may lie in changing the nature of the human race genetically, as well as behaviorally. The human brain, fashioned from information encoded in DNA, is beginning to refashion the DNA itself. We may one day be in a position to direct our own inheritance.

THE SOCIAL ENVIRONMENT

People have sought to change the nature and will of others and subordinate them since antiquity. It seems part of human nature to dominate others. Dominant males control the destiny of baboon and chimpanzee tribes, and dominant people have always regulated human behavior, usually through physical or psychological strength. Science has now given us the capacity to regulate behavior in more subtle ways—ways possibly offensive and even repugnant within the context of our present cultures.

There will be a controlling element in any society, be it an individual or a committee. In a small Pacific island culture, the leadership may be elected or chosen, whereas in the complex cultures of western civilization the leaders may rule by fiat, but it is human nature to lead and be led. The nature of the submissives of society is to seek leadership for their own security, protection, and survival.

Leaders of old assumed power from strength or, in the rare occasions of democracy, from popularity . It is entirely possible that future control may be directed by the wielders of genetic or behavioral authority.

Genetic Potential

We have stressed the basic genetic nature of the human race and seen it as a product of its inheritance. But if human action were governed solely by instinct we would not be so flexible in our response to the physical environment, nor would such diversity be found in the different human cultures. To a very large degree, we are also a product of our social and physical environment, in other words, our ontogenetic learning. Were it not for the flexibility and maleability of human behavior patterns, we would be enslaved as other animal species by the slow process of genetic adaptation.

Other creatures have adapted to their surroundings, but at a considerable sacrifice. Birds gained wings and conquered the air, but it was at the expense of their forelimbs. Whales mastered the sea but no longer move on land. Sloths move freely in the trees but not on the ground. The early hominids developed mental capability and the ability to use this intellect to adapt and conquered all the elements without surrendering any physical trait. They used their intellect to adapt to every environment and developed cultures initially compatible to them.

The potential for behavioral adaptation superimposed on a genetic base is part of each individual, and provides the basis for every culture. A newborn baby is born with numerous innate qualities. It knows hunger and love, it responds to pain and fear, it possesses a basic intellect and has an innate "passion for survival." Genes influence its behavior and set limits to its physical structure, temperament, intelligence, and special abilities.

Psychiatrist Alexander Thomas of New York University finds that babies show a characteristic temperament from their earliest days that he considers inborn. Other characteristics and emotional responses are largely the product of their behavioral and cultural associations. The social environment to which they are exposed influences their attitudes and behavior, their likes and dislikes, and their concern or unconcern for others. The food they eat is the food they savor, whether termites, grubs, or beef. Their taste is conditioned by what they eat. The gods they worship are the gods they know. As we mature, we respond to certain sexual stimuli, but even this response may vary according to childhood experience.

Genetic and Environmental Interaction

The interaction between environment and heredity makes it difficult to delimit where one influence leaves off and the other begins. Nearly all behavioral traits depend on several different genes and their interactions. The environment, with its behavioral experiences, regulates the degree to which the individual achieves the potential of his or her genes.

A human child remains virtually helpless for a much longer period than any other animal, and throughout its early years it is exposed to the teachings of its family and society. Its developing mind is molded in their image. More than any other animal then, humans are less a product of inheritance than of social environment.

Molding Behavior

The social environment determines the character of the individual, and the human mind is molded by it within the framework of a genetic base. Likes, dislikes, customs, acceptance of others, and according to behaviorists such as B. F. Skinner, aggressive, egoistic, or altruistic nature can be encouraged by early training by positive reinforcement. Skinner has documented this tenet sufficiently that the potential for psychologically molding human behavior as we desire is generally accepted. In other words, the technology is available to make a "better person." But the social mechanisms for effecting this are lacking. Assuming the mechanisms for improving the cooperative nature of humans were available and practiced, what might be the consequences?

The results might be likened to the takeover of trusting American Indian cultures by western civilization beginning in the fifteenth century. Any altruistic culture molded by behavioral engineering would lack the competitive attitude necessary for it to be dominant—such a society would soon be subservient to any of the remaining egocentric, materialistic cultures that might still abound. Most likely, the new society would be dictated by the behavioral engineers who "knew" what was best for them, or the individuals on whom, perhaps because of a stronger innate egoism, the brainwashing was unsuccessful.

GENETIC MANIPULATION

It might at first glance seem simpler to mold people than to mold their minds. Theognis of Magra proposed in 548 B.C. that the inborn qualities of people could be improved, and a century later Plato advanced the idea further. The concept of eugenics—improving the human species through the control of hereditary factors in mating—originally related primarily to the selective breeding of humans. The concept is sometimes extended to include the modification and reengineering of genes.

Rollin Hotchkiss of Rockefeller University asserts that the gene pool of mankind is public property and may have to be the subject of general purview. People should "begin to think of altering genetic outcomes." Hotchkiss suggests possibilities of mate selection, controlling offspring (eugenics), control of gene expression, and genetic intervention (gene therapy).

Mate selection and eugenics are the most rational of these possibilities. Eugenic control of mating would slowly reduce the prevalence of the recessive undesirable genes which may have accumulated in the gene pool, if such traits can be identified and forbidden (negative eugenics). At the same time, desirable traits could be encouraged (positive eugenics). Application of eugenics could theoretically alter the gene pool rapidly to produce a more intelligent subculture, or a stronger one, or more tolerant population. Perhaps social logic would never tolerate eugenics. Subsidies and grants to participants, however, or test tube reproduction, could go far toward encouraging desirable mating combinations and producing better humans.

Gene Modifications

We have begun to unlock the most fundamental processes of life and ultimately may be able to manipulate and alter them. Doing so could control cancer, correct genetic defects, lessen the distresses of old age, and expand the prowess of minds and bodies. Defective genes may some day be burned out by pinpoint laser beams and replaced by segments of DNA made in test tubes and introduced by viruses serving to transfer genetic information from test tubes to the control center of the cell. In an effort to treat children who had the heritable inability to produce the enzyme arginase, associated with mental retardation, researchers have infected two youngsters with a natural virus, the Shope papilloma, which contains DNA that triggers arginase synthesis. One might wonder, though, if a virus gene carrier could become promiscuous and pick up and transfer other than just the desired gene message; or might it invade the sex cells and become a component of the human gene pool?

Limited genetic control may not be too remote. Dr. Sol Spiegelman of Columbia University has synthesized an artificial virus that is indistinguishable from its natural model, and Arthur Kornberg of Stanford created DNA in the laboratory in 1967. Molecular biologists are learning to map the location of specific genes in the human DNA strands and determine the genetic code of each. They have also created synthetic genes in the test tube; the next step should be to perform genetic surgery. Molecular geneticists now look forward to the day when they might alter the nature of their species with laboratory-created genetic instructions.

A gene change of even low effectiveness might satisfy some human cell deficiencies to a reasonable degree. Such gene products as insulin or other hormones, blood-clotting proteins, or some enzymes might well suffice for nearly normal life at below-normal levels even if the new genes were only partly effective.

Gene changes of any kind are far more complex than sometimes inferred. Genes are probably only regions in a continuum of almost similar DNA. The interaction of DNA sequences effects genetic characteristics and may be more influential in determining a character than a particular segment. The idealized pure genes visualized may exist only in the minds of the molecular geneticist.

Cloning

Short of tampering with the basic nuclear substance, another mechanism for modifying humans is being investigated. This is *cloning*, duplicating individuals from nonsexual cells. Whole new carrots can be grown from a single cell, why not a whole new person from a cell scraped off a finger? Conceivably, the cell could be implanted in an artificial womb and bottled in amniotic fluid to develop like a normal fetus. The potential for cloning humans is with us. It may be only a matter of time before refinements in technology make it practical. Societies might clone their most eminent politicians, their best scientists, or most avid workers or soldiers. The fallacy in this obviously lies in that while the clonal individuals might possess the basic intelligence and physique of the donor, the social environment that developed the donor's intellect and character could never be duplicated. The "offspring" would be no more like the "parent" than the identical twins separated at birth and thrust into different environments. We are far more than the simple product of a genetic substance.

A more valid justification for cloning would be to replace lost organs. A new arm or leg might be grown, or a new kidney to replace a diseased one. Carrying the potential one step further, an entire new individual might be cloned at birth and kept in deep freeze until the organs might be needed. This grotesque possibility has been suggested more than once, but effecting it is still remote.

Knowledge Transfer

Why should knowledge go to waste? If knowledge were stored as memory in the brain, it should be transferable. Memory transfer apparently has been demonstrated in flatworms and mice. In one classic experiment, which has come under considerable question, University of Michigan's James McConnell conditioned flatworms to contract when a light was flashed. The worms were then ground up and fed to untrained worms. The worms fed this "knowledge" learned to contract twice as fast as their predecessors. McConnell theorized that the first batch of worms formed new RNA which synthesized new proteins containing the message that light was a signal to contract. Having consumed these memory proteins, the second group did not need to manufacture so much of their own.

The work of neurochemist Georges Ungar of Baylor was similar. He conditioned mice to shun the darkness they normally preferred, then made a broth of their brains. This was injected into the abdominal cavities of mice which now reacted with a similar aversion to the darkness. The more of the brain broth injected, the faster was this response learned.

If memory molecules could be found, the secret of memory would be revealed. At first whole brain tissues might be ground to transmit knowledge, but ultimately knowledge proteins could be synthesized so one might learn simply by swallowing the appropriate knowledge pills. Conceivably, sufficient knowledge should enable us to better cope with the increasing complexities of greater populations and diminishing resources.

Either by this means or by altering genes, babies might be born possessing rote knowledge—language skills, mathematical background, etc.—just as birds apparently emerge from the egg already programmed genetically for celestial navigation. Intelligence might also be enhanced by increasing brain size either through genetic manipulation or transplanting brain cells to newborn infants or to the fetus. Such cells might be grown in the laboratory. The main limitation to brain size, the size of the adult female pelvis, might be averted by brain cell implants after birth or a genetic manipulation of the pelvis.

Correcting Genetic Defects

Daniele Petrucci of Bologna, Italy has kept a fertilized egg growing in a laboratory for 29 days. The experiment was terminated only when the fetus was clearly becoming monstrously deformed. With improved techniques another embryo was kept alive for 59 days before it died from a laboratory mistake. Many scientists believe such "progress" is justified. If life is considered to begin at conception, scientists have produced life artificially out of the womb. The rationale of such genetic manipulations or creation of life lies not so much in bettering the human species, but in controlling the many diseases caused by genetic aberration, or predisposed by genetic character.

In the United States alone, over 50,000 children are born each year with genetic diseases; many more are mentally retarded. Cancer kills over 300,000 in the United States each year. If cancer is an aberration of normal cellular growth, as many suspect, genetic engineering should be able to control it. According to this hypothesis, normal cells manufacture RNA that migrates to nearby healthy cells where it provides a template which serves as a protovirus. If the wandering RNA transmits the wrong message after entering the cell, it can cause the production of altered DNA that orders the cell to grow abnormally. Removing such defective genetic imperfections, or improving the general level of intelligence, are major goals for the genetic biologist, and provide justifications for continued research.

Nature aborts the worst genetic mistakes, but modern medicine is saving more borderline cases each year. About 5 of every 100 babies are born with some genetic defect. The most obvious can sometimes be detected from chromosome abnormalities even before birth. Doctors can examine cells from the amniotic fluid of the fetus and identify over 70 different genetic disorders plus several "gene-associated" defects. But many disorders involve inconspicuously defective genes whose expression is more subtle.

If the lives of those with defective genes is extended, the chances of perpetuating this condition in the gene pool are increased. Compassion in one generation may lead to the decline of the next. If modern medicine is to continue intervening with nature, it may be necessary to take the next step and sterilize those with some hereditary diseases. The right to have children has been questioned not only for those with defective genes, but even among normal individuals. As the population becomes larger, reproduction may have to be viewed as a privilege, not a right. Perhaps prospective parents might have to prove their competence.

Natural selection favors the differential survival of some genotypes at the expense of others. This serves as the most significant agent of evolution. In primitive societies, infectious diseases and starvation commonly cause 50 percent infant mortality and are the principal factors checking population growth. Infectious disease has probably been the main agent of natural selection of people during the past 5000 years. Since urbanization, diseases associated with crowding and sanitation have become most important. Resistance to such diseases that affect both the young and old gradually builds up in a population, since resistant genotypes are favored. Degenerative diseases such as arteriosclerosis and some forms of cancer are not selective because they usually kill only after the childbearing years. In a natural population, the unfit perish. We might consider abandoning the seemingly benevolent goal that everyone must live. Then there would be no need for genetic tailoring. Nature would take care of the defective gene carriers as it has before.

The use of genetic engineering to further select resistance and to control defects of genetic fate is accepted in today's society. Few argue against research designed to cure cancer or diabetes or to correct faulty gene mechanisms that control the amino acid synthesis vital to normal life. Organ transplants are now a widely accepted tenet, and such artificial organs as the kidney are widely used at least outside the body to prolong life. The next step of producing natural organs artificially might raise more questions of immortality, as does cloning whole individuals for the same purpose.

PSYCHOLOGICAL CONTROL

The strongest innate human drive is the will for survival. This fundamental will, or need, may be interrelated with potential human aggressiveness. Aggressiveness may have been responsible for human success on the planet, but it may also lead to our doom. Controlling or even curbing aggressiveness may be more important to human survival than enriching intellect.

A program to develop nonaggression traits either through behavioral or genetic manipulation would provide an ideal mechanism for producing a population of subservient workers. It would foster a controllable society but destroy its freedom.

We are born with brain mechanisms to control violent behavior—to turn it on or off. Medical science now almost routinely taps the brain cells controlling violence. Surgery can remove these cells, and electric current transmitted to these cells through implanted electrodes can turn them on or off. Such procedures can extend far beyond the control of violent behavior.

Today's technology has discovered the ultimate pleasure. Psychologist James Olds at McGill University implanted electrodes in specific "pleasure centers" in the brains of rats, and the animals were allowed to stimulate themselves by pressing a lever. Given a choice, they preferred the lever to food, water, or sex. Some pressed the lever as often as 8000 times an hour, stopping only when they collapsed from fatigue. The potential of using such a mechanism of mass brain electrode implants for controlling society through positive and negative reinforcement of behavior, work obedience, and subservience is infinite, even if repugnant.

The danger from genetic and psychological control may easily outweigh any advantages. Not only are the psychological aspects foreboding, but our very survival may be at stake. A world is conceivable in which people pursue only artificially induced pleasures, where arts have died and books are no longer read, and human beings no longer think or govern themselves.

THE FUTURE

Biologist James Bonner of the California Institute of Technology believes that "biologists are on the verge of finding a way to eliminate senility, thus facilitating a human life span of 200 years." A more extreme view is that humans might live forever. Aging and natural death are genetically and physiologically regulated, and science is at the threshold of understanding and controlling them. With the replacing of parts and repairing faulty arteries, and a myriad of other overhauling operations, our life-span has already been extended greatly. Only the degeneration of the brain, organs, and connective tissues, and cancer, remain to be conquered. Eventually, the only cause of deaths may be accidents. Pressure on the human environment would then be enormous and call for drastic responsive measures.

If age can be extended greatly, there may also be a need to terminate life. At the moment, death control seems repugnant. This applies particularly to establishing when a person must die. But attitudes change, and they may become obsolete in the same way as technological discoveries. Will it eventually be acceptable to kill the infirm or anyone over a set age?

Genetic engineering is more than correcting defects or prolonging life. It encompasses also human dreams to breed a better person. What constitutes a better person? One more like ourself or what we think we should like to be? No two people would agree, and a person put together by a committee would probably look it. Would we combine athletic prowess with great intellect? Animals have been selected for desirable traits for centuries—cattle for weight gain or milk production, hogs to be fat, pineapples built to fit a can, and horses for speed; but here we know what we want. The same might be done for humans, but success could only be measured by the success with which the new person fits into the environment or culture. Then we must ask, "for what environment is the person intended?" Appropriately coordinating genetic manipulation with behavioral regulation, he or she may be better qualified for some activities than could be expected from the random chance of natural reproduction. But would the person be as human, and who is to define the qualities of humanity?

We would have destroyed free agency, but is this new? What choice does one have in selecting parents? We might choose to produce more reliable and efficient people who were content in their predetermined roles. It would cost our freedom, but this might not concern a generation in which this value was bred out or other values were held in greater esteem. The freedom of the individual might be sacrificed for the welfare of the species.

MORAL JUDGMENTS

Many scientists agree with molecular biologist Francis Crick that basic morals and common sense will prevail in utilizing genetic knowledge. Others fear that our newfound genetic knowledge will be used selfishly for the material gain of a few at the expense of more. It is still more likely that research will continue uncontrolled, bringing to reality many of the awesome possibilities discussed, and that knowledge will accumulate at a faster rate than our wisdom to manage it. As the gain of knowledge accelerates, the gap widens between our new knowledge and the ability to handle it wisely. The chasm separating knowledge and wisdom will become even more perilous. In the words of molecular geneticist David Suzuki of the University of British Columbia, "We must create the means of preventing further input of technological progress instead of trying to control it after it has created problems. We must anticipate problems and stop them before they are created."

Scientists have traditionally been concerned with the uses of their work, but there are many who practice science for the sake of learning new truths alone with no regard for the application of their findings. This is considered someone else's problem. Gain in knowledge is sought as an end in itself just as material gains are sought in business. The argument that science must always move forward is no more valid than the argument that economies must always grow. Too often the scientific elite not only fail to translate their work for the layman but discourage those who attempt to do so. Interpretation is left to less-qualified science writers and politicians. Scientists can no longer deny their responsibilities to make their work known to the public and understood.

Human beings are the only animal who can satisfy their curiosity with experimentation. This is science, and in practicing it, one is as uniquely human as when writing, painting, or composing, but in exercising this privilege of finding new truths, scientists have an obligation to make their work known to society and assure us it is in the public interest. The practical application of the scientists' work must be known to prevent its misuse.

CONCLUSIONS

We are in the position of developing the capability to steer our own destiny. Evolution no longer need be opportunistic. Human, or inhuman, manipulation would have both good and bad consequences—but very likely the consequences would be irreversible. Our fate is on the verge of no longer resting in DNA or in destiny, but in the hands of people. The value of this self-regulation to the species might be argued, as might the effects on human beings. Genetic manipulation could make us more mechanistic than ever before, but better adapted to fit into an almost inevitable "plastic and tinsel world."

In the final analysis, it may be our innate curiosity and egoistic nature to move ahead unfettered by moral restraint. The question "should one play God?" is then academic. If we can, we will; it is our nature. There are those who may be content to let others play God, and there are those who would question their wisdom.

Our genetic endowment has allowed us a long learning period of behavioral flexibility that has given us the capacity to shape our own destiny as individuals and in response to our environment. But what we do with this capacity may remain largely a function of our previous inheritance.

Natural selection is slow, perhaps too slow to keep up with changes in the environment, but humans might be altered to adapt more rapidly. There is little doubt now that we have the capacity to change our basic nature to a degree—to sharpen our intellect or to curb possible innate characteristics including aggressiveness. Human nature can be modified either physically or psychologically. Some of the changes may seem frightening in the context of today's culture, but are likely to be entirely acceptable in the framework of tomorrow. Even now, some alterations that might better adapt us to our environment appear highly desirable to us, yet might have seemed grotesque to our parents.

SELECTED READINGS

Anonymous. 1971. Man into superman. *Time*. April 19, 1971, pp. 33–52.

Downs, James F. *Cultures in Crisis*. (New York: Glencoe Press, 1971).

Hotchkiss, R. D. 1970. Man's Part in His Own Biological Future. pp. 35–54. In *Environment Man Survival*. Grand Canyon Symposium. L. H. Wullstein, I. B. McNulty, L. Klikoff (eds.). Biology Department, University of Utah.

Lasker, G. W. (ed.). *The Processes of Ongoing Human Evolution*. (Detroit: Wayne State University Press, 1960).

Rivers, Caryl. Grave new world. *Saturday Review*, April 18, 1972.

Spilhaus, A. 1970. The Next Industrial Revolution (editorial). *Science*, vol. 167, p. 1673.

Chapter 22

Confidence in
Tomorrow

Those who cannot remember the past are condemned to repeat it.

George Santayana

Already in the 1920s, the roaring days of the flapper and speakeasy, the Model T and the Charleston, there were those who were apprehensive of the growing complexities of society and who feared for human rights. Justice Oliver Wendell Holmes argued that as human numbers became greater and greater, one's responsibilities to the group became greater; in turn a person would have to lose some rights as an individual for the good of the whole. We have seen that our increasing numbers are at the heart of more values than our personal freedom, and that the freedoms we have enjoyed for millennia underlie the potential catastrophes of unchecked breeding, depletion of resources, and global pollution.

When human numbers were few, none of these hazards seemed imminent, but as our numbers increased, more and more cooperation was needed for survival. It is true of cells in the organism and of organisms in society. Furthermore, as life becomes more complex due to increasing numbers, we have fewer choices of direction. As with the differentiating cell, the further we progress toward a specialized end, the less options we retain to alter our social structure. There is no turning back. Modern agriculture, technology, and industrialization become the only means of supporting the ever-increasing populations; society and the environment must continue to adjust to meet the need.

Biologically, socially, and economically, the world is constantly changing. We have reviewed this global evolution of mankind and seen where we have been and where we are. Does this give us some idea of where we are going? Possibly! Where we go depends partly on where we want to go and the direction we take now, but most of all on our biologic, including our behavioral, potential.

THE STAGES OF CIVILIZATION

Humans have tried since antiquity to improve the quality of life—to fulfill the physiologic and psychological needs seemingly inherent in our gene pool. Since the industrial revolution, every nation has sought relentlessly to capitalize on its technology to improve life with near total disregard for the environmental consequences. How much longer can this go on? How much longer can humans survive? More dolorous, can our way of life survive? Is western civilization doomed to vanish as the Sumerians, Incas, or Romans? Or is all civilization to perish? Of approximately twenty major civilizations that have existed during the course of human history, only two or three now remain. Most have been destroyed by the expansion of western civilizations. Countless simpler cultures— Hottentots, Hopi, Tasmanians, and more, have also been lost.

Arnold J. Toynbee has suggested that civilizations have a life cycle much as any other viable biological entity. His studies indicate that civilizations pass through a common pattern of evolution. A civilization is born, then slowly enters a period of vigorous expansion, increasing in size and power both internally and externally at the expense of its neighbors, until gradually a crisis of organization appears. If the crisis is passed, a period of weakened vigor and morale is reached, after which the civilization becomes stabilized and eventually stagnant.

Western civilization followed this course through a period of crisis (Hundred Years War and plague), after which it emerged upon a new period of expansion beginning in the fifteenth century. According to the historian Carroll Quigley, it did this several times, most strongly in the nineteenth century and again in the twentieth—each age of expansion marked by four kinds of growth: (1) of population, (2) of geographic area, (3) of production, and (4) of knowledge.

Limiting Factors

The decline in the rate of expansion of a civilization marks its passage into the age of conflict characterized by a declining rate of expansion, growing tensions and conflicts, increasing wars, growing pessimism, and superstition.

Additional limitations may now further characterize decline: pollution, population growth, and resource depletion. Pursuit of material goals at the expense of our resources cannot continue indefinitely and will ultimately lead only to annihilation. There are many courses of action available to avert decline, each with different consequences.

Management professor Jay Forrester of Massachusetts Institute of Technology and his group have attempted to assess the consequences of taking various courses, assuming they are possible (Figure 22-1). Forrester developed a dynamic computer model to simulate and interrelate the major forces influencing us—natural resources, pollution, food production, population, capital investment, and geographic space. He simulated the interaction of these social, technological, and natural systems and projected the changes that might be expected if various actions were taken affecting each of these factors.

The basic question asked was how long a population and industrialization could continue to grow on a finite planet. John Mill posed the question in 1857: "Toward what ultimate point is society tending by industrial progress?" What factor would be most likely to limit growth; and how might the quality of life be affected? If the assumption were made that growth will continue in the same direction as it has in past centuries, Forrester asserts that civilization will first and most clearly be restrained by limitations of natural resources. As resources become scarcer, more capital must be spent on procuring raw materials, leaving

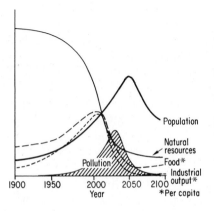

Figure 22-1 Jay Forrester's "standard" world model, assuming no major change in the physical, economic, or social relationships that have historically governed the development of the world system. Food production, industrial output, and population grow exponentially until slowed by diminishing resources and a rise in death rate after a lag period. *(Based on D. H. Meadows et al., The Limits to Growth: A Report for the Club of Rome's Project on the Predicament of Mankind, 1972.)*

less money for investment and new development. Investment would gradually fall behind the rate of obsolescence, and the industrial base would begin to collapse. The demise of the equipment of technology also will cause agriculture to lag, and food production will be unable to keep pace with population growth. A solution of slowing down production might seem obvious, but Forrester points out that the obvious "solutions" will not suffice. "The dynamic characteristics of complex social systems frequently mislead people." Relieving one set of symptoms may only create a new mode of system behavior with still more unpleasant consequences.

As nations strive to improve the quality of life through industrialization, they encounter increased pollution. If industrialization is curbed, crowding and food shortages ultimately ensue. If production were slowed to conserve resources, many nations would never achieve the standard of living sought. More significantly, technology is essential to obtaining maximum food production. Without tractors and gasoline, food supplies will never be adequate to feed the expanding population.

Increasing food production alone is of no value for at least two reasons. First, as discussed earlier, this would mean more people could be fed in the short run simply to starve in the long run. Less obviously, the higher availability of food would allow capital to be directed toward a higher material standard of living, hastening resource depletion and a pollution crisis.

Even population control alone is inadequate to stave depletion. Alone, birth control does not reduce material growth; more likely it increases the rate of capital investment, which in turn increases industrialization and pollution and accelerates depletion of natural resources.

Because of the interaction of all the forces, they must be treated collectively, not singly. Population must be limited, raw materials conserved, and the pollution of affluence all suppressed concomitantly. If global trends in population growth, industrialization, pollution, and resource depletion continue unchanged, limits of growth will be reached sometime in the twenty-first century, or even sooner.

Equilibrium

The MIT group concludes that global equilibrium is at least conceptually possible. They suggest it can be achieved by reducing the resource usage rate by 75 percent, pollution generation by 50 percent, capital investment generation by 40 percent, food production by 20 percent, and reducing the birth rate by 30 percent.

Chemical engineer Thomas J. Boyle of McGill University, using the MIT data but correcting for the pollution factor, which he maintained was 10 times too high to be used as it was, is more optimistic. He projected that the world population would stabilize at 6 billion people, natural resources would decrease, but pollution would be under control and technology would forestall such crises as famine and industrial collapse. The world of 2100 would see better days than ever before.

There are signs that reductions are already taking place. Population growth is most notably beginning to slow. On a global basis, population growth rate of 2 percent of several years ago may now have declined to 1.8 percent. The largest cities in the United States have stopped growing, and several European countries are approaching zero population growth. East Germany reached it in 1969. Births in the United States are declining markedly. The Vietnamese are looking both to the short-term effects of underpopulation and the longer term prospects of population stabilization. There are indications in many other poor countries that population growth is slowing, but in many more it is not. Social and cultural factors in many countries make a decline in birth rate highly improbable. Also, history emphasizes that birth rates are not reduced voluntarily until living standards rise above a certain minimum level, but it is critical that population growth does subside. The global resource is fixed, so the more people there are, the less each can have.

Diminishing Growth

Kenneth Boulding describes a slowdown in economic development. He sees the last spurt of expansion as having already passed and the world now beginning a general slowdown as indicated by the recent decline in GNP in the United States. The greatest economic acceleration came in the period of 1880 to 1920 with the introduction of electricity, movies, automobiles, and planes. Major newer developments include principally television, computer science, nuclear technology, and spacecraft—all initiated before 1950. The vast technological advances in agriculture have also slowed.

Boulding points out that these were once-and-for-all changes. Once they have happened, they cannot happen again. They gave rise to a great economic spurt, but now they are gone, and the only alternatives are stagnation and possibly ecological disaster—or perhaps unforeseen advances generating growth anew.

Resource depletion, and higher costs of existing resources such as petroleum, is likely to reduce industrial growth over the next few generations despite a culture geared to a philosophy of growth. Increased costs of production caused by high wages, resource costs, and the expenses of pollution control are already cooling the furnaces of industry in the United States. West Europe and Japan are following the same course, as will other countries as they achieve affluence. As it becomes increasingly more expensive to produce quality goods in the United

States, the nation is turning elsewhere—to Japan for radios and television, to Hong Kong for clothing, Mexico for food, Germany and Japan for cars, etc. By 1974, production in the United States and Western Europe began to decline, and unemployment began to increase. The last year of "peak" production was 1973; 1974 and 1975 saw a decline. Increasing costs of the diminishing resources within the next few decades may further slow economic and industrial growth not only in the United States but in other industrial nations. Costs of materials in shortest reserve have already begun to rise. Petroleum products, timber, and mineral resources provide the most striking examples. Added monies required for such essential commodities are unavailable for luxury products, thus affecting the material quality of life.

RESOURCE ADJUSTMENT

Depletion of the mineral resources of the developed countries should greatly enhance the economies of any nonindustrial nations possessing these resources. As the sale of their resources becomes instrumental in shifting the balance of trade and dollars in favor of these countries, the industrialized nations will place an ever-increasing demand on their resources and become more dependent upon them. Saudi Arabia and other nations rich in petroleum are currently enjoying unprecedented power and wealth as their major resource becomes more critical.

Despite the reserves still available in many nonindustrial countries, Harrison Brown concludes that ". . . most of these countries will never, under any circumstances, be developed in the sense in which the United States is today." Unrelenting population growth is one reason, but the limitation of resources is still more critical. There is simply not enough coal or other energy resource available to provide for the high material well-being of 3 billion persons. Nor is there sufficient lumber, iron, aluminum, or any other natural resource to allow undeveloped nations to develop to the degree of the already industrial societies.

Many retain faith in the salvation of humans by technology. Economist Peter Passell questions the depletion theory and believes that long before we run out of known oil reserves, petroleum will be extracted from oil shale rocks and tar sands, and before these are gone, other energy sources will be found. As for other resources, "the technology of substituting plentiful materials for scarce ones grows every day." Silicates made from sand replace copper, polyurethane substitutes admirably for rubber, and plastics continue to encroach on the steel and aluminum industry, but many of these substitutions are dependent on petroleum, and all require heavy energy expenditures.

Passell argues that industrial growth is not necessarily injurious to the undeveloped countries. They need capital to buy industrial products more than they need their own raw materials. Their need for tractors, turbines, and fertilizer may far exceed their need for their reserves of oil or other resources. The economic development of the poorer countries can best be achieved through trade. Yet even with perfect balance of the world's resources, their supply remains finite.

Some authors, such as John Maddox and James Schall, believe that the nation's growing commitment to the environment is dangerous and will undermine the destiny and dignity of human beings. Schall argues that "we don't know what man can be, and when we limit our capacities and our future, we are basing this on the technological and social limits of today." Our thoughts and concepts are based only on the knowledge of today.

Political and social instability may restrain development far more than limitations of natural resources. Short-term governments and a chaotic social structure, controlled by an excessively rich minority, are particularly limiting to the material well-being of the general society.

Theoretically, it would seem that the nonindustrial countries (UDCs) that possess reserves of essential resources should gradually prosper to such a degree that their production costs, both in wages and pollution control, will be as high as in the industrial countries (DCs), thus making production costs comparable in all countries. The period of resource and economic adjustment should see a rise in the material standard of living of some countries possibly at the expense of the already industrial nations whose resources are waning. Such equalization of world wealth has already begun as is well illustrated by Kuwait. Kuwait, with a population of under a million, received about $7 billion in oil revenues in 1974. In the "Declaration of Lahore," they and 36 other Moslem states pledged to cooperate in eliminating poverty, disease, and ignorance from Islamic nations, thus taking a major step toward dispersing their wealth and improving and enhancing the quality of life in one group of developing countries.

SOCIAL COALITION

From their origins in small, widely scattered tribes, humans gradually aggregated into villages and cities, uniting in part for mutual benefit and protection and partly to prevent absorption by stronger tribes. Ecologically speaking, as the population increased beyond the carrying capacity of its original range, existing ranges overlapped more and more into that of neighbors, giving rise to conflict over the existing resources—food, space, minerals, etc. For the most part, we have modified our behavior and needs to adjust and overcome some of the potential conflict arising from such overlap.

Throughout most of the world, the result of overlap was much the same; cultures fused, and fighting diminished among the fewer groups— but only at a cost of some measure of personal freedom. There were notable exceptions, including the city-states of Greece and the short-lived Republic of Rome, but for the most part, wars established a strong minority in power. An emperor or king was an absolute sovereign with unlimited power. A bureaucracy of clerks, inspectors, and spies conducted the affairs of state and maintained the closest scrutiny over the inhabitants. The majority from Roman times through the feudal era had almost no rights. Freedom was relinquished in exchange for protection and security. Social justice came slowly with the formation of national monarchies, but even into the nineteenth century the serfs were sold with the land in parts of Europe.

Individual rights were rekindled only gradually as the merchants and manufacturers in the larger cities demanded greater profits, and the bankers grew more independent in supporting emerging business. It was from such a framework that capitalism arose, providing opportunities and social justice for a larger part of the population than ever before. Still, there were inequalities inherent in the systems, and these inspired the concepts of socialism and communism, which theoretically would lead to a well-ordered, stable social system.

Cultures have always been ruled by a minority, from the pharaohs of Egypt, the emperors of Byzantium, to the kings of Europe and bureaucrats of Washington, but in general the minority has become larger. A democratic government based on the sovereignty of the majority provides the best example of this.

At the same time, a greater number of smaller principalities around the world have merged to form nations. Similarly the provinces of China have merged into a single nation. More recently nations have cooperated to form federations for common goals, such as the European Common Market. As communication improves and the same information is shared globally, still further unions and alliances seem probable.

With every merging of nations and more powerful central authority, conflicts become less likely. For one thing, fewer major "tribes," or groups, are existent to clash. As social systems evolve to share more fundamental objectives, chances of war should be still further reduced, just as a biological ecosystem gains more stability as it matures and approaches equilibrium. As world resources and food supplies diminish, motivation for sharing and exchanging for depleted materials should be stimulated. As democracy and capitalism become increasingly socialized, and communism perhaps more liberal, areas of disagreement between these major systems of government will be reduced.

COMPETITION AND COOPERATION

In the words of biologist Garrett Hardin, "one world is a mirage." Competition is inescapable. The noble dream of unity is awakened by the inherent competitive nature of all life. A unification of nations simply would shift competition from nations to other groups such as social classes, "gangs," or identity groups. Competition would intensify between classes—perhaps between farmer and urbanite, white collar and blue collar, bureaucrat and subject, party member and citizen. The wisdom of next breaking down class competition would also be questioned since it would install a dog-eat-dog society according to Hardin. "Competition there must be and one world would be but a prelude to extinction."

It may be possible that ultimately we will learn to live harmoniously, but only when it becomes imperative to the survival of *Homo sapiens*. "That species which has succeeded in eliminating all other species as competitors, ends by becoming its own competitor." In the final analysis, it is the kind of competition employed that will decide our fate.

Yet the merging self-interests of the superpowers of today are tending more than ever to draw the world together. They are concerned with the population explosion of underdeveloped countries; the inevitable demise of resources vital to their material standard of living; nuclear arms of smaller countries; and the approaching domination of the United Nations by a growing majority of underdeveloped countries.

Despite differences in basic ideologies, the converging interest of the superpowers, mainly the United States and the U.S.S.R, may lead to the sharing of common goals. However, they also lead to direct competition and confrontation if these goals happen to be natural resources, land, or power over other countries. Despite ideological contrasts, parallelism of structure exists between capitalist and socialist systems. Major decision-making policies are arrived at through lobbies that have economic clout, political strength, and bureaucratic self-perpetuation rather than sagacious judgment or the sanction of public opinion. Despite differences, democratic and socialist societies reach major decisions more through the pressure of great lobbying blocks behind the scenes than by political assembly. Free and closed societies alike share a similar allotment of economic resources and government expenditures to defense and capital investment. Both share similar kinds of social structure and education leading to convergence, and both governments are run by an elite of educated experts and trained technicians. Both share the same problems of distrust or skepticism toward authority.

Both realize that outright war is not an effective means of achieving goals. Dependency on economic values or resources is far superior. Superpowers see the contrast widening between the have and have-not nations and realize the need for alliance with these countries for resources.

Throughout the course of 1500 years of western civilization, the trend toward political centralization has proceeded or evolved continually despite the increasing inefficiency of exceeding a certain critical size. Democratic policy has dominated for less than 200 years. During this era, material goals of affluence have been achieved by a majority to raise the standard of living. Nations lacking affluence are still struggling to achieve it. Europe is concerned with the material acquisition that was dominant in the United States a generation ago. Due to a generation of deprivation of even simple, basic wants brought on by two world wars and exposure to consumption levels of the have world, the post-war population has been obsessed by a desire for these wants. Nations possessing this standard are now able to reflect on their achievements, and a voice of rebellion against material gains is being heard. Equity can be achieved only when our creative capacities are directed toward benefiting the entire species.

THE INDIVIDUAL, THE UNIT OF SOCIETY

B. F. Skinner argues that free man is dying. He says that "basic rights are becoming increasingly irrelevant or even harmful to development of a future culture in which men of reason would want to live." Skinner would implement government control with both behavioral and genetic engineering as part of a design to remake human character. He would reinforce desirable actions by reward so that punishable behavior seldom or never occurs. By providing the proper social environment, or education, human nature might be altered faster than the slow genetic change of inheritance would permit.

Yet the individual is the basic unit of society. In situations of extreme stress, it is the individual who stands alone. Forced off their hunting-gathering lands to farm dry mountain slopes, the new life-style of the Ik tribe of Central Africa was contrary to their inherent and cultural template. No longer were they part of the natural environment. Their social structure collapsed and the family unit dissolved. The only social need left was their innate personal need for survival. Will the price of human survival be the loss of our humanity?

Behaviorists are concerned mostly for the social environment with little acceptance of our dependency on the total biotic and physical environment. The sacrifice of individuality for unified behavior regulated by a minority of behavioral technicians or power elite would be contrary to inherent human nature. Further, it would not serve our sustained well-being to ignore the natural environment.

ENVIRONMENTAL CONSCIENCE

A global political order might at first glance appear to be in the best interests of the environment. An enlightened government consciously concerned for the conservation of resources on a sustained basis could serve to the best interests of humanity, although not necessarily the individual. But even though governments might gradually be assimilated, whatever their philosophy, environmental conscience is no more assured than social conscience.

The newly industrializing countries are beginning to express some concern about pollution and realize that economic prosperity is not always worth the environmental costs. Older industrial nations also recognize the hazards, but many nations continue to be far more concerned with the positive values of production and profit than their negative consequences. The political system makes little difference; the totalitarian socialist countries of today show little concern for the environment—the profit motive is universal.

A viable, balanced environment can be sustained only if the desires of a concerned and enlightened majority are free to be expressed. Hence, social justice and environmental conscience are most likely to be expressed in a free society. Awakening to the existence of a total environmental problem is long overdue. Lewis Mumford states that "the unrestricted increase of population, the overexploitation of megatechnical inventions, the inordinate wastages of compulsory consumption, and the consequent deterioration of environment through wholesale pollution . . . have at last begun to create the reaction needed to overcome them."

Any program sufficient to reverse this "destructive success of technological affluence" will require more than knowledge of how to resolve the problems. It will demand social and economic changes in attitude. We have yet to emerge from the stone age of human relations. The time it takes to adjust our values will depend on how soon this reorientation begins and the mechanical world is balanced in harmony with the biotic and human world.

Author Jean-Francois Revel asserts that utopian ideals of world social justice, peace, and environmental conscience can only be attained through revolution—five revolutions which must take place simultaneously: "a political revolution; a social revolution; a revolution in culture, values, and standards; and a revolution in international and interracial relations." Only in America are these taking place.

The revolution in ecological values is most apparent. Stabilizing the birthrate, equalizing the standard of living, and protecting the earth's resources are part of this revolution, or social evolution. As in any biological system, evolution is inevitable. If allowed to progress uncontrolled, overpopulation and resource depletion will have obvious consequences: As technology declines with the depletion of resources that drive it, the quality of life will deteriorate, especially in the richer countries, and food shortages will be frequent, due in part to reduced production and in part to lack of food-purchasing money brought on by a failing economy or inflation.

The developing countries may be in a more favorable position with regard to environmental balance than the industrial ones—and be better able to survive any coming crisis from resource exhaustion. They are less dependent on natural resources and may continue to develop even with their limited availability.

FUTURE QUALITY OF LIFE

On a worldwide basis, the future quality of life is not dependent only on such obvious forces as pollution or crowding. Quality is more basically dependent on economic and social values and the capability to combat any deleterious environmental factors. Quality will be retained or achieved largely by developing universal cooperation in regulating the interacting forces of the environment.

Human survival is only partly dependent on these forces. Resource depletion, overpopulation, pollution, and famine are not likely to destroy us. If unchecked, they may bring about a sudden decline in our numbers and drag down much of the beauty of the biosphere with us, but they will not destroy us. The ultimate survival of the human race is less dependent on material shortages or pollution than on human ingenuity and human nature. Although human nature can be directed to a large measure by the appropriate social environment, should this collapse, we may well revert to the innate individual struggle to survive.

ECOLOGICAL LAWS

We can also have confidence in tomorrow only if western civilization manages its destiny in a rational fashion following known ecological laws. We cannot contradict these laws indefinitely. We must realize that further growth of population and industry may be undesirable. As stated by ecologist David M. Gates, "Profits for self interests can no longer be gained at the expense of resources, open space, clean air and water, and lack of freedom from crowding and neurological stress." Other goals must include global pollution abatement, mass-transit systems, recognition of land values for wilderness areas, parks and open space, massive redesign of urban areas, and avoidance of all wars and conflicts among nations. Only by assuring order and harmony, presumably through rigid social structure, can disorder be minimized and *Homo sapiens* persist.

We are scarcely beginning to understand and accept our position as part of nature, as part of the total human ecosystem or information grid. As environmental author René Dubos so eloquently puts it, "Earth and man are thus two complementary components of a system, which might be called cybernetic, since each shapes the other in a continuous act of creation." Human numbers are now of such a magnitude that the tendency for disorder is running away with the system. For the system to remain viable, or balanced, disorder must be minimized. We have the technological capability to do this, but probably not the social capability.

Initially DNA provided a molecule capable of duplication and effective in organizing matter in a manner most capable of fully utilizing the earth's resources. Now a descendent and highly evolved DNA regulates the "ultimate organism" capable of directing its own destiny. It has done this by superimposing upon the genetic information transmitted the great flexibility of ontogenetic learning. Humans have utilized this behavioral learning, or learning from experience, to improve the quality of their lives; they are gradually utilizing it to modify their heritage and DNA itself.

The prodigious increase in human numbers is so rapid that the genetic endowment of intellect may be inadequate to understand the system's complexity and curb the accelerating perturbations of the system before it collapses.

Our genetic nature itself might prevent us from acting in time to stabilize the system. Although ecosystems and their components have a remarkable capacity for self-healing, sometimes a species is lost to retain the viability of the system. Will human beings be such a species, or will we respond in time with the appropriate information input to retain our dominant position in the human environment?

Environmental problems may be generated more rapidly in modern society, but the human response also seems more rapid. The way in which signals that warn of major changes bring about changing attitudes that evoke action is well illustrated by the "energy crisis" of the 1970s. Though the information warning of an imminent shortage of fossil fuels had been available for many previous years, it was only when actual shortages of petroleum developed that the government and public responded. The danger was quickly, though forcibly, recognized, and countermeasures taken to maintain the stability, or homeostasis, of the system. This is exemplified by the 81 percent increase in the federal energy research and development program through 1975, with 189 and 262 percent increases in monies to be spent for studies of solar and geothermal energy sources. Many years will pass, however, before we can judge if the response was adequate in funding, or quick enough, to be effective.

Limitations of Complexity

Society may well be destroyed by the complexities associated with dense populations. As society becomes more complex, its organization must adjust to facilitate communication and transmit information among the larger numbers, whether bees, ants, or humans. Society must achieve order either by increasing complexity, or preferably splitting into manageable subunits. Confidence in tomorrow can only be achieved by dismembering government into units of manageable size that are comprehensible and responsive to the inherent human intellectual capacity. The human mind is not adapted to interpreting the behavior of our enormous social system. Human judgment and intuition have been genetically selected to deal with limited numbers and to look only in the immediate past for the cause of the problem.

One of the great problems of society from large cities to whole nations is the poor communication and unwieldiness of big government. Aristotle foresaw this in 322 B.C.. "To the size of states there is a limit, as there is to other things, plants, animals, implements." For each of these there is a critical size; if exceeded they wholly lose their nature. The frustrations and complexities of modern society coupled with rapidity of change are becoming more than our social system can handle. Most critical, the enormity of society leads to unbearable stress and individual surrender. The individual feels that the enormity of business, government, even personal problems, are too huge and there is no way to relate to anything any more. Anything one does as an individual seems to have lost its meaning; and our intellectual, moral, and spiritual freedom is lost in the vastness of society.

As economic social systems have become larger and more tightly integrated with one another, human freedom, individualism, and identity have had to be sacrificed. The self-reliant individual has sacrificed independence to become a conformist (the "organization" man). We have lost some of our opportunity for self-expression in capitulating to the security of the machine. Whether this is a corporate or government machine makes little difference since their function and self-perpetuating goals are the same. If anything, the government machine is more deadly since it is more inviable, larger, more complex, and less subject to control.

Personal Freedom

It becomes apparent that to remain viable, the system must reach equilibrium. For global equilibrium, population and capital must remain essentially stable, with the forces tending to increase or decrease them in a carefully regulated balance. The stationary state would make fewer demands on our environmental resources, but greater demands on our moral resources.

If cultural or social evolution is regulated, and the "megamachine" discussed by Mumford is gradually brought under control, concurrent with population and resource limitations, quality of life might conceivably be raised for a majority without impairing it for a minority.

Such regulations to preserve the environment and limit population will naturally impose greater restrictions on personal freedom in many societies and may therefore be self-defeating. The majority of the world has never achieved much personal freedom, and the minority has not had it for long. Freedoms have been gained or lost over a period of generations or at least decades so that for the most part we have gradually adjusted to the change. Adaptability is the nature of humans. Thus, although if we are thrust into an Orwellian "1984" overnight, the prospect is glum indeed; if imposed gradually over a period of years, or if we were behaviorally "conditioned," even "1984" might be entirely acceptable. To some degree, we are our own behavioral engineers. Even in the best of times we envision things better; in the worst of times we have more to envision. Although tomorrow's world is unlikely to improve within the framework of today's values, it may be even better if viewed in the framework of tomorrow.

We may have most confidence in tomorrow by tomorrow's standards. Measured by today's values, we have probably never had it better than those of us enjoying the prosperity of the twentieth-century industrialized social democracies of western civilization. The peak quality of life for many may even have been passed some decades earlier before the cities became congested and the wilderness trails became trampled with the footprints and debris of urban refugees.

The Iks of Uganda knew a better yesterday 30 years ago. Now starving, the dying society still finds satisfaction within the framework of the present, although laughter is mirrored more in the sadistic pleasure of others' suffering than in love and joy.

CONCLUSIONS

Natural selection chooses between strategies, "giving" advantage to that strategy that leaves the most viable and successful offspring. Humanity has largely supplemented genetic strategies with behavioral strategies that have enabled it to successfully occupy virtually every global habitat and niche. Over the course of human evolution, humans have used this ability to modify behavior to suit the constantly changing circumstances of the environment. We have adjusted to increasing numbers and the complexity of society by improving communication and understanding, and by ruling more by intellect than force.

Catastrophe is not imminent. The earth's oxygen supply seems assured, and the pollutants and carbon dioxide discharged into the air are unlikely to spawn a new Ice Age. Polluted lakes and congested cities are not new and are perhaps trivial to human survival. Prospects for more widespread famine seem to be unlikely. Problems may appear to arise faster than ever before, but human capacity to resolve them seems even quicker.

The greatest immediate threat, aggravated by a diminishing supply of resources, is to our life-style. Now it remains to be seen if we can share our remaining resources and limit our numbers to what the earth can comfortably accommodate, without reducing the quality of life for the affluent to the level of the despondent. Certainly humans are in a position to adjust their biological strategy for survival, but it may mean rationing of resources, limiting births, and increasing governmental control to maintain stability and minimizing the complexity of the system to maintain the viable exchange of information needed to sustain any biological system.

Adaptability has always been a major criteria for success. Populations, or societies, having the most adaptive systems are most likely to survive. Populations with the most efficient social organization or production may well prove to be the best adapted.

The sooner humanity chooses and implements the appropriate social and economic strategies, the greater will be the options of its choices of strategies. Also, the fewer will be the sacrifices needed for success, and the better will be the potential for maintaining what we now regard as a quality style of life.

SELECTED READINGS

Boulding, Kenneth. *Economic Imperialism.* (Ann Arbor: Univ. Michigan Press, 1972).

Boyle, T. J. Hope for the technological solution. *Nature*, vol. 245, no. 5421, pp. 127–128.

Branden, N. *Who is Ayn Rand?* (New York: Paperback Library, 1962).

Brown, Harrison. After the Population Explosion. *Saturday Review*, June 26, 1971, vol. 54, pp. 11–13, 29–31.

Forrester, Jay W. *World Dynamics.* (Cambridge, Mass.: Wright-Allen Press, 1971).

Gates, David M. Designing a decent planet. *National Gardner*, vol. 41, no. 2.

Hardin, Garrett. *Nature and Man's Fate.* (New York: Rinehart, 1959).

Meadows, Donella H., D. L. Meadows, J. Randers, and W. Behrens III. *The Limits to Growth.* (New York: Universe Books, 1972).

Mumford, Lewis. The Megamachine—IV. *The New Yorker*, Oct. 31, 1970, pp. 50–98.

Quigley, Carroll. *Tragedy and Hope—A History of the World in Our Time.* (New York: Macmillan, 1966).

Background Information

THE LAWS OF THERMODYNAMICS

The laws of thermodynamics provide a useful basis for understanding how energy is exchanged or transformed. Since energy exchange is at the heart of every life process, some knowledge of these laws is very helpful to understanding many environmental problems.

The first law of thermodynamics (known also as the law of conservation of energy) states that energy is neither created nor destroyed, but is merely changed from one form to another, as from electromagnetic, or solar, energy to chemical energy in molecular bonds, or from mechanical energy to electrical energy. This means that if a system gains or loses energy, then an equal amount of energy must be transferred from or to the surroundings. The total energy of a closed system insulated from its surroundings remains constant. The constancy of the total energy can be illustrated when coal is burned to generate steam. The steam, in turn, drives the turbines that generate electricity; the total energy does not change, but the form does. Some of it becomes electrical energy and some of it is converted to heat. In such processes energy is degraded at every step of the way to forms not useful for performing work. Mostly this "lost" or "wasted" energy is being expelled to the surroundings as heat, so in the end, less than a third of the initial energy that was in the coal is left to be transmitted as electricity.

This sequence also partly illustrates the second law of thermodynamics, that the fraction of energy available for use continually diminishes. The second law states that the conversion of energy from one form to another is never 100 percent efficient. As an example of this, no engine for converting heat to mechanical work can ever be built that will obtain 100 percent efficiency. Some of the heat will always be ejected in exhaust and some of the mechanical energy will be reconverted to waste heat in the friction of the machine.

We know from experience that work may be dissipated entirely into heat, but heat cannot be converted entirely into work. Nature seems to have a number of one-way streets—pathways along which no return is possible, or if it is, then only by the expenditure of a great amount of energy. Heat, for instance, always flows spontaneously from warm to cool regions, not the other way. Water always runs downhill. Gases under pressure always leak out through an opening spontaneously. Salts washed into the ocean from rivers tend to mix, but ocean waters never unmix into pure salt and pure water. Although it is perhaps conceivable that by chance alone, all the oxygen molecules of the air in a room could come together on one side of the room, all the nitrogen molecules on the other, no great probability value is assigned to this event. The gases are in a state of mixture naturally, and this condition constitutes a state of disorder compared to the ordered arrangement of the separate gases. *Such disorder is the rule of nature.* All atoms and molecules in the universe seek the most random or disordered state and the lowest energy level. Any spontaneous process becomes more random or disordered. Rock weathers, crumbles, becomes sand and silt, and mixes in the soil to be eventually washed to the sea. Likewise, the energy stored in coal, oil, gas, wood, food, chemicals, and other substances, when released dissipates into the surroundings. It has gone from a state of orderliness to one of disorder. This is clear when it is realized that heat is merely the motion of molecules.

Highly ordered molecular structures, such as organic molecules, fossil fuels, trees, and so on, contain tremendous amounts of energy in their chemical bonds. When burned, this energy is released and goes to the making of heat—the random motion of air molecules. The heat is dissipated like dust in a windstorm. This is the spontaneous direction of such events in nature. To reverse this process and build complicated molecules requires energy from an outside source. Plants capture sunlight for this energy to convert molecules of carbon dioxide into their food. Animals eat these plants or other animals for their energy.

When it is said that living, nonspontaneous systems seem to violate the second law of thermodynamics, it must be remembered that protein molecules, living cells, human beings, indeed all life, are highly ordered systems only because of the energy that initially entered these systems. The second law was not violated—the energy laws were obeyed because the primary energy received from the sun made possible the ordering of the life systems.

Energy from the sun makes possible the ordering of molecules and sustaining of life. But the captured solar energy, when the fossil fuels and wood are burned, is continually reradiated and dissipated into the earth's biosphere and into space. Human activities, especially since the industrial revolution, tend to hasten this process. As our numbers and activities increase, the potential arises that we may cause significant imbalance and disorder in the systematic flow of energy.

ENTROPY

Generations of students have encountered, and have been left troubled by, vague feelings of dissatisfaction and incomprehension concerning the concept of entropy. Although having a firm basis in physical and chemical terms, entropy remains mysterious, a mind-picture gray and swirling, like some impenetrable damp fog in a Victorian graveyard. Indeed, this "limbo model" of entropy is about all many of us ever grasp by way of a mental impression concerning it. "Entropy is disorder" we have learned, "chaos, randomness, homogeneity, degradation, sameness, uniformity, nonsense," and so on, into "death, decay, darkness, and the ultimate cold inertness of the absolute zero of temperature." That entropy is defined mathematically and is capable of calculation as a quantity does not help much. Where does this energy go that is calculated as "unavailable for performing useful work"? Such "lost" energy, although remaining in fact within the system of its origin, is visualized as somehow departing, like the spirit of some lost soul, never to return.

Because of these negative constructs of entropy, different types of environmental abuse, and indeed any unpopular condition, such as overpopulation, are sometimes given as examples of increasing entropy. This label is applied in a voice of rising alarm that calls for immediate action, lest we hasten our own doom, the irreversible rush to total entropy, the limbo of complete disorganization where litter, pollution, and destruction stretch to the horizon. Entropy serves in such arguments as an alarm word, usually equivalent to "environmental abuse," and it is suggested as "something-to-be-avoided-or-we-are-all-going-to-perish."

Such uses of the entropy concept are philosophically useful, but it must be said in all candor that physical scientists would consider it technically erroneous to invoke entropy in this fashion. The error lies in treating entropy as a state of existence possible of achievement. Certainly the disturbed conditions, pollution, environmental degradation, waste, depletion, erosion, overpopulation, and the endless list of other difficulties that threaten us are alarming, and even contributing toward increased disorder and energy waste. But entropy is an entity much more subtle and useful for the understanding of nature than is suggested by these images.

It is understandable that such mental images of entropy exist. Entropy is a concept that originally came out of the branch of physics that deals with the phenomena of heat, today known as thermodynamics. Early in the nineteenth century, the groundwork was laid by N. L. Sadi Carnot, whose studies in 1824 on the capability of hot bodies (or heat) to do work showed that not all the heat supplied to a heat engine, such as a steam engine, was converted to work. In 1850, Rudolph J. E. Clausius, a German mathematician and physicist, first clearly stated what we now call the first two laws of thermodynamics. Within a few years Clausius defined and named the property called entropy. Entropy, he said, is that property which is conserved in all reversible processes. He meant that for *fully reversible*, or cyclic, changes of state or other processes, there is no change in some quantity, a thing called entropy. From this, and from the second law of thermodynamics, he stated the principle of increase of entropy. The famous maxim of Clausius is what now forms the philosophical basis of today's troubled impressions of what entropy is: "The energy of the universe is constant; the entropy of the universe tends always toward a maximum." Since entropy is held to be the amount of energy in any given process that is unavailable for useful work, wasted, so to speak, it is clear that eventually the ultimate energy crisis is going to happen. "The universe is running down," said someone. "Entropy is time's arrow," said Sir Arthur Eddington.

Entropy, it developed, could never decrease. It could be zero for reversible processes and positive for irreversible processes. Besides these two properties of entropy, a third was eventually proved: Entropy depended only upon the initial and final states of the system being considered and was independent of the means by which the final state was achieved.

These three properties of entropy are immensely important in practical ways. Not only do they allow the actual determination of entropy itself, but they lead to the prediction of possible changes in the systems under study. For example, chemists once believed that the sign of the quantity ΔH, the heat of reaction for a given chemical event, determined the spontaneity of the reaction. If positive, the reaction would "go," and perhaps even release heat. If negative or zero, heat (energy) had to be supplied, or the reaction, if it "went," cooled and drew heat from its surroundings. When the second law of thermodynamics was propounded and the property of entropy was defined, it was seen that the true criterion of spontaneity in a chemical reaction was not the sign of ΔH but the sign of a quantity that depended upon entropy. This quantity was called Gibbs Energy, after its discoverer, and was designated ΔG. Gibbs Energy, which is the energy that *is* available to do useful work, is given by the equation $\Delta G = \Delta H - TS$ in which T is the absolute temperature of the reactants and ΔS is the change in entropy of the system. Naturally, ΔS is a quantity not easily discovered for most reactions, but it is calculated by determining the heat change for the process if carried out *reversibly* (ΔQ_{rev}) and dividing this quantity by the absolute temperature: $\Delta S = Q_{rev}/T$.

Any reaction or change of state (such as the melting of ice) is accompanied by a change in entropy; that is, the entropy of the substance before the reaction or change of state is different than after. If entropy is "wasted energy," perhaps lost to the surroundings as heat energy, it can be thought of as an increase in the disorder or randomness of the system. This is easy to visualize; heat, after all, is nothing but the random motion of molecules. Hotter objects are composed of more violently and rapidly moving molecules than are cold objects. Accordingly, higher temperatures result in more disorder among the molecules.

Disorder occurs too when substances are mixed. Who among us has not had the lid fall from our salt or pepper shaker into the soup, along with all the contents? In one instant, two well-ordered and separated systems (salt and pepper) become one disordered one. Entropy as disorder, chaos, randomness, homogeneity, and so on, is understandable by a simple experiment, which also may help in appreciating the very real nature of the energy involved in entropy changes. If the contents of two containers of differently colored, finely divided particles (say salt and pepper) are poured together and stirred, what happens? The two well-ordered systems become one disordered, random mixture. If someone were to sit down and attempt to separate the mixture, grain by grain, into its separate components again, the effort would be considerable. Of course, a simpler sorting device could be invented, one that could perhaps do the job in a minute or a few seconds, but nevertheless, energy would be required to restore order. Entropy can be thought of as this kind of energy. If a few ounces of salt and pepper mixed together produce a significant entropy change, what then is the entropy change in the burning of a forest or the melting of an iceberg and the mixing of all its molecules with those of the ocean water? Impressive though these examples may be in the light of the energy required to "restore" them, it is nevertheless true that these kinds of things have not and do not lead perceptibly to anything like that often-imagined cold and dark ultimate wasteland of final maximum entropy.

The disorder concept of entropy has appeared in another context in recent years: Information theory. As this discipline unfolded, an astonishing similarity to the theory of heat became evident. Information can be defined by the formula $I = K \ln P$, in which I is the information represented by one outcome of a situation that originally had P possible outcomes, all of equal probability; K is an arbitrary constant; and ln represents the natural logarithm to the base e. The identity in form of this expression to that describing the probability of a given heat distribution is more than coincidental—it reveals a profound relationship between the fields of information theory and thermodynamics. The probability of a given heat distribution in thermodynamics is the expression describing entropy: $S = k \ln W$ in which k is the Boltzmann gas constant, 1.38×10^{-23} joule per degree Kelvin; and W is the number of microscopic or infinitesimal ways in which the overall state corresponding to S can be realized.

The correspondence between the theory of information and the theory of heat is further demonstrated by the comparison of thermodynamic entropy with information. The second law of thermodynamics requires that entropy always increase in any spontaneous change, or remain constant if the change takes place reversibly. Similarly, information always decreases during communication; it never increases. It can remain constant in a perfect communication. Thus entropy and information are alike except for "sign"; the first always increases and the second always decreases. They are said to be isomorphic quantities. Not only are they isomorphic and analogous, it seems they may be the same thing.

Thus, when disorder is increased in some system, it may be thought of as a more random distribution of molecules or particles, or it may be thought of as a loss of information through the increase of "noise," say, or disturbance. The quantities of entropy that are measured in each system can be compared. It turns out that one unit of entropy of information, called a *bit*, is equal to about 10^{-23} joule per degree Kelvin of thermodynamic entropy. This is the smallest possible thermodynamic entropy change that can be associated with a measurement yielding one bit of information. A bit is merely a yes-or-no choice between two equally possible answers to a well-formed question. The relationship allows the calculation of energy requirements for ordering such disordered states as the mixed salt and pepper example. Entropy therefore enters into information theory to show that not only does it require energy to obtain information, but it requires information to effect an energy change.

In conclusion, it would be appropriate to emphasize some of the things that entropy is *not*.

It is not a place or state of matter that exists now, or possibly ever, a gray wasteland of dissipated energy.

It is not the driving force of evolution.

It is not the cause of extinction. Not entropy but competition and adaptive failure in the face of environmental change do this.

It is not the essence of environmental hostility toward living organisms. There is energy enough for organisms; it is not snatched away from them into entropy's limbo. Indeed, it may that there is too much energy; it is the energy *available* for performing work that drives hurricanes, tornadoes, floods, speeding automobiles, and exploding bombs.

Finally, entropy is not simple in living organisms. Life, it has been said, is a great conspiracy against the second law of thermodynamics. "The ability to decrease entropy," once suggested Ernst Schrodinger, "is the most characteristic feature of living systems." It appears that living organisms indeed reverse entropy. They build complex molecules out of simple ones; they organize complex bodies and communities; they have arisen in some primordial soup and have taken a long uphill road against inconceivable energy gradients to arrive, millions of years later, at a state of astonishing diversity and vitality, still increasing in numbers, kinds, and complexities. Wonderful though this is, it must be remembered that at no point in all this long process was the second law ever violated. Every process in a living organism that seems to do so, or to decrease entropy, has been, and will be found to be, coupled with other energy systems that fully and adequately compensate. Though not to be feared, entropy will not be cheated.

ESSENTIAL AMINO ACIDS[1]

Amino acids are the fundamental units of protein structure and are thus essential to normal development. The body is able to synthesize most of the amino acids, but not all. Those that we cannot produce must be obtained from foods that contain them. These amino acids are referred to as essential, and include the following: isoleucine, leucine, lysine, methionine, phenylalanine, threonine, tyrosine, tryptophan, and valine.

Proteins from different foods contain various amounts of the essential amino acids, but the amount of protein still provides a reasonable

[1]Based on Sherman, H. C. *Essentials of Nutrition,* 4th ed. (New York: Macmillan, 1957).

guide to the amount of essential amino acids present. Some indication of the protein content of a few common foods are shown below:

Food	Grams per 100 grams of sample	Food	Grams per 100 grams of sample
Almonds	18.6	Halibut	26.2
Apples	0.2	Ham	23.0
Bacon, cooked	30.4	Lamb	16.2
Bananas	1.1	Macaroni	3.4
Beans, dried	22.3	Milk	3.5
Beef	18.5	Oatmeal (cooked)	2.3
Beer	0.3	Peanuts, roasted	26.0
Bread, white enriched	9.1	Potato, baked	2.4
Candy, chocolate	4.5	Potato chips	5.3
Cheddar cheese	25.0	Rice, white	7.6
Chicken	23.4	Sardines	25.7
Corn	3.7	Soybean flour	42.5
Cornflakes	8.1	Spaghetti	3.4
Corn flour	7.8	Sugar	0
Crab meat	16.9	Tuna	27.0
Eggs	12.8	Yeast, brewers dried	36.9
Frankfurters	14.0	Yoghurt	3.0
Greens	2.0		

Looking more specifically at the relative amounts of some essential amino acids present in a few of these foods, the variation and content is shown below:

	Grams per 100 grams of food			
	Lysine	Tryptophan	Leucine	Valine
Beans, baked ($1/2$ cup)	0.38	0.046	0.41	0.32
Beef, hamburger (1 large)	2.2	0.308	1.76	1.21
Bread, enriched (4–5 slices)	0.22	0.076	0.63	0.37
Cheese, cheddar ($7/8$ cup, grated)	2.1	0.375	2.25	1.92
Eggs (2 med)	0.90	0.192	1.18	0.92
Frankfurters (2, cooked)	1.4	0.196	1.12	0.77
Greens ($1/2$ cup, cooked)	0.17	0.068	0.31	0.16
Milk, whole fluid	0.30	0.05	0.38	0.24
Oatmeal, cooked ($3/8$ cup)	0.08	0.03	0.18	0.12
Peanut butter (6 tbsp)	0.78	0.26	1.75	1.15
Potato, baked (1 med)	0.20	0.05	0.23	0.13

The value of animal protein over plant protein is readily apparent both as to total percent of protein and the content of essential amino acids. Of the plant products, only seeds are sufficiently high to provide a valuable and practical protein source.

THE PRODUCTIVE CAPACITY OF A NATION

The capacity of a country to feed itself depends on more than the amount of land available for agriculture. Most countries must supplement their food needs with imports plus what they can obtain from lakes, streams, and the sea.

Georg Borgstrom, Professor of Food Science at Michigan State University, calls this unmeasured land area "ghost acreage"—the nonvisible acreage which a country requires to supplement its tilled land in order to be able to feed itself. This "acreage" is the land-producing equivalent of food obtained from the sea or from trade.

The degree to which agriculture provides the feeding basis of a country is sometimes surprisingly low. Even the Netherlands, so often cited for its capacity to feed a relatively dense population (845 persons per square mile in 1974) is only 60 percent agriculturally self-sufficient. Thirteen percent of its food comes from the sea, and the balance from trade. Switzerland is 58 percent self-sufficient, Israel but 37 percent, and Japan 28 percent. In Europe, only Denmark is completely self-sufficient (at 108 percent).

The ghost acreage of some of the most highly populated areas is close to 100 percent. Hong Kong, for instance, provides for only a fraction of its needs to feed 10,221 persons per square mile. Macau, with 44,667 persons per square mile, must import virtually all its food. But their financial resources enable the population to import the needed food.

The amount of arable land varies tremendously from one country to another, and even among areas within a country. The productivity of a square mile of land in Mauritania in the Sahara desert is nil, while a similar area in Denmark supports over 300 persons. Even within a single large country, such as the United States, there is a marked contrast in food productivity between, say, the rocky New England coast and the Central Valley of California, although both may have a similar population density.

Water Quality Standards*

	Use	Standards of quality for coliform bacteria (at low water stage)	Required treatment of waste water before discharge (normal)
I	Industrial uses not needing high-quality water	None	Sedimentation and chlorination
II	Fishing and Recreation	None	Sedimentation, chemical precipitation, or biological treatment
III	Bathing, recreation	Coliform group: $\leq$ 1000/100 ml (monthly average, $\leq$ 20% $\geq$ 1000, none $\geq$ 2400 on any day)	Sedimentation, chemical precipitation, or biological treatment and chlorination
IV	Shellfish culture	Coliform group average $\leq$ 70/100 ml	Sedimentation, chemical precipitation, or biological treatment and chlorination
V	Drinking water and related household uses	Bacterial standard groups per 100 ml: monthly average $\leq$ 5000, $\leq$ 20% $\geq$ 5000, or $\leq$ 5% $\geq$ 20,000.†	Sedimentation, chemical precipitation or biological treatment and chlorination

*Federal water quality standards are constantly being revised, but the above table represents a simplification of the 1974 values.
†These values include representative coliform bacteria, not just the fecal type.

Background coliform bacteria counts in relatively pristine mountain streams in areas where there are few people are roughly in the range from 30 to 60 per 100 ml sample.

Glossary

Abiotic   Nonliving.

ADP (adenosine diphosphate)   Molecule storing and transferring energy in the phosphate bond.

Age structure   The percentage of people in different age groups of a population.

Aggression   Unprovoked, offensive behavior.

Altruism   The unselfish concern for the welfare of others; placing the success of others first.

Alveoli   An air cell of the lungs formed by the dilation of tiny air passageways.

Antibiotic   Any chemical substance produced by microorganisms that has the ability to inhibit development of other microorganisms, mostly fungi and bacteria.

ATP (adenosine triphosphate)   The chemical in organisms used to store and transfer energy.

Behavior   Manner of responding or acting.

BOD (biochemical oxygen demand)   The oxygen required by aerobic organisms, as those in sewage, to live and break down organic substances.

Biological control   The control of pest species, usually insects, by using natural enemies such as parasites, predators, or disease organisms to curb the population.

Bipedalism   Locomotion on two limbs.

Breeder reactor   Nuclear reactor that generates electricity by splitting atoms and in so doing produces fissionable elements such as plutonium 239 from nonfissionable elements, such as uranium 238.

Bronchitis   An inflammation of the bronchial passages of the respiratory tract.

Calorie   The amount of energy required to raise the temperature of 1 gram of water 1 degree Celsius; often used as a measure of the amount of energy needed to sustain life.

Carnivore   Animal that obtains its food requirements by eating other animals.

Chlorinated hydrocarbon   A chemical, often a pesticide, consisting of chlorine as well as hydrogen and carbon. The group includes DDT, aldrin, endrin, dieldrin, chlordane, and many more.

Chlorophyll   The green pigment of plants that can capture light energy.

Choline esterase   Enzyme that splits acetylcholine into acetyl and choline fractions, making the hormone ineffective and thus stopping, and regulating, the transmission of nerve impulses.

Chromosome   Gene-containing, filamentous structure in the cell nucleus.

Cloning   Duplication of an organism by reproducing nonsexual cells.

Codon   Any combination of the three nucleotide bases (adenine, thymine, guanine) in the messenger RNA that provide the "code" for producing a particular amino acid.

Coliform   Bacteria occupying the intestinal tract, especially the colon.

Communication   Transfer of information between any parts of a system or different systems.

Community   Group of organisms occupying the same area.

Consumers   Organisms feeding on organic food or other organisms.

Co-valent molecular bonds   The bond between atoms created by the sharing of electrons.

Cross over   Exchange or transfer of chromosome segments with each other.

Culture   The sum total of the experience of present and previous generations that is transmitted from one generation to the next.

Cybernetics   The science of control or self-regulation of systems.

Cytochrome   One of several enzymes that catalyze oxidation reactions.

DNA (deoxyribosenucleic acid)   The genetic carrier of information found in the chromosome.

Detergent   Cleaning agent manufactured synthetically not containing fats and oils.

Deuterium   Isotope of hydrogen in which the nucleus contains one proton and one neutron.

DDT (dichlorodiphenyltrichloroethane)   Chlorinated hydrocarbon widely used to control insect pests.

Dismal theorem   The theorem first proposed by Robert Malthus that human beings are ultimately destined to misery and poverty unless population growth is controlled.

Ecology   The study of the interrelationships of organisms to each other in their environment.

Ecosystem   A group of organisms living and interacting with each other and their environment.

Electron   A subatomic, or elementary, particle representing a unit of negative electric charge.

Element   Component, constituent, or member of.

Emphysema   Lung disease caused by a breakdown of the membranes forming the walls of the alveoli of the lung.

Energy   The capacity to do work.

Entropy   The loss or degradation of energy; the portion of heat energy unavailable to do work. Also, the measure of the orderliness of a system; (from Morowitz) "the state of maximum disorder is also the state of maximum entropy."

Environment   The total factors and forces, internal and external, biotic and abiotic, that influence an organism.

Essential amino acid   Amino acid required for normal human development but not synthesized by humans.

Estrus   A distinct "heat," or period of sexual receptivity, characterizing most primates but not humans.

Ethology   The study of animal behavior.

Eugenics   The improvement of the human species through control of hereditary factors in mating.

Eutrophication   Nutrient enrichment of an aquatic system. A normal process in the maturation (or aging) of a lake but often undesirable because of the excessive growth of algae generated.

Exponential   (see Geometric)

Feedback   Signal returned to a self-regulating system so that it will respond; mostly to return toward a former condition.

Fish protein concentrate (FPC)   High-protein powder made from fish meal in which the entire fish is utilized—used to fortify protein-deficient foods.

Fission   Process in which the nucleus of an element (principally uranium) is split into two lighter elements with a release of energy.

Food chain   A series of organisms depending upon each other for food, and consequently energy; transfer of food from one trophic level to another.

Fusion   Process in which the nuclei of two light elements (especially hydrogen isotopes) combine to form the nucleus of a heavier element with the release of energy.

Gamete   Reproductive cell that must fuse with another before it can develop to produce a new organism.

Gene   The repository of genetic information located on a chromosome.

Gene pool   Total genetic information contained in a reproducing population.

Geometric (exponential) growth   Growth by doubling, usually in numbers.

Geothermal   Pertaining to the earth's internal heat; energy derived from super-heated water or steam in the earth's crust.

Green revolution   General name for increased agricultural productivity of food crops brought about by using higher-yielding crop varieties.

GNP (Gross National Product)   The total expenditure on goods and services, plus savings, produced by a nation, usually during a year.

Growth rate   The difference between the annual birthrate and death rate of a population times 100.

Habitat   Place, or locality, where organisms occur.

Homeostatic   A self-regulative, cybernetic system; maintaining a steady state.

Hominid   A living or extinct human or humanlike type; relating to the "family" of *H. sapiens.*

Homoiothermal   Warm-blooded; having a constant temperature.

Hydroelectric   Electric power generated from falling waters turning turbines.

Information   The capacity to store and transmit meaning or knowledge.

Integrated pest control   Combining both chemical and biological control methods against a population of pests (usually insects).

Knowledge   Acquaintance with facts, truths, or principles, as from study or investigation.

Kwashiorkor   Disease of infants caused by protein deficiency.

Lacustrine   Pertaining to a lake; living or growing in lakes.

Lasky ratio (*A/G* ratio)   The principle that as the grade of an ore decreases arithmetically, its abundance will increase geometrically.

Membrane   Thin layer enclosing a cell or a cell part; consists of fat and protein.

Message   A discreet or continuous sequence of measurable events distributed in time; a linear array of symbols which may be a set of words, syllables, letters, phonemes, musical notes, experimental observations, amino acids in a linear peptide or any other defined sequence (from Wiener and Morowitz).

Messenger RNA   Nucleic acid molecules carrying genetic instructions from the chromosomes to the ribosomes.

Mitochondrion   The cell organelle where respiration takes place.

Monoculture   Cultivation of a single crop to the exclusion of others; such as of wheat, corn, rice, or another agricultural species.

Mutation   Change in the genetic substance of a species often causing variation among individuals in a population; a gene or chromosome change.

Natural selection   The evolutionary process by which some organisms give rise to more descendants than others.

Niche (ecological niche)   The role of an organism in its ecosystem; its relationship to the community and total environment.

Nitrolotriacetic acid (NTA)   Chemical substitute for phosphorus in detergents used to improve cleaning property.

Nuclear reactor   Device in which a nuclear fission chain reaction can be initiated, sustained, and controlled. Used to generate heat energy or useful radiation.

Nucleic acid   One of a class of molecules composed of joined nucleotide complexes.

Order   Sequence, disposition, arrangement, arranged or regulated condition.

Ordered systems   Sequential, regulated arrays of elements, energy, and events in space and time; arrangements in which a change in one variable will result in a change in at least one other variable.

Osmosis   The tendency of a fluid to pass through a semipermeable membrane into a solution where its concentration is lower.

Parasite An organism which derives its nutrition by feeding upon another living organism.

Pest Any organism, commonly an insect, considered undesirable often because of its feeding on crop plants.

Pesticide Any chemical used to control pests.

Petrolith Pictorial symbols painted on walls of cave dwellings or exposed sites.

Phenylketonuria Inherited, abnormal condition characterized by phenylketones in the urine and causing mental retardation.

Phosphate bond Bond with a phosphate atom that contains energy which can be released when the bond is broken.

Photochemical pollutant Mixture of atmospheric chemicals formed by the action of light energy (solar) on primary air pollutants such as auto exhausts.

Photon Quantum of electromagnetic radiation, or energy.

Photosynthesis Process in which light energy and chlorophyll are used to manufacture carbohydrates out of carbon dioxide and water.

Pictograph Pictorial symbols on walls of cave dwellings, or exposed rocks as produced by etching.

PCBs (polychlorinated biphenyls) Any of several biphenyl compounds containing chlorine, used in plastics, paints, protective coatings, etc., and accumulated in biological systems when present.

Predator Organisms obtaining their food by preying on other organisms.

Primate Any mammal in the order Primates; includes humans, apes, monkeys, etc.

Producer Organisms obtaining their energy directly from the sun; synthesizes organic substances from inorganic.

Protein A class of chemicals composed of many joined amino acids. The amino acids contained are essential to normal development.

Regulating mechanism One that maintains the value of one or more variables within a range or ranges that permit the continued existence of the system (from Rappaport).

Resistance (to pesticides) The development of individuals (as in a population of insects) resistant to certain chemicals caused by the presence and reproductive advantage of individuals already innately tolerant of a particular chemical (as DDT).

Respiration The oxidation of carbohydrates by organisms in which energy is released.

RNA (ribonucleic acid) Nucleic acid groups responsible for transfer of genetic information from the cell nucleus to the sites of protein synthesis.

Ribosome A cell organelle that contains RNA and is the site of protein synthesis.

Second law of thermodynamics Law stating that as energy is degraded, the fraction available for useful work continually diminishes, much being lost as heat.

Sense (from computer technology) To determine or locate the position or arrangement of.

Sickle cell Blood cell having a crescentlike shape due to the presence of abnormal hemoglobin.

Single-cell protein (SCP) Single-celled algae or fungi that can be cultivated for production of food supplements high in protein.

Smog   Smoke and fog. Used in a general way to denote any combination of air pollutants.

Succession   The changes in an ecosystem by which one population or community is replaced by another.

Swidden agriculture   The practice of clearing forests by cutting and burning to plant crop species.

Territoriality   An area of space defended against others as an exclusive preserve.

Thermodynamics   The science concerned with the relationship between heat and mechanical work, or energy, and with the conversion of one to another.

TIBA   Growth-regulating chemical that influences the overall shape of plants.

Transducer   An entity receiving energy from one system and transferring it to another; or with reference to bacteria, transfer of genetic material (information).

Transfer RNA   Nucleic acid molecules transferring genetic information as amino acids to the site of protein synthesis.

Utterly dismal theorem   The more we do to increase the world food supply, the larger will be the number of people who ultimately starve to death.

Variable   A single measurable dimension of an entity, not the entity itself (from Rappaport).

Vector   An organism, often an insect, that transmits a disease organism, as a bacterium or fungus, or virus.

Virus   A submicroscopic, noncellular particle composed of a nucleic acid core and a protein sheath; parasitic in host cells.

Index